Reluctant Host:

Canada's Response to Immigrant Workers,
1896-1994

Donald H. Avery

Dedication

For my parents, Howard Mellor Avery (deceased) and Evelyn Chittick,
who greatly enriched my life and inspired this study.

Canadian Cataloguing in Publication Data

Avery, Donald, 1938-
Reluctant host: Canada's response to immigrant workers, 1896-1994

Includes bibliographical references and index.
ISBN 0-7710-0827-9

1. Alien labour – Canada – History – 20th century.   2. Labour supply –
Canada.   3. Canada – Emigration and immigration – Government policy
– History – 20th century.   I. Title.

HD8108.5.A2A8 1995   331.6′2′0971   C94-932539-2

Printed and bound in Canada
Typesetting by M&S, Toronto

McClelland & Stewart Inc.
The Canadian Publishers
481 University Avenue
Toronto, Ontario
M5G 2E9

1 2 3 4 5   99 98 97 96 95

Contents

"Men who seek employment on railway construction are, as a rule, a class accustomed to roughing it. They know when they go to the work that they must put up with the most primitive kind of accommodation. . . . it is only prejudicial to the cause of immigration to import men who come here expecting to get high wages, a feather bed and a bath tub."

CPR president Thomas Shaughnessy, 27 October 1897

"We will employ the kind of immigrants on the line that the Government allows into the country. Am I opposed to the entrance of oriental labour, you ask? Well, you need cheap labour don't you, and why should we reject the oriental if we cannot get the supply we require from any other source?"

Grand Trunk Railway president Charles Hays, 28 September 1907

"The shortage of unskilled labour is already acting as a brake on production. . . . the mining industries . . . are all suffering from a shortage of men who are willing to work with their hands, and an over supply of those who are not so willing. It is certain that the type of immigrant coming into Canada will not undertake the kind of employment that the Italian, Hungarian, Galician, Pole, Russian, Bukovinian and Finnish labourers did before the war."

Canadian Mining Journal, 25 February 1920

"If . . . we find these hard-working immigrants accepting employment at wages or under conditions which Canadian-born citizens are reluctant to accept, there should be no outcry against these immigrants for accepting a lower standard of living. . . . They are being brought to this country on the condition that they do exactly this."

Owen Sound *Sun Times*, 8 August 1946

"The type of immigrant we have in mind has been the backbone of the labour force of the mining industry in the past . . . a man has to be physically fit; but his education is not too important, so long as he can read and write."

Canada, House of Commons, Special Joint Committee on Immigration, Hearings, Brief of the Mining Association of Canada, 16 February 1967

"Without immigrants . . . cutting timber, mining, building hydro projects and transportation facilities, and carrying out work essential to the exploitation of remote resources . . . developments will be slow and costly."

Ibid., Statement by Sydney Spivak, Manitoba Minister of Industry and Commerce, 31 January 1967

Introduction

As Canada approaches the end of the twentieth century, the debate over immigration policy looms large. How many immigrants and refugees should be admitted? What occupational skills are most required? Are these newcomers a drain on the economy? Do certain immigrant groups pose a special threat to Canadian society?

These questions have been asked before. Indeed, during this century Canadians have often been perplexed and concerned about the social implications of being one of the world's most active immigration nations. Generosity of outlook has varied over time, and with reference to a shifting standard of ethnic acceptability. Immigration policy has also been based on a high degree of economic self-interest – the economic utility of immigrant workers. This viewpoint was graphically expressed by a British Columbia mining executive in 1903, who claimed that "We need immigrant workers . . . for the jobs Canadians won't do."

This book is an historical analysis of how different pressure groups – business, labour, ethnic, political, bureaucratic – determined the priorities and direction of Canada's immigration and refugee policies. Throughout, an attempt has been made to compare Canada's immigration experience, at different periods, with that of other major immigration nations, most notably the United States. The present work also explores the conditions of work and residence of different jobs of immigrant workers as they tried to adjust to a Canadian environment that held both promise and frustration. Where possible, the views of migrant workers themselves have been cited, although no comprehensive treatment of this complex subject is possible in this study. Canadian opposition to the entry of immigrants from "non-preferred" countries is another important theme. Indeed, the charge that certain ethnic groups do not fit into Canadian society is a recurring refrain, even if the groups deemed "undesirable" have changed over time. The role of the Canadian state in trying to control certain groups of so-called "dangerous foreigners" is another important subject addressed here. Finally, emphasis is placed on the continuity and change both in Canada's immigration policy and in the response of Canadian society toward various groups of immigrant workers.

From its beginning the Canadian state assumed an important role in both the recruitment and control of immigrant workers. Deportation was used not only to export the unemployed, but also against immigrant workers who became involved in syndicalist, socialist, and Communist activity. This was especially true in 1919 when fear of a Bolshevik revolution in Canada produced a series of repressive measures. The events of the Great Depression confirmed that Canadian society harboured deep suspicions of its foreign-born, particularly those who dared challenge the prevailing free enterprise system.

Equally important have been the similarities in the Canadian and American experiences. Prior to 1914 European immigrants and native-born workers moved back and forth across the Canada-United States border in large numbers in search of work. The two countries also shared certain exclusionist policies based on race and ideology. Both countries effectively barred non-white immigrants until the 1960s. Fear of anarchists and Communists was pronounced in both countries in 1919 and during the 1930s; it was revived with the advent of the Cold War. The Canadian and United States governments also shared a pragmatic rather than humanitarian response toward German Jewish refugees and post-war European displaced persons.

The Canadian experience of immigrant workers during the twentieth century has been strongly influenced by racial and ethnic considerations. Prior to 1960 the Canadian consensus seems to have been that Asians and blacks were unassimilable. Their future in the country, to the extent that they were thought to have one at all, was that of the most grinding labour. By contrast, British, white Americans, and many western European immigrants were readily afforded high occupational and social status.

Eastern and southern European immigrants were allocated a middle position within Canada's vertical mosaic. They were allowed into the country because of their brawn and industry; and they were granted basic civil rights, being at once candidates for Canadianization. Yet as "foreigners" theirs was a decidedly mixed reception, the attitude of their hosts varying with time and economic circumstances. Language and culture clearly set the European immigrant apart in Canada. So, too, did occupation and place of residence. And this social distance was lengthened by the suspicion and hostility many newcomers felt when they discovered Canada could not deliver what they had come – or been led – to expect.

That so many immigrants should have found work as wage labourers in industry and agriculture is not surprising. Settling on the land was an expensive business in early twentieth-century Canada and few immigrants had the capital to become full-time farmers straight-away. In the critical settlement process temporary employment in railroad construction, mining, harvesting, or lumbering was for most prospective farmers an absolute necessity. On the other hand, the ideal of the family farm was not necessarily the immigrant's ultimate goal;

many were committed to industrial employment on arriving in the country and headed directly to the major transportation centres and company towns. In addition, large numbers of immigrants regarded their Canadian residence as temporary. A man's Canadian wages might support his relatives in Europe and give him the means to improve his lot when he went back home.

Geographical mobility and occupational pluralism typified the immigrant experience in this period. Such occupational diversity belies the simple division of the world of work into agricultural and non-agricultural categories. The unskilled immigrant worker had one basic commodity to exchange – "his physical strength, his brute force, to carry, pull, push." He exchanged it from sector to sector as the demand for "human machines" shifted to a rhythm he could not but obey. Prior to 1930, the most victimized groups of immigrant workers were Chinese, Japanese, and East Indian residents of the country. Their hardship was compounded by their virtual exclusion from the Canadian trade union movement. African-Canadian workers also found themselves marginalized until the 1960s.

Although the Second World War and the post-war years brought substantial improvements in Canada's human rights record and the gradual emergence of the welfare state, these changes were not necessarily reflected in the country's immigration policy and performance. While thousands of European displaced persons were allowed into the country between 1946 and 1952, they were not immediately afforded occupational and social equality. Indeed, their Canadian apprenticeship often began with frontier jobs. This was also the experience of the many immigrants who came from Italy, Portugal, and Greece during the 1950s. Less fortunate still were Caribbean workers who gained entry not as immigrants but as temporary migrant labour.

The 1967 and 1976 changes in Canada's immigration policy greatly improved the status of immigrant workers, both by removing the racist bias against Asian and black immigrants and by creating an immigration appeal system. That is not to say, however, that immigrant workers coming to Canada during the 1970s and 1980s did not experience exploitation and discrimination, especially since more and more of them were visible minorities. These realities of ethnic stratification in contemporary Canadian society have been aptly described by anthropologist Frances Henry: "Slowness of promotion and lay-offs in a period of economic decline affect ethnic group members most dramatically as they are subject to the 'last hired/first fired' principle, often employed as they are in those industries most sensitive to economic constraints. . . . nonwhite job applicants are rejected for employment far more often than are Canadian whites, even when qualifications and prior job experience are controlled."[1]

General Patterns of Immigration, 1867-1994

Canada at the time of Confederation was overwhelmingly British in ethnic origin. Anglo-Canadians also dominated the economic and political life of the country. This is not to say, however, that French Canadians in Quebec did not exert a powerful influence on federal politics. The long domination of the Conservative Party of John A. Macdonald (1867-73, 1878-96) and the Liberal Party of Wilfrid Laurier (1896-1911) bears witness to the importance of the French-Canadian bloc vote. Whether French Canadians obtained the appropriate social rewards from being a part of the ruling party is an ongoing historical debate. In immigration matters, at least, the answer is that they did not. Both the goals and recruitment strategies of immigration were determined by English Canadians – sometimes, in the face of opposition from Quebec.

Immigration recruitment in the three decades after Confederation was not very successful. A large majority of the emigrants from western Europe and Great Britain felt that economic and social opportunities were far superior in the United States. In fact, many nineteenth-century Canadians were similarly attracted by "the American way of life," and, by 1900, over a million former Canadians had located in the United States.

The election of Laurier's Liberal government in 1896 was followed by a marked expansion of immigration into Canada (see Table 1). The change in administration had coincided with a period of world-wide prosperity that, in a Canadian context, focused attention on the development of the West. To make this dream a reality, strong, willing workers were needed to cultivate the vast acres of virgin prairie, to build the new transcontinental railroads, and to supply the manpower for an expanding industrial system. Thus the new government turned with greater enthusiasm than its predecessors to attracting new immigrants not only from the traditional sources (Great Britain, western Europe, and the United States) but also from central and eastern Europe. One aspect of the immigration debate revolved around the importance of racial and cultural characteristics as the criteria for entry into Canada. Although many entrepreneurs pressed for the large-scale importation of non-white immigrants who would function as an industrial proletariat, Canadian public opinion was generally hostile to the entry of ethnic groups who were believed to be non-assimilable. The undesirable qualities of the non-white races, it was argued, sprang from genetic and racial determinants that would not be altered by contact with Canadian society.

Few restrictive measures were imposed against Caucasian immigrants. Despite some unsatisfactory behavioural traits ascribed to certain ethnic and national groups from Europe, Anglo-Canadian immigration boosters claimed that these traits were primarily based on their past cultural and environmental background. Time and Anglo-Canadian institutions, it was held, would

Table 1
Immigration by Calendar Year, 1852-1992

Year	Number	Year	Number	Year	Number
1852	29,307	1899	44,543	1946	71,719
1853	29,464	1900	41,681	1947	64,127
1854	37,263	1901	55,747	1948	125,414
1855	25,296	1902	89,102	1949	95,217
1856	22,544	1903	138,660	1950	73,912
1857	33,854	1904	131,252	1951	194,391
1858	12,339	1905	141,465	1952	164,498
1859	6,300	1906	211,653	1953	168,868
1860	6,276	1907	272,409	1954	154,227
1861	13,589	1908	143,326	1955	109,946
1862	18,294	1909	173,694	1956	164,857
1863	21,000	1910	286,839	1957	282,164
1864	24,779	1911	331,288	1958	124,851
1865	18,958	1912	375,756	1959	106,928
1866	11,427	1913	400,870	1960	104,111
1867	10,666	1914	150,484	1961	71,689
1868	12,765	1915	36,665	1962	74,586
1869	18,630	1916	55,914	1963	93,151
1870	24,706	1917	72,910	1964	112,606
1871	27,773	1918	41,845	1965	146,758
1872	36,758	1919	107,698	1966	194,743
1873	50,050	1920	138,824	1967	222,876
1874	39,373	1921	91,728	1968	183,974
1875	27,382	1922	64,224	1969	161,531
1876	25,633	1923	133,729	1970	147,713
1877	27,082	1924	124,164	1971	121,900
1878	29,807	1925	84,907	1972	122,006
1879	40,492	1926	135,982	1973	184,200
1880	38,505	1927	158,886	1974	218,465
1881	47,991	1928	166,783	1975	187,881
1882	112,458	1929	164,993	1976	149,429
1883	133,624	1930	104,806	1977	114,914
1884	103,824	1931	27,530	1978	86,313
1885	79,169	1932	20,591	1979	112,096
1886	69,152	1933	14,382	1980	143,117
1887	84,526	1934	12,476	1981	128,618
1888	88,766	1935	11,277	1982	121,147
1889	91,600	1936	11,643	1983	89,157
1890	75,067	1937	15,101	1984	88,239
1891	82,165	1938	17,244	1985	84,302
1892	30,996	1939	16,994	1986	99,219
1893	29,633	1940	11,324	1987	152,098
1894	20,829	1941	9,329	1988	161,929
1895	18,790	1942	7,576	1989	192,001
1896	16,835	1943	8,504	1990	214,230
1897	21,716	1944	12,801	1991	230,781
1898	31,900	1945	22,722	1992	252,842

SOURCE: Citizenship and Immigration Canada, *Immigration Statistics, 1992* (Ottawa, 1994).

ultimately erase these differences and facilitate the absorption of all-white immigrants into the Anglo-Canadian community. Most Canadians accepted these assurances, but there were certain elements in the country that reacted negatively toward these European newcomers. Organized labour, for instance, charged that immigration recruitment produced a continuous supply of cheap labour that permitted the business community to resist trade union demands for higher wages, better working conditions, and union recognition. Many French Canadians argued that instead of recruiting European immigrants, the Dominion government should assist Quebec farmers to relocate in the rural areas of western Canada. Concern was also expressed that the influx of these European immigrants would alter the bicultural character of the nation, especially in the West. But despite this opposition Canada's immigration policy remained expansionist until World War One.

The rapid growth in Canada's population and the accompanying ethnic diversification that occurred between 1896 and 1930 had critical implications for the future of the country. While the settled regions of eastern Canada retained their English-French cultural dualism, the developing regions to the north and west of the Great Lakes assumed many of the characteristics of a pluralistic society. The emergence of ethnic communities played a useful role in helping their members to adjust from one linguistic environment to another, and sometimes from a rural way of living to an urban one. However, in some cases, the ethnic community acted as a brake on the individual achievement and social mobility of its members. Economic and cultural discrimination from both the Anglophone and Francophone host societies also created difficulties for many immigrants, a trend exacerbated by the severe problems associated with the Great Depression.

Prior to 1930 Anglo-Canadians had often demonstrated concern over the slow rate of Canadianization among certain immigrant groups. During the First World War patriotic fervour had brought about the abolition of bilingual schools in western Canada and a temporary redefinition of the citizenship rights of European newcomers on the basis of wartime service. This suspicion of divided loyalties once again surfaced in the late 1920s when the Ku Klux Klan of Kanada, a weird hybrid of American and indigenous bigotry, enjoyed some success in Saskatchewan with its "anti-foreigner" campaign. Not surprisingly, the advent of the Great Depression intensified the fear of the alien, the more so since the spectre of unemployment and social demoralization seemed to threaten the fundamentals of Canadian society.

Xenophobia became particularly pronounced in the late 1930s when thousands of German and Austrian Jews fled the Nazi terror and sought sanctuary in Canada. Yet, despite anguished representation from a wide variety of Canadian humanitarian organizations and the favourable response of other "traditional" immigration countries, most notably the United States and Australia, the Canadian immigration gates remained virtually closed to these tragic refugees.

Fortunately, the post-war years witnessed a dramatic change in Canada's refugee policy. In keeping with their new commitments to the United Nations and to human rights, Canadians welcomed over 160,000 European refugees and displaced persons between 1946 and 1952 – a substantially higher ratio of acceptance than the United States. There was, however, a dimension of economic self-interest to this generous response. Displaced persons were expected to perform traditional immigrant types of work in agriculture and in the labour-intensive extractive industries. For many of the DPs, as they came to be called, adjustment to the Canadian environment was very difficult, especially for the professionals and skilled workers. Particularly frustrating was the attitude of those Canadians who underestimated their abilities because of their unfamiliarity with the English language and the Canadian professional associations, which were reluctant to certify European-trained doctors, dentists, lawyers, and teachers.

The continued expansion of the Canadian economy, the seemingly insatiable demands for unskilled and skilled labour, and the heady optimism that Canada was an evolving major world power encouraged an expansionist immigration policy in the 1950s and 1960s. Thousands of Dutch, German, Italian, Greek, and Portuguese immigrants came to this country with the expectation of a better life; the low level of re-emigration suggests that most realized their goals. But now it was not the prairie West that attracted most immigrants. Instead, over half of the newcomers gravitated toward the major centres of Ontario, most notably Toronto, which became, by 1970, the most culturally diverse city in the country. Significantly, most Canadians welcomed the increasingly pluralistic quality of Canadian society and most immigrants effectively adjusted to their new environment. A wide variety of ethnic organizations (churches, newspapers, voluntary associations) have assisted in this social transition, but perhaps the most important integrationist catalyst has been the Canadian educational system, that essential bridge between Anglo-Canadian and immigrant communities.

Five federal agencies have been responsible for immigration policy since 1949 – the Department of Citizenship and Immigration (1949-66), the Department of Manpower and Immigration (1966-77), the Canada Employment and Immigration Commission (1977-93), the Department of Public Security (1993), and the present Department of Citizenship and Immigration. Although most provinces have continued to accept Ottawa's primacy in immigration matters, the Quebec government during the 1960s Quiet Revolution established its own service in order to recruit as many French-speaking immigrants as possible and to ensure that immigrants who settle in Quebec form part of the Francophone community. Immigration regulations provide for the entry of three categories of immigrants: close relatives, independent applicants determined by skill, and refugees.

Since 1967, when Canada followed the lead of the United States in removing the discriminatory sections from the Immigration Act and its regulations, the selection of applicants for admission has been largely conducted on the basis of occupational training, with professional and skilled immigrants theoretically being granted entry regardless of their ethnic background. Although these principles were enshrined in the Immigration Act of 1976, there was still criticism that Canadian immigration procedures were arbitrary and discriminatory when applied to immigrants from Third World countries. As a result, since the 1980s the Immigration Bureau of the Department of External Affairs has become very much involved in those immigration programs that affect Canada's foreign policy. The Immigration Bureau helps to monitor the country's international commitment to allocate at least 10 per cent of its annual immigration quota for refugees. Indeed, since the 1950s Canada has accepted thousands of refugees from all parts of the world: Hungarians in 1956; Czechs in 1968; Uganda Asians in 1972; and more recently, Vietnamese boat people and refugees from Bosnia, Haiti, and Somalia. Political refugees from Latin American dictatorships, however, have not always been as fortunate.

As the nation approaches the end of the twentieth century the old debate over immigration policy and the ethnic character of Canadian society continues. Should Canada greatly expand its annual intake well beyond the 200,000 quota projected for 1995? How many should come from Third World countries? To what extent do Canadians wish to extend the pluralistic character of their society? Are racism and ethnic intolerance spent forces in this country or are they recurring phenomena that surface in periods of large-scale immigration? Given the complexity of these questions, it is little wonder that politically ambitious Ministers of Immigration often seek a quick exit from that portfolio.

Anglo-Conformity, Multiculturalism, and Immigration History

Since Confederation the writing of immigration and ethnic history in Canada has gone through a number of stages.[2] The first of these would be the British and French ethnocentric and patriotic works of the nineteenth century. Most of these emphasized the hardships associated with settlement and the value of their respective institutions.[3] With the arrival of thousands of immigrants from western Europe, English-Canadian writers and scholars began to change their focus somewhat. In general these authors approached western European immigrants sympathetically, although there was still the assumption that German, Dutch, and Scandinavian immigrants did not quite measure up to the cultural qualities of British immigrants or Anglo-Canadian society.[4] In the early years of the twentieth century the "stalwart" peasants from the Russian and Austro-

Hungarian empires became the source of intense controversy. Some Anglo-Canadian writers emphasized the great contribution these central Europeans had made on their homesteads and in the many frontier work camps.[5] In contrast, a wide body of literature portrayed these "foreigners" as a long-term "problem" that would not be easily resolved. The Great War intensified the debate.[6] With renewed immigration and the advent of the Great Depression there was a resumption of the argument that certain groups of immigrants were a serious threat to Canadian society. The most vicious attacks were directed toward the Canadian Japanese community, and it was not until after 1945 that books began to appear criticizing the federal wartime policies.[7] The post-war years also brought a reassessment of Canada's isolationist and uncharitable response to Jews and other refugees fleeing the Nazi terror.[8] This was paralleled by a resurgence of interest in the ethnic dimension of Canadian society, with many books written from the viewpoint of particular ethnic groups.[9] Another important trend was the growing number of scholarly works emanating from professional historians, sociologists, and political scientists.[10] John Porter's *The Vertical Mosaic* (1963) was the most outstanding example of this new interdisciplinary approach. Increasingly, concepts such as the vertical mosaic, institutional completeness, ethnic enclosure, and ethnic identity would be used by a wide range of scholars involved in ethnic studies.[11] American ethnic studies, which had been a thriving field during the 1960s, strongly influenced many Canadian scholars.[12] Since 1970 Canadian scholars have produced a rich body of literature dealing with immigration[13] and ethnic issues.[14] This has included provocative general works,[15] as well as studies dealing with the various aspects of multiculturalism in Canadian society, past and present.[16] Patterns of racism and discrimination in Canada have also been analysed by a number of writers.[17] Studies on the specific experiences of various visible minority communities have greatly enhanced the scholarly debate.[18] So, too, have newer books on European immigrant groups.[19] But perhaps the most important addition to the scholarly literature has been works describing the Canadian experience of immigrant women.[20]

Immigrant Workers and Canadian Society

Studies of immigrant workers and their adaptation to the Canadian work and social environment have changed appreciably during the past twenty years. In the early 1970s the traditional interpretations emphasized that Canada only recruited agriculturalists, who gravitated toward the rural areas of western Canada, occupying homesteads on a full-time basis. This simplistic view ignored the reality that many immigrants were involved full-time in the capitalistic Canadian labour market.[21] Nor was the Canadian experience of European immigrant workers in various forms of working-class militancy and radicalism seriously analysed. Even studies of the dramatic and important Winnipeg General

Strike of 1919 tended to dismiss the involvement of thousands of Ukrainian, Polish, Jewish, and German workers.[22]

Fortunately, Canadian immigration, ethnic, and labour historians have increasingly turned their attention to these subjects since the publication of *"Dangerous Foreigners"* in 1979. Some studies have examined more general themes associated with the migration experience and the world of work.[23] Others have concentrated on how specific ethnic groups adjusted to Canadian society.[24] Labour historians have provided useful accounts of the role immigrant workers assumed in Canadian trade unions and socialist organizations.[25]

The present volume has also drawn on the work of various theoretical studies of migration and the Canadian labour market. Of particular value has been the work of immigration historians such as W.R. Bohning, whose research on post-war guest workers from the Mediterranean littoral into the highly industrialized countries of western Europe suggests some interesting comparisons with this study. In Bohning's scheme of things the first wave of immigrant workers consists normally of single males. These are not only the most mobile group in the emigration society, but also the closest "to the locus of the 'grapevine' which sets in motion a chain migration." Once the apparent success of a particular migration has been established, more and more unaccompanied married workers join the stream, most of them intending to return to their wives and children after acquiring their "stake." In time the advantages of the host society not only delay their return but encourage them to send for their dependants.[26] This larger pattern, it will be seen, has numerous Canadian examples in the period under review.

This book also uses the concept of the capitalistic labour market that H.C. Pentland developed in his masterful 1959 article:

> By a capitalistic labour market is meant one in which the actions of workers and employers are governed and linked by the impersonal considerations of immediate pecuniary advantage. In this market the employer is confident that workers will be available whenever he wants them; so he feels free to hire them on a short term basis, and to dismiss them whenever there is a monetary advantage to doing so . . . labour to the employer is a variable cost.

To maintain such a market in Canada, Pentland argued, it was necessary to do much more than import large numbers of unskilled immigrants. In addition, these immigrants had to be of a type prepared to seek employment in the low-paying, exacting jobs associated with labour-intensive industries. Implicit in this argument was the idea that a permanent proletariat was not a bad thing.[27]

Another useful theoretical model is the split labour market interpretation developed by the American sociologist Edna Bonacich and modified by other scholars. According to Bonacich, "a split labor market refers to a difference in the price of labor between two or more groups of workers, holding constant their efficiency and productivity."[28] Under this scheme European immigrant workers were less costly than native-born workers; even cheaper were Asian and black workers. But as employers attempted "to replace dominant workers with 'cheap' minority labor, ethnic competition results in renewed ethnic antagonism and segregation of the labor market by labor unions."[29] This, in turn, was often followed by "added labour market segregation resulting from the effects of the racist discourse . . . and from the abandonment of low-paying positions for higher paying ones by . . . dominant workers." What often occurred was "dominant employers and their dominant employees developing common interest in economic discrimination against minorities."[30]

The seminal work of John Porter on ethnic and class stratification in Canadian society is also significant here. Porter's insightful comments on Canada's immigration experience in the twentieth century bear repeating: "immigration and ethnic affiliation have been important factors in the formation of social classes in Canada . . . [and] ethnic differences have been important in building up the bottom layer of the stratification system in both agricultural and industrial settings."[31]

Summary

Class, race, and ethnicity have been important factors in determining both Canada's policy toward different groups of immigrant workers and where foreign-born men and women subsequently found employment. While European immigrant workers are the primary focus of this study, the unique problems of Asian and Caribbean immigrants are also examined. The book also places Canada's policies within a comparative framework: the impact of U.S. immigration and refugee policies receives special attention throughout the book.[32]

Since the vast majority of these workers were male, this has meant that the Canadian experience of immigrant women has not received the treatment it deserved if the focus of this study had been urban, rather than rural. Nor has the world of the immigrant worker – occupational, residential, cultural – been analysed in any detail. Such an undertaking would require another volume. Some readers will note that the immigration debate in Quebec has been given only cursory treatment. This topic also awaits the specialists.[33]

PART ONE

Immigration Policy and Immigrant Workers, 1896-1952

Departmental Affiliation
Ministry of the Interior, 1896-1930
Ministry of Northern Affairs, 1930-49
Ministry of Citizenship and Immigration, 1949-66

Ministers responsible for immigration
Liberal government of Sir Wilfrid Laurier, 1896-1911
Clifford Sifton	1896-1905
Frank Oliver	1905-11

Conservative government of Sir Robert Borden, 1911-17
Robert Rogers	1911-12
William Roche	1912-17

Conservative government of Borden/Arthur Meighen, 1917-21
James A. Calder	1917-21
John W. Edwards	1921

Liberal government of William Lyon Mackenzie King, 1922-26
Hewitt Bostock	1922
Charles Stewart	1922-23
John A. Robb	1923-25
George N. Gordon	1925
Charles Stewart	1925-26

Conservative government of Arthur Meighen, 1926
Robert J. Manion	1926
Henry L. Drayton	1926

Liberal government of Mackenzie King, 1926-30
Robert Forke	1926-29
Charles Stewart	1929-30
Ian A. Mackenzie	1930

Conservative government of Richard B. Bennett, 1930-35
Wesley A. Gordon	1930-35

Liberal government of Mackenzie King/Louis St. Laurent, 1935-49
Thomas A. Crerar	1935-45
James A. Glen	1945-48
James A. MacKinnon	1948-49

CHAPTER 1

European Immigrant Workers and
the Canadian Economy, 1896-1914

Between 1896 and 1914 Canada experienced unprecedented economic growth: railway mileage doubled, mining production tripled, and wheat and lumber production increased tenfold. This economic expansion was accompanied by dramatic population growth; in the decade 1901-11 the nation's population increased by a remarkable 34 per cent. Much of this increase was attributed to immigration; in 1914, it was estimated that three million people had entered the country since 1896. Although a substantial number of these newcomers settled on the land, the vast majority derived some portion of their annual income from the wage employment offered by the booming agricultural and industrial sectors of the economy whose demand for labour, both skilled and unskilled, seemed insatiable.

Led by the spokesmen for labour-intensive industries, including agriculture, Canadian public opinion came to favour an immigration policy that went beyond the traditional open-door approach to the systematic recruitment abroad of men and women who could meet the challenge of a nation freshly embarked upon great enterprise. This opinion found expression in the immigration policies of successive Dominion governments. Although the official pronouncements of the Immigration Branch in this period stressed that only farmers, farm labourers, and domestics would be recruited, exceptions were frequently made to accommodate the needs of businessmen in the expanding sectors of the economy. That Canada's search for immigrant agriculturalists was largely in the hands of steamship agents in search of bonuses further qualified official policy;

many who entered the country as farmers and farm labourers quickly found their way into construction camps, mines, and factories.[1]

Ironically, agricultural immigrants were also turned toward wage employment by a settlement policy that tended to give priority to a central European peasantry too poor to establish itself directly on the land. For many who entered the country during these years the life of a yeoman farmer was either irrelevant or but a distant ideal that could be realized only through the slow accumulation of capital by wage labour. As W.F. McCreary, the Winnipeg commissioner of immigration, put it in 1897: "We have a long and wearisome task before us if we expect to settle this country with . . . men with even modest means. The settlement, if it comes at all rapidly, must come from men without means, who will earn in this territory itself the capital to enable them to homestead."[2] It was therefore assumed by both immigration officials and employers that many agricultural immigrants would initially, at any rate, provide a source of cheap seasonal labour. Industries such as commercial agriculture, railroad construction, mining, and lumbering all experienced peak annual work periods; their needs and the needs of the immigrants could be harmonized – or so it appeared at the turn of the century. In the event, this arrangement was not entirely satisfactory to either party. The immigrant workers were exposed to a labour market both highly unstable and fraught with physical difficulties. The ideal of the Canadian developmental capitalists of this era was the sort of labour market H.C. Pentland has described, where "the capitalistic labour market represents a pooling of the labour supplies and labour needs of many employers, so that all may benefit by economizing on labour reserves."[3]

Faced with the demands of projects such as the building of two new transcontinental railways, Canada's captains of industry required a work force that was both inexpensive and at their beck and call. To them the agricultural ideal at the root of Canadian immigration policy increasingly appeared obsolete. Supply and demand should be the new governing principle of immigration policy. The best immigrants would be those willing to roam the country to take up whatever work was available. This view ran against the deep-seated Canadian myth of the primacy of the land but it nevertheless prevailed. By 1914 it was obvious, even to immigration officials, that Canada had joined the United States as part of a transatlantic market.[4]

Immigration Trends

Statistics on the ethnic composition of this immigration and the regional concentrations of immigrants (settlers and resource workers), as well as their distribution within the occupational structure, bring to the surface the contours of what could be called "the specificity of the Canadian experience." In 1891, at an early stage in Canada's industrialization, the foreign-born population accounted for 13.3 per cent of the total population, a figure roughly comparable to that for the United States. However, this foreign population came overwhelmingly from British sources, as 76 per cent were British-born. During the following thirty years British immigrants continued to constitute the majority among the foreign-born population; but there was also a dramatic increase in the number of foreign-born coming from other European areas, most notably eastern and southern Europe. By 1921, these new trends were clearly reflected in the population statistics. The proportion of all foreign-born within the total Canadian population had jumped to 22.2 per cent (about 7 percentage points higher than that of the U.S.), while the foreign-born other than British now accounted for 46 per cent of all the foreign-born population.[5] The large-scale arrival of southern and eastern Europeans into Canada occurred significantly later than the massive movement into the United States. As well, despite their numbers, European immigrants were still overshadowed by the volume of immigrants of British origin. Indeed, it is important to remember that English Canadians often had to reconcile their status as nationalists and imperialists, given Canada's important role in the British Empire prior to 1920.[6]

Another factor was the spatial distribution of the foreign-born population during this period of major industrialization and economic growth. In 1901, for example, Ontario, the country's largest province, accounted for 46.3 per cent of all foreign-born; during the following two decades this share declined to 32.8 per cent. In contrast, the surge of immigrants into western Canada greatly changed the demographic character of these four provinces. In 1901 they had 31.5 per cent of all foreign-born in the country; in 1921 they had 54 per cent. Thus, despite the importance of industrial growth in central Canada, these population trends reflect the significant place that land settlement occupied in Canada's economic growth. The significance of these trends is confirmed when one adopts a rural/urban classification system to analyse the residential choice of immigrants. Compared to the ratio of the Canadian-born population (52 per cent rural and 48 per cent urban in 1921), the non-British foreign-born were 54 per cent rural and 46 per cent urban, while 65 per cent of British immigrants were attracted to the cities.[7]

Immigrant workers had a different impact on the various Canadian regions. The Maritime provinces, for example, received relatively few of the immigrants and sojourners who crossed the Atlantic between 1890 and 1930. The few that did come were primarily hived in the coal and steel complex on Cape Breton Island.[8] In Quebec quite a different situation existed. During the latter part of the nineteenth century there was a large-scale movement of French-Canadian workers to the expanding mining and lumbering communities of the Canadian Shield, a migration strongly encouraged by the province's Roman Catholic hierarchy. Although some immigrant workers found jobs elsewhere in Quebec, the majority gravitated to the Montreal metropolitan region, which soon became conspicuous for the complexity of its occupational structure and the cultural heterogeneity of its work force.[9]

Many of the same characteristics were evident in the experience of immigrant workers in the resource industries of northern Ontario and western Canada. In one year an immigrant worker might find himself in many roles: in February a lumber worker in northern Ontario; in June a railroad navvy along the Canadian Pacific mainline in British Columbia; in August a harvester in Saskatchewan; in November, a miner in northern Quebec. Significantly, this pattern of work coincided with the needs of the labour-intensive resource industries and transportation companies that largely determined Canadian immigration policies in these years.[10]

Immigration Policy and Resource Industries

Until World War One Canadian immigration policy had two determinants: the willingness of the Dominion government to give businessmen a free hand in the recruitment of the immigrants they needed for national economic development; and the determination of the Immigration Branch to recruit agriculturalists, particularly for the settlement of western Canada. The tendency to equate population growth through immigration with national prosperity was especially pronounced during the years 1896-1914. The Immigration Branch in these years was under the direction of men who reflected the expansionist outlook of western Canada: Clifford Sifton (1896-1905), Frank Oliver (1905-11), Robert Rogers (1911-12), and Dr. W.J. Roche (1912-14). In many ways Clifford Sifton established the pattern followed by his successors. The operational budget was expanded from a modest $120,100 in 1896 to a remarkable $900,000 in 1905, Sifton's last year as Minister of the Interior.[11] This increase was accompanied by personnel changes that saw many of Sifton's business and political associates assume key positions. Men such as James A. Smart (deputy minister of the interior), Frank Pedley (superintendent of immigration), W.F. McCreary (Winnipeg commissioner), and W.T.R. Preston (commissioner in London, England) shared Sifton's faith that the key to Canadian prosperity was the settlement of western Canada through expanded immigration and railroad construction. These men also accepted the notion that government officials and businessmen should work closely together to promote the opening of new agricultural regions and the development of resource industries such as lumbering and mining.[12]

Sifton and his hand-picked civil servants saw immigration in the most pragmatic terms; it didn't matter where immigrants came from as long as they could be made to fit Canada's economic priorities. Racial and cultural factors could not be ignored, but above all immigrants should be selected according to their ability to adjust to the environmental and occupational demands of the Canadian frontier. Sifton also stressed the advantages of the family model of immigration, both for economic and social purposes. Anglo-Canadians might resent the influx of Poles, Russians, and Ukrainians with their vastly different ways, but his utilitarian approach guaranteed their entry. Sifton's attitude was summed up in one remark: "I think a stalwart peasant in a sheep-skin coat, born on the soil, whose forbearers have been farmers for ten generations, with a stout wife and half-a-dozen children, is good quality."[13] By this standard British immigrants were a doubtful quantity. Many of them not only refused to go on the land, they also refused "heavy-handed work." In 1907, Dr. P.H. Bryce, the chief medical officer of the Immigration Branch, suggested that a high percentage of British immigrants were poor physical specimens, especially those from "classes which have been for several generations factory operatives and dwellers in the congested centres of large industrial populations."[14] Immigrants from the British Isles, the ancient homeland of so many English-speaking Canadians, continued to flow into the country. But for the Immigration Branch the "peasant in a sheep-skin coat" chiefly had to be found elsewhere. Under Sifton's direction Canadian immigration policy acquired a vigorous continental European dimension.

Between 1896 and 1914 approximately a million immigrant farmers were found for Canada's burgeoning agricultural economy. Immigration officials were particularly anxious to maintain a steady supply of farm workers since agriculture in Canada was labour-intensive and large numbers of men were required during both spring seeding and fall harvest. The demand for seasonal labour was most pronounced in the grain belt of western Canada and in the sugar-beet and fruit-farming regions of Ontario, Alberta, and British Columbia. The declining number of native-born family farm workers increased the demand for immigrant farm labourers.[15] This desperate shortage of agricultural workers was vividly described by one Alberta farmer in 1907: "The government is trying to bring settlers or farmers into the west all the time. What is needed is men to work for the farmers that are already here, or those who are here will have to go out of business.... I hired a man from the Salvation Army.... He is with me yet, but ... he knows he could get $3.00 a day if he were free, and reminds me of that fact quite often. He is the boss and I am the roust about, or chore boy."[16]

In its attempts to meet the mounting needs of Canadian farmers the Immigration Branch employed a variety of methods. The most common and traditional of these was the payment of a bonus to steamship agents and colonization organizations for each agricultural immigrant brought into the country.[17] Unfortunately, there was no way to guarantee that particular immigrants were agriculturalists or that, once in the country, they would be available for farm work. Many steamship agents assumed no responsibility beyond the bonus.[18]

In 1899 an attempt was made to provide a more systematic and responsible system for the recruitment of continental European agriculturalists, particularly from Germany, the Austro-Hungarian Empire, and the Scandinavian countries. This took the form of a clandestine agreement between the Canadian government and the North Atlantic Trading Company. By 1906, when the Dominion government backed out of the arrangement, the company had directed over 70,000 immigrants to Canada, most of them from the Austrian provinces of Galicia and Bukovina, and had been paid $367,245.[19] The elimination of the company signalled a return of chaotic market conditions in the immigrant industry, though the Dominion government continued to pay bonuses to a variety of organizations and agents to bring farm workers to Canada. One of the most controversial of these emigration organizations was the Salvation Army. In 1903 the "Army next to God" had created a Department of Migration and Settlement for the transportation and placement of the "deserving" poor of Great Britain. The Salvation Army was able to persuade the Dominion authorities to include it in the bonus scheme for bringing agriculturalists to the country. Bonus payments to the Army rose dramatically from $500 in 1903 to $9,052 in 1907 and $25,000 in 1914, despite continual charges from the Trades and Labour Congress of Canada that most of these "agriculturalists" soon became industrial workers.[20]

Organized labour was even more hostile toward the schemes of commercial emigration companies. One of these had at its head James A. Smart, Sifton's first deputy minister. In 1905 Smart was able to convince immigration officials to support a prepaid passage scheme whereby his agency would act simultaneously as immigrant bank, steamship agency, and labour bureau. Immigrants resident in Canada would purchase steamship and rail tickets for friends or relatives overseas through one of Smart's local offices. Those recruited in this fashion were then brought to Canada and placed in agricultural jobs by the Smart labour agency. For its efforts the company would receive both a commission on steamship tickets sold and a bonus from the Dominion government.[21]

In 1907, the Immigration Branch itself became directly involved in the recruitment and placement of British agricultural labourers in the provinces of Ontario and Quebec. Approximately 100 government agents were appointed, each of whom received a two-dollar bonus for every farm labourer placed. W.D. Scott, the superintendent of immigration, explained the new system in these terms: "Each agent is supposed to correspond with the [3,000] British booking agents pointing out the needs of his individual locality, the rate of wages there and to request the booking agent to direct suitable farm labourers to him. When the booking agent has succeeded in selling a ticket to an emigrant ... he immediately mails an advice form to the agent interested ... and delivers to the emigrant in question a card of introduction."[22]

In many ways this placement scheme was an attempt to attract a higher percentage of British agriculturalists to Canada. Conditions in Great Britain did not favour the emigration of such persons since agricultural wages and working conditions were often better than in Canada. Indeed, British farm labourers had little incentive to leave for a harsh new land where irregular employment, low wages, and poor accommodations were commonplace. Nor did Canadian farmers show themselves particularly willing to make the prospect of immigration more attractive for British labourers. In 1907, the Winnipeg commissioner of immigration became so annoyed with the outlook of Prairie farmers that he suggested a reduction in the efforts being made to recruit farm labour for spring seeding.[23]

His suggestion was neither economically expedient nor politically wise. In fact the opposite occurred. Pressure from the railway companies and Prairie farmers and businessmen led the Immigration Branch into further involvement in the farm labour market in conjunction with private labour bureaus such as the Canadian Pacific Employment Agency, the Grand Trunk Pacific Employment Agency, the Canadian Northern Employment Agency, Allons Employment Agency, and Hislop Employment Agency. The phenomenal increases occurring in wheat production ensured that business interests recruiting farm labour would have the active co-operation of the Immigration Branch. In 1901, 20,000 harvesters had to be induced into the fields; by 1914 the number had jumped to 50,000. The movement of seasonal workers on this scale required resources that only the Dominion government and the large railway companies could supply. Immigration officials and railway agents worked together to obtain the necessary manpower. On the government side a careful estimate was made each spring of the requirements of the following harvest. The major contribution of the railway companies was the harvest excursion rates by both rail and sea. In 1907, the CPR reduced its rates for British harvesters to such an extent that it incurred the wrath of the North Atlantic Shipping Convention.[24]

Yet from the point of view of both Canadian farmers and immigration officials the British harvesters left much to be desired. A common complaint of western farmers was large numbers of them "had no skill with the pitchfork, but great enthusiasm for the dinner fork," and that they soon abandoned farm work for easier jobs in urban centres. This in turn led to problems between organized labour and the Immigration Branch. In 1904, Arthur Puttee, the labour member of Parliament for Winnipeg, charged that urban wage earners were being required "to bear the whole brunt of carrying labour on a labour market for nine months in order that farmers may use it for two or three months."[25]

Continental European immigrants proved much more malleable. Work in the grain fields of more affluent Anglo-Canadian farmers provided these men with necessary subsistence and offered farmers the means to expand existing land holdings. One survey of rural settlement in western Canada revealed that 50 per cent of the 832 families interviewed had no money on arrival in Canada; another 42 per cent had less than $500. As a result, it was necessary for the Ukrainian

settler to seek temporary employment in farm labour, railroad construction, lumbering, or mining. The initial years of adaptation of one Ukrainian family in the Vonda district of Saskatchewan were typical of the experience of many continental European immigrants:

> When they arrived at Rosthern, Saskatchewan, they had not a cent left. Her husband could not get work on account of a strike of section labourers [July, 1901]. Later he managed to obtain farm work for 3 months from a German farmer near Rosthern. The money thus earned was their means of living for a whole year. They lived after this fashion for three years until they were settled on their own homestead.[26]

Steamship and railway companies assumed a central role in the recruitment and distribution of agricultural immigrants. By 1900, the British and European companies had thousands of agents and sub-agents circulating throughout the British Isles and continental Europe advertising economic opportunities in North America and the advantages of travelling with their company.[27] At European ports such as Rotterdam, Hamburg, and Trieste steamships received their human cargo for the still difficult transatlantic crossing. Upon arrival at Halifax or Quebec City the European peasants then boarded primitive railway coaches for their journey to the Golden West. At Winnipeg and other regional centres they set out for government homesteads, or to railway land, spread throughout the Prairies.[28] In *The Sowing* Emerson Hough offered this vivid account of the arrival of immigrant trains in Winnipeg:

> There is no more picturesque, albeit no more pathetic spectacle in the world than that afforded by the Canadian Pacific Railway Station in Winnipeg where most of the European immigrants make the first stop in their long journey to their chosen land. . . . In this gathering ground there are to be seen Swedes, Norwegians, Germans . . . numbers of Hungarians, Galicians, and others . . . their striking and bright-coloured costumes of silks and skin, their strange embroidered boots and bright head coverings. . . . A babel of tongues arises. Here wanders a helpless soul, with no record of any recent meal visible in his gaunt form or features, and no understandable human speech by which he may set himself right with the world.[29]

The attitude of the CPR toward immigration was typified in a comment made to Thomas Shaughnessy by Archer Baker, the European emigration manager in 1907: "We have done more in the last two years with reference to encouraging the immigration along intelligent lines from the United States, Great Britain and Europe than the whole Dominion Department of Immigration. . . ."[30] The company had many reasons for this level of involvement. The sale of its land was a major consideration; between 1896 and 1913 sales expanded from $216,081 to

$5,795,977. The CPR saw advantages in an arrangement whereby European immigrants would be directed by the Immigration Branch into the construction of colonization railways in the underdeveloped regions of western Canada. Here the immigrants would satisfy several needs: they would serve as a source of cheap labour in the construction of CPR branch lines; their crops would bring further business to the company; and, ultimately, they could be directed into complementary resource industries like lumbering and mining. From the point of view of immigration policy, work on railroad construction gangs would be a means of initiation whereby the newcomers could adapt to Canadian society. In 1900 the Winnipeg commissioner of immigration suggested that the presidents of the CPR and Canadian Northern should be informed that it was "their duty to employ all immigrants who have taken up land, whether they be English-speaking or foreign, in preference to importing labour of any kind."[31]

The initial response of the railway companies was favourable; settler-labourers seemed to meet their needs admirably in that they were "obedient and industrious." Docility was a virtue highly prized by both the railway companies and the Immigration Branch. In 1900, James A. Smart, deputy minister of the interior, made it clear to his subordinates that Slavic navvies should be actively discouraged from any attempt at collective bargaining: "They should be told when they need work they had better take the wages they are offered."[32] Consideration was also given in the Immigration Branch to a system whereby time spent on railroad construction work would count toward securing a land patent.[33]

In northern Ontario immigrants were distributed throughout the Clay Belt both by private railway companies and by the provincially owned Temiskaming and Northern Ontario Railway. Here, when the railway construction season ended, the immigrants often found work in logging camps and sawmills. Boards of trade and municipal governments in northern Ontario pressed continually for more immigrants who would adapt to the seasonal job market of the region. In 1901, for example, the Port Arthur Board of Trade made the following appeal to the Minister of the Interior: "So many pulp and paper mills have been building in the northern country, which by reason of its unlimited supply of spruce timber and paper trade, that labour is becoming very scarce, and we need immigrants who, whilst making pulp wood in clearing their farms, will also help to work the mills." The arrival of Finnish and Scandinavian "agriculturalists" experienced in "wood cutting and timber floating" and the cultivation of marginal lands soon provided an abundant source of manpower. Some of these immigrants also found their way in the winter months to the mining camps at Sudbury, Cobalt, and Timmins; others drifted west and joined with homesteaders and farm labourers from the Prairies in seeking employment in a rapidly expanding Rocky Mountain coal-mining industry.[34]

Recruiting Industrial Workers

By the turn of the century it was quite clear that a large percentage of the peasant farmers and farm labourers recruited by the Dominion government were not becoming full-time agriculturalists. Neither seasonal employment in farm labour nor subsistence agriculture was enough to sustain life; other means had to be found and the numerous railroad construction, lumbering, and mining camps scattered across the country provided the necessary outlets. But this adaptation of the immigrant to the Canadian environment had produced many dislocations. Commercial farmers bitterly complained about the lack of help during periods of peak production. Spokesmen for labour-intensive industries voiced a similar complaint. Occupational specialization rather than occupational pluralism was what both the established farmers and captains of industry required of the immigrant worker.[35]

The railway companies were loud in their demand that the priorities of the marketplace take precedence over those of immigrant adaptation. By 1900, the CPR had apparently decided that certain groups of immigrants made poor construction workers. British immigrants were especially suspect; not only were they unwilling to tolerate low wages and primitive working conditions, but they could use the English-language press to focus public attention on their grievances. In 1897, for example, the CPR was charged with gross mistreatment of Welsh and other British immigrants recruited for work on the Crow's Nest Pass Railway. The report of Justice R.C. Clute on the matter generally confirmed the accusations, particularly those with respect to sanitary conditions in the camps.[36] The CPR did not, however, meekly accept blame for the harsh working conditions. Instead, CPR president Shaughnessy claimed the type of worker, rather than the company, was at the root of the problem:

> Men who seek employment on railway construction are, as a rule, a class accustomed to roughing it. They know when they go to the work that they must put up with the most primitive kind of camp accommodation. . . . I feel very strongly that it would be a huge mistake to send out any more of these men from Wales, Scotland or England. . . . it is only prejudicial to the cause of immigration to import men who come here expecting to get high wages, a feather bed and a bath tub.[37]

Slavic and Scandinavian settler-labourers also became unpopular with the railway companies; their temporary commitment to railroad construction created an unstable labour market. Many of these men were available to the companies only during the late spring and earlier part of the summer; in August they quit their jobs to harvest their crops. Moreover, large numbers of them were gradually able to accumulate their money and to establish themselves full-time on the land. Ironically, in 1903 James A. Smart complimented the CPR on its generosity "to foreigners coming to this country, to such an extent that hundreds and perhaps thousands of them today are living in their own homes and are practically independent."[38] But the company was not to be denied. During the 1901 maintenance-of-way employees' strike, the CPR had imported hundreds of itinerant Italian navvies from the United States, despite anguished protests from immigration officials that these workers were undesirable racially and were taking jobs from "labourers who have taken homesteads." On this occasion, Mackenzie King, deputy minister of labour, had informed the CPR president that the private employment agencies that had recruited the Italian navvies had apparently violated the Canadian Alien Labour Law. Yet no action was taken against either the agencies or the CPR itself; quite clearly the Laurier government had accepted the advice of former Winnipeg commissioner W.F. McCreary that strained relations with the CPR "would be disastrous for Canadian immigration ventures."[39]

After 1901 the CPR systematically increased the proportion of Italian workers in its construction crews; many of these were supplied by Montreal-based labour agents such as Antonio Cordasco.[40] Between 1901 and 1904 Cordasco had a virtual monopoly in supplying labourers to the company; for his efforts the CPR paid him a salary of five dollars a day and expenses. He was also given the right to provision the Italian rail gangs. On this particular concession Cordasco made between 60 per cent and 150 per cent profit on each item sold. What Cordasco offered the CPR was not only a regular supply of unskilled workers, but men who could be controlled either by his interpreters or by Italian foremen. The outlook of Italian navvies was greatly appreciated by CPR officials. As George Burns, the company's employment agent, put it: "Italians are the only class of labour we can employ who can live for a year on the wages they earn in six months . . . if we have the Italians . . . there is no danger of their jumping their jobs and leaving us in the lurch."[41]

Pressure for the recruitment of "industrial" immigrant navvies mounted after 1907 when the Canadian Pacific, Grand Trunk Pacific, and Canadian Northern were all engaged in immense construction projects. During the next seven years between 50,000 and 70,000 railroad workers were engaged annually in completing the two new transcontinental railways, in double-tracking the CPR main line, and in building numerous colonization lines. In their insatiable demand for cheap unskilled labour all three companies pressured the Immigration Branch to facilitate the entry of immigrant navvies "irrespective of nationality." A survey of the labour demands of railroad contractors in 1909 revealed that the most popular immigrant workers were "non-preferred" southern European immigrants; these, it was claimed, "were peculiarly suited for the work." Wheaton Bros. of Grand Falls, New Brunswick, reported that it "would not employ Englishmen"; the Toronto Construction Company announced that it was entirely dependent "upon Italians, Bulgarians, and that class of labour"; while the Munro Company of La Turque, Quebec, expressed a preference for foreigners – "Polacks, Bulgarians, Italians."[42]

There were also several schemes to import large numbers of immigrant workers from Russia. In 1907, as a mark of his goodwill toward the Canadian government, Doukhobor leader Peter Veregin announced that he would recruit 10,000 Russian labourers for the building of the Grand Trunk Pacific. Nothing came of this plan, but Russian workers were brought into the country in 1909 and 1913 from Vladivostok.[43]

Dismayed at the growing percentage of "non-preferred" industrial immigrants entering the country, immigration officials embarked on a spirited defence of the settler-navvy. In 1908 they claimed that Slavic settlers were superior construction workers since they "could be had at more reasonable figures than many others who are either in large cities or who have had past experience in railway construction work and rates of wages." This line of argument appealed to the self-interest of railroad entrepreneurs. Wages had increased appreciably from the $1.75 daily wage of 1900. By 1907 they had risen to $3, and by 1913 some contractors were paying as much as $5. But for the railway companies a return to the older settler-labourer employment pattern did not offer a realistic solution to this problem. In fact, their answer represented a further retreat from the agricultural ideal that inspired official immigration policy. What they now demanded as a solution to their problem was the flooding of the labour market with itinerant workers who would be hired cheaply and thus keep costs down. In short, the railway companies became the outstanding spokesmen for an open-door immigration policy.[44]

This position was opposed both by organized labour, for economic reasons, and by nativist elements, for social and cultural reasons. Many of these immigrant navvies, it was charged, were nothing more than "professional vagrants" whose habits and attitudes were "repugnant to Canadian ideals." They were, in short, people who tended "to lower the Canadian standard of living." Gradually the Immigration Branch was forced into a position of reconciling the opposing demands of the railway companies and the advocates of a more selective immigration policy. The labour and nativist point of view was reflected in the introduction between 1908 and 1910 of new standards for admission to the country. Immigrants were now required to make a continuous journey to Canada and to pass a means test that required them to have an amount of money varying from $25 to $200, depending on place of origin.

Politically, the Dominion government had no choice but to acknowledge the strength of nativist opinion.[45] But on balance it came down on the side of the railway companies. This was clearly revealed in 1910 when Duncan Ross, the lobbyist for the powerful construction company of Foley, Welch & Stewart, convinced Prime Minister Laurier to reverse the decision of the Minister of the Interior and his immigration officials to stiffen the immigrant means test. The extent of the railway victory could be seen in a circular letter sent to all immigration border inspectors in July, 1910; this letter placed "railway labourers in practically the same position as farm labourers." Moreover, railroad navvies were defined as "those who are physically able to [endure] strenuous labour and [who] . . . must be able to handle a pick and shovel."[46]

The coming to power of the Conservatives in 1911 did not significantly disrupt the government-contractor relationship; indeed, the ability of the business lobby to influence immigration policy decisions was again clearly revealed in 1912. In that year immigration officials once again attempted to limit access to the country in response to a public outcry that immigrants from southern Europe "constituted a serious menace to the community." This time they were overruled by Robert Rogers, a politician whose corporate connections were myriad.[47]

By 1913 immigration officials were concerned that Canada was becoming increasingly committed to a guest-worker form of immigration. But the influx of itinerant immigrant workers continued. Indeed, in the spring of 1913 arrangements were made to bring immigrant workers from eastern Russia on short-term contracts that gave them a semi-indentured status. In fact, to prevent desertions both the Canadian Pacific and the Grand Trunk Pacific transported these workers from Vancouver to the Prairies in closed boxcars and with armed escorts.[48]

The mining and lumbering companies aided and abetted the efforts of the railway companies in seeking to keep the immigration door open. Corporate unity on this issue reflected economic interdependence; the transcontinental railway touched all segments of the developing resource-based industries of the "new" West and their point of view was widely shared. The movement of lumber and firewood, especially from British Columbia, provided the railways with a source of revenue that grew dramatically during this period. In 1896 the CPR moved 636,128,374 feet of lumber and 166,831 cords of firewood; by 1914 these figures were 2,953,125,699 and 287,910 respectively.[49] The rapidly developing metalliferous and coal mines of the Kootenays and Crow's Nest Pass provided an important new market for lumber. In 1910 a report of the Department of the Interior estimated that the coal mines in the Crow's Nest Pass alone were using "three million lineal feet of mining props and two and one-half million feet of board measure of lumber and dimension timber." The report also claimed that within five years this quantity would probably double, thereby requiring the product of 66,000 acres of forest. Thus the railway and mining companies had a common interest in seeing that the British Columbia forest industry had an ample supply of cheap reliable labour. The railway entrepreneur was, therefore, often the spokesman for a region whose views would be ignored by politicians at their peril.[50]

A particular concern of the transcontinental railway companies – the Canadian Pacific, Grand Trunk Pacific, and Canadian Northern – was that there should be no serious work stoppages in the mining industry of the West. Coal was an indispensable source of energy; lignite coal was an essential fuel in the harsh Prairie winter; coke was a necessary ingredient in smelting; and bituminous or steam coal gave motive power to the railways themselves. Hence the determination with which the railway companies attempted to guarantee a reliable mining operation and to meet their seasonal demands for coal. They did this in two ways, by effecting a secure corporate link with the coal producers and by going into mining themselves.[51] In 1908 the CPR opened its own mine at Hosmer, Alberta; in 1911, Canadian Northern acquired the extensive Dunsmuir holdings on Vancouver Island. The Hosmer mine was acquired by the CPR not only to ensure coal for its locomotives during the peak harvest season, but to provide additional coke for the silver-lead-zinc smelters at Nelson, Greenwood, and Trail, British Columbia. Indeed, the previous year the company had acquired the economic leadership in this region through the formation of the Consolidated Mining and Smelting Company. Not surprisingly, these corporate changes were accompanied by an intensification of the demand for an open-door immigration policy.[52]

Mining promoters welcomed this initiative as the labour traditions of the Canadian mining industry were well suited to the outlook of the railway companies. During the boom years from 1896 to 1914 mining companies became even more active in the recruitment of immigrant workers. One mining authority gave the estimate of the industry's labour situation: "Canadians won't work in the mines. They are quite willing to boss the job but they are not going to do the rough work themselves. . . . What we want is brawn and muscle, and we get it." The *Canadian Mining Journal*, the voice of the industry, continually maintained that the number of immigrant miners entering the country was insufficient. In 1907, the *Journal* argued that it was "quite feasible not only to select the proper class of workers across the ocean, but to place them where they are needed."[53] Although the Dominion government did not undertake the systematic recruitment of miners, it placed few obstacles in the way of the recruitment efforts of the mining companies themselves, even when strike-breaking was involved. By 1911 over 57 per cent of mine workers in Canada were immigrants; in British Columbia and Alberta the equivalent figures were 84 and 88 per cent. In Ontario, only 48 per cent of the mine workers were foreign-born. But these workers were concentrated in the northern part of the province; their presence gave that region a destructively "non-Canadian–non-British" character.[54]

The Rocky Mountain coal-mining region of western Canada was equally polyglot. In most of the mining communities those of British stock constituted less than 50 per cent of the population; Slavic and Italian workers were in the majority. A study prepared by the Royal Commission on Coal provided the information given in Table 2 below.

In their frantic search for immigrant unskilled labour the mining companies, in keeping with the traditions of Canadian big business, turned to private

Table 2

Ethnic Distribution in Alberta Mines: A Percentage Breakdown

	Crow's Nest	Lethbridge	Drumheller Park	Mountain	Brazeau	Edmonton
British	44	40	61	41.5	44.5	60
American	1	2	2	1	2	1
Slavic	25	32	26	36	17.5	19
French and Belgian	7	–	–	–	5.5	–
Italian	14.5	15	3	17.5	25.5	–
Others:						
European	8.5	8	7	4	5	18
Finnish	–	–	1	–	–	–
Oriental	–	3	–	–	–	–
	100	100	100	100	100	100

SOURCE: *Report of the Alberta Coal Commission, 1925* (Edmonton, 1926), 181.

employment agencies. In 1904 there were about 100 agencies in operation in the country; by 1913 the number had grown to over 300. Of these, Ontario had the largest number (97), followed by British Columbia (45), Manitoba (36), Alberta (32), and Quebec (26). Together the agencies were placing over 200,000 workers a year, most of whom were immigrants. These agencies recruited workers not only in Europe but in the United States, where they worked closely with similar labour bureaus. [55]

Agents supplying large industrial concerns often specialized in a particular ethnic group. Thus, the Dominion Coal Company of Nova Scotia was supplied with Italian workers by the Cordasco agency of Montreal, and with Armenian and Syrian workers from agencies operating in Constantinople. The approach of one of the Constantinople agencies was explained in a leading Armenian newspaper in these terms:

> The Dominion Company Ltd. of Sidney, Canada, North America, undertakes to furnish employment, which will pay you from $2.00 to $5.00 per day. Emigrants would have to go via Trieste (Austria) and there sign contracts concerning their future employment and wages. The steamship fare is $50.00 paid in advance. . . . Come, without losing time, to our office, American Travellers' Company, No. 2, Custom House, Galata, Constantinople, which is the greatest and most important of such organizations. [56]

Many of the immigrant workers who came by this route were transported first to St. John's, Newfoundland, where there was no immigration inspection; from there they travelled on the iron-ore carriers of the Dominion Coal & Steel Company to the company's piers at Sydney.[57]

During periods of industrial conflict the Dominion Coal Company and other mining concerns looked to the labour agencies for relief. Strike-breakers were frequently imported into the country despite the Alien Labour Act of 1897, which made it unlawful "for any person, company, partnership or corporation, in any manner to pre-pay the transportation of, or in any other way to assist or solicit the importation or immigration of any alien or foreigner into Canada under contract or agreement . . . to perform labour or service of any kind in Canada."[58] During the ferocious strikes in the metalliferous regions of British Columbia between 1899 and 1901 the mining companies blatantly imported Italian and Slavic strike-breakers through labour agencies in Fernie, Spokane, and Seattle. Organized labour strongly resented the recruitment of these "foreign scabs." In July, 1899, for example, the secretary of the Sandon (British Columbia) Miners' Union appealed to Prime Minister Laurier to enforce the Alien Labour Act: "1000 Canadian miners of the Slocan, with their wives and families, are being driven out of Canada by the importation of labour from the United States. . . . As British subjects we naturally resent the circumstances which are driving us from our native land. Will you, as First Minister of the Crown, secure for us the protection which the Alien Labour Law provides?"[59]

The degree of support the miners received from labour organizations across the country eventually forced the Dominion government to establish a royal commission under Justice R.C. Clute of the British Columbia Supreme Court to investigate the situation. But violations of the Alien Labour Act remained a feature of life in the region. In 1901, the mining companies expanded their recruitment of alien strike-breakers, most of whom were Italians. The blunt comment of Edmund Kirby, the manager of the War Eagle Mine, showed the importance of these new industrial recruits to the position of local capital: "How to head off a strike of muckers or labourers for higher wages without the aid of Italian labour I do not know." Nor were the companies deterred either by the protests of organized labour or by warnings from Mackenzie King, the deputy minister of labour, that the Alien Labour Act would be enforced "to prevent wholesale importation of labour." Despite two convictions under the Act the mining companies achieved their goal: sufficient strike-breakers were secured to re-open the mines and crush the offending union.[60]

The events of 1901 in British Columbia revealed much about the power politics of Canadian immigration. When large industrial concerns, possessing appreciable political power, were determined to import workers, even for the purpose of strike-breaking, they would usually get their way. This principle would be demonstrated on many occasions, most notably in the metal-miners' strike in Cobalt in 1907, the CPR machinist strike in 1908, the coalminers' strike in Nova Scotia in 1909, the dockworkers' strike in Port Arthur in 1910, the coalminers' strike in Crow's Nest Pass in 1911, the railroad navvy strike in British Columbia in 1912, and the coalminers' strike on Vancouver Island in 1913.[61]

Immigrant Recruitment and Work Camps: The Critique

The most comprehensive contemporary examination of the impact of immigration on North American society was the U.S. Senate *Report of the Immigration Commission* of 1911, better known as the Dillingham Commission Report. After a three-year study of North American and European conditions, this Commission concluded that most new immigrants were not coming to the United States to settle on the land but to sell their labour in "a more favourable market." It also claimed that large numbers of immigrant workers were essentially sojourners who regarded their stay in North America as temporary and who used their wages to effect an elevation in their own social status when they returned to Europe. According to the Commission one of the most important influences on this transatlantic labour market was the activity of shipping and labour agents who made excessive profits at all stages of the immigration process.[62] They received commissions from steamship companies, kickbacks from money-lenders in Europe, labour agency fees from immigrant workers themselves and from the American companies for whom they acted, and interest from ethnic bankers for handling remittances and pre-paid tickets. In order to deal with these "human traffickers," the Commission recommended state laws regulating both employment agencies and immigrant banks. It further recommended that the Bureau of Immigration and Naturalization monitor more effectively the Alien Labor Act.[63]

The report of the Dillingham Commission had a decided impact on those advocating reform of Canadian immigration laws and practices. Under the Canadian Immigration Act of 1869 and subsequent amendments, various types of undesirables were excluded from the country. These included paupers, criminals, and the diseased. The immigration of Chinese, East Indians, and Japanese was also controlled.[64] These restrictions were enforced by immigration officials employed at the major ports and border crossings. At the request of municipalities, immigrants who became public charges could be deported. There was also the Alien Labour Act of 1897. In the long run, however, this legislation proved to be a great disappointment to Canadian trade unionists concerned about the problem of cheap labour. There were two reasons for this: the Act only applied to workers coming from the United States; and the Dominion government failed to establish effective administrative machinery for the enforcement even of this limited arrangement.

The anger of Canadian unionists over the foreign labour problem was clearly revealed during the 1901 strike of the maintenance-of-way employees of the Canadian Pacific Railway. On this occasion the Brotherhood of Railway Trackmen complained to Dominion authorities that the CPR practice of recruiting Italian navvies constituted a blatant violation of the Alien Labour Act. This view was strongly endorsed by the Winnipeg Trades and Labour Council; indeed, in Winnipeg pitched battles occurred between resident workmen and Italian scabs. Yet the Dominion government did nothing more than protest to the CPR president. In CPR tradition, this protest was politely ignored.[65]

The controversy also focused attention on the role of the private employment agency, which could mobilize from its urban base a pool of unskilled labour in both Canada and the United States. The growth of these agencies was noted in the *Labour Gazette* of 1904. According to this source about 100 agencies in operation in the country could be divided into three groups: those placing female domestics; those placing skilled workers; and those placing unskilled workers.[66]

The search for immigrant domestic servants was an important activity for charitable and patriotic organizations such as the Salvation Army and the British Women's Emigration Association (BWEA). By 1911 over one-third of domestic servants in Ontario, and a whopping three-quarters in the West, were immigrants. The vast majority of these were of British working-class background, who viewed domestic service as "the main bridge to Canada for women of limited funds." Dominion authorities were impressed with the consensus that existed between rural and urban residents: both wanted a steady supply of cheap and respectable homecare workers. As a result, generous bonuses were paid by the government to steamship and labour agencies for recruiting immigrant domestics; as well, subsidies were given to the Salvation Army and to BWEA reception homes. In turn, these reception centres "segregated domestics from other immigrants so they would not acquire notions about better opportunities in other kinds of work."[67]

Between 1905 and 1908 there were a number of incidents involving the importation of skilled immigrant workers.[68] The 1905 amendments to the Alien Labour Act relating to misrepresentation applied only to agencies located in Canada, and this became a source of difficulty in itself. British employment agencies such as Grahaeme Hunter of Glasgow and Louis Leopold of London were outside Canadian jurisdiction.[69] This was remedied somewhat when William Lyon Mackenzie King was sent by the Laurier government to negotiate an agreement with imperial authorities that brought British agents into line.[70]

Another important change in 1906 was the removal of W.T.R. Preston from his position as Superintendent of Emigration in Great Britain. Preston had held this position since 1899, and had become the *bête noire* of organized labour in Canada. Specifically, he had become discredited in the eyes of Canadian unionists because of his connection with Louis Leopold's Canadian Labour Bureau.

Not only was Preston's office next door to that of the Canadian Labour Bureau, but he and Leopold shared the same telephone, thereby bringing to a new height of perfection the network that existed between Canadian businessmen and civil servants.[71] Once this became public knowledge, Prime Minister Laurier was deluged with petitions from Canadian trade unions demanding that Preston be fired. Even the backing of the Canadian Manufacturers' Association (CMA) and the Montreal Builders' Exchange was not enough to save Preston's hide; he was discreetly transferred to Hong Kong as the representative of the Department of Trade and Commerce.[72]

The Canadian Labour Bureau, however, survived Preston's decline. In fact, in 1907 Leopold was placed in charge of the newly opened London labour office of the CMA; the president of the Association, C.M. Murray, even went so far as to suggest to the Minister of the Interior that Canadian immigration officials "refer potential emigrants to Mr. Leopold."[73] The direct involvement of the CMA in overseas labour recruitment was short-lived, partly because of the recession of 1907-08 and partly because of a campaign against it by the Canadian Trades and Labour Congress.[74] Nevertheless, skilled workers continued to be readily available for Canadian employers even during strikes.[75]

While the recruitment of immigrant domestics and British skilled workers periodically embarrassed federal authorities, the most serious problem was the treatment of unskilled alien workers by Canadian labour agencies and railroad, lumber, and mining companies. For its part the Dominion government seemed prepared to allow the companies a free hand in the industrial use of immigrant workers, particularly in the railway camps. The rapid completion of the Grand Trunk Pacific and Canadian Northern was regarded by both the Laurier and Borden governments as a crucial economic and political priority. So great was the commitment of the government in this regard that Dominion authorities rarely questioned the characterization given by employment agencies of life in the railway work camps. In April, 1910, this description of working conditions in the Grand Trunk Pacific camps appeared in the British newspaper *Answers*.

> Life in the camps is strictly teetotal. . . . But the feeding provided is not only unstinted, but of the best obtainable, and on a scale undreamed of by the navvy in this country . . . there is an unlimited choice . . . of fresh meat, fresh vegetables, groceries, butter, eggs, milk, bread and fruit. . . . After work, the men amuse themselves to good purpose, with sing-songs in the shorter days of spring and autumn, and with games and sports, fishing and shooting during the long summer.[76]

The reality of immigrant life in Canada was rather different. Foreign workers were frequently cheated out of their wages and subjected to harsh and dangerous working conditions. In the spring of 1904 the evils associated with the immigrant traffic were dramatically revealed when the Italian labour agencies of

Antonio Cordasco and Alberto Dini, vying for steamship and employment commissions, lured thousands of Italian labourers to Montreal. These men soon faced unemployment and destitution; in time, their condition became so desperate that both the municipal and Dominion authorities were forced to intervene. Although a royal commission appointed to investigate this episode documented the many problems with unregulated labour agencies, and legislation was passed providing severe penalties for anyone "inducing people to come to Canada by false representations," the abuses continued. [77]

In 1907, the Austrian consul-general in Ottawa registered an official complaint about the treatment of Austrian nationals in Canada by Ukrainian and Bulgarian labour agencies operating out of Montreal and by foremen in various railway camps. What had happened, he asserted, was so cruel and exploitative "as to make my blood curdle and . . . bring shame and dishonour upon your country." His specific charge related to the recruitment by the Davis & Nagel agency of Montreal of hundreds of Ukrainian, Polish, and Hungarian immigrants for work on the construction of the Temiskaming and Northern Ontario Railway. Some of these workers had been engaged by the bureau after they had landed in Montreal; others had been sent to Montreal by labour agents in the United States. Before leaving Montreal for the construction camps in northern Ontario these immigrant workers had signed contracts with the Davis & Nagel Company. [78]

By the time they had reached the job site many of the men had already spent all their money on labour agency fees, rail fares, and hotel accommodation. The cost of these latter two items had been grossly inflated by kickbacks to labour agents. The situation of the workers had been made worse by the fact that Davis & Nagel had misled them into believing that they would receive a refund for their transportation costs from the McRae, Chandler & McNeil Construction Company. No such refund was ever forthcoming. In addition, the construction company and the labour agency had conspired to prevent the workers from leaving the campsites. Many of the foremen and sub-contractors had used firearms to intimidate recalcitrant workers, and most of these camps had jails where "unruly" workers had been confined after kangaroo court proceedings. Workers who had managed to escape from camp had often been tracked down by special constables and detectives engaged by their employers. These "specials" were often assisted by local police and justices of the peace. The police state tactics used in the construction of the railway had been clearly revealed in June, 1907, when a group of thirty Slavic workers had been seized for violation of their labour contracts. One of the captured men described his experience as follows:

> On the 20-th inst [*sic*] at night, 12 men who represented themselves as policemen came again to our place and began to make a wholesale arrest, firing revolvers at the Immigrants. . . . 35 men of us were arrested and packed into a fright [*sic*] car, for a whole long night with no water and no place to

rest or even sit upon. In the morning, as they made preparations to take us away, we began shouting, whereupon said policemen entered the car and putting the muzzles of their guns to our mouths, threatened to shoot if we continued our alarm. A number of us have been beaten with sticks . . . we have obtained our release, but only after . . . binding ourselves to pay each $17 for transportation and $35 for the policemen who had beaten and fired at us.[79]

The investigation conducted by the Immigration Branch provided evidence substantiating much that the Austrian consul-general had alleged. It was shown that Davis & Nagel had indeed been guilty of misrepresentation and that their agents had been guilty of physical intimidation. The quasi-judicial activities of McRae, Chandler & McNeil were also censured. Yet no attempt was made to prosecute either the labour agency or the construction company. Both Dominion and provincial officials argued that it was the responsibility of the victimized immigrant workers themselves to take legal action. This, of course, was impossible: the men were virtually without money and were scattered across the country.[80]

The coercive measures employed against immigrant navvies were characteristic of their harsh and dangerous lives.[81] The accident rate at "the end of steel" was particularly shocking. Between 1904 and 1911, for example, out of a total of 9,340 fatal industrial accidents in Canada, 23 per cent were related to the railway industry. But even these statistics do not tell the whole story. It was not until 1912 that the Dominion government required contractors receiving public funds to register fatalities occurring in their camps. Yet even this provision did not produce accurate statistics: "Oh, some Russian is buried there" was the passing remark that commonly designated an unkempt plot in the vicinity of an erstwhile camp.[82]

There were also numerous complaints about the level of wages and the accommodation in the construction camps. Although there was an obligation on the part of the head contractor who accepted Dominion funds to grant wages that were consistent with local standards, to maintain a reasonable level of sanitation, and to provide medical facilities, it was difficult to enforce these measures.[83] Labour alleged that government inspectors visited the camps only infrequently and rarely came into contact with immigrant navvies. The foreign worker was particularly vulnerable to this type of exploitation. He was often unable to communicate in English, was frequently manipulated by an "ethnic straw boss," and often had a basic mistrust of state officials. For the navvies, the government inspector simply did not offer a viable channel of protest.[84]

Immigrant mine workers faced similar problems. This was especially true of the smaller mines, the so-called "gopher holes." In these, in addition to irregular employment, it was not uncommon for the companies to declare bankruptcy and forfeit on wages. Within the mines the power of hiring and allocating contract places usually rested with the foremen and shift bosses. There were numerous allegations that these men exploited their positions and extracted bribes from desperate workers. These conditions were compounded by the danger of the workplace. The reports of the Ontario, Alberta, and British Columbia mining inspectors throughout the period 1896-1914 were generally critical of the prevailing high accident rates, especially among the foreign workers. This criticism was most effectively stated in a 1914 report of the Ontario mining inspector:

> Anyone looking over the list of mining statistics . . . cannot but be struck by the large percentage of names of foreign origin. . . . In part this may be due to unfamiliarity with the English language and the difficulty of comprehending quickly spoken orders in an emergency. Mental traits have also to be reckoned with, and the fact that few of these men were miners before coming to this country. . . .

The report neglected to state that many mine managers were reluctant to maintain costly safety regulations. The apparent lack of solidarity among the mine employees because of ethnic differences reinforced this callous approach.[85]

The lumber companies also employed large numbers of immigrant workers, especially Scandinavians, Finns, and Slavs, most of whom were recruited by labour agencies in Vancouver, Victoria, Winnipeg, Port Arthur, Ottawa, Montreal, and Sault Ste. Marie. There were numerous complaints about the working and living conditions, especially in the "long timber" industry of British Columbia. In 1918 the *British Columbia Federationist* gave this description of a typical camp: "muzzle loading bunks . . . pigs, lice and other vermin all over the place . . . the stench of drying clothes and dirty socks . . . enough to knock a man down."[86]

Conclusion

Between 1896 and 1914 Canadian immigration policy served, above all else, the dictates of the capitalist labour market. Under the banner of economic growth thousands of immigrant workers were encouraged to enter the country to meet the labour needs of commercial agriculture, railroad construction, lumbering, mining, and other labour-intensive industries. Increasingly, the long-standing goal of bringing into the country only the settler-labourer type of immigrant was displaced by a policy of importing an industrial proletariat. Immigration statistics reveal that the percentage of unskilled labourers entering Canada increased from 31 per cent of total immigration in 1907 to 43 per cent in 1913-14, while the percentage of agriculturalists decreased from 38 per cent to 28 per cent. This change from settler to worker immigrants was accompanied by a change in ethnic composition. In 1907, 20 per cent of the immigrants were from central and southern Europe; by 1913, when 400,000 men and women entered the country, this figure had advanced to 48 per cent.[87]

In the minds of many Anglo-Canadians the arrival of these "hordes" of foreigners stirred deep suspicion. The immigrants seemed to present a serious challenge to Canadian institutions, particularly in the rapidly growing urban centres of western Canada and northern Ontario.

CHAPTER 2

Asian Immigrant Workers
and British Columbia Society

Of the many immigration problems that faced the Laurier and Borden governments, none was more intractable and none politically more dangerous than that of the movement of Asians into British Columbia. Part of the problem, from Ottawa's perspective at least, was the concentration of the country's Asian population along the Pacific coast. In 1891 approximately 98 per cent of the Chinese population was in British Columbia; although it declined somewhat during subsequent decades, 60 per cent of Canada's Chinese were still in the province in 1921. In contrast, over 90 per cent of Canada's Japanese and East Indian populations lived in British Columbia until the Second World War. [1]

The dispute over Asian immigration had started long before Laurier came to power; but the economic boom that began after 1896 intensified the existing conflict and in the years 1907-08 brought it to a head. Hence it was a more pressing and complex issue for Laurier and his ministers than it had been for any of their predecessors. On one side stood the spokesmen of the mining, forest, salmon canning, and fruit farming industries of British Columbia, who demanded a steady supply of cheap, unskilled Asian labour. This lobby enjoyed the support of powerful central Canadian manufacturing and transportation interests anxious for a closer trading relationship with the Orient. On the other side of the issue stood the forces of a vociferous and uncompromising British Columbia nativist movement, rooted in, but by no means confined to, the organized labour movement of the province.

By the turn of the century the advocates of a white British Columbia had gained the ascendant in provincial politics. On the national political scene the potential divisiveness of the issue was shown in 1908 when British Columbia gave a majority of its seats for the first time since 1891 to the Conservatives. In contrast to the temporizing of Laurier, Borden stood squarely on the principle of a white British Columbia – or so it seemed to nativist opinion in the province. But the reality of the division between the national political parties on the issue by 1908 was more complex; in effect, the Asian immigration question had become one of those issues in Canadian politics that could be readily taken advantage of in opposition but not so easily solved in office. Thus, when the Conservatives came to power in 1911 they assumed the same brokerage role as their Liberal predecessors both nationally and internationally – to the disappointment of some of their more rabid British Columbia supporters. That they did so is indicative of the interplay of national and international considerations that made the Oriental question *sui generis* in the myriad range of immigration issues facing Canada's policy-makers.

Significantly, the Canadian response to immigration from Asia varied from country to country. In the case of China, Canadian policy had, only generally speaking, to take account of economic and humanitarian considerations. But the Dominion's relations with Japan were affected both by a treaty of trade, commerce, and navigation Great Britain had negotiated with Japan in 1894 and, after 1902, by the Anglo-Japanese Alliance. The policy with respect to immigration from the Indian subcontinent was influenced by the common membership of Canada and India in the British Empire. Again, the community of interest that existed between British Columbia and the Pacific states of the United States on the Oriental immigration issue became increasingly important after the turn of the century; in 1908 it occasioned an important but ultimately unsuccessful attempt by the United States to effect common Anglo-American action to restrict Japanese immigration. For Canada the crisis over Asian immigration that arose in 1907-08 occasioned a participation in world politics that was as unaccustomed as it was unexpected.

Another dimension was the reaction by organized labour in British Columbia to the presence of Asian workers. On the one hand, there was intense opposition to Chinese, Japanese, and East Indian workers because they were cheap competitors who undermined the wage structure and threatened the existence of trade unions. On the other hand, in the coal mines of Vancouver Island white miners used Chinese workers to do some of the most arduous and repetitive jobs, while still demanding the termination of Asian immigration. The reaction of Chinese workers to this ethnically based split labour market is difficult to document.[2]

Major Trends, 1885-1907

The first Asians to arrive in Canada were the Chinese, many of whom came north from California during the British Columbia gold rush of the 1850s.[3] The Japanese began arriving in the 1880s but their numbers did not become large enough to make their presence a political issue until the next decade. East Indian immigrants did not begin arriving in sizable numbers until 1905. The Dominion government's approach to Asian immigration was markedly different from its policy with respect to American and European immigration. No agents were commissioned, no promotional literature was distributed, and no plans were made for the agricultural settlement of Asians.[4] On the contrary, much of the impetus for the mass movement of Asians into Canada was provided by syndicates in the Asian countries themselves; these found Canadian allies in the employment agents of labour-intensive industries. The advantage Canadian entrepreneurs saw in the Asian workers was admirably summarized in an 1885 description of them as "living machines."[5]

Given this exploitative attitude on the part of the importers of Asian labour, it is not surprising that their machinations soon met with strong local labour resistance, though the opposition that developed in Canada to Asian immigration was racial and cultural as well as economic. Naturally, the legislature of British Columbia became the focal point of this opposition. Extra-parliamentary opposition to Chinese immigration manifested itself in the emergence of the Workingmen's Protective Association in 1878 in Victoria; the purposes of this organization were "the mutual protection of the working class of British Columbia against the great influx of Chinese" and the use of "all legitimate means for the suppression of their immigration."[6] The Association collapsed after only a year's existence but its work was later taken up by other labour and exclusionist bodies, most notably the Knights of Labor and the Asiatic Exclusion League.[7]

Not surprisingly, anti-Asian sentiment in the province soon found legislative expression. In 1878, for example, the employment of Asians on provincial public works was prohibited; at the same time legislation was passed placing a special tax on Chinese residents. These attempts to make Asians unwelcome ran counter to the priorities of the Dominion government.[8] Moreover, under the British North America Act the Dominion authorities had sole legislative jurisdiction over matters pertaining to the regulation of trade and commerce, the rights of aliens, and the treaties of the Empire. Hence, between 1878 and 1914 successive Dominion governments used the power of disallowance eighteen times against British Columbia.[9] In the process the Dominion government became the defender of a variety of business interests who wished to import large numbers of Asians into British Columbia. This was clearly revealed in 1881 when Andrew Onderdonk, the contractor for the western section of the Canadian Pacific Railway, began to import Chinese coolies by the thousands.

His actions produced an angry outburst from the province but this was ignored by the Dominion government. Having been warned by Onderdonk that the CPR would be delayed "twelve years longer than necessary" if the contractors were not given a free hand in the recruitment of Chinese labour, Prime Minister John A. Macdonald acquiesced in what was being done; it is estimated that between 1881 and 1885 10,000 Chinese were brought into British Columbia. [10]

If Macdonald gave the interests of the contractors priority, he could not ignore opposition opinion in British Columbia entirely. Accordingly, on July 5, 1884, after his hands-off policy had satisfied the economic need and ensured the future of the CPR, he appointed a royal commission composed of J.A. Chapleau, his Secretary of State, and J.H. Gray of the Supreme Court of British Columbia to investigate the situation. Their report was duly presented to the House of Commons and found legislative embodiment in the Chinese Immigration Act of 1885. Popular support for regulation was acknowledged by the imposition of an entry tax of $50 per head; restrictions were also placed on the number of labourers that ships arriving in Canadian ports could land. [11] But opposition opinion in British Columbia was not satisfied with these concessions, and during the next three decades pressure mounted for the complete exclusion of Asians. The demands of the advocates of a white British Columbia became ever more shrill when the Chinese, and later the Japanese and East Indians, began, in increasing numbers, to find employment in the coal mines, lumber camps, salmon packing plants, and fruit and dairy farms of the province. Labour spokesmen continually alleged that Orientals were displacing white workers in these industries because they were willing to accept lower wages, to work in unhealthy and unsafe conditions, and to act as strike-breakers during industrial conflicts. [12] By contrast, British Columbia industrialists sought to convince Dominion authorities that without a steady supply of Asian labour the entire economy of the province would be jeopardized. [13]

In this effort they had a powerful ally in the Canadian Pacific Railway Company. With its profitable steamship service between Canada and the Orient and its extensive investment in the labour-intensive mining and fruit-farming industries, the CPR had good reason to support an open-door immigration policy. [14] Thus in a letter to the editor of the Vancouver *World* in 1896, the president of the CPR, Sir William Van Horne, argued that "an abundance of cheap labour" was "absolutely necessary to the rapid progress of the country." This abundance could only be "had from China and to a small extent Japan." Van Horne also argued that Canadian workers would not be adversely affected by this influx: "for every three Chinese labourers brought in, a demand will be created for one white working man for employment in capacities better than ordinary labour with pick and shovel." [15] Moreover, the Chinese labourers were superior in several important respects to their counterparts from southern Europe, an alternative source of supply for Canada's voracious manpower requirements: "We of the Canadian Pacific Railway Company have had a pretty large experience with Chinese and European labourers, and we know . . . that an average Chinese labourer spends much more than one Italian labourer, and no objection is made to the latter, although they come here with a view to earning a certain amount of money and going home again, as is the case with the Chinese. And in point of morality and good behaviour, the Chinese can give this class odds." [16]

Four years later Thomas Shaughnessy, Van Horne's successor, protested to Laurier against any increase in the Chinese entry tax. Such a change, Shaughnessy charged, would mean the loss to the CPR steamship service of "one hundred thousand to one hundred and fifty thousand dollars per annum." [17] This, in turn, would entail the discontinuance of the China service and a serious loss to Canadian trade. On this issue, however, the CPR and the other advocates of an open-door policy were fighting a losing battle; in 1900 the Chinese entry tax was increased to $100 and in 1903 it was raised to a prohibitive $500.

Yet, the CPR's Pacific steamship service was not destroyed. Although the company's Chinese traffic was appreciably reduced, this loss was more than off-set by a phenomenal expansion in the trade and passenger service with Japan and the Indian subcontinent. Indeed, between 1901 and 1907 the CPR increased the number of its Pacific steamships, all of which were manned by Asian crews, and dispatched traffic agents to the major ports of Japan and India. The major func-tion of these traffic agents was to funnel Asian unskilled labourers by way of CPR steamships to the British Columbia labour market. [18] Needless to say, this system touched off a new wave of protest. Thus, in 1907 it was alleged that the recent influx of East Indian labourers was directly related to the recruitment efforts of CPR steamship agents:

> According to their own story . . . [they] were induced to come to Van-
> couver by Canadian Pacific Railway Agents. . . . l am reliably informed
> that the . . . Company in this matter did not bring these Hindus to British
> Columbia to meet a scarcity of labor; but that they started this immigration
> solely in their interest as carriers. . . . The Canadian Pacific Railway Com-
> pany set the ball rolling to replace their diminished Chinese steerage traf-
> fic which almost ceased after the imposition of the $500.00 head tax. It
> will now continue on its own accord. [19]

Nor was the CPR interested simply in passenger revenue; its own operations in British Columbia required a large and steady supply of unskilled labour. During the economic boom of 1906-07 CPR officials seriously contemplated the importation of residents of Hong Kong "for the purpose of meeting the great scarcity of labourers and servants in British Columbia." [20] But an attempt by company officials to have these immigrants exempted from the head tax because they were British subjects proved abortive. On the other hand, using the services of employment agencies such as the Canadian Nippon Supply

Company, the CPR was able to obtain large numbers of Japanese labourers; by 1903 over 30 per cent of the construction workers in the company's Pacific Division were of Japanese origin.[21] Japanese immigrant workers were also increasingly employed by other British Columbia industrial concerns, most notably those involved in the coastal salmon-packing industry and in the coal mines of Vancouver Island. It was this dramatic development that touched off the explosion of 1907.

Concern over the Japanese influx had been growing for several years. Not surprisingly, the organized labour movement had taken the lead in this agitation. Significantly, the Japanese were denounced by labour spokesmen as a more serious threat to the working classes of British Columbia than the long-abused Chinese. This distinction is attributable to two factors: the aggressive behaviour of Japanese workers in obtaining semi-skilled and skilled jobs in a variety of industries; and the ease with which they seemed to be entering the province, despite repeated efforts by the legislature to control their movement.[22]

That the Dominion government should have been hesitant to restrict Japanese immigration too overtly reflected the exigencies of world power politics. Japan's emergence as a world power had encouraged other countries, Canada included, to treat her nationals with a respect they did not always feel it necessary to accord those of China. Canadian immigration policy toward Japan also had to take account of two imperial agreements: the Anglo-Japanese Treaty of Commerce and Navigation of 1894 and, after 1902, the Anglo-Japanese Alliance. By the terms of the 1894 agreement the subjects of each power were granted "full liberty to enter, to travel or reside in any part of the dominions and possessions of the other contracting party."[23] This provision proved seriously embarrassing to successive Dominion governments. On the one hand, the Dominion authorities had been forced either to disallow or to reserve any provincial legislation designed to exclude Japanese immigrants. On the other, they had failed to negotiate an arrangement whereby Canadian immigration regulations respecting the entry of labourers would take precedence over the terms of the Anglo-Japanese Alliance. Yet another difficulty facing Canadian policy-makers had been a somewhat ambiguous imperial policy on the issue.[24] By 1906, however, both the Canadian and imperial authorities were committed to a non-discriminatory policy toward Japanese immigrants, the more so since Japan had adopted a policy of voluntary restriction of the number of emigrants leaving her shores for Canada.

What Canada wanted – and momentarily seemed to have achieved – was the best of both worlds: to respect the spirit of the Anglo-Japanese Alliance by not discriminating against Japanese nationals but to limit the number of Japanese entering the country.[25] This compromise, which typified the foreign policy outlook of the Laurier government, was undermined by two factors: the implacable opposition in British Columbia to *any* Japanese immigration; and the ability of employment agencies to manoeuvre their way around every obstacle placed in their path. Thus, Japanese immigrants continued to pour into British Columbia from the American protectorate of Hawaii, where they were not subject to the control of Japanese officials. Moreover, agencies such as the Canadian Nippon Supply Company were able to work covertly through emigration companies in Japan itself. The most notable of these, the Tokyo Society, was alleged to have "as managers and stockholders . . . the leading businessmen and politicians of Japan."[26] The ability of private agencies seeking to profit from the labour-hungry British Columbia market to convince Japanese officials to relax emigration regulations pertaining to labourers is not really surprising: they could claim to have contracts with Canadian companies closely associated with both the Dominion and British Columbia governments, most notably the CPR, the Grand Trunk Pacific Railway, and the Dunsmuir coal mines.[27]

The effect of this on public opinion in British Columbia was entirely predictable: allegations were soon circulating that a conspiracy existed to flood the province with cheap Japanese, Chinese, and East Indian labour. These charges grew when a new bill passed by the British Columbia legislature restricting the entry of Orientals was reserved by Lieutenant-Governor James Dunsmuir, himself a leading importer of "Oriental" labour.

With rumours circulating that additional shiploads of Asians were waiting to disembark, the newly formed Vancouver branch of the Asiatic Exclusion League organized a rally for September 7, 1907.[28] This rally soon became a riot; white mobs swept through the Chinese and Japanese sections of the city, destroying property and indiscriminately assaulting residents. The incident presented Laurier and his ministers with the gravest crisis any Dominion government had ever faced on the Pacific coast.

National and International Implications

The Laurier government reacted to the violence in British Columbia with a variety of measures. Its first action was designed to reassure Japan that the 1906 agreement would be honoured. W.D. Scott, the superintendent of immigration, was sent to Vancouver to report on the situation, and on October 2 orders issued by the immigration authorities there prohibiting the landing of Japanese were rescinded on the grounds that they contravened the 1906 agreement.[29] In the meantime W.W.B. McInnes, a prominent Vancouver Liberal, had started a secret inquiry for the Dominion government into the causes of the outbreak in general and the activities of the American-based Asiatic Exclusion League in particular.[30] Then, on October 12, it was announced that Mackenzie King, the deputy minister of labour, would go to Vancouver to investigate the losses suffered by the Oriental population in the rioting, and that Rodolphe Lemieux, the Postmaster General and Minister of Labour, would undertake a mission to Japan.[31]

Ultimately, King chaired three one-man royal commissions appointed to investigate the west coast situation: the Royal Commission on Methods by which Oriental Labourers Have Been Induced to Come to Canada; the Royal Commission Into Losses Sustained by the Japanese Population of Vancouver; and the Royal Commission Into Losses Sustained by the Chinese Population of Vancouver. In general, King supported the demands of organized labour in his recommendations. Thus, he warned that "unless methods are adopted sufficiently effective to prohibit . . . the importation of contract labour from Japan . . . the Canadian Nippon Company and other like concerns will carry on a traffic in Japanese labour the like of which has not been equalled in the importation of any class of coolie labour that has ever been brought to our shores."[32] King was particularly impressed by the warnings of the local labour movement that the continuation of the Asian influx would precipitate a class war in British Columbia and might in time lead to the secession of the province from Canada.[33] He made similar observations about Chinese and East Indian immigrants, but the diplomatic problems surrounding Japanese immigrants were obviously of a different order than those surrounding these other groups. This was clearly shown in the events that followed Canada's decision in October, 1907, to send a mission to Japan. At stake was nothing less than the integrity of Canadian immigration policy – the authority of the Dominion government to determine which ethnic and racial groups could enter the country.

On the surface, the crisis between Japan and Canada appears to have been easily reconciled. In November, 1907, Lemieux submitted a memorandum to Count Tadaju Hayashi, the Japanese Foreign Minister, through the British embassy. This memorandum reviewed the assurances Canada had been given and requested Japan to render these effective "by restricting the immigration of labourers and artizans" to a number that could be absorbed by British Columbia "without unduly disturbing" its existing racial balance.[34] In December a provisional agreement was reached; this was confirmed by an exchange of notes in Tokyo on January 20, 1908, after Lemieux had returned to Ottawa and persuaded a hesitant Laurier to accept it. Part of the agreement was embodied in a letter Hayashi addressed to Lemieux on December 23, 1907. While maintaining that the 1906 agreement guaranteed Japanese subjects "full liberty to enter, travel and reside in any part of the Dominion of Canada," Hayashi agreed "to take efficient means" to restrict emigration, "having particular regard to circumstances of recent occurrences in British Columbia." What this meant in practice was that the influx of Japanese labourers would not exceed 400 annually.[35] Lemieux announced the conclusion of this agreement to the House of Commons on January 21, 1908.[36]

It was at this point that the Asian immigration question intruded into Canadian-American relations. Tension between the United States and Japan had been mounting since 1906 when the San Francisco Board of Education had overtly branded Japanese-American children as undesirables. This episode had quickly created a situation in which a violent confrontation between the two countries seemed possible. During the summer of 1907 the war scare in the United States had been heightened by alarming rumours about Japanese intentions emanating from German and other European sources. Japanese-American relations had been still further aggravated during the summer of 1907 by the existence of a suspicion in Washington that Japan did not intend to honour the "Second Gentleman's Agreement" of February, 1907, by which she had agreed to restrict emigration voluntarily.[37]

In the face of these developments President Theodore Roosevelt now attempted to enlist the support of Canada and Great Britain in building an English-speaking common front to stem the flow of Japanese immigrants. In characteristically unorthodox fashion, Roosevelt did not work through normal diplomatic channels. Instead, he outlined his proposals in a series of remarkable interviews with Mackenzie King during January and February, 1908.[38] In these discussions Roosevelt stressed the importance of both the American and Canadian governments coming to grips with the problems of "Oriental" immigration. If, he said, the two countries were insensitive to the feeling against Asiatics on the Pacific coast, a new republic embracing British Columbia and the Pacific states of the United States would be formed between the mountains and the sea.[39] Roosevelt also informed King that Canada could serve as a valuable intermediary in the establishment of a joint Anglo-American position on the issue of "Oriental" immigration:

> What I would like to accomplish is not merely an understanding for today, but some kind of Convention between the English-speaking peoples, whereby in regard to this question, it would be understood on all sides that the Asiatic peoples were not to come to the English-speaking countries to settle, and that our people were not to go there. . . . If Japan understands that on this question the two great English-speaking powers, Great Britain and the United States, have a common interest, there will be peace.[40]

Roosevelt also stated in his meetings with King that Great Britain, as the ally of Japan, could help to ease the existing tension by explaining to the Japanese government, in a friendly way, the intensity of feeling on the Pacific slope of North America against Asian immigration. To persuade Great Britain to do this, he obliquely suggested that King should go to London to impress the urgency of the situation upon the British Foreign Office, offering to give him "some strong messages" to carry to Sir Edward Grey, the Foreign Secretary, if he were to undertake such a mission.[41]

Although Roosevelt was ultimately successful in having King go to Great

Britain, his plan for an Anglo-American common front against Japan was never taken up by the Foreign Office. [42] Roosevelt, however, was not easily discouraged and for several weeks after his initial meeting with King preached the doctrine of Anglo-American solidarity against Japan at every available opportunity. On February 10, 1908, he told three Canadian members of Parliament who were visiting him that the American fleet was being sent to the Pacific in the interests of British Columbia and Australia as well as California. Asked by one of the Canadians if this meant that the Monroe Doctrine applied to the Pacific coast, he replied: "Yes . . . and to Australia as well – if it doesn't, I'll make it apply." [43]

The possibility of renewed anti-Japanese agitation in British Columbia should the American fleet visit Vancouver greatly alarmed both Canadian and imperial officials. But this threat was effectively removed by the announcement in the spring of 1908 that the American fleet would visit Japan itself. This latter development, indeed, marked a turning point in the Japanese-American dispute. From March, 1908, onward the anti-Japanese agitation in the United States rapidly disappeared and Roosevelt dropped the subject of Anglo-American co-operation as suddenly as he had raised it. [44] In November, 1908, the Root-Takahira Agreement signalled the return of Japanese-American relations to a more satisfactory footing.

In the meantime, King's mission to London had produced a stiffening of the regulations governing the flow of immigrants from India to British Columbia. A neglected portion of the Indian Emigration Act of 1885, which prohibited Indians from leaving their country under contract, was revived. Moreover, the imperial authorities sanctioned two exclusionist orders-in-council issued under the Canadian Immigration Act. These excluded immigrants not coming directly to Canada from their country of birth or naturalization and Asian immigrants who did not have $200 in their possession, excluding those "with whose countries the government of Canada has special arrangements." [45]

By the end of 1908 the Laurier government had apparently resolved the crisis over immigration from Asia. Although the immigration gates were not completely closed, international agreements and legislative enactments appeared to restrict the entry of all but a small number of Asians. But this compromise had satisfied neither nativist sentiment in British Columbia, which was suspicious of any Asian immigration, nor the ambitions of Canadian corporations to profit from the human traffic on the Pacific. The CPR, for example, showed little willingness to reduce its transpacific passenger service, despite the sense of outrage in British Columbia about it. Indeed, only strong pressure from both Dominion and imperial authorities dissuaded the company from establishing direct steamship service between Vancouver and Calcutta. [46] The CPR and other industrial concerns also continued to complain about the shortage of unskilled labour in the coast province and to demand the entry of additional Asian workers. [47] The Canadian government resisted this pressure, but seemingly only because of the uproar increased immigration would provoke in British Columbia. That the government may not have opposed Asian immigration *per se* was clearly shown in 1909 when Laurier rejected a bid by Charles Hays, the president of the Grand Trunk Pacific, to import Asian navvies.

> The condition of things in British Columbia is now such that riots are to be feared if Oriental labour were to be brought in. You remember that in our last conversation upon this subject I told you that if the matter could be arranged so that you could have an absolute consensus of [Premier] McBride, the dangers would probably be averted, but with the local government in active sympathy with the agitators the peace of the province would be really in danger and that consideration is paramount with me.[48]

Frustrated in their attempts to turn the government from the course of political expediency, many employers secured the services of Asian immigrants illegally. In 1910, for example, it was revealed that thousands of Chinese labourers had entered British Columbia without paying any head tax by successfully posturing as merchants, a stratagem made possible by the existence of an organization that provided immigrants with credentials and funds.[49] Shaken by these revelations, the Laurier government belatedly decided to remove the administration of the Chinese Immigration Act from the Department of Trade and Commerce. But King's proposal that "control of the Oriental Question should be placed with the Department of Labour" was rejected; instead, jurisdiction was shifted by order-in-council to the Immigration Branch of the Department of the Interior, a decision that greatly angered organized labour.[50] The Liberal government's credibility was further reduced in British Columbia by this episode and it was no surprise when the Conservatives won all the seats in the province in the federal election of 1911. Laurier's long search for a compromise solution to the immigration problems on the Pacific coast had ended in a political rout.

Borden's Policies

After 1911 it was Prime Minister Robert Borden who had to find a course through the perilous shoals of provincialism and racism, while Laurier was free to play the opportunist. After 1907, Borden had consistently maintained that his party recognized "the provincial character of the question of Asian immigration and the right of the Province to regulate it, provided only that the method of doing so does not conflict with national or Imperial interests." The Conservative view was that British Columbia must remain a "white man's country" and that the province deserved "the same measure of justice . . . as is meted out to any other part of the Empire."[51] Conservative opposition to the Lemieux agreement, which stood in contrast to their nominally pro-imperial stance, was undoubtedly a factor in the political success enjoyed by the party in British Columbia in the elections of 1908 and 1911.[52] Yet in office Borden's path was by no means straight on the "Oriental" question, and as late as the Imperial Conference of 1921, when Arthur Meighen advocated the dissolution of the Anglo-Japanese Alliance, the Conservatives were still attempting to bury the issue.[53] Indeed, the mettle of the new government on the issue was severely tested by the Vancouver coal strike of 1913 when some of the companies involved brought in Japanese and Chinese strike-breakers. Bloody riots ensued and the militia had to be used to restore order.[54] By this time many white merchants, businessmen, and farmers were themselves becoming alarmed by the upward mobility of the Japanese. The activities of the powerful Mitsui Company in the province was a source of special concern.[55] Apprehension was also growing over the increased Japanese ownership of prime agricultural land. In August, 1913, Borden was informed that the Boards of Trade in the Okanagan Valley had approached the provincial government with a demand for an "Oriental" land exclusion law modelled on the California Land Act of 1913.[56] The bill did not materialize but the incident occasioned this expression of concern about the Japanese immigrants from Borden to Sir Joseph Pope: "These energetic people are reaching out in every direction throughout the Province and are continually engaging in new associations under such conditions that the white races cannot possibly compete with them."[57]

Agitation also developed in British Columbia after 1911 over the prospect of further immigration from the Indian subcontinent. In 1913, a rumour circulated that a direct passage connection was about to be established between Calcutta and Vancouver, an innovation that would subvert the direct-journey regulation in effect since 1907-08.[58] It was also claimed that Sikh nationalists intended to provoke incidents in British Columbia to inflame resentment at home against British rule.[59] These fears produced yet another clamour for restrictive measures. The Vancouver City Council contended that only the total exclusion of Sikhs would be acceptable; indeed, it strongly advocated the amendment of the Immigration Act to prevent any Asians from entering the province.[60] Premier McBride now suggested that the Dominion government should itself pass a Natal Act.[61] Both the immigration officials and governing politicians in Ottawa were sympathetic to these proposals, but international factors restricted their freedom of manoeuvre. Borden had attacked the Lemieux agreement in 1908 but as Prime Minister in 1913 he was not prepared to run the risk of a breach with Japan.[62] Nevertheless, a new order-in-council concerning Asian immigration was issued in October, 1913. This prohibited the landing at any port of entry in British Columbia of any immigrants who were either artisans or labourers. Initially, this regulation was to apply until March, 1914, but it was later extended until September of the same year.[63] Not surprisingly, it drew a sharp reaction from Japan. In December, 1913, the Japanese consul-general in Ottawa,

T. Nakamura, protested to Borden that the Canadian government was violating the spirit of the Lemieux agreement.[64]

Borden's difficulties were increased in May, 1914, when the s.s. *Komagata Maru*, with 376 Sikh immigrants on board, arrived at Vancouver. When the immigration officials began the deportation of some of these people, the rest of the passengers seized control of the vessel and repulsed attempts by the Vancouver police to come on board. A bloody confrontation was narrowly avoided by the intervention of prominent members of the Vancouver Sikh community. Ultimately, the Indian immigrants accepted the ruling of the Canadian courts upholding the immigration regulations and returned the ship to its Japanese crew. In return, the federal government provided $4,000 of supplies to enable the ship to return to Calcutta.[65]

The *Komagata Maru* incident revealed the extent to which the political parties could adjust their policies to meet the exigencies of either government or opposition. Thus, Frank Oliver, the former Liberal Minister of the Interior and the member for Edmonton, attacked the Borden government for being too lenient with the defiant Sikhs, while Laurier chided the government for not having negotiated "gentlemen's agreements" with India and China like the one his government had negotiated with Japan.[66] In the British Columbia provincial political arena the Liberals took advantage of the situation to accuse the Conservatives, both nationally and provincially, of being pro-Asian.[67] Quite clearly, the Asian immigration issue still had a great future in Canadian politics. But as with so many other traditional issues, attention was momentarily diverted from it by the coming of war in 1914.

Between 1885 and 1914 the Asian immigration controversy in Canada clearly passed through several stages.[68] The original policy of 1885 of restricting but not prohibiting Chinese immigration had been extended to Japanese and Indian immigrants. Moreover, pressure from British Columbia for the total exclusion of Asians had grown progressively stronger. The CPR had got its way in the use of Asian navvies, but the Grand Trunk Pacific was largely refused the same advantage, despite its immense influence in Ottawa. Exclusionist sentiment was rooted in both economic and cultural factors. It was the misfortune of the Asian immigrant in British Columbia to be a pawn in one of the rawest struggles between capital and labour to be seen anywhere in a country in which the wishes of big business were seldom denied. The fact that the captains of industry, people like the Dunsmuirs and Charles Hays, regarded the Asians as the stuff of an ideal industrial proletariat aroused the fear and hatred of white workers. As Asians began to move out of the extractive industries and into agriculture and commerce, the opposition to their presence and continued immigration multiplied. In a cultural sense many British Columbians not only regarded Asians as impossible to assimilate but maintained that the presence of large blocks of such aliens would prevent the creation of a pan-Canadianism.

A Legacy of Racism

The legacy of this conflict over Asian immigration was complex and bitter. For white British Columbians the continued presence of Asians within the province was an unacceptable reality. Less "civilized" people might have considered mass expulsion; institutional discrimination seemed more "Christian." The process of maintaining rigid social segregation and political marginalization required many different tactics. One of these was to perpetuate the negative stereotypes of Asian immigrants as genetically and culturally inferior. Another was to portray them as sojourners with no stake in the life of the province. If this was not the case, it was asked, why did the Chinese and Japanese remain in their ethnic ghettos?

What most white British Columbians did not see was the rich and varied social environment in these ethnic enclaves. As Kay Anderson has observed, "'Chinatown' is not 'Chinatown' only because the 'Chinese' whether by choice or constraint live there. Rather, one might argue that Chinatown is a social construction with a cultural history and a tradition of imagery and institutional practice that has given it a cognitive and material reality in and for the West." [69] Her portrayal of the growth of Vancouver's Chinatown from a population of 114 in 1884 to over 1,000 by 1911 highlights the indignities the community had to endure from civic officials. These included special business licences, arbitrary health inspections, de facto school segregation, and police harassment. The following 1905 protest from Vancouver's Chinese Board of Trade captures their sense of frustration and hurt:

> The members of our board are law abiding citizens. Many of them have been residents of this country for a number of years and are large holders of real estate, payers of taxes and other civic assessments. The members have been constantly annoyed by what we believe to be an unjustifiable intrusion of certain members of the Vancouver Police Force. . . . We are subjected to indignities and discriminating treatment to which no other class would submit . . . . [70]

In relative terms this small middle class was well off, at least when compared to the vast majority of Chinese Canadians, who were manual labourers. Most were bachelor workers who toiled to supply the needs of their families back in China. "The art of saving their meagre wages taxed the mental agility of even the most frugal. . . . Forced to return from their low-paying jobs to crowded dismal unsanitary rooming houses, many lonely and despondent labourers turned to opium as an alternative to madness." [71] And then there was the danger and alienation of the workplace where many Chinese deaths resulted "either from premeditated negligence or simple incompetence on the part of . . . other white labourers or the company itself." [72] One Chinese immigrant described the difficulty of his life in British Columbia: "We were poor and starving, and we needed money at home. We had to borrow money to come over here, and when we came over here, we had to work hard to pay back the money that we owed."[73]

This contract system usually meant a long period of indentured labour, with little opportunity for independent action until the debt was paid. Not surprisingly, Chinese workers readily accepted any jobs that labour contractors such as the Chinese Consolidated Benevolent Association provided, even if it meant displacing white workers in the Dunsmuir coal mines of Vancouver Island. By 1906, Dunsmuir Collieries, which owned the mines in Cumberland and Extension, employed over 500 Chinese; in many instances, the company "paid the head tax and passage fare ... in return deducting seventy-five cents a day from the daily salary of $1.25.... (and) provided Chinese miners with company housing in Chinatown ...."[74]

The Chinese who worked for Dunsmuir Collieries found themselves in a split labour market, a situation that has been described as follows: "As employers replace higher-paid (dominant) labor with lower-paid (minority) labor, class conflict between capital and labor is transferred to market conflict between dominant and minority workers, which in turn generates ethnic antagonism. . . . Whether dominant workers support politics of ethnic antagonism or politics of class solidarity depends primarily upon the articulation of the racist discourse and the dependence of political parties on minority votes."[75] According to sociologist Peter Li, Chinese workers faced formidable occupational barriers, many of which were erected by British Columbia governments responding to the political pressure of B.C. unions. "For example, the Coal Mines Regulation Act of 1903 forbade Chinese to work underground, or to occupy various skilled jobs in mines, but Chinese could continue to work as unskilled labourers above ground. Despite frequent complaints ... white workers were the first to hire Chinese when the former became small contractors."[76]

The use of Chinese mine workers became particularly controversial during the bitter Vancouver Island coal strikes of 1912-13. While wages and working conditions were the major issues, the union, District 23 of the United Mine Workers of America, was also concerned that the Wellington Collieries Company had increased the number of Asians working underground from 21 per cent to 44 per cent of the total labour force.[77] This practice was denounced by the UMWA not only because of its threat to mining as a "calling," but also because it posed an additional safety threat at an already dangerous mine.[78] When on September 16, 1912, the strike began, the issue of Asian mine workers became even more intense, especially as the company began to promote Chinese and Japanese workers to the status of bona fide miners. In August, 1913, the *British Columbia Federationist* claimed that at one sitting of the Miners Examination Board over fifty Asians became certified miners.[79] On August 13, 1913, striking miners, in a demonstration of solidarity and frustration, marched to Extension;

after attacking company property they launched an attack on Chinatown, forcing the inhabitants "to flee to the nearby woods." This riot provided the McBride government with the excuse to call out the militia to restore order; 256 striking miners were subsequently arrested.[80]

Chinese workers were a pawn in this fierce confrontation between capital and labour. But did they have any choice? The refusal of the UMWA to accept Chinese members meant that there was little possibility they could or would co-operate with white miners. Instead, their commitment was to the Chinese Benevolent Association (CBA), which helped them survive in Canada. "Without it destitute Chinese labourers had nowhere to turn for help; the sick would be left to die . . . lawlessness would have been the norm." And it was through the CBA, which acted as a clearing-house for remittances sent home to China, that many of these labourers maintained contact with their families. That is not to say, however, that they were docile: "Chinese labourers would also take on Chinese companies if they thought they had been cheated."[81] But in general they accepted their place, even though they recognized that "traditional Chinese life could not be transplanted to the overseas country."[82]

Because of the onerous head tax, few Chinese could bring their wives to Canada. This meant an incredible imbalance in the sex ratio, which by 1911 was 2,790 males for every 100 females.[83] For those women who managed to get into the country, their Canadian experience was often very difficult, even for those like Margaret Chan, who was sponsored by wealthy relatives:[84]

> My father was a gambler and he smoked opium too. He was not able to support his two daughters. So he gave me away. I became the adopted daughter of my relatives . . . (who) brought me over to Canada when I was eight years old. They didn't treat me good. . . . Finally, they were going back to China and they were going to sell me to some people with a lot of children – so I run away to the Oriental Home . . . run by the Women's Missionary Society in Victoria. . . . I went to school. . . . After I finished grade eleven, I went to Vancouver to work in a fruit store. . . . we worked hard – cold! Then we were half starved. . . . After I finished normal school, I went back to work in a fruit store again. . . . In those days in Canada, they discriminate against us Chinese . . . don't give us a chance to teach here. I taught in Hong Kong.[85]

By the time of the Great War, Chinese Canadians in British Columbia had even more grievances. Provincial statutes excluded them from acquiring crown lands, from decent jobs in the mining and forestry industries, from being hired on public works, from admission to provincially established homes for the aged and infirm, from holding liquor licences, from the professions of law and pharmacy, and, above all, from the provincial franchise. At the same time that they

were denied most civil rights, the Chinese population was still heavily taxed both within the province and by the immigration head tax.[86]

Because they were unable to compete for well-paying jobs, many Chinese workers moved into ethnic enterprise – hand laundries, restaurants, groceries.[87] This, in turn, encouraged a movement toward urban communities in the Prairie West, as the following case history illustrates:

> I came to Moose Jaw in 1913. . . . First I washed dishes, making $35.00 a month. I worked from fourteen to sixteen hours a day. . . . Then after that, I went to Simpson (Sask.), at harvest time. . . . I worked on a farm. I got up at six o'clock in the morning, milked the cow, and came back to the house to cook breakfast for my boss. . . . He was not a very friendly person. . . . It was no good, so I quit. I came back to Moose Jaw to work for my brother for $50.00 a month for twelve hours a day. At night I scrubbed the floor and waited on tables. Then in 1918, I went back to China to get married.[88]

But Saskatchewan was no haven for Canada's Chinese. By 1914, the province had also passed laws excluding Chinese residents from the franchise and prohibiting them from hiring white females in their ethnic enterprises.[89]

The outbreak of World War One would further threaten the status of Canada's Chinese, Japanese, and Sikh populations.[90]

CHAPTER 3

European Immigrant Workers and
Labour Protest in Peace and War, 1896-1919

The transatlantic migration of thousands of immigrant workers between 1896 and 1914 greatly altered the social and economic fabric of Canada and the United States. In both countries much of the rapid economic progress in railway construction, mining, lumbering, and secondary manufacturing during this time can be attributed to immigrant manpower. Yet the immigrants themselves paid a high price for North American economic gains.[1] In *Men in Sheepskin Coats*, Vera Lysenko graphically described the plight of these foreign workers: "they were systematically underpaid . . . tortured by physical labour, torn by nostalgia for the old country, crushed by loneliness in a strange land, and by the fear of death which [they] often looked in the face." This theme of exploitation and alienation has fascinated many historians of immigration.[2]

"A Sort of Anthropological Garden"

The inferior occupational positions and the low social status afforded European immigrant workers in Canada prior to the Great War were essentially functions of Anglo-Canadian immigration priorities. As John Porter persuasively argued in *The Vertical Mosaic*, the most important factor in determining entrance status for immigrant groups was "the evaluations of the 'charter' members of the society of the jobs to be filled and the 'right' kind of immigrants to fill them."[3] Quite clearly, in this period most Anglo-Canadians recognized the importance of having an available source of cheap unskilled labour for use in both the agricultural and industrial sectors of the economy. Combined with this, however, were a number of reservations about the movement of immigrant workers within Canadian society. Throughout the latter part of the nineteenth century Canadian politicians and immigration officials had assured the public that Canada's recruitment of immigrants would be confined to Great Britain and to northwestern Europe, a selective policy that would be greatly superior to the American open door.[4] In 1890 Sir John A. Macdonald had deplored the influx of millions of Slavic and southern European immigrants into the United States: "It is a great country, but it will have its vicissitudes and revolutions. Look at that mass of foreign ignorance and vice which has flooded that country with socialism, atheism and all other isms."[5] In contrast, Canada would seek only those vigorous northern races who were culturally sound and who could quickly conform to the norms of Anglo-Canadian life.

The employment boom at the turn of the century, with its insistent demand for Slavic and Italian workers, shattered this vision of a culturally harmonious Canada. Not surprisingly, the Anglo-Canadian response to these new immigrants from central and southern Europe was initially hostile. The Toronto *Mail and Empire* set the tone in 1899 when it branded Clifford Sifton's immigration policy as "an attempt to make of the North-West a sort of anthropological garden . . . to pick up the waifs and strays of Europe, the lost tribes of mankind, and the freaks of creation."[6] Organized labour had particular fears; as the guardian of the rights of Canadian workingmen it stood squarely against the importation of cheap labour. The fears, prejudices, and emotions of Canadian trade unionists were epitomized in a 1904 article of *The Independent*, a Vancouver labour newspaper: "This question of alien immigration . . . strikes at the foundation of every labour organization in the Country. . . . This labour is generally garnered from the slums of Europe and Asia, and thus thrown into direct competition with all kinds of Canadian labour. The immigrants having been brought up under conditions which no Canadian . . . [would] tolerate – work for wages upon which no Canadian could . . . exist."[7]

Many Anglo-Canadians were also disturbed by evidence of social deviance among immigrant workers. The ethnic ghettos, which quickly sprang up in the major Canadian cities and almost all single-enterprise communities west of the Ottawa River, were increasingly thought of as a breeding ground for "filth, immorality and crime."[8] The reports of the Royal North-West Mounted Police (RNWMP) from western Canada frequently stressed the tendency of foreign workers to take the law into their own hands; according to these accounts the prevalence of knives and guns could turn even minor disagreements into violent confrontatións. When the foreign worker was brought into contact with liquor, especially at festive occasions, social anarchy ensued.[9] This situation was vividly described by the Reverend C.W. Gordon (Ralph Connor) in his famous novel, *The Foreigner*:

In the main room dance and song reeled on in uproarious hilarity. In the basement below, foul and fetid, men stood packed close drinking while they could. . . . In the dim light of a smoky lantern, the swaying crowd, here singing in maudlin chorus, there fighting savagely to pay off old scores or to avenge new insults, presented a nauseating spectacle.[10]

Outraged by these conditions, Gordon and other Anglo-Canadian reformers such as J.S. Woodsworth sought to alleviate the lot of the immigrant workers. Their vision of immigrant life accords well with the notions of the historian Oscar Handlin, who has written of the period: "Immigration had transformed the entire . . . world within which the peasants had formerly lived. From surface forms to inmost functioning, the change was complete. . . . In the process, they became, in their own eyes, less worthy as men. They felt a sense of degradation that raised a most insistent question: Why had this happened?"[11] That the lives of immigrant workers had been seriously disrupted cannot be doubted, but was the transformation as complete as reformers such as Gordon and Woodsworth and historians such as Handlin would have it? Any attempt to answer this question in the Canadian context must of necessity take account of the reasons why emigrants left Europe for Canada, and of the social and economic adaptations they made on Canadian soil.

The World of the Immigrant Worker

The majority of European immigrant workers who came to Canada between 1896 and 1914 were of peasant background. Generally speaking, they came from regions where agricultural technology was primitive, crop productivity was low, and peasant landholdings were very small; for many, emigration was "an alternative to the restrictive opportunities of [their] traditional agrarian societies." In the case of immigrants from the Austro-Hungarian Empire, about 60 per cent were Slavs from the provinces of Galicia and Bukovina, regions where most of the landholdings were below the five hectares necessary for subsistence. A similar situation prevailed in other areas of high emigration, most notably in southern Italy, Slavonia, and the coastal regions of Sicily.[12]

The peasant face of all these societies belies the true nature of their employment patterns. Thus, while the traditional life of the land was the focus of work, economic circumstances forced many peasants to become migratory industrial workers for at least part of the year. The produce of the land and the industrial wage had for some formed the economic package by which they and their families were sustained. Modernization had intruded on these societies, and rural proletarians could "feed themselves from their own soil for only a few months, and for the rest of the year . . . worked as hired labour for 'others'."[13] In their search for casual employment these peasant workers had considerable geographical mobility both within their own and neighbouring countries. In 1908 alone some 300,000 Slavic workers from the Austro-Hungarian Empire crossed into Germany seeking short-term employment in the Junker farms of East Prussia and in the coal-mining and steel-producing regions of the Ruhr and Saar. Such labour mobility had transformed traditional peasant life in many parts of central and southern Europe. By 1900 the closed nucleated village of the nineteenth century had been replaced by a relatively open community whose residents "continuously interacted with the outside world and tied their future to its demands." In time, this "outside world" became transatlantic as well as continental.[14]

Returned sojourners acted as a source of information about economic conditions in North America and were of great importance in chain migrations whereby prospective migrants learned of job opportunities, were provided with transportation, and had initial accommodation in North America arranged for them. This adaptation of "familial and dyadic patronage" significantly influenced immigrant behaviour across the Atlantic. One familiar aspect of this was the creation of a series of "Little Italies" and "Slavtowns" in the towns and cities of the United States and Canada; another less well explored aspect was the carving out of ethnic niches within the North American job market.[15] *The Social Survey of Ukrainian Rural Settlement in Western Canada* (1917) showed that the kinship and village patterns of the Old World clearly influenced settlement patterns in the New. Similarly, Reino Kero's study of Finnish immigrants from the commune of Karvia has revealed that the majority gravitated toward three communities: Port Arthur and Nipigon in Ontario and Covington in Minnesota. Close familial and fraternal ties persisted among these immigrants, the international boundary notwithstanding.

The role of the ethnic intermediary or go-between, whether *padrone*, steamship agent, employment agent, or village sponsor, was also important in the movement of migrants from southern and eastern Europe to Canada. The revelations of both the Royal Commission to Inquire into the Immigration of Italian Labourers in Montreal, and Alleged Fraudulent Practices of Employment Agencies (1904) and investigations by the Immigration Branch showed that labour and steamship agencies annually facilitated the movement of thousands of immigrant workers to Canada through the issuance of prepaid tickets and the arrangement of jobs.[16] Nor did the relationship between the intermediary and the immigrant end with the latter's arrival in Canada; the intermediary, whether agency or individual, provided a variety of services for the migrant in the old homeland.[17] In 1907, for instance, $55.3 million was received in the Austro-Hungarian Empire from immigrant banks located in North America, while another $6 million was paid in postal money orders.[18] The intermediary also facilitated departure from North America both for those who had satisfied their economic ambitions and for those who were forced back across the Atlantic either by unemployment or infirmity. [19]

There were many similarities between the experiences of British and European immigrant workers in Canadian society prior to 1914. [20] As immigrants, both groups were forced to adjust to a new occupational and social environment. Both groups transported their unique cultural baggage. While British immigrant workers had a much easier entry into Canadian society, they still identified themselves, and were perceived, as being a distinct group. [21]

This ethnocentrism, combined with their early arrival and occupational skill, helps to explain why British immigrant workers had such a powerful influence on the development of trade unions and socialist parties in Canada. This was particularly pronounced at the latter part of the nineteenth century, at a time when momentous changes were occurring within British society itself. Between 1889 and 1900 the number of British trade unionists increased from 750,000 to two million. Moreover, many of these workers, especially in the new industrial unions, demonstrated considerable militancy in their struggle with both the business community and the state. [22]

After 1900, thousands of British workers moved back and forth across the Atlantic in response to economic opportunities. [23] As one British engineer put it, "You are only six days older when you land (in North America), and what is 3,000 or 4,000 miles for a young man?" Nor was the adaptation difficult for these skilled workers; the availability of jobs and the similarity of culture allowed them to enter Canadian society as equals, and, at times, even as important catalysts for working-class organizations. [24] This transfer of trade union and socialist party experience was an important aspect of the cultural adaptation of British immigrant workers to the Canadian environment, which was often reinforced by periodic trips back to the old country or by exposure to the lectures of prominent British labour organizers such as John Burns, Tom Mann, and Keir Hardie. [25] Other British-born activists came to the Canadian labour scene after having spent some time in the United States. This trend was quite pronounced in the western Canadian coal and hard-rock mining industries, where British-born workers moved back and forth across the border in search of work. As a result, they often transferred to the Canadian industrial environment not only their British cultural baggage but also their experiences in many American labour struggles. [26]

Prior to 1914, most labour and socialist political candidates in western Canada were British-born. This was evident during the federal election of 1900 when Ralph Smith and Arthur Puttee were elected from British Columbia and Manitoba working-class constituencies. Both represented the labourism tradition of the British Labour Party: "Less of a doctrine than a persuasion, labourism had several sources – Christian ethics, Gladstonian radicalism and Marxism. . . .

labourites were primarily reformers, committed to an immediate amelioration of social conditions under capitalism."[27] The pragmatic approach of Smith and Puttee was, however, quickly challenged by the more doctrinaire stance of the Socialist Party of Canada, founded in Vancouver in 1903. Despite its unwillingness to compromise its Marxist principles, the SPC was a potent force in the political life of western Canada prior to the Great War, particularly in the mining towns of the region and in the working-class neighbourhoods of Vancouver and Winnipeg. By 1909 the SPC had expanded its base of support into the industrial areas of Ontario and in scattered pockets in Quebec and Atlantic Canada. It had also drawn Ukrainian, Finnish, and Jewish socialists within its orbit. This success, however, was short-lived. By 1914 a combination of ethnic particularism, the rivalry of the more flexible Social Democratic Party, and serious internal schisms had virtually shattered the SPC as a national force.[28]

European immigrant workers also developed many responses to a Canadian environment that both promised and threatened. Going home was one method of dealing with economic exploitation and social discrimination. This return migration was not confined to sojourners who had accumulated savings; it also included many who were forced out of Canada by depressed economic circumstances. The lack of unemployment benefits in the Dominion and the existence of ample means to deport public charges and alien radicals further swelled the ranks of the returners.[29]

But of much greater importance were the wide range of cultural and working-class institutions that various groups of immigrant workers created in Canada. These ranged from the rather conservative ethnic churches to the more assertive mutual aid societies and political organizations.[30] The transfer of Old World values and ideas was also closely associated with the emergence of the immigrant press. At the turn of the century, many of the newspapers circulated among European immigrant workers were imported from the United States or from Europe, but by the First World War a distinct Canadian ethnic press had emerged.[31]

One aspect of the encounter of immigrants with industrializing Canada is associated with the growing presence of eastern and southern Europeans in the urban economy. For major ethnic groups composing this new flow of immigration – such as Jews and Italians – their experience in Canada became inextricably associated with the rapidly changing urban environment.[32] For example, during the first three decades of the twentieth century eastern and southern Europeans made up about one-fifth of the labour force at CPR installations in Montreal; yet, three out of four worked at unskilled jobs, usually as general labourers and car washers. A recent study of Italians working at the various CPR sites has shown the extent to which this labour market was characterized by instability and precariousness, with many dead-end jobs whose performance only required physical strength and a willingness to submit to the dictates of foremen and departmental bosses. It is not surprising, therefore, that 60 per cent of these employments lasted less than six months and 41 per cent less than three months. In part, this segmentation process was a result of managerial policies that favoured a constant supply of new workers. But even more important was the extent to which this severance of contact was worker-initiated. For the thousands of Italian immigrants who entered and left the Montreal economy between 1900 and 1914, unskilled CPR jobs were often only a temporary expedient until something more rewarding and stable came along. [33]

Italian immigrants involved in the capitalist labour market of Montreal, Toronto, Hamilton, and other Canadian urban centres often experienced economic and social exploitation. [34] Yet there was a low level of work-centred group militancy among these workers, a phenomenon that can be explained in a number of ways. First, only a small percentage of Italian skilled workers and artisans were among these immigrants, and the Italians lacked pre-migration radical political experience. Research on the place of origin of Montreal's Italian community, for instance, has shown that the great majority had a peasant background and most originated from the mountainous villages of the Abruzzi-Molise and Campania regions – areas little touched by the political and ideological ferment that swept Italy in the late nineteenth and early twentieth centuries. [35] A second factor was the lack of significant numerical concentrations of Italian workers in specific industrial sectors. There is, however, some evidence to suggest that when Italians did become a significant element within the labour force – such as occurred in the Montreal garment industry – the potential for union organization and labour militancy was greatly enhanced. [36] The highly unstable and precarious labour market in which most Italian workers operated was still another factor precluding union organization and militant collective action. Cut off from the major labour and political movements of both Italy and Canada, most Italian immigrants sought other means of survival and advancement, relying primarily on kinship solidarity and on village-based forms of co-operation. That this associational life was usually dominated by the local ethnic petty bourgeoisie and the Catholic clergy obviously reinforced the impulse toward conservative solutions. [37]

The Canadian experiences of Italian immigrant workers and Jewish immigrants present some striking contrasts. In demographic terms, Jewish immigrants were even more concentrated in large metropolitan centres, most notably Montreal, Toronto, and Winnipeg. Even more important was the level of their political involvement at both the local and national levels. Jewish immigrants established new militant trade unions, assumed leadership roles in radical political organizations, and in general acted as a sort of vanguard in the broader Canadian socialist (and later Communist) movement in ways that parallel significantly the experience of their U.S. counterparts. [38]

The involvement of European immigrant workers in railroad construction, harvesting, and the extractive industries represents another important aspect of the Canadian experience. Prior to 1920 these were the industries with the most acute labour shortages and the least appeal for the native-born and skilled immigrants. Only the European workers seemed prepared to face the irregular pay, high accident rates, crude living conditions, and isolation characteristic of work in these expanding parts of the Dominion's economy. In time, many of the immigrants moved on from the lumber and mining camps and railroad gangs to more stable opportunities in the steel mills and packing plants of urban Canada.[39]

According to the 1911 census, 57 per cent of the country's mine workers were immigrants: in Ontario, 48 per cent of the miners were foreign-born, but in British Columbia and Alberta the equivalent figures were 84 and 88 per cent. The Rocky Mountain coal-mining region of western Canada was especially polyglot, and in most of the mining communities those of British background constituted less than 50 per cent of the population. Within the mines, eastern and southern European miners were generally allocated the most arduous and dangerous jobs. The reports of the Alberta, British Columbia, and Ontario mining inspectors throughout the period 1900-14 document the prevailing high accident rates among foreign workers.[40] Yet another factor was the high degree of ethnic segregation and clannishness that characterized most of the frontier single-enterprise communities, a situation that often enabled Canadian employers to play one ethnic group off against another.[41]

Quite clearly it is not a simple matter to analyse patterns of collective protest among European immigrant workers, given the extent of ethnic diversity and the geographical divisions. The spectrum of protest among groups of railroad navvies, miners, and lumber workers in Canada ran from primitive and clannish to highly sophisticated and intensely ideological. On the other hand, it is readily apparent that some occupational contexts fostered working-class consciousness more than others. It has been said that miners everywhere have "a pre-existing tradition of conflict" and that their work, by its very nature, "gives them a powerful capacity for collective enterprise." During the period 1900-40 this thesis was certainly borne out in the mine fields of Cape Breton Island, northern Ontario, and western Canada. But the response of immigrant miners to the Canadian environment was by no means uniform. Cultural factors were also important, above all, the extent to which communal values in the old European homeland had been affected by industrial capitalism. Many Ukrainian and Finnish immigrant workers, for instance, came from societies where collective action against economic and social exploitation was an established fact. For others, the exploitation and alienation associated with the Canadian work environment were the most important catalysts in the development of working-class militancy and radicalism.[42] Moreover, common involvement in frontier single-enterprise communities as well as a common sense of peasant folk culture often provided a basis of communication between different linguistic and ethnic groups. This growth of worker comradeship has been vividly described by Vera Lysenko:

> In the evenings, the men smoked, chewed gum, told jokes at the expense of the foreman, went for joyrides with hand cars, read newspapers, wrote letters to their families, played poker with matches . . . there were always a few musicians among them [and] the men joined in singing in a mixture of many languages . . . the Hungarians with their wild Magyar songs, the Roumanians and Ukrainians sang theirs in turn.[43]

Recent scholarship has analysed the importance of male bonding among industrial workers, "a conception of 'manliness' " that could lead them "not only to accommodate themselves to the conditions of their labour, but also to challenge authority when its exercise by supervisors impinged on a man's dignity." Co-operation and comradeship became particularly important in the face of difficult and dangerous labour situations, although the fears and insecurities were often channelled through an acceptable masculine outlet "in drinking, arguments, rough play, or fighting."[44]

Numerous incidents could be cited from the period 1896-1914 of immigrant workers in the rail, mine, and lumber camps resorting to collective action to remedy specific grievances.[45] In many cases worker demands were accompanied by violence or the threat of violence. Action was directed against employers and ethnic intermediaries alike. A 1908 report of the Dominion Police gives this account of the response of Bulgarian navvies to an attempt by Sava Angeloff, a labour agent, to extract an additional commission from them:

> Last week he [Angeloff] went down to La Turque to collect some board money owing him by some of the Bulgarians and they got after him to mob him, but he drew a revolver and kept them off, and while he was at the camp the men poured coal-oil all about the place with a view to setting fire to it and burning him up, but on a promise to refund from $5.00 to $10.00 to each man, which he did, they let him go back to Montreal.[46]

Prior to 1914 the most spectacular attempts to organize European immigrant workers in Canada were undoubtedly those made by the Industrial Workers of the World (IWW), the famous American-based syndicalist movement. In this work the "Wobblies" had a number of advantages. In the first place, their approach was entirely class-oriented; unlike the situation in most Canadian craft unions, there was little Anglo-Saxon hostility toward ethnic workers. As one Prince Rupert Wobbly exclaimed, "when the factory whistle blows it does not call us to work as Irishmen, Germans, Americans, Russians, Greeks, Poles, Negroes or Mexicans. It calls us to work as wage workers, regardless of the country in which we were born or colour of our skins." The second great advantage of the IWW was the extent to which its organization was geared to the migratory work patterns of the foreign worker: its initiation fees and dues were low, the membership cards were transferable, and the camp delegate system of union democracy made it possible for an immigrant worker to become "a full time organizer while he wandered." Nor did the IWW waste time in sterile ideological controversy; despite its syndicalist underpinnings the IWW concentrated on specific grievances. Moreover, IWW organizers usually waited until a labour disturbance erupted before launching a recruiting drive. [47]

The IWW entered the hard-rock mining regions of the Kootenays in 1907, but it was their involvement in the spectacular Canadian Northern railway strike of March, 1912, that put them on the front lines of Canadian labour. Worker protest against low pay and harsh working and living conditions resulted in a bitter dispute involving over 7,000 workers. This massive confrontation was to test severely the IWW's ability to organize unskilled labour in western Canada. Initially they seemed to stand a reasonable chance of victory, thanks to the remarkable degree of labour solidarity. An article in the *British Columbia Federationist* of April 5, 1912, hailed the walkout as "an object lesson as to what a movement animated by an uncompromising spirit of revolt . . . can accomplish among the most heterogeneous army of slaves that any system of production ever assembled together." On the other hand, these workers were responding to specific grievances and few had any real knowledge of unionism; they were also vulnerable to the threat of destitution and displacement by strike-breakers. Ultimately, a hostile British Columbia government helped crush the strike by arresting more than 250 IWW activists. [48] Although the IWW had failed, the memory of its involvement and the syndicalist creed of industrial unionism cast a long shadow over future industrial relations in western Canada. [49]

Beyond the unions were the various socialist parties that actively operated among European immigrant workers, especially in western Canada and northern Ontario. The most successful of these organizations were usually located in single-enterprise communities or major urban centres, drawing much of their support from the ethnic enclaves. [50] This was particularly true of regions with large numbers of Ukrainian and Finnish immigrants. [51] In both cases, emphasis on cultural and ethnic values enabled the socialists to secure considerable popular support throughout western Canada and northern Ontario; thus, the socialist hall was not only a political but a social institution. [52]

Finnish women were also involved in the various socialist parties. As early as 1907 a female branch of the SPC had been organized in Toronto and campaigned for both economic and political reform in the city. Other Finnish women were active in SPC locals in Sudbury and Port Arthur, as well as in western Canada. The extent that women were afforded equal rights with the Finnish left greatly impressed the SPC, especially the editors of its newspaper, *The Western Clarion*.

"The Finnish comrades have taken a high stand in the matter of discouraging smoking and drinking, and in making their socialist gatherings a meeting place for both sexes of all ages."[53]

Eastern European Jewish women garment workers demonstrated considerable militancy in the needle trades of Toronto, Montreal, and Winnipeg and organized themselves into a variety of trade unions. This was not an easy task, given an industry characterized by economic instability and intransigent management, as well as problems with ethnic rivalries, anti-Semitism, and the difficulty of overcoming the timidity of women garment workers, the poorest paid and most vulnerable segment of the labour force. According to Ruth Frager, one of the major reasons why so many Jewish women were involved in socialist organizations was because so many of them had been radicalized in the European ghettos, "not only in response to class consciousness, but also in response to the oppression they faced as Jews." On the other hand, she points out that Canadian Jewish labour organizers recognized the danger of concentrating on Jewish rights "precisely because it would weaken the working class by dividing Jewish workers and non-Jewish workers." Women union organizers also had another problem: how to carry their struggle "against class oppression and anti-semitism," while having to cope with the onerous "triple day of labour" (job, home, union). In addition, there was the reality that many of Toronto's Jewish women unionists allowed themselves to be "incorporated into the Jewish labour movement on the basis of an implicit acceptance of their own subordination."[54] Notable exceptions to this pattern were Becky Buhay and Annie Buller of Montreal, both of whom later became prominent members of the Communist Party of Canada.[55]

In 1908 Winnipeg gained notoriety when Emma Goldman, one of North America's most famous anarchists, visited the city. What was notable about this was not her lecture, but rather the frantic attempts by Winnipeg civic officials to have her barred from the country. Mayor J.H. Ashdown, a prominent local businessman, articulated the views of the city's Anglo-Canadian elite when he criticized the Immigration Branch for not excluding such "professional agitators":

> . . . we have a large foreign population in this City, it consists approximately of 15,000 Galicians, 11,000 Germans, 10,000 Jews, 2,000 Hungarians and 5,000 Russians and other Slavs and Bohemians. Many of these people have had trouble in their own country with their Governments and have come to the new land to get away from it but have all the undesirable elements in their character that created the trouble for them before. They are just the right crowd for Emma Goldman or persons of her character to sow seeds which are bound to cause most undesirable growths in the future.[56]

Emma Goldman was eventually allowed into Winnipeg, but this incident cleared the way for a 1910 amendment to the Immigration Act, which provided for the exclusion and deportation of those professing anarchist views. The amendment was a portent of what was to follow in 1919.[57]

The War Years

The economic status of immigrant workers on the eve of World War One was not favourable. By 1912 the unsettled state of European affairs had helped produce a prolonged economic slump in the transatlantic economy. This recession was particularly felt in western Canada, a region very dependent on foreign capital for its continued prosperity. By the summer of 1914 there was widespread unemployment in the area, the more so since over 400,000 immigrants had arrived in the previous year.[58] Before long many Prairie and west coast communities were providing relief to unemployed workers.[59] But worse was to follow – especially for those immigrants unlucky enough to have been born in those countries that took up arms against the British Empire.

The outbreak of war in August, 1914, forced the Dominion government to adopt a comprehensive set of guidelines for dealing with the enemy alien residents of the country. Of those classified as enemy aliens, there were 393,320 of German origin, 129,103 from the Austro-Hungarian Empire, 3,880 from the Turkish Empire, and several thousands from Bulgaria.[60] The government's position was set forth in a series of acts and proclamations, the most important being the War Measures Act of August, 1914. This measure specified that during a "state of war, invasion, or insurrection . . . the Governor in Council may do and authorize such acts . . . orders and regulations, as he may . . . deem necessary or advisable for the security, defence, order and welfare of Canada." Specific reference was made to the following powers: censorship on all forms of communication and the arrest, detention, and deportation of dangerous enemy aliens. Subsequent orders-in-council in October, 1914, and September, 1916, prohibited enemy aliens from possessing firearms and instituted a system of police and military registration. By the end of the war over 80,000 enemy aliens had been registered, though only 8,579 of these were actually interned. This number included: 2,009 Germans, 5,954 Austro-Hungarians, 205 Turks, 99 Bulgarians, and 312 classified as miscellaneous. These prisoners of war were located in twenty-four different camps, although most were placed in either Kapuskasing, Ontario, or Vernon, B.C.[61]

There were very few incidents of sabotage or espionage on the home front during the war, but enemy aliens soon became the object of intense Anglo-Canadian hostility.[62] This was particularly true of those enemy aliens categorized as Austrians since most of them were immigrants of military age who retained the status of reservists in their homeland.[63] Throughout the fall of 1914 there were also alarming reports about what was afoot in the German-American communities of several American cities; one agent reported from Chicago that "should the Germans achieve a single success I believe that we in Canada are in danger of a repetition of the invasion of 1866 on a larger scale." What made the threat from the United States even more ominous was the steady flow of migrant labourers across a virtually unpatrolled border; many of those on the move were either enemy aliens or members of alleged pro-German groups, such as Finns. [64]

The fear of a fifth column among unemployed and impoverished enemy alien workers was also widespread. [65] Conversely, strong support existed in the country for enemy aliens who had jobs to be turned out of them; in 1915 there were many dismissals for "patriotic" reasons. This policy was popular among both Anglo-Canadian workers and immigrants from countries, such as Italy and Russia, now allied with the British Empire. [66] Some labour-intensive corporations, however, held a different point of view. [67] The Dominion Iron and Steel Company, for example, resisted the pressure to dismiss their enemy alien employees on the grounds that Nova Scotia workers "would not undertake the rough, dirty jobs." [68] It was only when the company obtained an understanding from the Immigration Branch that it could import even more pliable workers from Newfoundland that it agreed to join temporarily in the patriotic crusade. [69] Elsewhere, corporate resistance was even stronger. In June, 1915, English-speaking and allied miners threatened strike action at Fernie, B.C., and Hillcrest, Alberta, unless all enemy alien miners were dismissed. The situation was particularly tense at Fernie, where the giant Crow's Nest Coal Company initially balked at this demand. Eventually a compromise was achieved: all naturalized married enemy alien miners were retained; naturalized unmarried enemy aliens were promised work when it was available; the remainder of the enemy alien work force, some 300 in number, were temporarily interned. Within two months, however, all but the "most dangerous" had been released. [70]

This action indicated that, despite severe local and provincial pressure, the Borden government was not prepared to implement a mass internment policy. The enormous expense in operating the camps and an antipathy to adopting police-state tactics partly explain the government's reluctance. There was also a suspicion in Ottawa that many municipalities wanted to take advantage of internment camps to get rid of their unemployed. Arthur Meighen articulated the view of the majority of the cabinet when he argued that instead of being interned, unemployed aliens should each be granted forty acres of land that could be cultivated under government supervision; he concluded his case with the observation that "these Austrians . . . can live on very little." [71] By the spring of 1916 even the British Columbia authorities had come around to this point of view. One provincial police report gave this account of how much things had quieted down: "From a police point of view, there has been less trouble amongst them [aliens] since the beginning of the war than previously, the fact that several of them were sent to internment camps at the beginning of the war seemed to have a good effect on the remainder.... In my opinion, if there is ever any trouble over the employment of enemy aliens, it will be after the war is over and our people have returned."[72]

But the changed attitude in British Columbia also reflected a dramatically altered labour market. As the war progressed serious labour shortages developed in the province and throughout the country. In the summer of 1915 there was a demand for about 10,000 harvest labourers in the Prairie provinces. Many of those who came to do the harvesting were unemployed enemy alien workers from the slums of Vancouver and Winnipeg who had their transportation subsidized by the federal and western provincial governments.[73] Government involvement in the recruitment of such workers was increased in 1916 when it became apparent that the supply of labour available on the Prairies would again be insufficient to meet the harvest demands. The Immigration Branch now began placing advertisements in United States newspapers urging Americans to look northward for employment. Instructions were also issued to the agents of the branch that the money qualifications of the Immigration Act were to be relaxed. By the end of September 1916, over 5,000 harvesters, attracted by generous wages ($3.50 a day) and cheap (one cent a mile) rail fares from border points, had crossed the international border.[74]

Increasingly, the practice of securing industrial workers from the United States was also regarded as essential to the maintenance of the Canadian war economy. By an order-in-council of August, 1916, the Alien Labour Act was temporarily shelved to facilitate the movement of industrial labour northward. Thousands of American residents were soon streaming into Canadian industrial communities.[75] But with the entry of the United States into the war in 1917 this source of labour supply was abruptly cut off. Of necessity, the focus of Canadian recruitment efforts now shifted overseas, most notably toward Asia and the West Indies. The most ambitious proposal called for the importation of thousands of Chinese workers on a temporary basis. But this solution met with the same violent objections it had always encountered from organized labour and nativist opinion, and was ultimately rejected by the Dominion government.[76]

With an overseas solution seeming impossible, the new labour situation put a premium on the surplus manpower available in the country. This made the alien worker, whether of enemy extraction or not, a very desirable quantity indeed. The implementation of conscription in the summer of 1917 only aggravated an already difficult situation; by the end of the year the country faced an estimated shortage of 100,000 workers. From the spring of 1917 on, foreign workers found themselves not only wanted by Canadian employers, but actually being "drafted" into the industrial labour force by the government.[77] As of August, 1916, all men and women over the age of sixteen were required to register with the Canadian Registration Board, and in April, 1918, the so-called "Anti-Loafing Law" provided that "every male person residing in the Dominion of Canada should be regularly engaged in some useful occupation."[78]

As early as 1916, the government had adopted the practice of releasing non-dangerous interned prisoners of war under contract to selected mining and railway companies, both to minimize the costs of operating the camps and to cope with labour shortages. Not surprisingly, this policy was welcomed by Canadian industrialists since these enemy alien workers received only $1.10 a day and were not susceptible to trade union influence.[79] One of the mining companies most enthusiastic about securing large numbers of the POW workers was the Dominion Iron and Steel Corporation. In the fall of 1917 the president of the company, Mark Workman, suggested that his operation be allocated both interned and "troublesome" aliens since "there is no better way of handling aliens than to keep them employed in productive labour." In December, 1917, Workman approached Borden, before the latter left for England, with the proposal that the POWs interned in Great Britain be transferred to the mines of Cape Breton. Unfortunately for the Dominion Steel Company, the scheme was rejected by British officials.[80]

The railway companies, particularly the Canadian Pacific, also received large numbers of POW workers. The reception of these workers harked back to some of the worst aspects of the immigrant navvy tradition of these companies. During 1916 and 1917 a series of complaints were lodged by POW workers, and on one occasion thirty-two Austrian workers went on strike in the North Bay district to protest dangerous working conditions and unsanitary living conditions. Neither the civil nor military authorities gave any countenance to these complaints; the ultimate fate of these workers was to be sentenced to six months' imprisonment at the Burwash prison farm "for breach of contract."[81]

This coercion was symptomatic of a growing concern among both Anglo-Canadian businessmen and federal security officials about alien labour radicalism. Not surprisingly, a 65 per cent increase in food prices between August, 1914, and December, 1917, created considerable industrial unrest, and the labour shortages that began in 1916 provided the trade unions with a superb opportunity to strike back. In 1917 there was a record number of strikes and more than one million man days were lost. Immigrant workers were caught up in the general labour unrest, and in numerous industrial centres in northern Ontario and western Canada they demonstrated a capacity for effective collective action and a willingness to defy the power of both management and the state. The coming of the Russian Revolution in 1917 added to the tension in Canada by breathing new life into a number of ethnic socialist organizations.[82]

By the spring of 1918 the Dominion government was under great pressure to place all foreign workers under supervision, and, if necessary, to make them "work at the point of a bayonet." The large-scale internment of radical aliens and the suppression of seditious foreign-language newspapers were also now widely advocated.[83] In June, 1918, C.H. Cahan, a wealthy Montreal lawyer, was appointed to conduct a special investigation of alien radicalism. In the course of his inquiry Cahan solicited information from businessmen, "respectable" labour leaders, police officials in both Canada and the United States, and various members of the anti-socialist immigrant community in Canada. The report Cahan submitted to cabinet in September, 1918, was the basis of a series of coercive measures: by two orders-in-council (PC 2381 and PC 2384) the foreign-language press was suppressed and a number of socialist and anarchist organizations were outlawed. Penalties for possession of prohibited literature and continued membership in any of these outlawed organizations were extremely severe: fines of up to $5,000 or a maximum prison term of five years could be imposed.[84]

The Red Scare

The hatreds and fear stirred up by World War One did not end with the armistice of 1918; instead, social tension spread in ever-widening circles. Anglo-Canadians who had learned to despise the Germans and Austro-Hungarians had little difficulty transferring their aroused passions to the Bolsheviks. Though the guns were silent on the Western Front, Canadian troops were now being sent to Siberia "to strangle the infant Bolshevism in its cradle."[85] Within Canada, there was widespread agitation against potentially disloyal aliens and those involved in socialist organizations. An editorial in the *Winnipeg Telegram* summed up these sentiments: "Let every hostile alien be deported from this country, the privileges of which . . . he does not appreciate."[86]

In the early months of 1919 the Borden government was deluged by a great wave of petitions demanding the mass deportation of enemy aliens. Inquiries were actually made by the government concerning the possible implementation of a policy of mass expulsion. Surveys by the Department of Justice revealed that there were over 80,000 enemy aliens registered, 2,222 of whom were located in internment camps. There were also 63,784 Russian subjects in Canada, many of whom officials in Ottawa believed to be potentially hostile.[87] The policy of mass deportation was rejected, however, both because of its likely international repercussions and because of the demands it would make on the country's transportation facilities at a time when the troops were returning from Europe.[88]

The need to find jobs quickly for the returning soldier also affected the situation of the foreign worker. Both politicians and businessmen faced a powerful argument in the claim that all enemy aliens should be turned out of their jobs to make way for Canada's "heroes"; but their actions were also motivated by the fear that the veterans would be radicalized and lured into socialist organizations if their economic needs were not immediately satisfied. By February, 1919, the British Columbia Employers' Association, the British Columbia Manufacturers' Association, and the British Columbia Loggers' Association had all announced that their memberships were prepared to offer employment to returned soldiers by dismissing alien enemies. This pattern was repeated in the mining region of northern Ontario, where in the early months of 1919 the International Nickel Company, for instance, dismissed 2,200 of its 3,200 employees, the vast majority of whom were foreigners.[89] Even the CPR joined the "patriotic crusade" of dismissals. As vice-president D.C. Coleman put it, "The aliens who had been on the land when the war broke out and who went to work in the cities and towns, taking the jobs of the men who went to the front . . . [should] go back to their old jobs on the land."[90]

But not even the land of the "men in sheepskin coats" was now safe for the immigrant worker; rumours were abroad that the government intended to cancel large numbers of homestead patents, and assaults on aliens by returned soldiers were commonplace.[91] Even the usually passive *Canadian Ruthenian* denounced the harsh treatment that Ukrainians and other foreigners were receiving from the Anglo-Canadian community and the government:

> The Ukrainians were invited to Canada and promised liberty, and a kind of paradise. Instead of the latter they found woods and rocks, which had to be cut down to make the land fit to work on. They were given farms far from the railroads, which they so much helped in building – but still they worked hard . . . and came to love Canada. But . . . liberty did not last long. First, they were called "Galicians" in mockery. Secondly, preachers were sent amongst them, as if they were savages, to preach Protestantism. And thirdly, they were deprived of the right to elect their representatives in Parliament. They are now uncertain about their future in Canada. Probably, their [property] so bitterly earned in the sweat of their brow will be confiscated.[92]

By the spring of 1919 the Borden government had received a number of petitions from ethnic organizations demanding either British justice or the right to leave Canada. The *Toronto Telegram* estimated that as many as 150,000 Europeans were preparing to leave the country. Some Anglo-Canadian observers warned, however, that mass emigration might relieve the employment problems of the moment but in the long run leave "a hopeless dearth of labour for certain kinds of work which Anglo-Saxon will not undertake."

Concern about the status of the alien worker led directly to the appointment of the Royal Commission on Industrial Relations on April 4, 1919. The members of the Commission travelled from Sydney to Victoria and held hearings in some twenty-eight industrial centres. The testimony of industrialists who appeared before the Commission reveals an ambivalent attitude toward the alien worker. Some industrialists argued that the alien was usually doing work "that white men don't want" and that it would "be a shame to make the returned soldier work at that job." But in those regions with high unemployment among returned soldiers and where alien workers had been organized by radical trade unions, management took a strikingly different view. William Henderson, a coal-mine operator at Drumheller, Alberta, informed the Commission that the unstable industrial climate of that region could only be reversed by hiring more Anglo-Canadian workers, "men that we could talk to . . . men that would come in with us and co-operate with us. . . ." Many mining representatives also indicated that their companies had released large numbers of aliens who had shown radical tendencies; there were numerous suggestions that these aliens should not only be removed from the mining districts, but actually deported from Canada.[93]

In the spring of 1919 Winnipeg was a city of many solitudes. Within its boundaries rich and poor, Anglo-Saxon and foreigner lived in isolation. The vast majority of the white-collar Anglo-Saxon population was to be found in the south and west of the city; the continental Europeans were hived in the North End. This ethno-class division was also reflected in the disparity between the distribution of social services and the incidence of disease. Infant mortality in the North End, for example, was usually twice the rate in the Anglo-Saxon South End. The disastrous influenza epidemic that struck the city during the winter of 1918-19 further demonstrated the high cost of being poor and foreign.[94]

During January and February, 1919, there were a series of anti-alien incidents in the city. One of the worst occurred on January 28 when a mob of returned soldiers attacked scores of foreigners and wrecked the German club, the offices of the Socialist Party of Canada, and the business establishment of Sam Blumenberg, a prominent Jewish socialist.[95] Reports of the event in the *Winnipeg Telegram* illustrate the attitude adopted by many Anglo-Canadian residents of the city toward the aliens. The *Telegram* made no apologies for the violence; instead, the newspaper contrasted the manly traits of the Anglo-Canadian veterans to the cowardly and furtive behaviour of the aliens: "It was typical of all who were assaulted, that they hit out for home or the nearest hiding place after the battle."[96] Clearly, many Anglo-Canadians in the city were prepared to accept mob justice. R.B. Russell reported that the rioting veterans had committed their worst excesses when "smartly dressed officers . . . [and] prominent members of the Board of Trade" had urged them on. Nor had the local police or military security officials made any attempt to protect the foreigners from the mob.[97]

At the provincial level Premier Norris's response to the violence was not to punish the rioters, but to establish an Alien Investigation Board that issued registration cards only to "loyal" aliens. Without these cards foreign workers were not only denied employment but were actually scheduled for deportation. Indeed, the local pressure for more extensive deportation of radical aliens increased during the spring of 1919, especially after D.A. Ross, the provincial member for Springfield, publicly charged that both Ukrainian socialists and religious nationalists were armed with "machine guns, rifles and ammunition to start a revolution in May."[98] The stage was now set for the Red Scare of 1919.

The Winnipeg General Strike of May 15 to June 28, 1919, brought the elements of class and ethnic conflict together in a massive confrontation. The growing hysteria in the city brought with it renewed propaganda against aliens, a close co-operation between security forces and the local political and economic elite, and finally, attempts to use the immigration machinery to deport not only alien agitators but also British-born radicals. The sequence of events associated with the Winnipeg Strike has been well documented: the breakdown of negotiations between management and labour in the metal trades was followed by the decision of the Winnipeg Trades and Labour Council to call a general strike for May 15. The response was dramatic; between 25,000 and 30,000 workers left their jobs. Overnight the city was divided into two camps.[99]

On one side stood the Citizens' Committee of One Thousand, a group of Anglo-Canadian businessmen and professionals who viewed themselves as the defenders of the Canadian way of life on the Prairies. Their purpose was clear: to crush the radical labour movement in Winnipeg. In their pursuit of this goal the Citizens' Committee engaged in a ferocious propaganda campaign against the opposing Central Strike Committee, both through its own newspaper *The Citizen* and through the enthusiastic support it received from the *Telegram* and the *Manitoba Free Press*. The committee's propaganda was aimed specifically at veterans, and the strike was portrayed as the work of enemy aliens and a few irresponsible Anglo-Saxon agitators.[100] John W. Dafoe, the influential editor of the *Free Press*, informed his readers that the five members of the Central Strike Committee – Russell, Ivens, Veitch, Robinson, and Winning – had been rejected by the intelligent and skilled Anglo-Saxon workers and had gained power only through "the fanatical allegiance of the Germans, Austrians, Huns and Russians." Dafoe advised that the best way of undermining the control the "Red Five" exercised over the Winnipeg labour movement was "to clean the aliens out of this community and ship them back to their happy homes in Europe which vomited them forth a decade ago."[101]

The Borden government was quick to comply. On June 15, the commissioner of the RNWMP indicated that 100 aliens had been marked for deportation under the recently enacted section 41 of the Immigration Act, and that thirty-six were in Winnipeg. In the early hours of June 17 officers of the force descended on the residences of ten Winnipegers: six Anglo-Saxon labour leaders and four "foreigners" were arrested.[102] Ultimately none of these men were summarily deported, as planned. In the case of the Anglo-Saxon strike leaders, an immediate protest was registered by numerous labour organizations across the country. Alarmed by this uproar, the Borden government announced that it did not intend to use section 41 against British-born agitators either in Winnipeg or in any other centre.[103]

The aliens arrested were not so fortunate. The violent confrontation of June 21 between the strikers and the RNWMP, in which scores were injured and two killed, encouraged the hard-liners in the Borden government. On July 1 raids was carried out across the country on the homes of known alien agitators and the offices of radical organizations. Many of those arrested were moved to the internment camp at Kapuskasing, Ontario, and subsequently deported in secret.[104] In its attempts to deport the approximately 200 "anarchists and revolutionaries" rounded up in the summer raids of 1919, the Immigration Branch worked very closely with United States immigration authorities. This co-operation was indicative of a link being forged between Canadian and American security agencies; the formation of the Communist Labour Party of America and the Communist Party of America in the fall of 1919 further strengthened this connection.[105] This RNWMP and military intelligence also maintained close contact with the British Secret Service. Lists of undesirable immigrants and known Communists were transmitted from London to Ottawa. Indeed, the Immigration Branch had now evolved from a recruitment agency to a security service.[106]

Immigration "Reform"

The events of 1919 produced a spirited national debate on whether Canada should continue to maintain an open-door immigration policy. Since many Anglo-Canadians equated Bolshevism with the recent immigration from eastern Europe, support grew for policies similar to the quota system under discussion in the United States.[107] The Winnipeg Strike, the surplus of labour, and a short but sharp dip in the stock market removed some of the incentive for industrialists to lobby for the continued importation of alien workers. Even the Canadian Manufacturers' Association, a long-time advocate of an open-door policy, sounded a cautious note: "Canada should not encourage the immigration of those whose political and social beliefs unfit them for assimilation with Canadians. While a great country such as Canada possessing millions of vacant acres needs population, it is wiser to go slowly and secure the right sort of citizens."[108] Ethnic, cultural, and ideological acceptability had temporarily triumphed over economic considerations. Whether Canada was prepared to accept a slower rate of economic growth to ensure its survival as a predominantly Anglo nation now became a matter of pressing importance.

Among the European workers themselves the enemy alien hysteria and the Red Scare produced great bitterness. This was especially true for Ukrainian, Finnish, and Russian immigrants, many of whom had considered returning to Europe in the spring of 1919. The unsettled economic and political conditions in their homelands had, however, ultimately prevented their exodus. But their future prospects in Canada looked anything but promising. Certainly there seemed little reason to believe that they could ever become part of the mainstream of Canadian life. In these circumstances, some of their ethnic organizations offered an alternative to the "Canadian Way of Life" – an alternative that found sustenance in the achievements of Soviet communism.[109] The distinctive outlook of Slavic and Finnish socialists in Canada was described as follows in a 1921 RCMP intelligence report:

> If in earlier years they came sick of Europe, ready to turn their back on their homelands, and full of admiration for the native Canadian and Canadian civilization, they have changed their point of view. The war and revolution have roused their intense interest in Central Europe. They belong almost wholly to the poorest element in the community, and it is highly exciting to them to see the class from which they come, composed in effect of their own relatives, seize control of all power and acquire all property.[110]

Such was the legacy of 1919 – the floodtide of radical labour politics in Canada.

Table 3
Immigration Trends Prior to World War Two

A. PERCENTAGE OF IMMIGRATION ARRIVING IN DIFFERENT PERIODS, **1896-1939**

1896-1906	*1907-14*	*1914-19*	*1919-25*	*1926-30*	*1931-39*
924,554	1,984,182	315,032	637,576	731,450	147,238
19.5%	41.9%	6.6%	13.5%	15.4%	3.1%

B. OCCUPATIONAL BACKGROUND OF IMMIGRANT MALES
ARRIVING IN CANADA, **1907-35**

Farmers	*Labourers*	*Mechanics*	*Clerks*	*Miners*	*Others*
947,064	547,004	318,799	130,145	43,298	117,458
45%	26%	15.1%	6.2%	2.1%	5.6%

C. BACKGROUND OF FEMALE DOMESTICS COMING TO CANADA, **1904-61**

	Total	*British*	*W.European*	*E.European*	*S.European*
1904-14	117,568	90,028	8,094	15,387	1,110
1919-30	123,982	74,179	14,179	30,814	1,989
1951-61	82,937	7,479	10,487	35,116	27,160

SOURCES: Annual Reports of the Immigration Branch, Department of the Interior, and Department of Immigration and Colonization, 1896-1939; Marilyn Barber, *Immigrant Domestic Servants in Canada* (Ottawa, 1991), 2.

CHAPTER 4

The 1920s:
New Immigrants, Old Problems

In June, 1919, Canadian immigration policy was dramatically revised. Whereas before 1914 economic considerations had been paramount, now the principal criteria became political and cultural acceptability. Previously acceptable ethnic groups, most notably Germans, Ukrainians, Russians, and Finns, were either barred from the country or had stringent entrance requirements placed on them. [1] The prevailing view of those who designed immigration policy was that sufficient numbers of Anglo-Saxon agriculturalists and industrial workers could now be secured either within the country or from the United States and Great Britain. This notion assumed a new role for the Dominion government in both land settlement and the distribution of labour; the instruments of this new role were to be the Soldier Settlement Branch of the Department of Reconstruction and the Employment Service of Canada, which fell under the Department of Labour.

The high hopes of an ethnically pure Canada were soon dashed. In the immediate post-war period the urbanization of native-born Canadians continued at an accelerated rate, and relatively few entered the country from the Anglo-Saxon homelands of Great Britain and the United States. Indeed, thousands of Canadian workers, both rural and urban, abandoned the country and its mounting economic problems for the United States. In time these developments strengthened the position of the old open-door lobby of transportation and resource-based industries. By 1925 spokesmen for these interests had managed to achieve the removal of all disabilities from Germany and its wartime allies. In September of that year the government entered into an agreement with the Canadian Pacific

Railway and the newly formed Canadian National Railways that allowed these companies a free hand in the selection and distribution of central European agricultural immigrants. In the next six years approximately 370,000 continental European immigrants entered the country.[2]

The arrival of thousands of continental European workers between 1925 and 1930 had significant economic and social ramifications. Resource-based labour-intensive industries were once more allowed access to cheap unskilled labour. The price of this free hand for business was partly paid by Canadian workers who were already facing the challenges of technological change and scientific management. But, as before 1914, the interests of the immigrant workers themselves were the first consideration to be swept aside in the name of Canadian economic progress. Immigrant workers drifted across the country in a desperate search for jobs. Many searched in vain, unable to accumulate enough money either to settle on the land or to return to Europe. These "new Canadians" also encountered a notable hostility on the part of some Anglo-Canadian trade unionists and farmers, who joined forces with nativist organizations to lobby against the railway agreement. The ideological garb of this new agitation was racial: Canada's Anglo-Saxon character, it was claimed, was being destroyed. That the percentage of people of European origin in western Canada had increased from approximately 29 per cent in 1921 to 35 per cent in 1931 only lent credence to the exclusionist argument.[3] Since Yugoslavs, Czechs, Slovaks, and Hungarians had followed the earlier practice of Ukrainians and Russians in forming communities within communities, whether in town or country, the threat seemed visible enough.

Not surprisingly, the advent of the Great Depression intensified the existing fear of the foreigner, the more so since unemployed foreign workers seemed to be the natural constituency of the Communist Party of Canada and other radical organizations. Between 1929 and 1931 the Dominion government once more reversed its immigration policy. In 1931 the Railway Agreement was cancelled, and only bona fide farmers with ample capital were allowed into the country. Simultaneously, a program was implemented to deport thousands of indigent immigrants back to their European homelands. This was accompanied by an expanded use of section 41 of the Immigration Act, especially against those alien radicals associated with the Communist Party. By 1931 it was evident that Canada had not only closed its doors to the foreigner, but that the social and political rights of non-British immigrants were in jeopardy.

"Keep out the Foreigners, Bring in the Anglo-Saxons"

That section 41 should have come so much to the fore in the 1920s reflected its central importance in the changes made in the Immigration Act in 1919. Under the terms of this section, "any person other than a Canadian citizen [who] advocates ... the overthrow by force ... of constituted law and authority" could be deported from the country.[4] This sweeping provision reinforced section 38 of the Act, which gave the Governor General in council authority "to prohibit or limit ... for a stated period or permanently the landing ... of immigrants belonging to any nationality or race deemed unsuitable." This section had been invoked consistently to exclude either U.S. or West Indian blacks from the country.[5] In 1919, section 38 was also used to exclude various European immigrants. By order-in-council PC 1203, Germans, Austrians, Hungarians, Bulgarians, and Turks were excluded because of their wartime associations; PC 1204 barred Doukhobors, Mennonites, and Hutterites because of "their peculiar customs, habits, modes of living and methods of holding property."[6]

These measures reflected prevailing Anglo-Canadian opinions. Pejorative terms such as "Bohunks," "Huns," and "Dagos" abounded in the popular writing of the time. One very successful work, *Breaking Prairie Sod*, by the Reverend Wellington Bridgman, even went so far as to charge that all Germans and Austrians were capable of "unnameable treachery and crime." Bridgman also attributed the industrial unrest of 1919 to the foreign workers and predicted that Canada would never achieve industrial stability until they were swept from the country.[7] Nor was this an isolated outburst. In the summer of 1919 *Maclean's* magazine ran a series of articles exposing the evil associations of alien radicals, especially those of Finnish, Ukrainian, and Russian background.[8] The same spirit prevailed in the Department of Immigration and Colonization. F.C. Blair, the departmental secretary, wrote that immigration from Finland was being discouraged because "a number of Finnish people seem to be very busy spreading IWW propaganda and occasionally one is found doing something worse." Ukrainians and Russians, especially those who lived in Soviet-controlled territory, were seen in a similar light.[9] Even Italians were now suspect, not only for an alleged propensity for crime, but also because the Bolshevik menace had spread to their homeland. In September, 1920, Blair informed the president of the Algoma Steel Corporation that "hundreds of industries have been seized in Italy by workers and there is a good deal of unrest in that country at the present time." In future, he warned, Italian immigrants would "be carefully examined regarding their attitude towards organized government."[10]

Increasingly, immigration restriction was also justified for racial and eugenic reasons. During the 1919 immigration debate there had been numerous references to Madison Grant's pseudo-scientific diatribe *The Passing of the Great Race* and to the ethnocentric arguments of the U.S. Dillingham Commission. Similar arguments had been forthcoming from British theorists such as Francis Galton and organizations such as the British Eugenics Society.[11] Although a Canadian chapter would not be created until August, 1930, the eugenics movement attracted a number of important scientists, social workers, educators, and civil servants during the twenties. Public health, educational reform, and immigration selection were areas of common concern. [12] The convergence of these fields was evident in a 1920 editorial of the *Canadian Journal of Mental Hygiene*, which observed that the feeble-minded, insane, and psychopathic found in the province of Manitoba came out of all reasonable proportions from the immigrant class, and it was found that these individuals were playing a major role in such conditions as crime, juvenile delinquency, prostitution, pauperism, certain phases of industrial unrest, and primary school inefficiency. [13]

A similar message was forthcoming from Dr. Peter Bryce, chief medical officer of the Department of Immigration, who emphasized the important role immigration could perform in eradicating "the weakling from the race." Bryce also pointed out that not only did inferior immigrants, with their large families, burden Canada with massive social problems, "they also perversely lowered the fertility of Anglo-Saxons who had to limit their own family size if they were to pay through taxes for the support of others." What Bryce and the other eugenicists wanted was an immigration policy that rigorously differentiated between "preferred" British and western European immigrants and "non-preferred" eastern and southern Europeans. [14]

Yet, despite these arguments, the flow to Canada from non-preferred regions continued even during the post-war recession. Part of the "problem" was that during the war the European inspection offices of the Immigration Branch had been closed. Hence, the Dominion government lacked information even about the departure of immigrant workers. Undesirable immigrants could, of course, be rejected at Canadian ports of entry; but in this regard the government proved highly susceptible to the pressure tactics of both big business and ethnic organizations. [15] In October, 1919, for example, despite the opposition of immigration officials, the Shepard & Morse Company of Ottawa was able to secure the services of Finnish immigrant workers by arguing that they could not obtain the workers they needed in Canada. [16] Mining companies were even more aggressive in their search for cheap and malleable labour. In September, 1919, the Dominion Coal Company requested the admission of large numbers of continental European miners into Cape Breton. These men were needed not only because of labour shortages of cheap unskilled labour, but because many of them came from allied countries and had lived in the region during the war. The company got its way despite the protests of the miners' union and local immigration officials. [17]

Similar pressure tactics were employed by mining companies in northern Ontario, both through direct lobbying in Ottawa and Toronto and in the pages of the *Canadian Mining Journal*. In February, 1920, the *Journal* claimed that unless the immigration doors were opened wider the mining and metallurgical industries of northern Ontario would be seriously disrupted. [18] Significantly, this grim prediction was supported by published reports of the Ontario Department of Labour indicating that one-third of the mines of northeastern Ontario were operating below peak capacity because of the shortage of unskilled labour and their high turnover rate. According to the deputy minister of labour, the province's solution to this problem was "to get a steady class . . . of foreigners," especially Italians. These he described as ideal mine workers because of their great physical strength and deep commitment to occupational mobility within the industry. They are quite capable, he wrote, of "advancing themselves from jobs as muckers to the high positions of machine runners, joistmen, cage tenders etc." In October, 1920, this same official recommended that 2,000 European miners should be brought into northern Ontario. [19]

The railway companies were equally insistent. In the spring of 1920 the Railway Association of Canada petitioned the government for the immediate admission of 20,000 Italian navvies: "Canadian Railways are rapidly approaching a very serious situation . . . of obtaining an adequate supply of track labour to carry out the heavy maintenance and improvement work. . . . The difficulty arises out of the steady exodus to Europe of those classes of foreign-born persons upon whom the railways have long been dependent for track work . . . and the aversion of the native-born and other Canadians toward this class of work." [20] Another industry petition suggested that the Russians, Czechs, and Poles, who had served with the "White Armies" in Vladivostok and were now retreating homeward across Canada, also be drawn into the railroad construction labour market. [21]

The immediate response of the government to these proposals was quite favourable, but the strenuous opposition from organized labour and Great War veterans and other patriotic organizations soon forced a change of heart. [22] In November, 1920, the *Labour Gazette* reported that 10.2 per cent of organized workers in Canada were unemployed; by April, 1921, this percentage had increased to 16.3 per cent. [23] This was clearly a time for caution in immigration policy and the strict application of existing regulations. In January, 1921, an order-in-council required even a British immigrant arriving in Canada to have at least $250 in his possession. [24] Two years later, faced with an even more severe domestic economic situation, the government, through PC 183, established firm occupational guidelines to restrict further the entry of European immigrants. Only the following would be admitted into the country. [25]

1. A bona fide agriculturalist . . . [with] sufficient means. . . .
2. A bona fide farm labourer entering Canada to follow that occupation and has reasonable assurance of employment.
3. A United States citizen entering Canada from the United States provided it is shown to the satisfaction of Immigration Officer in Charge, that his labour is required in Canada.
4. Any British subject entering Canada directly or indirectly from Great Britain, or Ireland, Newfoundland, the United States of America, New

Zealand, Australia or the Union of South Africa who shall satisfy the Immigration Officer in Charge at the port of entry that he has sufficient means to maintain himself until employment is secured.

Asians were specifically excluded from the provisions of this arrangement, and in the same year a Chinese Immigration Act was passed that virtually stopped all immigration from that source.[26]

According to the 1923 legislation, the entry to Canada of "persons of Chinese origin or descent irrespective of allegiance or citizenship" was confined to members of the diplomatic corps, Chinese children born in Canada, merchants, and university students. The Act also stipulated that every person of Chinese origin was required to register with Dominion officials within twelve months after the Act came into effect. Any Chinese Canadian wishing to leave the country had "to give written notice to the Controller before departure, specifying the foreign port or place he planned to visit and the route he intended to take." Those leaving for more than two years would lose Canadian domicile.[27]

The genesis of this legislation is complex. In part, it was rooted in a long-term antipathy toward Asian immigrants that was most pronounced in British Columbia but had also become quite strong in the Prairie west and in Ontario during the post-war years. Hard times in the coast province, combined with a volatile political situation, helped to foster a virulent anti-Oriental campaign. Now, however, business organizations such as the B.C. Board of the Retail Merchants of Canada rather than trade unions were the ones denouncing unfair Chinese competition: "To us, it is not merely a question of competitive merchandising, aggravated by a lower standard of living. It is in fact a struggle of far deeper significance in which home, family, and citizenship considerations outweigh mercenary motives."[28]

There were also renewed charges that the existing head tax system had not worked: that thousands of Chinese workers were entering the country by fraud. These allegations were confirmed by immigration officials who favoured, from a management point of view, total exclusion.[29] Perhaps most important of all, there was a political consensus when in the spring of 1922 two members of Parliament, H.H. Stevens of Vancouver and W.G. McQuarrie of New Westminster, introduced a bill for the exclusion of Chinese immigrants.[30] Nor was the King government prepared to oppose public opinion, especially once it had separated trade and immigration issues.[31] Despite the spirited lobbying efforts of Chinese consul-general Dr. Chilien Tsur and the Chinese Association of Canada for a Sino-Canadian gentleman's agreement and the extension of full civil rights to all Chinese Canadians, their cause was doomed. When the Chinese Immigration Act went into effect on July 1, 1923, Chinese communities across the country marked the day as "Humiliation Day."[32]

Black immigrants from the United States and the Caribbean also found

Canada an inhospitable milieu during the tribal twenties.[33] Not only was it difficult to get into the country; black workers also found themselves channelled into certain low-status occupations. This was certainly the experience of Caribbean immigrants in Sydney, Nova Scotia, who were forced to accept the most arduous and unpleasant jobs in the coal mines and steel mills of the region. Domestic workers from Jamaica and Guadeloupe, who were recruited for employment in the homes of the middle class in Toronto and Montreal, also experienced wage and social discrimination, with little chance of job mobility.[34] Nor was the situation any better in the railway industry, an occupational ghetto for many blacks. In Montreal, for example, it was estimated that in 1928 about 90 per cent of adult males worked for either the CPR or the CNR, most as sleeping car porters. But it was a vulnerable job, with the CPR, in particular, insisting on an individual contract that allowed the company to terminate employment "without notice and without assigning any reason." And to ensure that it maintained a sufficiently docile labour force, the CPR continually recruited in the southern United States on the grounds that "there were not sufficient black men of experience and character in Canada to meet its labour force needs."[35]

Another motive for the CPR was its determination to prevent the Canadian-based Order of Sleeping Car Porters and the even more powerful Brotherhood of Sleeping Car Porters from gaining a foothold among its employees. This tough stance was evident in 1919 when the company abruptly fired thirty-six porters who were involved in union activity, and when it created its own company union. But the CPR's most effective strategy was to maintain a steady flow of malleable black labour from the American South, a policy that encountered no government opposition.[36] Nor was the Minister of Immigration, W.A. Gordon, swayed when the chairman of the Brotherhood wrote him in July, 1932:

> For a number of years it has been the practice of the Canadian Railways to insert advertisements in certain important daily newspapers. . . . Canadian citizens who applied for such positions were invariably advised that the Railway had succeeded in obtaining all the help of this class they required. . . . the Railways would then make representations to the Department of Immigration, claiming that they were unable to obtain in Canada the class of labour required and asking to be granted permission to bring large numbers of United States negroes into this country. . . .[37]

During the 1920s the Immigration Branch also demonstrated that it was not prepared to adopt a generous refugee policy. Part of the problem was that the Canadian government did not recognize a legal or administrative definition of refugee status. Another was that immigration officials could exclude those seeking sanctuary under the provisions of PC 2669 (1921), which stipulated that except for immigrants from Great Britain and the United States, all others must be "in possession of a valid passport issued in and by the Government of the country of which such person is a subject or citizen, such a passport to be presented within one year of the date of its issue." It was also necessary for these immigrants to have their passports visaed abroad.[38]

Prior to the enactment of PC 2669, considerable numbers of Polish and Romanian Jews had managed to gain entry.[39] But this had required intense lobbying and guarantees by the Canadian Jewish Congress and affiliated organizations that the refugees would not become public charges. Equally fortunate were about 20,000 Russian Mennonites who had the backing of the influential Canadian Mennonite Board of Colonization and the Canadian Pacific Railway. In quite a different category were two groups who had been driven from their homelands – over 200,000 anti-Soviet Russians and upwards of one million Armenians.[40]

Throughout the 1920s the League of Nations attempted to find homes for these stateless and helpless people, especially through the issuance of the so-called Nansen passport. This identity certificate was issued annually; it identified the holder's ethnic and national identity and allowed the person to move from one country to another. But while other countries honoured these passports, Canadian immigration authorities viewed them as a kind of trojan horse enabling thousands of European refugees to pour into the country.[41] This viewpoint was expressed in 1921 by Minister of Immigration and Colonization James Calder:

> at the present time . . . there are . . . in the ports of Europe, hundreds of thousands of people awaiting entry into either Canada or the United States. Many of these people are war refugees; many of them have lost everything they had in the world, and are looking out over the world to find a new country in which they can make a home. Many of them are penniless. . . . They are weary of Europe and all that it means to them, and they want to get away. We have set up two restrictions in an endeavour to hold back that flood. . . . The Order in Council now in force provides that, with the exception of farmers, farm labourers and domestic servants, all other classes of skilled and unskilled labourers, must have $250.00 in cash. In ordinary times the money qualification is only $50.00. . . . The other qualification . . . requires people coming from a foreign country to come on a through ticket, by continuous passage.[42]

These regulations were imposed with particular vigour against desperate Armenian refugees, largely because they were categorized as "undesirable" immigrants on the erroneous assumption they were an Asiatic race.[43] Nor did the lobbying efforts of the influential Armenian Relief Association of Canada change this restrictionist policy; during the decade only 1,300 Armenians were allowed into the country.[44] It made little difference that Canadian immigration officials endorsed the 1926 intergovernmental agreement to improve the system of refugee identification certificates. On the contrary, they continued to insist on the right to exclude refugees in accordance with their level of returnability. As the assistant deputy minister, F.C. Blair, bluntly put it, "the Nansen Passport must be valid for the return of prohibited immigrants the cause of whose deportation arises within five years after entry."[45] By taking this hard line, Canada rejected the humanitarian and internationalist principles advocated by the League of Nations and opted instead for a utilitarian and isolationist approach to the refugee problem.[46]

Planning Manpower and Immigration Policy

The entry of the government into programs of direct unemployment relief through the Employment Service of Canada, established in 1918, and by other means gave Dominion officials a greater awareness of the economic repercussions of large-scale immigration than they had before 1914. Between 1920 and 1923 the government assumed the burden of one-third of a municipality's costs for the relief of the unemployed. This was, however, said to be a temporary measure and the theory of the system remained that unemployment was "fundamentally a municipal responsibility."[47] That a high percentage of the unemployed were immigrants placed the federal government in an awkward position in the matter. Traditionally, the welfare of immigrants had been its responsibility, and this matter could not now be disentangled from these questions. During the 1920s the government continued to place immigrant agriculturalists on Canadian farms and to house them in the twelve immigration halls located in western Canada.[48]

Ottawa was also deeply involved, through the Employment Service of Canada, in the problems of economic adaptability being faced by immigrant workers. In the pre-war years some immigration officials tried to protect European workers from unscrupulous employment agents and employers, a paternalism exemplified by the passage of PC 1028 in May, 1913. This order-in-council had required all employment agencies dealing with immigrant workers to obtain a licence from the superintendent of immigration. Such agencies also had to keep an accurate record of the workers registered with them and could not charge a labour placement fee of more than one dollar. An additional requirement forbade the dispatching of workers until there was written proof that the jobs to which they were being sent actually existed. Violations of these guidelines could result in the loss of an agency's licence and fines for its owners.[49] During the war the government had gone further in asserting its control over the recruitment and placement of immigrant workers, most notably with the National Registration Act of 1916 and the so-called "Anti-Loafing Law" of 1918, which required all adult males residing in Canada to be gainfully employed.[50] Another order-in-council, issued in 1918, provided for the establishment of public employment offices on a Dominion-provincial basis. According to T.W. Crothers, the Minister of Labour, it was in the national interest that the existing labour exchanges of Quebec, Ontario, Manitoba, Saskatchewan, and British Columbia "be linked up with a clearing house in Ottawa" and that the Dominion government "should contribute to the expense of establishing and maintaining them." Under the new legislation funds were provided on a graduated scale: $50,000 in 1918-19; $100,000 in 1919-20; and $150,000 in each succeeding year to the end of the decade. Between 1924 and 1930 the Employment Service of Canada provided jobs for over 1,879,791 male workers. [51]

Incidentally, this new government initiative in the labour market provided for a more systematic and equitable method of placing immigrant workers. It did not, however, remove many of the major problems of the pre-war years, especially the seasonal nature of employment available to unskilled workers. During the 1920s about 25 per cent of those workers placed by the Employment Service held their jobs for less than one week. Nor did the advent of national employment planning mark the downfall of the private employment agency, although initially many of the smaller agencies were forced out of business by the new government regulations and the competition offered by the public system. [52]

The immediate post-war years did not favour the old free-enterprise immigrant labour traffic. Between 1919 and 1925 Canadian immigration policy discouraged the entry of both European workers and agriculturalists. The government's purpose now was to re-establish the Anglo-Saxon character of the country. What this meant in immigration terms was selective recruitment in Great Britain and the United States. British immigrants, it was felt, could be attracted in large numbers since Canada offered them superior economic opportunities and an attractive social milieu. [53] This expectation was not realized; indeed, during the 1920s British immigration only amounted to about 50,000 a year, or about 45 per cent of pre-war levels. Moreover, many of the British immigrants who did come later moved on to the United States, joining the thousands of Canadians who were likewise attracted by high-paying jobs.

The pessimistic viewpoint toward British immigration in the interwar years was perhaps most forcefully stated by former Minister of Immigration Clifford Sifton in a letter to John W. Dafoe in November, 1920:

> The farmer class in England will not emigrate; they are doing too well. . . .
> There is left only the Agricultural labourer; they are a diminishing quantity. Their wages have lately doubled and they are going to stay put. They will not emigrate. There remains only the mechanic, the artisan, and the drifter in the Southern towns. These are the people that Frank Oliver got in by the thousand and which flooded Canada and would have precipitated a crisis in labour if it had not been for the war. The worst blunder on earth would be to encourage their immigration. They are hopelessly incapable

of going on farms and succeeding. Pretty nearly all the Great War Veterans Associations that are making trouble are composed of these fellows who enlisted in the Canadian Army when the war came and want the country to support them for the rest of their lives.[54]

Because of the difficulty of placing British immigrants in agricultural regions the British and Canadian governments agreed in the Empire Settlement Act of 1922 to co-operate in a variety of colonization programs. By 1931 about 127,654 had come to Canada under these schemes; most of these received reduced transportation fares, agricultural training, and placement on Canadian farms. The effect of this imperial legislation on the transportation fare was particularly dramatic; the Liverpool-to-Winnipeg fare was reduced from $120 to $30. Yet cheap transportation was not sufficient to guarantee that those who left Great Britain would become Canadian farmers and farm labourers. In the 1931 census it was observed that immigrants from the British possessions showed the least inclination to go into agriculture, and less than 10 per cent "were found to be farmers." In the 1920s British immigrants also shied away from railway construction, mining, lumbering, and unskilled labour in the cities;[55] in Montreal, for example, the percentage of British workers in the construction industry fell from 20 per cent in 1920 to 12 per cent in 1931.[56]

The 1920s also witnessed a decline in the number of British domestics, although they still represented about 60 per cent of household workers in Canada. The Empire Settlement Act, with its assisted passage for domestics, had, however, promised a steady supply of experienced domestics. But with better wages and benefits in Britain, there was little incentive for the experienced household workers to emigrate. As a result, many of the British women recruited by the Women's Division of Immigration and Colonization were more attracted by cheap fares and a sense of adventure than by the prospect of working in Canadian homes. The search for better-paying and more flexible jobs began once they became conditioned to their new environment. The high turnover of British domestics meant that Canadian employers turned more and more to European household workers. In western Canada, Ukrainian, Polish, and other eastern European women welcomed the economic opportunity and the chance "to learn English and to become acquainted with Canadian household appliances and food preparation."[57] Mennonite and Finnish domestics in Ontario were likewise attracted to these jobs, especially the latter. Indeed, during the 1930s Finnish maids represented two-thirds of all Finnish women who worked outside of the home.[58]

The Impact of U.S. Policies

Canada was strongly affected by the major changes in American immigration policy that occurred between May, 1921, when President Warren Harding signed the Emergency Immigration Restriction Act, and 1924, when the permanent policy of selected and limited immigration came into effect.[59] The restrictionist campaign involved influential members of Congress, patriotic organizations such as the American Legion, and the American Federation of Labor. And their message was often direct and nasty. A congressman from Maine, for instance, stated:

> God intended, I believe, [the U.S.] to be the home of a great people. English-speaking – a white race with great ideals, the Christian religion, one race, one country, and one destiny. . . . a mighty land, settled by northern Europeans from the United Kingdom, the Norsemen, and the Saxons. . . . The Africans, the orientals, the Mongolians, and all the yellow races of Europe, Asia, and Africa should never have been allowed to people this great land.[60]

During the next three years arrangements were made to substitute the emergency legislation with a permanent quota system that would give the "old" immigrant groups from Britain and western Europe an advantage over those coming from eastern and southern Europe. This was achieved by basing the new quotas on the census of 1890 rather than staying with the previous system, which had used the 1910 census as the reference point. The Immigration Act of 1924 – the Johnson-Reed Act – easily passed Congress and was signed into law by President Calvin Coolidge. This restrictionist measure had an immediate impact on the flow of immigrants from southeastern Europe, which was reduced from 155,585 in 1921 to only 20,423 in 1924. In addition, all overseas immigrants were required to obtain visas that allowed "for administrative screening of immigrants prior to their entry into the U.S."[61] The 1924 Act also differentiated between European quota immigrants and non-quota immigrants from the Western Hemisphere. For Canadian residents this new status created an additional incentive to consider moving to the United States.[62] Indeed, between 1925 and 1932 over 496,203 Canadians headed south, 83.5 per cent of whom were native-born Canadians.[63]

In 1924, however, most Canadians did not know how the new American immigration laws would affect their country. Advocates of an active Canadian immigration policy like the Montreal *Gazette* saw the American policy as a misguided experiment and reasoned that "with Canada encouraging good immigrants and South America drawing immigrants from Europe, the United States is making an economical and sociological mistake to restrict immigration too sharply."[64] In contrast, Canadian immigration officials quietly congratulated their American counterparts for limiting "the admission of certain classes"; at the same time, they wondered how they could prevent many of the so-called non-preferred European immigrants from using Canada as a backdoor to the United States.[65]

There was also another issue: would the National Origins Act apply to Canada, or would the Western Hemisphere exemption be maintained? The matter was of special concern to the Windsor-based *Border City Star*, which, in a January 11, 1924, editorial, predicted dire consequences if Canada were included in the new quota system. These concerns, however, proved premature. In April, Esme Howard of the British embassy in Washington informed Ottawa that the recently passed House of Representatives bill (the Johnson Bill) posed no immediate threat in that it granted exemption to both native-born and naturalized Canadians.[66] But for some Canadians, like wealthy businessmen Joseph Flavelle, the most menacing feature of the U.S. law was not its exclusionist dimensions but the incentives it provided for Canadians to abandon their country.[67] In a December, 1924, letter to an English banker friend Flavelle was more explicit:

> Until the United States adopted the policy of strict limitation of immigration of all except native born Canadians, we always welcomed the promise of great activity in the United States because it was followed some months later by somewhat similar conditions in Canada. During the last two or three years, however, . . . with increasing activity, and sectional shortages of labour, important numbers of Canadians are attracted to the United States. The trouble is, our loss is chiefly in men between twenty-five and thirty years of age.[68]

For Americans, the real problem was not so much the influx of Canadian skilled workers but the rapid increase in the numbers of Mexican unskilled workers. In April, 1924, Prime Minister King was advised that although neither the Senate nor the House of Representatives would take any immediate action against Canadian immigrants, legislators had begun to reassess Western Hemisphere immigration, largely because agricultural interests were "bringing in peon labour from Mexico by the trainload."[69] Nor was this an idle warning. In his 1924 report the Secretary of Labor, James J. Davis, called for an amendment to the Immigration Act so that the "quota law would be applicable to Canada, Mexico and Central and South America, thus closing the door which now invites the activity of surreptitious entrant and the smuggler of aliens." Instead of free access, Davis called for a systematic and controlled immigration policy that would reflect changing economic and social conditions in the United States.[70]

Davis was, however, prepared to co-operate with Canadian officials in resolving a variety of transborder controversies. One of these was whether Canadian Indians would be allowed, under the terms of the 1924 Act, to cross the boundary for seasonal work since they were initially placed "in the same category as Japanese, Chinese and other races ineligible for citizenship."[71] Another issue was the large-scale entry of British immigrants from Canada; particular exception was taken with those who had received assistance from the Overseas Settlement Office and who had not "repaid the advances made to them."[72] Even more contentious was the smuggling of illegal Europeans – especially Italian, Polish, and Jewish immigrants who sought to join relatives and friends in the United States.[73]

During the 1920s the American labour movement became one of the major advocates of immigration restriction, not only from Mexico but also from Canada. In early 1924, for instance, AFL president Samuel Gompers "reluctantly" demanded that Canada be covered by the quota stipulations, and he had strenuously lobbied for the Senate bill that contained this provision.[74] Support for this initiative among border labour councils also grew, especially in cities such as Detroit.

In contrast, Canadian trade unionists remained opposed to any measures that restricted their easy entry into the American labour market. In January, 1925, for example, the Allied Trades and Labour Association of Ottawa urged the King government to defend "the right of free entry of citizens between Canada and the United States . . . so long as either country can absorb those who desire to make the change."[75] From the mayor of Windsor came an even more anxious letter:

> All municipalities on the American boundary are seriously alarmed over the introduction of a bill by Congressmen Box . . . which if passed would prevent the employment of Canadian citizens in the United States. It is estimated that four thousand residents of Windsor would be affected and besides creating an alarming labour situation would strain the present cordial relations between Canada and the United States.[76]

New Policy, New Immigrants

The failure of the Canadian government's Anglo-Saxon immigration strategy to satisfy the labour requirements of the country produced renewed agitation from Canadian farmers and businessmen to open the immigration door wider. Farmers and businessmen were not, however, united on the question of the long-term effect of immigration from continental Europe. The United Farmers of Manitoba and the United Farmers of Alberta, both Anglo-Saxon to the core, enthusiastically endorsed the efforts of the Western Canada Colonization Association to attract American farmers, despite the WCCA's being "composed chiefly of large corporations and wealthy individuals."[77] The *Grain Growers' Guide*, the official voice of the UFM, continually called on the government to expand the British harvester scheme of 1923 into an annual event. Neither of these plans, however, was able to supply a steady source of Anglo-Saxon farm labour. The British hired hand was in great demand, but despite every exhortation central Europeans continued to form the bulk of the farm labourers in western Canada, cultural antipathies not withstanding.

If some farmers were still troubled by the social and cultural implications of such a policy, few spokesmen for the transportation companies and the labour-intensive industries shared their concern. On the business front the tone was set in 1922 when Clifford Sifton made his famous speech to the Canadian Club in Toronto in which he claimed that western Canada needed another 500,000 "stalwart peasants." These people, he argued, should be immediately brought from "Central Europe, particularly Hungary and Galicia." Sifton's opinions were strongly endorsed by Sir Thomas Shaughnessy, chairman of the CPR Board of Directors; in his view continental Europe could supply Canada with "thousands of rugged, splendid people."[78] If anything, the mining companies were even more confident than Shaughnessy of this result. In the words of the *Canadian Mining Journal*:

> We want to see the doors opened not only to farmers and farm labourers, but also to such an extent in other directions as will enable our manufacturers and businessmen to secure the skilled workers and other help they require in their industries. At present they cannot get these. Nor will they early be able to do so, if the Labour unions in this country can work their sweet will. We have a shrewd idea that it is the fear of these Labour unions that has been responsible for the lethargy and the laxity that the Government has so long displayed in this matter of immigration.[79]

Although the "immigration boosters" did not immediately gain their objective, they did force the King government to remove gradually most of the barriers against large-scale European immigration. In 1923, PC 1203, which restricted the entry of immigrants from Germany and its wartime allies, was repealed. More significant still were the modifications of PC 183; the regulations under this order were now interpreted to allow the entry of more immigrants from continental Europe. In 1924 the Dominion government entered into a number of agreements with the railway companies to facilitate the recruitment of immigrants from the source. A joint farm-labour scheme brought 6,727 farm labourers to Canada "under the auspices of the Canadian National Railways and Canadian Pacific Railway Company." Various ethnic organizations within Canada were also used as recruitment agencies, most notably the Lutheran Immigration Board, the Canadian Mennonite Board, the Association of German Catholics, and the St. Raphael Ukrainian Society. This was considerable change, but the appetite of the transportation companies remained unsatisfied.[80]

In February, 1925, Edward Beatty and Sir Henry Thornton sent Prime Minister King a joint letter urging the government to assist their companies in

Sikh railway workers in western Canada, 1912. (*National Archives of Canada* (*NAC*) - *PA 139833*)

Group visiting hydro construction project at Great Falls, 1922. (*Provincial Archives of Manitoba* (*PAM*)/*Foote Coll. 483/Neg. no. N 2083*)

Ukrainian women cutting logs for prairie homesteads, 1930. (*NAC - C 19134*)

Great War Veterans Association demonstration at City Hall, Winnipeg, 1919.
(*PAM/Foote Coll.1671/Neg. no. N 2737*)

Sir Edward Beatty meets CPR workers, 1927. (*PAM/Foote Coll. 1000/Neg. no. N 2600*)

British harvesters for prairie wheat fields, 1928. (*PAM/Foote Coll.447/Neg. no. 2047*)

New technology for Manitoba's sugar beet industry, 1940. (*PAM/Foote Coll.723/Neg. no. N 2323*)

Royal Canadian Navy seizes fishing boat of Japanese-Canadian, December, 1941. (*NAC - PA 112539*)

European displaced persons leaving Bremen for Canada, 1950. (*NAC - PA 165211*)

"No More Bars": 267 displaced persons are admitted after three months in this Halifax detention centre, 1949. (*York Archives*)

Expectant Italian immigrants crowd Canada's visa office in Rome, 1954. (*York Archives, Toronto Telegram, Box 282, file 1970*)

Belgian women hard at work on an Ontario poultry farm, 1950s. (*NAC - PA 124821*)

Hungarian "Freedom Fighters" complete their transatlantic airlift to Canada, 1956. (*NAC - PA 125700*)

Immigration Minister Ellen Fairclough welcomes new Canadians at citizenship ceremony, late 1950s. (*NAC - PA 117803*)

Poster condemns Canada's racist immigration policy, 1955. (*NAC - PA 139579; courtesy of Mr. Kalmen Kaplonsky.*)

Protest agains the 1975 Immigration Green Paper. (*NAC - PA 126346*)

developing the millions of acres of unused land in Canada. [81] This development, they asserted, required large-scale recruitment of continental European farmers and farm labourers, and they volunteered their services in a new colonization undertaking. Specifically, the railway companies proposed that the overseas officials of the colonization departments of the CPR and CNR be granted the authority to issue certificates showing that prospective immigrants met the occupational and guaranteed employment requirements of PC 183. The government's own immigration officers would henceforth restrict their activity to the issuance of medical certificates and visas.

The initial government response to this bold initiative was negative, largely because officials of the Department of Immigration and Colonization resented the prospect of losing some of their administrative prerogatives. The railway presidents, Beatty especially, were not easily deterred. King's approach was most conciliatory. On August 7 he reassured Beatty and Thornton that he agreed "entirely with both views. . . . With respect to immigration, I have in mind making a vigourous declaration on the first occasion I speak in public and shall indeed be pleased if it serves to further the efforts of agencies at present involved in colonization and help to remove some of the obstacles you are meeting at present." On August 27, 1925, Beatty increased the pressure when he warned King that unless the Liberal government made "a vigorous declaration" in favour of expanded immigration the two major railway companies would be forced to dismantle their colonization departments, a development that "would be disastrous to Canada." Implicit in his message was the warning that with an election campaign in progress the Liberal Party could not afford to alienate the transportation giants and their corporate allies. [82]

On September 5, 1925, the Dominion government and the two transcontinental railway companies signed an agreement giving the CPR and CNR control over the recruitment of "bona fide" European agriculturalists until September, 1928, at which time the agreement could be renewed. Under this arrangement the representatives of the transportation companies could now issue occupational certificates to immigrants from those countries that had previously been designated "non-preferred" by the Department of Immigration and Colonization. As a result of these changes, prospective immigrants from Estonia, Latvia, Lithuania, Russia, Poland, Czechoslovakia, Yugoslavia, Austria, Hungary, Romania, and Germany were now on the same footing as those in western Europe. [83]

The railway companies had made an important gain, but the Immigration Branch, fighting a rearguard action, was still able to impose certain restrictions on them. The companies were instructed to recruit only from those nationalities, races, and modes of life "readily assimilable into the population and citizenship of Canada." Another memorandum was even more blunt. "From Russia, Mennonites and German Russians and from Romania, the German and Hungarian types are the only ones desired." Immigrants recruited by the companies could also be deported if they did not secure farm employment or settle on the land within one year of their arrival. In such cases the cost associated with their deportation would be assumed by the railway companies.[84]

Public reaction to the Railway Agreement varied.[85] There was substantial support for it from pro-business newspapers, boards of trade, and leading industrialists. In western Canada newspapers such as the Edmonton *Journal* and the Calgary *Herald* applauded the new immigration policy.[86] On the other hand, some Canadians regarded the agreement as a sell-out to the transportation interests and predicted dire consequences for their country. Organized labour was especially critical of the agreement. Throughout the early 1920s Tom Moore, the president of the Trades and Labour Congress, had warned that any attempt to recruit large numbers of agriculturalists from central Europe would be in effect a conspiracy "to rush in a heterogeneous conglomeration of people to furnish cheap labour for the farms, coal mines, railway construction and other industrial activities."[87]

Labour's opposition found many echoes in cultural and religious institutions. The newly formed United Church of Canada publicly criticized "the handing over of the promotion of immigrations from the British Isles and European countries to the transportation companies." Nor did all agrarian organizations welcome the change. The *Grain Growers' Guide* criticized the extent of power given to the railway companies and claimed that a massive influx of central European peasant farmers would not improve agricultural productivity in western Canada. Such immigrants, it asserted, could only adapt to an agriculture condition of "a crude nature, and on a small scale."[88] Most critical of all were the reactions of immigration officials, such as the deputy minister, W.J. Egan, who saw the agreement as a "pernicious attempt to destroy the selective immigration policy, and to return to the chaotic labour market which existed in the pre-war years." The next five years were to provide ample evidence to support this gloomy analysis.[89]

Between 1925 and 1930 about 185,000 central European immigrants entered the country under the terms of the Railway Agreement. In most respects the CPR and CNR adopted similar tactics in their immigration work. Prospective immigrants were initially approached by representatives of the railway companies, normally steamship agents who were paid five dollars for each bona fide agriculturalist. The prospective immigrants then proceeded to the major European ports, primarily Danzig, Riga, and Hamburg, where they were screened by officials of the railway companies who had the responsibility of issuing occupational certificates. They were then checked by Canadian immigration officials to ensure that they were medically sound and their passports were in order. They were transported to a Canadian port either on CPR steamships or on vessels of steamship companies associated with the CNR.[90] They then travelled by rail to the major transportation centres of western Canada to be met by representatives of the railway colonization departments and, if possible, placed on the land. Some found their way into the employment of western farmers who had previously requested agricultural workers; in these requests, or nomination certificates, the farmer described the location of his farm, the wage he proposed to pay, and the type of accommodation he could provide. The farmer could also specify preference for farm workers of a specific ethnic or national background.[91] Religious, ethnic, and local organizations often acted as intermediaries between farmers, employers, transportation companies, and European workers. The CPR worked closely with organizations such as the Lutheran Colonization Board, the Hungarian Slovak Colonization Board, and the Ukrainian Colonization Board, while the CNR established close working relations with the Lutheran Immigration Board and the German Catholic Immigration Board.[92]

Perhaps the most extensive fusion of transportation, agricultural, and ethnic interests developed in the sugar-beet region of southern Alberta. To secure the necessary immigrant labour the CPR, sugar-beet growers, boards of trade, and the Hungarian Colonization Board established the Colonist Placement Service Association (CPSA). This was a multi-purpose organization, but it was above all else an extension of the CPR's Colonization Department. Significantly, the CPR co-ordinated the recruitment and selection of immigrant workers and provided financial support for the Hungarian Colonization Board.[93] The CPR also made use of this board to secure unskilled workers for its own section gangs, as the following extract from a 1927 report of the Dominion Land Settlement Branch reveals:

> Those arriving under the Canadian Pacific are met on Train No. 1 arriving at four o'clock in the morning by a Mr. Schwartz, Manager of the Calgary Hungarian Colonization Board. They are directed by him to rooming houses and they are invited to register with him for ultimate naturalization. These people "mill" around Mr. Schwartz' office and the streets until they are placed. . . .
>
> Mr. O. Hanson, who keeps the Canadian Pacific Employment Office one block away, whenever he requires men for Extra Gangs, telephones over to Mr. Schwartz who sends him the number of men required.

The report also indicated that Schwartz gave preferential treatment to Hungarians, Poles, and Slovaks in distributing CPR jobs; in return for such favours the men were required to pay a labour placement fee and to buy their provisions through Schwartz's store at greatly inflated prices.[94]

The CPR had a particular interest in this type of recruitment because it wanted to avoid having to return its clients to Europe since the return passage would be paid by the company. In May, 1927, the Land Settlement Branch indicated that 75 per cent of the continental European immigrants who had arrived in Calgary under the terms of the Railway Agreement had obtained jobs with the company. Another report of the branch pointed out that companies doing business with the CPR were expected "to give new immigrants the first chance of jobs"; this was especially true for immigrants who had "come in on CPR ships."[95] The CPR's anxiety not to give the impression of exacerbating the country's unemployment situation by flooding the country with immigrant workers created severe problems within the immigrant community itself.[96] Thus, when the CPR dumped large numbers of new immigrants in the lumber camps of northern Saskatchewan it not only depressed local wages but also displaced an earlier wave of immigrant workers who were attempting to open up the land of the region: "these settlers rely solely on bush work during the winter to enable them to carry on for the first few years of settlement. If this work is not available for them, lack of capital will force the relinquishing of their holdings and mean that they must seek other work on which they can support their families." The CPR's immigration strategy also meant that there was an ample supply of foreign workers in the country who could be used as strike-breakers. In 1926, for example, large numbers of recent Hungarian immigrants were said to have taken the place of striking miners in the Nordegg mines in Alberta.[97]

The influx of immigrant workers seems to have made the employment situation in the Rocky Mountain coal-mining region particularly volatile. In March, 1927, the Alberta Department of Labour reported on the depressed condition of the numerous coal towns in the region as follows:

> Recently a number of immigrants from Europe . . . have come to The Pass Camps seeking employment. The argument is that if the natural production of The Pass Coal Camps was mined by the men who are making their homes in The Pass, and not by temporary or non-resident men, then there would be ample employment and reasonably good conditions in The Pass Towns, instead of frequent periods of slack work in the Mines, with consequent hard times and requests for relief from the Government.[98]

Canada's employers also had access to cheap immigrant labour outside the terms of the Railway Agreement. In 1926 an amendment to PC 183 provided for the admission under permit of any immigrant "whose labour or service was required in Canada." From 1926 to 1929 thousands of immigrant workers entered the country by this means.[99] General Hervey, an influential Ontario railway contractor, made 300 requests for the necessary permits, many of which were endorsed by representatives of the CNR and CPR. In June, 1926, W.J. Black wrote to the Immigration Branch on behalf of both General Hervey and the Morrow & Beatty railway construction company:

The applications are apparently not in any way identified with the project of any steamship line or other agency to secure immigration for the benefits which accrue in transportation.

With these two contractors we have the opportunity of placing a total of 500 workers to be made up of Poles, Czechs, Slovakians, Yugoslavs and Ukrainians. We have assurances that the conditions of employment are satisfactory and are, therefore, prepared to give to you our assurances that the number mentioned will be placed by us with these contractors under conditions such as usually prevail in the business of railway building.[100]

As was so often the case, however, the reality of the employment situation was so much different. The immigrant workers who were permitted into the country as a result of this appeal were charged excessively for their transportation, paid well below the advertised wage level, and given only eight days' work. Destitute and unemployed, they soon became dependent on municipal charity.[101] Immigration officials such as F.C. Blair were shocked by such blatant disregard for the immigration standards the government was trying to maintain:

The Permit business still flourishes. If there is any present day desire close to my heart, it is the desire to wipe out this cursed business at one strike.... With unemployment . . . it seems a terrible thing to have to issue Permits day after day for the admission of Italians, Greeks, Jews and others of the less desirable classes of immigrants, and merely because some Member of Parliament or other influential gentleman demands that it be done.[102]

Dissatisfaction with the permit system and Railway Agreement intensified during the spring of 1927. Immigrant workers, it was argued, were displacing established labourers not only in resource industries but also in the manufacturing sector. In Oshawa it was reported that some companies had dismissed half of their labour force in order to secure cheap immigrant replacements. In Winnipeg some immigrant workers were so destitute that they were even working below "the minimum wage of women" in the garment industry.[103]

Such accusations strengthened the hand of the Immigration Branch vis-à-vis the transportation companies. In June, 1927, F.C. Blair told his deputy minister that public opinion was once again insistent on a more selective immigration policy and that instead of fighting with their backs to the wall the moment had now come to carry "the war into the other camp." Blair even suggested that the Immigration Branch launch a campaign to have the Railway Agreement terminated: "There will be a terrific outcry from the Railway Companies if the thing is cancelled. On the other hand there is bound to be a worse situation created by public opinion in Canada if the present conditions are allowed to continue." Ultimately, however, a prosperous economy permitted the transportation companies, at least for the moment, to weather this particular storm; but the debate continued.[104]

In the spring of 1926 the CPR, CNR, and the Canadian Bankers' Association had launched their own campaign "to endeavour to overcome the opposition of farmers and their organizations to an active and aggressive immigration policy." The purpose of such publicity was "to influence Western Dailies by various means to refrain from featuring unemployment stories, local crop inquiries, etc. which find their way into the European press and neutralize propaganda overseas." Another approach was "to interest Western provincial governments through pressure of public opinion in constructive co-operation regarding colonization." Local boards of trade could help matters by fostering "a more tolerant attitude towards supporting unemployed immigrants" and pushing the view that "unemployment was a more or less temporary by-product of active immigration efforts."[105]

The central figure in this publicity campaign was C.W. Peterson, editor of the Calgary-based *Farm and Ranch Review*. Peterson distributed the news releases and arranged speaking tours for the immigration lobby. By December, 1926, he had distributed articles to 216 dailies with a circulation of 1,112,234 and to 126 weeklies with a circulation of 848,489. The funds for this activity were provided by the transportation companies and the Bankers' Association through a discrete account with Royal Trust in Calgary. In this regard Colonel Dennis of the CPR issued instructions that the funds were to be handled in such a manner that it could never be claimed that "payments are being made by either of the railway companies or the Bankers' Association directly to Peterson."[106]

One of the most spectacular initiatives by the immigration boosters occurred during the summer of 1928 when the transportation companies, agrarian organizations, and imperial settlement officials proposed that some 10,000 unemployed British coalminers be transported to the harvest fields of western Canada. This scheme went ahead despite the strenuous opposition of immigration officials such as F.C. Blair, who argued that "it was folly" to bring in a lot of green Britishers with the hope of getting five or six weeks of harvest work. The opposition of the civil servants was once more overcome. Between August and September, 1928, about 8,500 British harvest-miners came to Canada. Half the transportation costs of these workers was paid by the Overseas Settlement Branch, while the Canadian Land Settlement and Employment Service was committed to finding them jobs with farmers in western Canada.[107] Not surprisingly, the scheme was hailed as a great imperial undertaking, and patriotic organizations like the Orange Lodge called on their members to assist these harvesters in every possible way. The United Farmers of Manitoba also endorsed the scheme while the *Grain Growers' Guide* enthusiastically declared that these harvest excursions from Great Britain would soon become "an annual event with ever increasing success."[108]

Evidence, however, indicated that the harvest excursions had not been such an unqualified success. The Trades and Labour Congress claimed that the economy of the country could not "absorb these workers after the harvest had been garnered," and that the manpower needs of Prairie farmers could be met from within the country.[109] There were also reports that the British harvesters had faced numerous problems in adjusting to the living and working conditions in rural regions of western Canada. Increased use of combines and threshers had substantially reduced the demand for harvesters; but even in areas where more traditional methods were employed these British harvesters were said to have suffered from a lack of suitable work experience.[110] Finally, it was charged that British workers had been discriminated against in areas dominated by central Europeans. As one disgruntled harvester put it: "we were engaged by a German farmer or a Polack but the minute one of their own people could be secured, we were fired and our jobs taken by those who could speak the language of this bunch." The *Toronto Telegram* went one step further and claimed that there was a conspiracy against the British harvester scheme "to make it that much easier for the European hordes to fill jobs and desirable farms in Saskatchewan." The fact that about 75 per cent of the harvesters returned to England tended to give credence to these charges.[111]

These observations were indicative of a growing anti-alien sentiment that had developed among many Anglo-Canadians, especially in western Canada. In 1928 various patriotic and religious organizations launched a new assault against the Railway Agreement; in the forefront of this campaign was George Lloyd, the Anglican bishop of Saskatoon. One of Lloyd's persistent charges was echoed by organized labour: that the existing immigration policy created "a great deal of unemployment among our British friends due to the low wages the foreigner will work for."[112] The same view was dressed up in scholarly clothes in a series of articles by Professor A.R.M. Lower of Wesley College. Applying Sir Thomas Gresham's monetary theory to Canadian immigration policy, Lower came to this conclusion:

"Cheap men" will always drive out "dear" men. The men with the higher standard of living cannot compete with the man with the lower. Broadly speaking, all immigrants are "cheap" men in this sense, for it is noticeable that a man arriving in the country should take what he can get in the way of a job. . . .

The gradual displacement of the English speaking farmers from the small farms and soils by Central Europeans who demand less from life is an illustration of the principle of the "cheap" and "dear" man.

In the sphere of labour . . . the immigrant's handicap is the employer's advantage, for the employer gets a man who must at all costs hold his job. Wholesale immigration productive as it is simply turns us into a training ground for American citizens. The time has come for us to sit down and think over the terms of our national future. What more likely to determine that future than the policy which will decide who should be our citizens?[113]

Canadian citizenship was also much to the fore with the nativist organizations. The National Association of Canada charged that thousands of Canadian workers had been forced "to seek employment under the Stars and Stripes while the CPR & CNR Railways flooded the country with the riff-raff of Europe." The Native Sons of Canada called for a stop to any immigration that tended "to make Canadians a mixed or coloured race or lower the standards of living, education or morals."[114] In a class by themselves were the statements of the Ku Klux Klan of Kanada. Between 1927 and 1929 a number of Klan locals were organized in Canada. The Klan had its greatest success in Saskatchewan, where it was estimated that it had a membership of 10,000. According to one study of this phenomenon, "joining the Klan gave hundreds a vent for ingrained prejudice in the semblance of safeguarding all that was admirable in British institutions, Protestantism and the Canadian Way of Life."[115] J.H. Maloney, one of the most successful Canadian Klan organizers, offered this account of his views of central European immigrants:

I am loyal to Canada and the British Crown – a Canada composed of those strong virile men of the north, the Nordic or Anglo-Saxon race . . . men whose forefathers fought for this country by expenditure of British blood and treasure, whose sons died on Flanders field. . . . but I am not loyal to a Canada composed of men who jabber all the tongues that destroyed the tower of Babel, men who tighten their bellyband for breakfast, eat spaghetti and hot dog and rye bread for lunch and suck in his [sic] limburger cheese for supper – men who crowd our own people out . . . by offering to work for ten cents an hour, men who come to Canada with tags on them telling you their destination. . . . we are a great melting pot, but let us see that the slag and scum that refuse to assimilate and become 100 percent Canadian citizens is skimmed off and thrown away.[116]

Charges of a Catholic conspiracy also found a receptive audience where the separate school issue was ever-virulent. The Klan did not hesitate to draw connections between the increasing militancy of Catholic separate school advocates in Saskatchewan and the massive influx of central European Catholics; this movement was, in fact, part "of their world-wide Romanization campaign." The immigrant assault was also held responsible for rising crime rates and the growing power of the Bolshevik elements. The conviction of the Finnish Communist, Arvo Vaara, in December of 1928 for blasphemous references to the British monarchy was regarded as symptomatic of the type of "disloyalty and sedition" being fostered across the country.[117]

The nativist campaign against the Railway Agreement intensified during 1928. At the 1928 annual convention of the Trades and Labour Congress there was considerable discussion about the increasing encroachment "of non-English speaking immigrants . . . a majority of whom seek employment in urban centres and industrial activities, which [was] in violation of the agreement." The problem was there for all to see; solving it was another matter. On one hand were those at the convention who proposed that the TLC bring pressure to bear on the Dominion government to adjust its policies so as to ensure "that not less than 75 per cent of immigrants coming into Canada shall be English speaking." Some of the restrictionists went even further and advocated the enactment of a measure by which immigrants who had not been naturalized after five years in the country would be deported. On the other hand, many delegates did not wish to stand in the way of workers from other countries "bettering their lot in life." They tended to see quota systems and deportation procedures as reactionary. Ultimately the restrictionists were defeated at the convention, though they remained a strong grassroots minority.[118]

The 1928 TLC convention also went on record against the recommendation of the chiefs of police of Canada that all European immigrants be fingerprinted on entering the country. Moreover, the convention reaffirmed labour's belief that those who induced immigration into the country should be responsible for their welfare. Two resolutions were passed in this regard: one recommended that "any company, society or individual bringing settlers to this country for gain shall be answerable for the maintenance of the immigrant or immigrants for a period of twelve months." The other demanded "that the Federal Government or the railways or shipping companies be made responsible for the support of all immigrants brought in by them for a term of not less than two years."[119]

In a similar vein the 1928 convention of the United Farmers of Alberta recommended that all future farm labourers admitted to the country have "a knowledge of the English language." William Brownlee, Premier of Alberta, publicly criticized the Dominion immigration policy for being "overwhelming in favour of the middle European races."[120] In Ontario, Premier Ferguson indicated his displeasure over the Railway Agreement when he openly criticized the transportation companies for bringing out immigrants "without due regard to the Provinces."[121] In Ottawa, R.B. Bennett, the new leader of the Conservative Party, warned that continuing central European immigration would seriously threaten the Anglo-Saxon character of the country: "we must still maintain that measure of British civilization which will enable us to assimilate these people to British institutions, rather than assimilate our civilization to theirs."[122] The chorus of complaint was completed by the representatives in Canada of various European countries. They spoke disparagingly of a system that left immigration to private enterprise, claiming that many of their nationals who had come to Canada under the Railway Agreement had experienced unnecessary hardship and exploitation.[123]

In the face of all this pressure the King government decided to have the subject of immigration policy examined by the Select Committee on Agriculture and Colonization. Between February 29 and May 22, 1928, some twenty-nine representatives of the transportation companies, patriotic organizations, churches, and other groups appeared before the committee. Not surprisingly, there were sharp differences of opinion about the national implications of the Railway Agreement. Edward Beatty claimed that "the country had not erred in free immigration; . . . we have been careful; we have made it as selective as possible and we have proceeded on the assumption . . . that if we have more people . . . the prosperity of Canada will be increased."[124] By contrast, Canon C.W. Vernon, general secretary of the Council for Social Services of the Church of England in Canada, referred to the alarming increase in the percentage of non-British immigrants; this group, he claimed, had risen from 22 per cent in 1923 to 50 per cent in 1927. Vernon warned the committee that unless immediate steps were taken to reverse this trend Canada would find itself in the same dilemma as the United States: "In the neighbouring Republic, where the preponderating proportion in immigration from central Europe has already become a most serious problem . . . [there are] warnings that we should profit from their experience and not flood the country with immigrants who will produce the puzzling problems with which they are already confronted."[125] In the course of its work the committee also investigated the charges made by alderman M.J. Coldwell of Regina that "a regular traffic was carried on at Ottawa of the sale of permits to admit men who were not ordinarily eligible for entry into Canada . . . for a sum of $100. each." No charges were ever laid in this regard, but the evidence before the committee had a decided effect on its findings.[126]

On June 6, 1928, the committee submitted its final report to the House of Commons. It made two major recommendations: the first called for the modification of the Railway Agreement; the second for stricter control over the issuance of permits or letters of assurance of employment.[127] Anticipating this recommendation, the Department of Immigration and Colonization had already curtailed the numbers of European workers entering the country. In January, 1929, the transportation companies were informed that they would have to reduce by 30 per cent the numbers of immigrants they had recruited in 1928. In the case of the Prairie provinces the transportation companies were issued more specific guidelines.[128]

In October, 1929, in a deteriorating employment situation, the railway quota was reduced another 25 per cent, and instructions were issued cancelling all visas in the hands of prospective European immigrants.[129] During the 1930 federal election campaign the Conservatives had strongly attacked Liberal immigration policy as being too lax. Now, as Prime Minister, R.B. Bennett had to provide alternative policies while not alienating big business. In October, 1930, the railway companies were informed that the government was cancelling its agreement with them. W.A. Gordon, the new Minister of Immigration and Colonization, offered this defence of government policy in a joint letter to Beatty and Thornton:

> analysis showed that of the total immigration of 221,561 people admitted to Canada in the sixteen months ending with July 31st of this year no less than 99,367 were males over eighteen years of age, and of this latter number 25,305 had entered in the first four months of the present fiscal year. It is clear, therefore, beyond peradventure that either substantial numbers of immigrants who have recently arrived in Canada are in the ranks of the unemployed, or conversely, they have displaced Canadians who are now unemployed.[130]

Significantly, the Canadian Manufacturers' Association also removed itself from the immigration booster lobby. At the 1929 annual convention L.W. Simms, the CMA president, questioned the necessity of importing unskilled workers in view "of the marvellous mechanical progress in automatic machinery and in serialization of processes."[131]

Conclusion

In many ways immigration trends during the 1920s were a continuation of pre-war patterns. Despite attempts to concentrate on the recruitment of British and American immigrants, sustained pressure by the railway and resource companies forced a change in policy by 1925. Nor was the Trades and Labour Congress willing or able to oppose the Railway Agreement, or even the recruitment of unskilled labour for the mines and manufacturing plants. Canadian craft workers seemed more interested in securing high-paying jobs in the United States than in seeking work in northern Ontario or western Canada.

Canada also maintained its racist exclusionist immigration policies, as the 1923 Chinese Immigration Act demonstrated. Similarly, the immigration gates were shut to the so-called "Asiatic" Armenian refugees and to West Indian or U.S. black immigrants, unless they had guaranteed jobs on CPR passenger trains.

CHAPTER 5

Closing the Gates:
Canada's Response to Immigrants and
Refugees During the Great Depression

In the early part of the twentieth century the Canadian and American immigration experiences had many similarities. Before 1914, native-born workers and European immigrants moved back and forth across the Canada-United States border in large numbers in search of work. The two countries also shared specific exclusionist policies: both resolved to stop mental defectives, paupers, and avowed anarchists, at all costs, and strictly limit the number of Asian and black immigrants.

After the war the two countries drifted further apart in their policies. During the 1920s the United States government established an elaborate quota system, which sharply reduced the numbers of immigrants coming to the country from southern and eastern Europe. In contrast, Canada remained a self-proclaimed homeland for immigrants who would shoulder the burden of its work, and thousands of British and European immigrants entered the country in the decade. [1] With the advent of the Great Depression, however, the immigration policies of the two countries once again converged. Both closed their gates to immigrant workers; both favoured the native-born worker over the foreigner. Fear of communism was also rampant, especially among business groups and law enforcement agencies. Arrest and deportation of alien radicals were widespread in Canada and the United States during the 1930s.

Another common feature was the relative indifference of the Canadian and American governments to the thousands of European refugees, victims of Nazism and Communism. This topic has received considerable attention from scholars on both sides of the border, especially in recent years. Most Canadian studies have been highly critical of Ottawa's actions. For example, Gerald Dirks in *Canada's Refugee Policy* declares that humanitarian factors, though present in Canada's policy, are difficult to assess and indeed may not have been genuine.[2] A more biting indictment comes from Irving Abella and Harold Troper in *None Is Too Many*:

> Like the other western liberal democracies, Canada cared little and did less. . . . In the prewar years, as the government cemented barriers to immigration, especially of Jews, Immigration authorities barely concealed their contempt for those pleading for rescue. There was no groundswell of opposition, no humanitarian appeal for a more open policy. . . .[3]

Immigrant Workers and the Great Depression

By 1930 Canada, after much debate and rancour, began to close its immigration gates and to monitor its foreign-born. In part, this was a response to political pressure. The newly elected Prime Minister, R.B. Bennett, felt compelled to make good on his criticism of Liberal policy. And he received much support for his restrictive approach from a variety of powerful organizations. As a sign of the times, the Canadian Manufacturers' Association president, R.J. Hutchings of Winnipeg, called for a complete halt to immigration from central Europe: "Large numbers of unemployed and illiterate people," he stated, "are liabilities and not assets. Employment, at fair remuneration, should be the keynote of our immigration policy. It is not economic to import farmers to compete with those now on the land . . . nor is it wise to congest cities with people unless industry is encouraged to expand and provide them with employment." Hutchings might have added that in Winnipeg and other centres, Anglo-Canadian businessmen were becoming increasingly disturbed by the threat that large numbers of unemployed central European workers posed to social order.[4]

An association between European immigration and unemployment was now being made in many parts of the country. At the Western Unemployment Conference held in Winnipeg in January, 1930, immigration authorities were censured not only for gutting the labour market, but also for allowing "the immigration societies to gather up all the available jobs for the people they brought in." A few days after the conference the Manitoba legislature unanimously passed a resolution branding unemployment a national problem; "the flow of immigrants into Western Canada, many of whom had been admitted as agricultural labourers, and who have undertaken farm work for a short time only," was the root of the problem.[5] In Ontario, Premier Ferguson went one step further, announcing that his government would not extend relief payments to unemployed immigrant workers. No attention, he informed one correspondent, had been paid "to our views to the matter."[6] On March 31, 1931, order-in-council PC 695 stipulated that "the landing of immigrants of all classes and occupations is hereby prohibited."[7] This was a direct response to the formal presentation by representatives from municipalities from Ontario, Manitoba, Saskatchewan, Alberta, and British Columbia with evidence that unemployment and immigration were linked. The representatives from Winnipeg and Vancouver, cities that bore the brunt of the relief of destitute immigrant workers, were to the fore in this confrontation. In the case of Winnipeg, relief costs had increased from $31,394 in 1927-28 to $1,683,836 in 1930-31.[8]

The transportation companies had already responded to the crisis, but their motivation was not so much the welfare of the immigrant worker as the fear that they might have to pay for their return to Europe.[9] During the winter of 1930-31 CNR offices in North Bay and Winnipeg had found jobs for immigrant workers with fifteen large lumber companies in northern Ontario; between October and December, 626 of these men had been placed, most of them Slavs and Finns. As the depression advanced, however, the placement of these men became more and more difficult not only because of the scarcity of jobs but because of their destitution. Robert England, the western colonization manager of the CNR, gave this account of the situation to W.J. Black: "This year [1930] the wages being paid are rather lower compared to other years and no doubt this has had a great effect on the financial position of immigrants generally. At freeze-up time a lot of immigrants find it impossible to outfit themselves in winter clothing . . . ."[10]

In the context of the depression the efforts of the transportation companies and private employment agencies on behalf of immigrant workers only intensified anti-alien sentiments among Anglo-Canadian workers. In May, 1931, the employment of foreigners on a reforestation project near North Bay drew an angry response from residents of the area. Canadian workers, it was alleged, had "to stand around and starve while foreigners get the first privilege."[11] The fact that large concerns like INCO and the CPR worked through private agencies rather than the Employment Service of Canada only exacerbated the situation.[12] Private employment agencies also favoured immigrant workers because they were more malleable and willing to pay kickbacks. As a group of Russian workers recounted their experience in securing employment through the Sudbury labour agency of Manor & Carmichael:

> We had talked to this man at the Employment Office and he said then that he would fix us up with a job later. When we went and knocked at his door, he told us to come in; we went in and sat down; we could not talk much English, so we did not speak much. He held out his hand and we both give him a ten dollar bill. . . . We figured it was better to pay for a job than to be around a soup kitchen.[13]

With the municipal and provincial governments now lined up against them, immigrant workers had no choice but to fall in line with the "padrone" system. In

September, 1934, the City of Winnipeg announced that it intended to discontinue relief payments to 500 families and 1,600 single men who had entered the country after January 1, 1929; the vast majority of these people were central Europeans.[14] In Sarnia, central European immigrants were not only denied financial assistance, but were fired from local public works in large numbers because of the hostility of the Anglo-Canadian community. The Sarnia *Observer* frequently ran editorials calling for the deportation of unemployed foreigners, especially those who were involved in radical immigrant organizations like the Ukrainian Workers' Council.[15]

W.B. Hurd's census monograph, *Racial Origins and Nativity of the Canadian People*, offers further insight into the desperate plight of central and eastern European immigrants in this period. Using data from the 1931 census, Hurd shows that the annual level of unemployment of central Europeans was far above the national average. Thus, while in 1931 Ukrainians, Poles, and Russians were unemployed for 20.12, 19.68, and 17.16 weeks per year, respectively, the average for those of British nativity was only 9.09 weeks and for those from "preferred" European countries like Norway and Sweden only 13.80 weeks. His analysis also showed that among central Europeans "the highest level of unemployment existed among those immigrants who had arrived during the boom years 1926-29." In addition, 51 per cent of the central European population in Canada in 1921 had been naturalized, but the equivalent figure for 1931 was only 39 per cent. What was even more shocking to Hurd was the apparent propensity of these unemployed and alien people to become involved in crime and civil unrest. His pessimistic conclusion was that these problems could not be solved by economic means alone because they were partly racial in nature: "every South, eastern and Central European race . . . exceeded the average by over 60 p.c. [which] tends to support the view that the propensity to crime is in some measure at least a product of racial background."[16]

What Hurd neglected to mention was that vagrancy was the most common crime for which central Europeans were being charged. During the years 1929-32 thousands of immigrant workers rode the rails desperately seeking employment, and finding nothing but rejection and discrimination. A Polish immigrant's account of how arrest and deportation might be welcome typified their desperation:

I have travelled 1200 miles for work. I never knew I would come to this life. I wish I could get back. They can't even find work for there [*sic*] own Canadians I have spoke to Indians Poland French and they were down and out and good fellows. I cant [*sic*] go on like this. I will have to do something to get deported. Will you see what you can do now I think I will close now if you want to find out where I am put the police on me I cant put know [*sic*] address because I won't know where I shall be.[17]

By 1931 many immigrant workers believed they would be better off in Europe, and the movement of people back across the Atlantic became a feature of Canadian life. It was also significant that several European countries, most notably Germany and Poland, considered schemes to repatriate their destitute nationals in Canada. A letter from the Berlin chief of police to a Canadian official caught the spirit of the times:

> What are you doing to these young men. . . . We sent you clean, vigorous young fellows, the cream of our manhood. They wished to start life in a new, virile country like Canada. Now, when that country cannot give them employment, they are being deported to us branded with the stigma of a conviction under your laws. We are happy to welcome them home, where they find it easier to subsist among their friends, but help them to come home with unblemished records. [18]

Yet another problem facing European immigrant workers was the closing of the American immigration gates. In 1929 the National Origins Plan had finally become operational, which meant a decline in the annual European quota from 356,952 in 1921, to 161,422 in 1924, to 150,491 in 1929. [19] With the advent of the Great Depression, there was strong pressure in the U.S. Congress to reduce the quotas by between 60 and 90 per cent, or to suspend independent immigration altogether. Although no legislation was passed, the State Department exercised its new control over immigration by strictly enforcing the public charge clause before granting a visa. As a result, there was a drop of 62 per cent in quota immigration between 1930 and 1932; and during the decade "those immigrants coming into the United States exceeded repatriated immigrants for a net total of only 68,693." [20]

Non-quota immigrants from Mexico and Canada also faced new obstacles, [21] although Canadian-born workers remained a privileged group until 1933, despite growing pressure from the American Federation of Labor for more restrictive measures. [22] By this stage, there was widespread support for domestic affirmative action practices that excluded Canadian immigrants and commuters, among others.

Ironically, the long-awaited opening of the passenger bridge between Windsor and Detroit provided additional ammunition for those who argued that Canadian-based commuters undermined the Detroit economy – and that the situation would become much worse. "Easy accessibility via the Ambassador Bridge," it was argued, "combined with the liberal liquor laws on the Ontario side of the Detroit River, may ultimately attract a number of people now living in Detroit to establish their residence on the Canadian shore." [23] Predictably, the commuter "bashers" included Frank Martel, president of the Detroit Federation of Labor. In August, 1929, Martel and his supporters had tried to have the Toronto AFL convention endorse his resolution that U.S. quota laws should include Canadian workers.[24] Unsuccessful, he once again resorted to local pressure. On March 4, 1930, the *Detroit News* reported his demand that the City Council carry through with its policy of firing all alien workers and that it remain resolute against the lobbying "of certain elements who run to Washington and protest in behalf of the Canadian immigrants every time an attempt is made to preserve Detroit jobs for Detroit labouring men."[25]

Although this nativist policy was ultimately defeated, the status of the commuters remained precarious, especially as bill after bill appeared before Congress demanding an end to all immigration.[26] In the spring of 1931 the most sweeping measure of all was passed by the Michigan legislature. The Alien Registration Law (or Spolansky Act) stipulated that each of Michigan's 241,000 aliens must register with the Commissioner of Public Safety; it also required aliens to be photographed and fingerprinted.[27]

American policy toward the Communists also influenced Canadian attitudes. In August, 1930, H.M. Wrong of the Canadian legation in Washington informed O.D. Skelton, undersecretary of state for external affairs, that in the United States "there has been a considerable increase in the number of prosecutions of 'reds.'" As a result, the American government had established a special committee of inquiry into Communist influence, especially among the immigrant working class. Wrong's own response was light-hearted; the more responsible newspapers had "treated the investigation with indifference or as a subject for levity which served to enliven their columns during the season when there is a scarcity of news."[28] By January, 1931, however, Wrong's report had acquired a more serious tone. The American investigators had shown that the Communist Party had an active membership of about 12,000 in the country, backed up with "500,000 to 600,000 Communist sympathizers." The recommendation of the American investigators was that the Communist Party be outlawed and that immigrant members of it, "whether naturalized or not [,] be deported from the country."[29]

Deporting Radicals from Canada

Confrontations were symptomatic of the years 1929-31.[30] The Communists were on the rise and their business and political opponents were more determined that they should be suppressed.[31] The climax came in August, 1931, when ten of the leaders of the Communist Party of Canada were charged with seditious conspiracy and the Party was declared an illegal organization. Simultaneously, efforts were made to drive foreign-born Communists out of the country, hundreds being deported under section 41 and the vagrancy provisions of the Immigration Act. The main instrument of Communist retaliation was the Canadian Labour Defence League (CLDL). This organization provided funds for bail, fines, and legal fees, and sought to mobilize public opinion for the victims of "capitalist oppression." That its success was only marginal was evident in the steady stream of "foreign" Communists heading back across the Atlantic, many to fascist countries.[32]

Toronto and Winnipeg, as well as the industrial communities of northern Ontario and British Columbia, were the major arenas in which the struggle between Canadian communism and the forces of law and order was fought. In Toronto, as elsewhere, anti-communism and anti-alien sentiment were closely linked. In January, 1929, Brigadier-General Denis C. Draper, chief constable of Toronto, announced that in future "all proceedings and addresses at all public meetings [were] to be in the English language"; he also stipulated that "no disorderly or seditious reflections on the form of government or the King, or any constituted authority [would] be allowed." These measures were soon implemented. Many public halls and "places of public amusement" that had allowed Communist meetings to be conducted "in a foreign language" now had their licences suspended. When the Communists resorted to impromptu streetcorner meetings the police were there with their clubs and horses. This tough response received widespread support not only from traditional patriotic organizations like the Orange Lodge and the Canadian Legion, but also from the city's newspapers.[33] A January, 1929, editorial of the *Mail & Empire* caught the mood of the times: "The majority of those who have a gripe about police interference . . . are not Canadian by birth or persons who have lived all their lives under British institutions. They need reminding that the laws of Canada are binding upon them. No sovietism or other form of anarchism they have been indoctrinated in alien countries or by alien teaching will find a footing here."[34]

During the spring and summer of 1931 pressure for government intervention against the Communists grew. In April, Mayor Colonel Ralph Webb of Winnipeg warned Prime Minister Bennett that unless decisive action was taken by the federal government Winnipeg's Anglo-Saxon community might resort to force to defend its property and to prevent "Moscow interference with the citizens and the development of our country."[35] Provincial governments soon joined this crusade. In June, 1931, Premier S.F. Tolmie informed the Bennett government that the labour unrest in British Columbia was almost out of control; the province had been pushed to the brink by "foreign agitators" – "some of whom were adopting English and Scotch names [thus] giving the public a false impression." Deportation, Tolmie argued, had two advantages: it would remove "foreign agitators without waiting for conviction by court or jury," and it would encourage the loyal Anglo-Saxon population. It is difficult, he wrote, "to say how long we can hold back the law abiding population from themselves dealing with this element and [the] public results would be terrible."[36] The Taschereau government in Quebec issued a similar appeal, though its tendency was to blame Communist activity on Jewish radicals.[37] But the support of the Ontario government put the anti-Communist campaign over the top.[38]

The Bennett government was already moving in the same direction.[39] In March, 1931, the deputy minister of immigration asked the commissioner of the RCMP to keep him informed when "budding revolutionaries" were applying for passports. "We will probably find," he wrote, "that some of them are Canadian born but we will undertake to make things very interesting for them in establishing their status under the Immigration Act if they leave Canada and seek to return."[40] Yet another aspect of the Canadian policy of restriction was the introduction into the Senate of the Alien Identification Bill: under this measure "all aliens in Canada would be required to register." This measure, it was argued, would make it possible for the RCMP "to know what people arrive from Moscow or some other foreign place." The bill did not pass because it "stigmatized all newcomers to Canada."[41] But this did not mean that the government was backing down. During 1931 the number of foreigners deported under sections 40 and 41 of the Immigration Act increased significantly; section 40 was used most extensively because, as A.L. Jolliffe, superintendent of immigration, informed his officers, "in these types of procedures very little background information would be required."[42]

Arrests and deportation of suspected Communists soared during the spring and summer of 1931. On July 11, 1931, the *Ukrainian Labour News* charged that the Bennett government had already prepared a list of prominent Communists "to be deported." On August 11, eight days after Parliament had adjourned, the RCMP, Ontario Provincial Police, and Toronto Municipal Police raided the offices of the Communist Party and its affiliates. By the end of the day eight of the leaders of the Party had been arrested and charged under section 98 of the Criminal Code of being members of an unlawful association and of being involved in seditious conspiracy. On November 14, the "Toronto Eight" were sentenced to five years' imprisonment; deportation was also recommended for those not native-born once they had served their prison terms.[43] That same month the commissioner of the RCMP sent to the Immigration Branch a list of thirty-five foreign-born Communists designated for deportation.[44]

While Canadian public opinion generally applauded these stern measures, many Canadians eventually would become concerned over the tendency of police forces across the country to disregard the civil rights of the foreign-born. Among the immigrants themselves there was widespread alarm that the techniques of arrest and deportation were used as a "corporate lash" to maintain labour docility.[45]

Canadian Refugee Policies, 1933-38

While European refugees had often found it difficult to enter Canada during the 1920s, the situation became even worse during the depression years. One of the first examples of Canada's resolve to close its immigration gates occurred in the fall of 1929 when Russian Mennonites looked toward Canada in their desperate attempts to escape the forced collectivization and political repression imposed by Soviet authorities and the threat of being deported to Siberia.[46] But despite their reputation as industrious agriculturalists and the lobbying efforts of the Canadian Mennonite Board of Colonization, only a small number of the 13,000 asylum seekers found refuge in Canada. The reason: poor economic conditions; political and social resistance in western Canada; and the timidity of the King government. In 1929, and in subsequent incidents, King was not prepared to champion unpopular immigration causes or to confront the provinces. He was particularly impressed by the opposition of J.T.M. Anderson, the newly elected Premier of Saskatchewan, who on November 9, 1929, informed Ottawa that his province was not interested in receiving any more immigrants unless the federal government would look after them:

> Realize many excellent Mennonite citizens in this province, but feel time most inopportune to admit destitute immigrants. Saskatchewan, in view assistance now being given to citizens already here, feels guarantee to our satisfaction must be submitted. Is federal government prepared to assist in relief measures now being carried on among recent arrivals, including Mennonites?[47]

Canada's response to the plight of German and Austrian Jews was even less generous – less than 4,000 were admitted prior to the outbreak of war. Anti-Semitism, xenophobia, and isolationism were deeply rooted in Canadian society, although they were more pronounced in Quebec. That English Canadians were more circumspect in their prejudice does not mean that they were more generous toward the thousands of Jewish refugees who sought sanctuary. On the contrary, as historians Irving Abella and Harold Troper have demonstrated, "the federal cabinet, fully aware of the extent of anti-Jewish feeling throughout the country," was unwilling to open the immigration gates even when Nazi terror mounted. This callous response was particularly evident during the Evian Conference of 1938, which attempted to find possible solutions to the refugee problem: Canadian representatives expressed much "sympathy" but offered no places.[48]

The plight of over 400,000 refugees who fled Germany between 1933 and 1939 has been discussed in many books and articles. One aspect of this subject that has received particularly good treatment is the movement of Jewish intellectuals to Great Britain and the United States.[49] Less is known about the Canadian experience, although in many ways it demonstrates the bias against Jews among both federal authorities and influential groups in Canadian society.

Prior to the outbreak of war there was considerable agitation for a more generous Canadian refugee policy, especially after the intensification of Nazi brutality against German Jews in November, 1938. One of the most eloquent calls for Canadian assistance came from the newly formed Canadian National Committee on Refugees and Victims of Persecution (later renamed the Canadian National Committee on Refugees). In a December, 1938, resolution sent to Prime Minister Mackenzie King the CNCR claimed:

> that the immigration of carefully selected individuals or groups of refugees to Canada will prove of inestimable value in our national economy by introducing skilled workers and new arts, crafts and industries. . . . the assimilation of selected refugees constitutes no serious problems for Canadians since they would come from countries where thrift and frugality have been notable [Germany and Austria], while many would be highly skilled in a variety of techniques and conversant with many languages; further that their devotion to the methods of democracy would be unquestioned.[50]

Indeed, the King government had already recognized that the views expressed by the CNCR were gaining in popularity. In a November memorandum prepared for the cabinet by officials of the Department of External Affairs and the Immigration Branch, the argument was put forward that "for the time being, at least, public opinion expects the government to make some appropriate contribution toward the solution of the problem which the Christian and civilized countries now find upon their doorstep." The report did, however, indicate a determination to retain existing ethnic ratios. "We do not want to take too many Jews, but in the present circumstances, we do not want to say so. We do not want to legitimatize the Aryan mythology by introducing any formal distinction for immigration purposes between Jews and non-Jews." In December, 1938, Thomas Crerar, the Minister responsible for immigration, briefly broke ranks with the rest of cabinet and recommended that Canada accept upwards of 10,000 refugees.[51] This initiative paralleled an Australian announcement that it was prepared to admit 15,000 refugees over the next three years.[52] But under intense pressure from his French-Canadian colleagues, and recognizing the political perils associated with this opening of the immigration gates, King chose to repudiate Crerar's proposal. The familiar arguments were put forth: serious unemployment, opposition of provincial governments, and the necessity of restricting Jewish refugees "lest it might ferment an anti-Semitic problem."[53] For King and his cabinet the safest approach politically was to leave the decision of how many Jewish refugees would be admitted in the hands of deputy minister F.C. Blair. The outcome was predictable.[54]

Between January and November, 1938, the amount of capital required for a Jewish family to enter Canada increased from $5,000 to $15,000. Moreover, even gifted intellectuals, scientists, and businessmen who claimed that they had knowledge and inventions that would enhance Canadian industrial performance were usually rejected. For example, in April, 1939, A.L. Jolliffe, the commissioner of immigration, assured concerned scientists at the National Research Council that his department was "rigidly enforcing the regulations in order to conserve for Canadians any available openings."[55]

Refugee Scientists in Canada

Canadian scientists had long been aware of the plight of German refugee academics both through the newspapers and through direct contact with the Academic Assistance Council, formed in April, 1933. It helped that Ernest Rutherford, who still had a powerful influence on Canadian scientists and academic administrators, was one of the founders and president of the organization. One of Rutherford's more celebrated statements was his public endorsement of A.V. Hill's December, 1933, letter to *Nature*, which questioned how it was possible "in a great and highly civilized country, that reasons of race, creed, or opinion, any more than the colour of a man's hair, could lead to the drastic elimination of a large number of the most eminent men of science . . . many of them men of the highest standing."[56]

By 1934 a number of national organizations had joined the British Academic Assistance Council in trying to place German refugee scientists.[57] These included the U.S. Emergency Committee in Aid of Displaced German Scholars (ECADGS), the Comité National de Secours aux Réfugies Allemands (France), the Bureau voor Duitsche Intellectueelen (Holland), the Notgemeinschaft Deutscher Wissenschaftler im Ausland (Switzerland), and the League of Nations organization, the High Commission for Refugees from Germany. Of these, the New York-based ECADGS was one of the most active and successful in placing German physicists, chemists, mathematicians, and medical researchers, despite high levels of unemployment in the United States among university graduates.[58] The Emergency Committee negotiated with individual universities that had requested a specific scientist from lists circulated by the Committee. Not surprisingly, preference was given to the scientific super-stars, the "well-off and well-connected." Thus, among the 100 physicists who found U.S. jobs, for example, the names of Albert Einstein, Enrico Fermi, James Franck, Edward Teller, Victor Weisskopf, and Hans Bethe loom large. Nor was the situation any different for German chemists or mathematicians.[59]

All of these scientists were able to gain entry to the U.S. by means of a loophole in the Immigration Act of 1924, which exempted university teachers from quotas, and by means of grants from the Rockefeller Foundation, which as early as April, 1933, had become concerned over the fate of displaced German scholars.[60] It was, however, a delicate business. In 1935 MIT president Karl Compton warned about the "tactical danger of having too large a proportion of the mathematical staff from the Jewish race, . . . that this arises not from our own prejudices in the matter, but because of a recognized general situation which might react unfavourably against the staff and the Department unless properly handled."[61]

Canadian university administrators and scientists were aware of British and U.S. attitudes and policies toward refugee scientists. But for a variety of reasons they did not create the Canadian equivalent to the British Academic Assistance Council or the American Emergency Committee. Instead, the Canadian response was more localized and fragmented; it was also less charitable and enlightened.

One of the more fortunate German academic refugees to be admitted to Canada was the physicist Gerhard Herzberg of the Physical Institute of the Technische Hochschule at Darmstadt. By the summer of 1934 Herzberg was facing imminent dismissal from his academic position for having "committed race treason" by marrying a Jew.[62] Yet, despite having endorsements from some of the world's greatest physicists, Herzberg was unable to obtain an academic position in either Britain or the United States. He had better success in Canada, largely because John Spinks of the University of Saskatchewan, a former student, intervened on his behalf and convinced university president Walter Murray of the advantages of obtaining this "brilliant physicist . . . an international authority on spectroscopy."[63] Herzberg was offered a position as guest professor for two years under the Carnegie Foundation system and immediately accepted.[64] During the next eleven years Herzberg published a number of outstanding papers and his well-regarded *Atomic Spectra and Atomic Structure* (1937).

Although the Carnegie guest professorship provided an avenue out of Nazi Germany, it still required host universities to guarantee permanent jobs. This was regarded as a heavy burden by many Canadian universities during the Great Depression because of their pressing financial restrictions. The University of Toronto Senate, for example, decided that in 1935 only two Carnegie positions would be offered.[65] One of these went to Dr. B. Haurwitz, formerly of the Geophysical Institute of Leipzig and "one of the few authorities on mathematical meteorology in the world."[66] During the thirties the University of Toronto added a few more German refugee scientists, and at the June, 1938, University of Toronto convocation, the university president, Cody, appealed for greater tolerance and compassion and denounced anti-Semitism at home and abroad.

While the University of Toronto was more receptive to refugee scientists than most Canadian universities, it was clear that Jews had to demonstrate exceptional ability to be hired. One example of this anti-Jewish bias was Charles Best's 1939 letter to Sir Henry Dale, requesting the services of an organic chemist for the Connaught Laboratories: "There are presumably expatriate Jews available but we would wish to be sure of the personality and ability of a candidate. These matters are easier to arrange in the University when there is not too high a proportion of Jewish blood."[67] Fortunately, Robert Julius Schnitzer, the subject of debate, was hired.

The controversy over Jewish refugee scientists was most intense at McGill University. In part, it was based on well-founded allegations that some university administrators were xenophobic and anti-Semitic. One of the most outspoken and influential was Ira MacKay, Dean of Arts and Science and formerly a constitutional law professor, whose negative views on Jewish students had already been conveyed to Sir Arthur Currie, the McGill principal from 1920 until his death in 1934, and the Board of Governors in April, 1926:

> Canada needs scientific men of initiative and intuition, engineers, builders, agrarians and workers, while the population of the Jewish community is almost altogether engaged in the professions and in money lending and trading occupations. . . . we do not need more of this class in Canada. . . . The experience of all Universities in the United States shows unquestionably that wherever the Jews begin to come in any very large numbers into the libraries, students unions, clubs, debating societies . . . the Christian students immediately begin a steady continuous retreat. . . .
>
> I think that you will recognize, then, that the problem is a very comprehensive one affecting not only the life of the University but the life of the community and of the whole of Canada and must, therefore, be fairly met.[68]

Nor did MacKay change his mind when, in July, 1933, the British Academic Assistance Council approached McGill with a list of German Jewish scientists who required positions. "I do not think that we need or should answer them at all," he advised Currie, "why should we import . . . Jewish university professors? . . . the Jewish people are of no use to us in this country."[69]

There is no evidence that Currie shared these views; but he was obviously not offended by this "straight talk."[70] At the same time, Currie was prepared to serve on the American-based Emergency Committee as long as no effort was made "to bring these men to this Continent in any wholesale numbers."[71] Nor did his successors attempt to hire more refugee scholars, despite pressure from the McGill faculty and from organizations such as the Canadian Fund for Refugees, which included such scientific luminaries as Frederick Banting and H.M. Tory.

Pressure on McGill and other Canadian universities to change their policies mounted in 1939. In January of that year Principal L.W. Douglas of McGill was asked to join a consortium of fifteen U.S. universities and their "proposed program for joint action by the American universities to provide an asylum for those refugees from European countries who are distinguished members of the international community of scholars."[72] The McGill Senate cautiously endorsed the spirit of the program, "subject to such reservations as may arise out of the formation of a procedure aimed at making the principles effective." But when the registrar suggested that McGill might raise the issue during the forthcoming conference of Canadian universities, he was sharply rebuked by Principal Douglas, that this was "a controversial, even dangerous subject, on which much embarrassment might develop from public discussion."[73] But Douglas had no reason for concern. In May, 1939, the National Conference of Canadian Universities, at their annual meeting, endorsed a resolution "calling on the government not to admit any of these refugees unless it guaranteed that no Canadian teacher, professor, scientist, mathematician or musician would lose his job."[74]

By the fall of 1939, however, more Canadian scientists supported a relaxation of immigration restrictions. This was evident in the survey conducted by R.W. Boyle, director of the Physics Division at the National Research Council.[75] It was also evident in the response of Frederick Banting, who as chairman of the NRC Associate Committee on Medical Research had been asked by immigration officials during the previous year to assess the abilities and job possibilities of refugee scientists. By August, 1939, Banting was now prepared to give the refugee the benefit of the doubt. "We are . . . not greatly impressed," he wrote F.C. Blair, "with the work of Dr. Jungermann. However, from the reprints of other investigations, it would appear that Dr. Jungermann's substance is of some value, and I see no reason why he should not be admitted as we are in need of pharmaceutical chemists in Canada."[76] But unless Dr. Jungermann had found sanctuary in Britain, it was too little, too late.

Refugees and Security

European Jews were not the only refugees to have the Canadian immigration gates slammed in their face. In 1939 the King government did not show much enthusiasm in placing about 600 anti-Fascist Sudeten German refugees, despite the political pressure and the financial support of British authorities.[77] Part of the problem was the time-consuming screening procedures and the task of co-ordinating the activities of the Immigration Branch and the CPR's land branch, the Canada Colonization Association.[78] Another factor was that the British were concerned their efforts to place the Sudeten Germans would be compared unfavourably with their response toward German Jewish refugees. This dilemma was not lost on Joseph Kennedy, the American ambassador in London, who criticized this attempt to place "non-Jewish emigrants to certain British Dominions where it would not be possible to send in more Jews," especially since "other countries of settlements, notably those of Latin America, would immediately express preference to receive non-Jewish refugees and no place would be left open for Jews."[79]

In September, 1939, another refugee crisis emerged when the Canadian government received numerous appeals to help the 250,000 Spanish exiles, located primarily in France. Most reports emphasized that unless the international community acted these refugees would be forcibly returned to Spain to face "the same terror and persecution ranging from assassination to long term imprisonment the Franco-government is meeting [sic] out to thousands of those who supported the Loyalist cause during the Civil War."[80] On this occasion, Canadian High Commissioner Vincent Massey gave qualified support to the proposal to accept Spanish refugees and argued that Canada might secure from the Spanish refugee camps "men of eminence in the world of science, education, literature and the arts in whose availability [Canadian] universities might be interested."[81] But as always, Immigration Branch director F.C. Blair seemed to have the last word in keeping out refugees who might be a financial burden, a disruptive influence, or a bureaucratic problem. His most convincing argument, however, was directed toward the French-Canadian members of cabinet, already suspicious of the "Godless" Spanish Republicans, who were impressed by Blair's warning that "there would be a tremendous amount of opposition if anything were done to open the door to these penniless refugees who have been opposing Franco."[82]

This bias against left-wing refugees and immigrants was, of course, of long standing. So, too, was the view that the Immigration Act could be used to protect the country from Communist, Nazi, and Fascist infiltrators. Naturally, the easiest and most common approach was to exclude suspected subversives at the point of entry, usually on the basis of information provided by British security agencies and the American Federal Bureau of Investigation.[83] Deportation was another way of dealing with foreign agents and alien radicals, at least until most of Europe became the domain of the Axis powers. Political deportation, of course, had a long Canadian legacy, and had been used extensively in 1919 and during the Red Scare of 1931.[84]

By 1939 the Naturalization Act also became an even more popular weapon to ensure that the foreign-born, both alien and naturalized, made loyalty to Canada their over-riding consideration. Enforcement of these laws and regulations was generally the responsibility of the Royal Canadian Mounted Police, long an authority in dealing with "dangerous foreigners."[85]

One of the first official expressions of concern that European refugees could pose a serious security threat came from T.A. Crerar. In December, 1938, while meeting with the Canadian National Committee of Refugees, Crerar gravely predicted that "certain foreign states would not be above sending certain people to Canada for subversive purposes."[86] The image of the refugee as a destabilizing force had already become a matter of intense debate in various parts of the country. In Quebec, for example, the radical right, as part of its anti-Semitic campaign, charged that recent Jewish refugees had substantially reinforced the Communist movement in the province.[87] In Ontario, even the respectable *Globe and Mail* encouraged this type of insidious propaganda when it declared, in a November, 1937, editorial, that "although it cannot be said that a majority of

Jews are Communists, the indications are that a large percentage, and probably the majority of Communists are Jews."[88]

Actually, by the end of 1938 the federal government had devised a wide variety of measures to deal with all subversives who threatened national security. In a May, 1939, memorandum, Norman Robertson, in his capacity as liaison between the RCMP and the cabinet, set forth an even more comprehensive list of guidelines to deal with seditious activities. One of these was the recommendation that immigration and naturalization regulations now be used against Nazis and Fascists "in the same way that police now check the records of persons believed to be of radical or Communist sympathies."[89] Not surprisingly, the leadership of the Communist Party was outraged that their movement was "accused of being in a 'sinister combination' with the fascists to weaken the defences of Canada."[90]

Within the King government, however, the Communists continued to be viewed with intense suspicion, and the RCMP was particularly suspicious. In August, 1939, as the international situation became more critical, the commissioner of the RCMP recommended that the CPC be outlawed and its leadership interned. At the time, however, moderates such as Norman Robertson of External Affairs and J.F. MacNeill of Justice argued that this hard-line approach was both undemocratic and inefficient.[91]

Canadian anarchists were another group of "leftists" who became the target of Canadian security agencies, and in several cases the deportation weapon was applied. In October, 1939, the RCMP and the Immigration Branch attempted to deport Attilio (Arthur) Bortolotti, a member of an Italian anarchist group in Toronto. The Bortolotti case quickly assumed national and international importance for a number of reasons. One was the allegation that the incriminating information used against Bortolotti had been provided by Italian Fascists in retaliation for his activities in the 1936 exposure of "fascist attempts to inculcate their ideas in the separate schools of Windsor and Toronto." Bortolotti's lawyer, J.L. Cohen, went even further and charged that within "the police organization in Toronto there has been a good deal of sympathy with both the Italian and French Canadian Fascists." In contrast, Cohen asserted, when dealing with leftists these police officers seemed "to be afflicted with some kind of monomania."[92] There was also the fact that the criminal charges against Bortolotti and his three colleagues, submitted under the Defence of Canada Regulations, had been thrown out of court; the defence claimed, therefore, that the subsequent deportation order was both unjustified and vindictive. Yet another dimension, which was pointed out in a February 13, 1940, editorial of the *Toronto Star*, was that to deport Bortolotti to Italy "would be condemning him to prison for anti-Fascist activities in Canada."[93]

F.C. Blair, however, was not swayed by these arguments. Bortolotti was, in his opinion, a menace to national security, "the author of some very dangerous literature," and a man who had a long record of radical activity in both Canada and the United States. Blair made particular reference to an RCMP report that in 1929 Bortolotti had been dismissed from his job at the Ford Motor Company "on account of his arrest by the Detroit Police for the distribution of subversive literature . . . on the second anniversary of the execution of one, Sacco Van Zetti [*sic*]." Fortunately, there were those within the Canadian government, most notably O.D. Skelton and Norman Robertson, who found Blair's reasoning intolerable and spoke out in defence of Bortolotti's civil rights and Canadian justice. Was it not true, they asked, "that Immigration authorities in both Canada and the United States have been very reluctant to deport persons to the totalitarian countries who are likely to suffer there for their political ideas. . . . Now we are at war it is perhaps more important than ever to maintain these principles."[94] The combination of public pressure and the intervention of the Ottawa mandarins resulted in the release of Bortolotti on April 29, seven months after his arrest.[95]

This incident demonstrated that there were sharp divisions between the Immigration Branch and External Affairs over the status of refugees from Fascist-controlled regions. It also demonstrated that the federal government still assumed that enemy alien refugees did not constitute a security threat since "their sympathies, in the event of war, by reason of racial considerations or political opinions, would not be with enemy powers."[96] This blanket clearance covered both German and Austrian Jews as well as refugees from Czechoslovakia and Poland. By May, 1940, however, the Interdepartmental Committee on Alien Propaganda had become more security conscious and instructed all government departments "to make available all information . . . relating to enemy aliens, including refugees," to the RCMP.[97] Nor was Canada prepared to accept many new refugees. In part, this was in response to the September, 1939, British declaration that "during the war Germany will permit the emigration only of persons whose departure would relieve economic pressure or who would actively further the German cause abroad."[98]

The Soviet-German Non-Aggression Pact of August, 1939, placed suspected left-wing refugees in an even more vulnerable position. The situation was not improved when the Canadian Communist movement stopped describing the war as anti-Fascist and began calling it an anti-imperialist conflict that Canada had to avoid. This meant that Communist organizations in general, and groups like the Ukrainian Labour-Farmer Temple Association in particular, were now legitimate targets under the security provisions of the Defence of Canada Regulations. In January, 1940, the round-up of Communists and anarchists began; on June 4 the Communist Party and most of its front organizations became illegal. Under order-in-council PC 2667 the Custodian of Enemy Property was given control of the property of all banned organizations – including that owned by the ULFTA.[99]

Conclusion

In March, 1941, Immigration Director F.C. Blair provided his own definition of refugee, based on his experience since 1933.

> In the first place there is no such term as 'refugee' in our statistical compilation. . . . Our statistics are kept mainly by race. The League of Nations adopted a definition which was not strictly adhered to and the Evian Conference set up at the suggestion of President Roosevelt adopted an entirely different definition of 'refugee'. The term has now come to include pretty much every person who is seeking to change his place of residence, not only because of war, but because of economic, racial and religious difficulties. From this angle, practically all the people who have come to Canada, whose homes originally were in Europe, belong to the refugee class.[100]

Although Blair was aware that the rise of fascism during the 1930s had created additional problems for his department in coping with the flood of refugees, his administrative record does not indicate that he appreciated their desperate plight. Yet, according to his colleagues and associates, Blair was not a malevolent person; but his world view was parochial, ethnocentric, and self-righteous. Admission to Canada, Blair believed, was a privilege to be awarded those who met his occupational and cultural standards, namely, hard-working immigrant workers who would assimilate quickly. By this standard German Jews and Spanish Republicans did not fit, and Sudeten Germans were suspect. Above all, Blair was anxious not to admit refugees who were politically controversial.

One must remember, however, that Blair was a bureaucrat, not a cabinet minister, and that immigration policy was ultimately determined by W.A. Gordon and T.A. Crerar. There was also the influence of Ernest Lapointe, the Minister of Justice, who was concerned about the intensity of anti-Semitism in Quebec. Nor was Prime Minister Mackenzie King prepared to advocate a more generous policy in the face of hostile public opinion in Quebec and in other parts of the country. King's sense of political expediency was reinforced by his own ethnocentric bias.

Deporting the radical foreigner was a popular policy during the Bennett years. While it became less pronounced during King's administration, the security dimensions of Canadian immigration policy became quite pronounced as the war clouds loomed on the horizon. This trend was particularly threatening for Canadians of German, Italian, and Japanese background, as the prospect of being labelled an enemy alien soon became a frightening reality.

CHAPTER 6

Keeping Out the Subversives: The Security Dimension of Canada's Immigration Policy, 1939-1952

National security considerations had a powerful impact on Canada's refugee policies during the Second World War and the early stages of the Cold War. For those refugees who fled from Germany and Austria prior to September, 1939, and were fortunate enough to gain entry to Canada, there was the likelihood of being classified as enemy aliens. Although this meant a variety of restrictions on civil rights, most immigrants in this category were left relatively undisturbed. Not as fortunate were the 4,000 enemy alien refugees who were transported from Britain to Canada in June, 1940, for safekeeping. At the very least, these men were interned for six months, until they could qualify either for return to Britain or for release in Canada. Those who chose the latter option had no guarantee of permanent sanctuary. A final group, numbering about 2,500, came from a wide assortment of backgrounds: diplomats from Czechoslovakia, engineers and technicians from Poland, and, of course, Jewish refugees trying to escape the horrors of Hitler's "final solution."

Irving Abella and Harold Troper have provided a strident critique of Canada's wartime refugee policies: "Even . . . the mounting evidence of an ongoing Nazi program for the total annihilation of European Jewry did not move Canada. Its response remained legalistic and cold. . . . And with the Allies' victory the remnant of European Jewish survivors found no welcome, no succour in Canada."[1] Reg Whitaker has attacked the Canadian record on other grounds: its right-wing agenda.

The immigration screening process was put in place in the immediate aftermath of the Second World War. . . . Yet some forty years after the screening process was put in place, there was sufficient public disquiet regarding its effectiveness that a Royal Commission was established to discover whether war criminals had in fact entered Canada despite screening. There is good reason for this disquiet. The screening process was, in truth, a bird with one wing; an anti-Communist wing.[2]

These are thoughtful and provocative analyses, but clearly much more research remains to be done about Canada's response to refugees between 1939 and 1952. How, for example, did the Canadian record compare to that of the United States, with particular reference to David Wyman's challenging indictment of the performance of the Roosevelt administration in these years?

Until the Nazis blocked the exits in the fall of 1941, the oppressed Jews of Europe might have fled to safety. But relatively few got out, mainly because the rest of the world would not take them in. The United States, which had lowered its barriers a little in 1938, began raising them again in the autumn of 1939. Two years later, immigration was even more tightly restricted than before 1938. In fact, starting in July, 1941, America's gates nearly shut. The best chance to save the European Jews had passed.

Blame for this callous approach, in Wyman's opinion, is attributed to nativism, anti-Semitism, and widespread fear that many of the refugees were actually Nazi infiltrators – a potential "fifth column."[3]

World War Two

If it was difficult for European refugees to gain entry to Canada after the outbreak of war, it became virtually impossible after the German Blitzkrieg of May, 1940. From Belgium, the Netherlands, and France came reports of a sinister German fifth column working behind Allied lines. After his flight to Britain, Sir Neville Bland, former ambassador to the Netherlands, warned his countrymen not to trust any German or Austrian "however superficially charming and devoted."[4] This same message was soon conveyed to the House of Commons by Prime Minister Winston Churchill: "After the dark and vile conspiracy which in a few days laid the trustful Dutch people at the mercy of the Nazi aggressors, a wave of alarm passed over this country, and especially in responsible circles, lest the same kind of undermining tactics and treacherous agents of the enemy were at work in our Island."[5] Not surprisingly, these developments profoundly affected Canadians. Public concern and panic were clearly evident in the hundreds of letters and petitions sent to Prime Minister King by a wide variety of organizations.[6] One Toronto resident wondered whether private citizens could "kill at sight enemy agents damaging utilities." Even organizations such as the Canadian Legion indicated that they intended to form protective units that would, if necessary, "take the law into their owns hands and act against all aliens in Canada, including naturalized citizens."[7] This threat of vigilante action was taken very seriously by the King government. On June 27, 1940, an important memorandum suggested a number of alternative policies; but the message was one of concern:

> The fact that the German advance since May 10 has been assisted by saboteurs in invaded territories naturally caused concern about aliens in Canada. The success of German efforts resulting in the occupation of half of Europe, even threatening the United Kingdom with invasion, gave Canadians a serious emotional shock. That was natural. What was unnatural was that some interests have exploited people's apprehensions in an effort to embarrass the Government, thus doing Hitler's work.[8]

Part of the government's response was to move against the different enemy alien populations under the Defence of Canada Regulations. On June 4 various Fascist organizations were declared illegal, as were Communist and anarchist organizations.[9] The large German-Canadian community found itself, for the second time in the century, classified as enemy aliens and forced to abide by security regulations. But only about 800 were arrested and interned, in part because Canadian Germans as a group were regarded as anti-Nazi.[10] Not so fortunate was the Italian-Canadian community, which had dramatically increased to 112,000 during the interwar years, especially in Montreal and Toronto. But Mussolini's June 10 decision to fight alongside Hitler placed Italian Canadians at risk: public condemnation, mob violence, and internment of about 700 suspected Italian Fascists soon followed.[11] Although Japan and Canada were not yet at war, Canadian security officials had already made plans for the internment of security risks among the 22,000 members of the Japanese-Canadian community if the military situation so required.[12] In June, 1940, Hugh Keenleyside, a rising star in the Canadian foreign service and a supporter of extending civil rights to the Nisei (Canadian-born Japanese), accurately predicted why the Canadian government would eventually order mass internment: "If Japan should enter the war against us . . . there would certainly be danger of subversive activities on the part of some elements in the Japanese community. The police are not in a position to ferret out the dangerous Japanese as they have done with the Germans and Italians. . . ."[13]

These security measures were directed against enemy aliens already in Canada. But what about the thousands who sought refuge in Canada after the fall of France? What security standards would be applied to these desperate people? This problem greatly concerned Canadian officials throughout the summer and fall of 1940 as they sought to ferret out possible spies and subversives. Significantly, much of the information used by the RCMP and immigration officials came from British and American sources.[14] In June, 1940, for example, the RCMP was informed by British intelligence that a Jewish refugee, William Roth, who had been admitted six months previously, might be a Nazi agent since he had been observed "making rather large cash payments to suspicious characters" while travelling between Montreal and New York.[15] The activities of Soviet agents were of equal concern, as this March, 1940, message from O.D. Skelton of External Affairs to F.C. Blair shows:

> I am informed by the French Legation that a Miss Sophie Burnstein, who is of Russian birth and has been living in Paris in recent years, has left for the United States on some errand for the Comintern. It is understood that she plans later to apply for entry into Canada as a well-to-do refugee. I have already passed on this information to the Royal Canadian Mounted Police, but thought you might wish to have advance notice of the lady's intentions.[16]

Other refugees who caused External Affairs and immigration officials considerable difficulty were those who had the support of powerful religious and political groups within the country. In October, 1940, Skelton informed the RCMP and the Immigration Branch that Professor Mordrat, a suspected agent from Vichy France, had applied for entry as a political refugee and that his application had been endorsed by a number of prominent people in Quebec, including Liberal Senator Raoul Dandurand.[17] Under these circumstances Skelton suggested that the application should be approved: "With some misgivings, Mr. Blair and I concluded that Mordrat might be a more effective propagandist for the Vichy government as a soldier of France prevented from re-joining his Canadian wife and family by Canadian Immigration authorities, than as an active agitator in the Province of Quebec."[18]

Canadian policies toward European refugees were also strongly influenced by developments in the United States and Great Britain. In both countries the outbreak of war in September, 1939, resulted in a drastic change in government policies. This was most notable in Great Britain, where friendly enemy aliens and refugees increasingly became suspect. In the United States the hard-line approach was somewhat delayed and immigration policy remained reasonably tolerant throughout 1939, even toward those refugees who had entered the country illegally. In November, 1940, for example, Loring Christie, the Canadian chargé d'affaires in Washington, reported that the United States Department of Labor was even "permitting anti-fascist Italians and anti-Franco Spaniards who are illegally in this country to remain here, since they claim that they are on the blacklist of their respective governments because of their political activities."[19]

Unfortunately, this humanitarian approach would soon end as Americans became increasingly concerned over the possibilities of Nazi and Soviet espionage and sabotage. In some ways this hysteria was a reaction to the belief that Nazi success in Europe had been greatly assisted by a fifth column; it was also in response to the draconian anti-refugee policies adopted by the British government in June, 1940. There is considerable evidence as well that various American nativist and racist organizations used the fifth column scare as a means of justifying their long-standing views "that foreigners should be kept under close surveillance and that immigration should end." [20] These views found expression both in Congress and in the press. Beginning in August, 1940, for example, the *American Magazine* presented six articles on the internal Nazi threat under such titles as "Enemies Within Our Gates" and "Hitler's Slave Spies." Not to be outdone, the pro-business journal *Fortune* published a series of articles on Fascist and Communist activities in the United States. [21]

This agitation had a powerful impact on American immigration policy. In June, 1940, the Alien Registration Bill or Smith Act was passed, "virtually without debate and without division," which gave American security authorities greatly expanded powers to deport suspected radicals and subversives, and called for the "registration and fingerprinting of aliens." [22] Worse was to follow. In mid-June, 1940, Attorney General Robert Jackson declared that the idea that a refugee might be admitted to the United States unless he posed a danger to the country "must at least temporarily yield to the policy that none shall be admitted unless it affirmatively appears to be for the American interest." In the summer of 1940 the Roosevelt administration shifted the Immigration and Naturalization Service from the Labor Department to the Justice Department "to ensure more effective control over aliens." [23] The authority to issue the all-important immigration visa was, however, entrusted to officials of the Visa Division of the State Department. Unfortunately for the refugees, assistant secretary Breckenridge Long and his subordinates often "brought strongly nativist attitudes to the situation" and appeared obsessed with the fear of an alien fifth column. [24]

This negative stereotype was reinforced early in 1941 when there were renewed reports that Germany had established an elaborate network of "unwilling" spies and saboteurs in the United States "by forcing people who had relatives in Nazi territory to serve as German agents under threat of harm to their loved ones." During the May, 1941, session of the House Committee on Un-American Activities one left-wing refugee testified that "it was impossible for anyone to be released from a Nazi concentration camp unless he signed a pledge that he would help the Gestapo." A similar warning emanated from Laurence Steinhardt, American ambassador in Moscow: "Soviet authorities would not issue visas to potential immigrants to the United States unless they had guarantees that these people could be used as espionage agents." [25]

The State Department required little prodding. On June 5, 1941, it began to reduce substantially the number of visas granted to refugees who had "parents, children, husbands, wives, brothers or sisters resident in territory under the control of Germany." These restrictive measures, in the words of David Wyman, "crushed the hopes of thousands who had looked to the United States for asylum."[26]

Not surprisingly, both External Affairs and immigration officials were influenced by American reports that the Nazis and Soviets were using refugees as a fifth column. On May 31, 1941, for example, Hume Wrong of the Canadian legation in Washington forwarded to Ottawa a confidential memorandum prepared by Avra M. Warren, chief of the U.S. State Department Visa Division, on the dangers associated with refugees temporarily located in the Far East:

> There are at present approximately 22,000 European refugees in Shanghai and 2,000 in Japan. . . . Of the 22,000 in Shanghai, roughly 8,000 are known to be Japanese agents, and of the remaining 14,000, one in four obtained transit through Russia upon the written undertaking that he would become a Russian agent in the Americas should he succeed in reaching this hemisphere. Large numbers have admitted this fact to the American Consuls before whom they applied for United States visas. These admissions have been in many cases corroborated by other means.

The memorandum went on to claim that "of the approximately 2,000 refugees in Japan, more than half are Jewish rabbinical students who escaped from Poland over a period of many years. All refugees in Japan are working in full collaboration with the Japanese against Russia."[27]

Developments in Britain also had important ramifications on Canada's wartime refugee policies. Of greatest significance was the British government's decision in the summer of 1940 to send about 4,500 interned civilian enemy aliens and prisoners of war to Canada for safekeeping. Of these, the most tragic were the 2,600 civilian refugees in the so-called "C" category, mostly Jews, who until the dark days of June, 1940, were regarded as safe or friendly enemy aliens. The complex reasons why the British government so dramatically reversed its September, 1939, policy of interning only "agents, members of foreign organizations and special 'dangerous individuals' " has been thoroughly discussed in a number of British and Canadian studies. What is of central importance here is the impact those category "C" internees had on the internal and external policies of the Canadian government.[28]

As early as March, 1939, British security agencies such as MI-5 warned the Home Secretary that "the Germans were anxious to inundate this country with Jews with a view of creating a Jewish problem in the United Kingdom." After September, 1939, MI-5 and military intelligence intensified their demands for wholesale roundups of enemy aliens despite the arguments of the Home Secretary and the Foreign Office that such draconian measures were unnecessary and harmful.[29] Christopher Andrew, in *Secret Service: The Making of an*

Intelligence Community, effectively summarizes the major factors associated with the mass internment:

> The home secretary Sir John Anderson, anxious to avoid the anti-alien hysteria of the First World War, told the cabinet that none of the intelligence services had found any evidence of Nazi plans to infiltrate German and Austrian refugees. Nor, as a group, were the refugees potentially dangerous.... The chiefs of staff, however, insisted that alien refugees were 'a most dangerous source of subversive activity'.... Churchill sided with the chiefs of staff....[30]

The placement and administration of the 2,600 friendly enemy aliens created immense problems for Canadian military and civilian authorities. First, the "hundreds of professionals, mingled with baffled schoolboys and mid-European peasants," did not fit into the preconceived model of dangerous aliens who had to be guarded and not integrated back into either British or Canadian society. Second, the British government, or, more specifically, the security agencies, had the exclusive authority to screen the internees, and the vetting process was long and laborious. Third, conditions in the eight internment camps were often unsatisfactory from the point of view of both the internees and the officials and staff of Canadian Internment Operations, and later the Commission of Refugee Camps.[31]

Not surprisingly, there was intense bitterness among the internees over their treatment in both Britain and Canada, a condition Saul Hayes of the Canadian Jewish Refugee Agency patiently explained to director of operations General Panet. "As you will understand there is a considerable amount of agitation because of the position in which these Jews, themselves first victims of Nazi oppression . . . now find themselves." What made the situation even worse was that the screening of internees had not been very thorough and Nazis, Fascists, Social Democrats, and Communists were often placed in the same camp. Author Eric Koch, himself an internee, describes the controversy at the Farnham camp:

> We had pressed for the removal of the Nazis and nothing had been done, and we realized that unless they were removed there were bound to be more ugly incidents. . . . As for the majority, this was a highly emotional issue touching on a fundamental principal, namely our status as refugees. To most of us it was irrelevant that a small number of communists were making the most of the confrontation. Jews and gentiles felt equally strong about this principle.[32]

Between the fall of 1940, when the British government sent Alexander Paterson to assess the status of the category "C" internees, and the end of 1943, when the refugee camps were closed, Canadian authorities had three main responsibilities.[33] One was to facilitate the gradual repatriation of those internees who wished to return to Britain and who passed the security assessment of MI-5.[34] A second problem was how to meet the demands of those refugees who had American visas and wanted to proceed to the United States.[35] The third difficulty was how to deal with those refugees who wished to remain in Canada, either in wartime jobs or as university students.

The most challenging and controversial of these was the latter, especially since the cabinet subcommittee had in September, 1940, made it clear to the British government that it opposed the permanent residence of these internees since there was such strong public opposition "to the admission of any large proportion of Jews."[36] Nor did the official position change substantially in 1941. A request sent to Colonel Stethem in May for the use of Jewish artisans in Montreal factories brought a curt and negative response from the director of internment operations: "Up to the present, the Canadian Government has not consented to permit any of these internees to be released in Canada, except those who had first degree relatives, or one or two skilled craftsmen, where their services were urgently required in war work." In his opinion there would probably be difficulties if they were given industrial jobs: "they are of German nationality, although anti-Nazi, and they would have to be registered as enemy aliens. Whether the other workmen in the factory would object to their presence or not, I do not know."[37]

By the end of 1941, with almost total segregation of the refugee internees from prisoners of war, a much more enlightened policy was adopted to use the diverse skills of these men.[38] F.C. Blair, in a September, 1942, memorandum to officials of the Department of Munitions and Supply, indicated that of those refugees who chose to remain in Canada, 150 were students, 100 were in farm jobs, and another 350 were "in various industries where their services might be useful . . . in the war effort." He did emphasize, however, that the greatest care was taken, as extensive screening occurred before these men were released:

in any case the Home Office in London is consulted to obtain their approval, where the record overseas is satisfactory and the camp record here is good, we proceed with release depending of course on the refugees' qualifications. Every refugee is required to register with the police and to report regularly wherever he may be placed. No man is permitted to leave his employer without obtaining our consent and that consent is rarely given because we are determined to prevent these men from drifting about from place to place. We have endeavoured (and I am glad to say with some success) to impress upon these individuals that they . . . have an obligation to live up to the conditions under which their release was granted. Those who fail to do it face the possibility of return to the camps and already at least half a dozen have been returned.

In discussing the procedure for security screening Blair provided an interesting argument, particularly in light of his obvious bias against the entry of Jewish refugees:

> I would estimate that at least 90% of those released are of Jewish racial origin, although some of them are of mixed race such as a Jewish father and a German mother. In every case where the race is not Jewish particular care has been taken to check up on the reliability and the attitude of the individual to Nazism. In no case have we yet found any reason to suspect the conduct of persons who have been released. [39]

The task of integrating the refugees into the economy was carried out by immigration officials. They proved to be tough assessors, even in employment situations where refugees complained about "exploitation and oppression . . . under-pay and harsh treatment." In case after case the managerial argument about the importance of maintaining labour stability was accepted rather uncritically. This rigid stance was clearly evident in the case of a Montreal factory where three refugee workers were charged with fomenting unrest "in a manner that indicated they hold and expound the old view of communism that taught that all employers were tyrants and oppressors." As a result, these men were temporarily returned to the internment camps for "behaviour modification."[40]

Refugee students were much more fortunate, especially after the summer of 1941 when Canadian and British authorities had agreed that it would be better to allow refugee students "to continue with their studies in Canada rather than waste valuable time behind barbed wire." The original plan was that 100 would be admitted to Canadian universities after their records were screened by the Home Office, the Commissioner of Refugee Camps, and the Director of Immigration.[41] In his 1942 report on this program Colonel Fordham, the Director of Internment Operations, laconically commented that few pre-war immigrants "have had their histories as thoroughly investigated." The program worked as follows:

> A responsible sponsor, residing in Canada, was found for every student released for the purpose of attending a Canadian university. The sponsor had to be a reputable citizen possessed of assets who would undertake to guarantee the cost of maintenance and the tuition fees of a student. That was to prevent a student from becoming a public charge. . . . The sponsors were usually found through the agencies of . . . the Central Committee for Interned Refugees. . . . Every sponsor had to meet with the approval of Mr. F.C. Blair . . . before being accepted. [42]

Although the scheme was praised by Canadian security authorities and those university administrators who had internee students, public criticism was soon forthcoming.[43] In March, 1943, Tommy Church, the combative member of

Parliament for Toronto Broadview, attacked Minister of Defence J.L. Ralston in the House of Commons for giving enemy alien students preferential treatment. He also warned that it was "unwise to enrol these enemy prisoners in our universities and permit them, where so inclined, to get all kinds of information from mingling with the students and staff and . . . making use of our science courses and laboratories."[44] Behind the scenes, C.J. Mackenzie, president of the National Research Council, reminded university officials of the NRC's policy "not to employ enemy aliens in any work having contact with secret information," no matter how brilliant they were. To charges that Canada was more concerned with security precautions than its allies, Mackenzie provided a robust if facetious rebuttal:

> It is true that there are a few aliens of enemy origin working in the United States on secret war projects, but they are very few and most of them have been in the country for some time. Also, they are only allowed to have knowledge of a very partial field of secret projects. As a matter of fact, several distinguished Britishers who have lived for years in the United States had to be formally associated with our Research Council before they could be admitted to certain secret war projects in the United States.[45]

Developments: 1943-45

Between 1943 and 1945 the Canadian government was much less concerned about the activities of enemy aliens, in particular, and the foreign-born population, in general. There had been no alien subversion or sabotage. Vast numbers of the foreign-born had enlisted in the Canadian armed forces, and the fortunes of war had swung to the Allies. As well, the propaganda and citizenship work of the Department of War Services, especially its Nationalities Branch and Committee on Co-operation in Canadian Citizenship, appeared to be working. Both sought to monitor and mould public opinion among Canada's ethnic groups by providing "Canadian news for the domestic foreign-language press" and by providing "immigrant groups with information about their homelands without reviving nationalistic ambitions or antagonism." While some eastern European intellectuals were employed by these organizations, the executives were solidly Anglo-Canadian.[46] They also made no excuse for their anti-communism or for supporting the goals of ethnic nationalist organizations such as the newly formed Ukrainian Canadian Committee (UCC).[47]

This anti-communism would be modified after June, 1941, when the Soviet Union became Canada's ally in the common struggle against Fascism. The new pro-Russian sentiment was most evident in the work of the National Council for Canadian Soviet Friendship, which had branches in eighteen urban centres across the country and an executive that included such Anglo-Canadian luminaries as Sir Ellsworth Flavelle as president and John David Eaton as vice-president. Within the King government, External Affairs officials were especially anxious to establish cordial relations with the U.S.S.R. and often became impatient and even hostile toward anti-Soviet agitation in Canada.[48]

This new legitimacy for the left in Canada also affected the status of enemy alien refugees. In October, 1943, officials of External Affairs suggested that "steps should be taken to remove as far as possible, the restrictions imposed on refugees from the United Kingdom." This proposal reflected growing public pressure for unconditional release. On December 10, 1943, an order-in council granted the refugees a renewable one-year permit to remain in Canada and specified that they would "be released from any restraints or conditions."[49]

Yet, many of the interned refugees did not wish to remain in Canada. Instead, they wanted to join relatives and friends in the United States, but American authorities had already demonstrated, in the 1940 case of Hermann Bondi, that they were not prepared to facilitate the entry of any group of European refugees, especially those who came from Canadian internment camps. In the Bondi case, the justification for exclusion was twofold: he had not arrived at an American port, and he had not been interviewed and given security clearance by American authorities prior to coming to the United States.[50] In the fall of 1941 British envoy Alexander Paterson sought to circumvent these exclusionist regulations when he visited with American officials in Washington. He was, however, thwarted by the Allan Bill, which "stipulated that nobody could be admitted to the USA during the war who had relatives in Germany or German occupied Europe, and no alien could enter the country who had not been a free man for at least a year."

Between 1941 and 1944 Canadian officials, on various occasions, attempted to carry out Paterson's plan, but with no success. In July, 1944, Norman Robertson, undersecretary of External Affairs, informed the Canadian ambassador in Washington, Lester B. Pearson, that he was now convinced that "the continuous difficulties, delays, errors and apologies that have arisen in this matter lead me rather to doubt whether the State Department is actually interested in achieving an arrangement under which entry of refugees is possible." In his reply, Pearson confirmed that the American State Department appeared to have no intention of altering its hard-line approach toward this unique group of refugees:

> Despite the assurances given us on several occasions it is evident we are up against the ill-will of the Visa Division to deal fairly with these applications. Although it is difficult to assess the reasons for this attitude, it may be attributed, in our opinion, to the resentment caused in the Visa Division by the establishment of the War Refugee Board. As you might recall, the creation of the Board was regarded as an implicit criticism of the work performed in that field by the State Department, e.g., the Visa Division. As

the Visa Division, however, is responsible for the final decision in each specific case, it can be appreciated that each one is scrutinized with the utmost care and without too great sympathy.[51]

But were Robertson and Pearson justified in criticizing American refugee policies when the Canadian record was so unimpressive? Quite clearly in Robertson's case, he was not only aware of Canada's meagre response to Europe's war victims but personally embarrassed that his country had not done more. In October, 1944, for example, Robertson reluctantly transmitted a report to the British deputy high commissioner on the numbers of refugees admitted into Canada since 1939. "In passing this information which you have requested, I feel I should mention my misgivings about the use to which your Government wish to put it."[52] And well he should have misgivings, for at this stage in the war Canada had admitted only about 2,700 temporary refugees. They consisted of the following seven groups:

1. 60 Belgium and Dutch refugees from Spain and Portugal.
2. 100 Czechoslovak officials and nationals from the United Kingdom and the Iberian Peninsula.
3. The members of the crew of the Norwegian Whaling Fleet brought to Canadian ports when Norway was invaded, this personnel totalling about 300.
4. 665 Polish engineers and technicians from France and the Iberian Peninsula, following the overthrow of the first mentioned country; some of these were accompanied by their families.
5. 150 Polish nationals from the Far East.
6. 966 civilian internees brought to Canada from the United Kingdom in 1940 and released for employment or for educational purposes in this country.
7. 447 Jewish refugees from the Iberian Peninsula and Tangier.[53]

Two of these groups merit particular analysis – the 665 Poles and the 447 Jewish refugees from the Iberian Peninsula and Tangier. In each case, they reveal important aspects of the economic utility and security dimensions of Canada's refugee policies.

Between 1940 and 1943 Canadian authorities attempted to bring hundreds of Polish engineers and technicians who had fled to unoccupied France and Britain after June, 1940. The initiative came from the London-based Polish government-in-exile and its Canadian representative. In September, 1940, Victor Podoski, the Polish consul-general, informed the Canadian government that there were, in France, many "chemical and mechanical engineers, technicians of all types and experts in munitions production." His message found a receptive audience in the Department of Munitions and Supply and in the Department of

External Affairs. In November, 1940, approval was given for the entry of seventy engineers and their dependants from Vichy France. However, prolonged discussion over which government would assume the transportation costs and Nazi pressure on Vichy thwarted the repatriation efforts.[54] Gerald Dirks describes the situation:

> The speed with which these arrangements were concluded reflected both the eagerness of the Canadian companies in the manufacturing and munitions industries to acquire skilled labour and the fear of the Polish government-in-exile [that] . . . Germany would pressure Vichy to hand over the skilled refugees to the Gestapo, which in turn would force the Poles to work in the Reich's own war industries. In January 1942, these fears were shown to be well justified. A Vichy decree prohibited the emigration of all men under the age of forty five. . . . By mid-January all attempts to acquire exit permits for these much desired refugees were dropped.[55]

Having lost out on the initial lottery for skilled war workers, the Canadian government was quite responsive to a subsequent Foreign Office suggestion that they accept a few hundred Polish "experts" in Britain who had not yet been absorbed into high-priority jobs in the British war economy. During 1941 and 1942, 400 skilled technicians and 265 scientists and engineers came to Canada under the same terms that had been worked out for the Vichy-based group. All of these men quickly found employment, and by 1945 they had become prime candidates for permanent domicile and Canadian citizenship because of valuable wartime service.[56]

In 1943 and 1944 the debate surrounding the entry of Jewish refugees from Spain, Portugal, and Tangier was an even more striking example of the dictum inherent in Canada's refugee policy. On one hand, the King government had to respond to the demands of humanitarian groups such as the Canadian National Committee on Refugees and newspapers such as the *Winnipeg Free Press* that the time had come "when we have to stop talking about doing something about refugees and get down to action."[57] In contrast, there were strong isolationist and xenophobic forces within the country that resisted the entry of almost all refugees, but specifically Jews. There were also the messages being sent by Canadian security officials that certain European refugees remained a serious security risk.[58]

In the spring of 1943 the Canadian government was pressured by British authorities to grant asylum to greater numbers of European refugees. One major argument was that the few unoccupied countries of Europe, such as Sweden, Switzerland, Spain, and Portugal, were being overwhelmed by the economic and social burdens associated with the maintenance of the victims of Nazism. In April, 1943, representatives of Great Britain and the United States met at Bermuda "to discuss proposals aimed at establishing a more adequate multilateral assistance scheme for European refugees."[59] Although the Bermuda Conference and the subsequent actions of the Intergovernmental Committee on Refugees produced few solutions for the desperate plight of European Jews and other victims of Nazism, it did force Canadian authorities to open the immigration gates a crack. In particular, arrangements were made to reopen the Lisbon immigration office and to select a limited number of both Jewish and non-Jewish refugees.[60]

Yet even this pathetically small movement caused great agitation in Canada, most notably in Quebec. In the fall of 1943 the leader of the Union Nationale, Maurice Duplessis, publicly charged that there was a conspiracy between an "international Zionist brotherhood" and the federal government "to place 100,000 Jewish refugees in Quebec."[61] In March of 1944 Duplessis went even further when he introduced a motion in the Quebec legislative assembly calling for a moratorium on large-scale immigration because of the dilatory effect it would have on French Canadians. Duplessis's use of the Jewish refugee bogey was quickly endorsed by right-wing newspapers such as *Le Bavard*:

> Evidently Mr. Duplessis stirred a hornet's nest when he dared to attack openly a Jewish project to invade our province. . . . It is enough to know the plan of the Jews and to follow the march of events in order to be convinced that a sinister and powerful organization does not hesitate to take in the dark all the possible means for the entire execution of the plan.[62]

Despite extensive and persuasive refutations of Duplessis's malicious propaganda, it was an important issue during the 1944 provincial election and a factor in the Union Nationale victory.[63]

Criticism of the movement of Jewish refugees emanated from another source – the Royal Canadian Mounted Police. The RCMP was particularly interested in the refugees sponsored by the Montreal Jewish Labor Committee (JLC). Indeed, in March, 1943, it requested assistance from the Federal Bureau of Investigation in checking certain JLC refugees against a "master list of known subversives maintained by the Bureau."[64] The RCMP was also interested in the status of the Jewish Labor Committee of New York City, which was affiliated with the JLC. Although both organizations were given a clean bill of health by the FBI, officials of the RCMP remained convinced that they were dealing with dangerous subversives. This message was quickly conveyed to the Immigration Branch by assistant commissioner F.C. Mead, who alleged that many JLC refugees appeared to have been affiliated with the Jewish Social Democratic Party in Poland, "an organization of revolutionaries, and although not connected with the Communist International, its aims are somewhat similar to the latter." The policy was obvious: reject all JLC-sponsored refugees.[65]

The movement of over 400 Jewish refugees from Lisbon in June, 1944, some of whom were sponsored by the Montreal Jewish Labor Committee, caused even more consternation for the RCMP. On June 1, 1944, Commissioner Wood wrote the Minister of Justice, Louis St. Laurent, expressing concern over the ability of the RCMP to ascertain "the bona fides of refugees entering Canada . . . with the object of preventing persons who might be enemy agents from taking up residence here." His complaints were both specific and general. The RCMP had received only a one-day notice prior to the arrival of 276 refugees in Halifax. No background information about the refugees had been forwarded by either British or American security agencies, and the Force did not have available "the skilled manpower to do an adequate job of screening." Wood reinforced his dire warning by pointing out that among the refugees there were at least four possible "Gestapo agents."[66]

St. Laurent took these warnings seriously and advised Norman Robertson that while it was "no doubt necessary to do whatever may be compatible with the safety of our State for the relief of persons persecuted in occupied Europe, there seems to be some danger that the admission of these refugees might be used for the purpose of introducing espionage agents in this country."[67] Robertson countered with the proposal for an interdepartmental committee composed of officials from External Affairs, the RCMP, and the Immigration Branch to investigate all incoming refugees. He also suggested that "complete information should be secured from the United Kingdom Security Organization as soon as possible concerning all people who have thus far been brought to this country."[68]

From the Canadian security point of view the problem of a refugee fifth column was substantially reduced in the fall of 1944 when the Lisbon screening office was closed and the movement of Jewish refugees from the Iberian Peninsula was curtailed. Immigration officials had no difficulty justifying this decision:

> . . . with the progress of the war refugees not actually in enemy hands are not now in danger of persecution or loss of life and that as the termination of the war might be expected within a reasonable period, a continuance of the movement of refugees to Canada would not be warranted; they would only reside in this country a comparatively short time before the question of return to Europe would have to be considered.[69]

At this juncture, the main concern of immigration officials and the RCMP was the post-war repatriation of those refugees who had been admitted only for the duration of the war. But this joint investigation soon proved to be a fiasco. In September, 1944, a somewhat embarrassed Commissioner Wood informed A.L. Jolliffe, the new director of immigration, that the RCMP could not even locate the majority of the 447 Jewish refugees brought from Lisbon in the spring and summer of 1944:

It was anticipated that we would be able to keep in touch with these people through the offices of the Canadian Jewish Congress and the Jewish Immigrants' Aid Society but we are now advised that these offices do not maintain contact with refugees who are not in receipt of assistance and, therefore, under the circumstances, it will not be possible for us to keep advised of the whereabouts of those refugees who are not enemy aliens. . . . the thought occurs that you may have some suggestion to make in this regard and your comments therein will be greatly appreciated.

Jolliffe was of little assistance, and all he could suggest was that the RCMP contact the Canadian National Committee on Refugees, which might "be able to furnish the addresses to which the individual families were directed."[70] Fortunately for all concerned, the repatriation procedures were not implemented after J. Allison Glen, the Minister responsible for immigration, urged that refugees admitted during the war be granted permanent residence.

Post-War Security: 1945-50

The security apparatus used to screen wartime refugees was greatly expanded after 1945. According to Reg Whitaker, who has written extensively on the subject, the post-war policies were different in that they provided for "the systematic application of specifically political criteria as a basis for mass exclusion from Canada of categories of persons."[71] Initially, most of the emphasis was placed on excluding Nazis, collaborators, and war criminals. All this changed by the spring of 1946 when revelations that a Soviet espionage ring had been operating in Canada, combined with the lingering fear of left-wing subversion, prompted the federal government to establish more rigorous apparatus for screening out Communists in the country. A Security Committee was established, which had as one of its functions the job of co-ordinating the task of keeping Communist subversives from Canadian shores. Under the umbrella of the new agency representatives of Immigration, Labour, External Affairs, and the RCMP came together to review policy in this important area. The Department of Justice was also consulted on "the question of authority for rejecting persons deemed undesirable on security grounds." By the end of September, 1946, RCMP officers were accompanying Canadian inspection teams to Europe in the hope that their own relative inexperience in counter-espionage would be offset by "the ready cooperation of the United Kingdom Passport Control Office in understanding the examination of any suspects."[72] These security officers soon found, however, that the vast workload (over 6,000 cases in the first month) and the slow rate of conducting effective file checks (about thirty cases a day) created an impossible situation. Yet the government was insistent that more

Communists be found among the ranks of the displaced persons who wanted to come to Canada. [73] On May 22, 1947, the cabinet authorized withholding, "without explanation," an immigration visa if the RCMP discovered that the prospective immigrant had "a record of Left Wing activities." The definition of such activities was left to the RCMP on the grounds that this fell within their area of expertise. [74]

Granting the RCMP such wide discretionary power over incoming refugees had many implications. One was the virtual exclusion of refugees from Soviet-controlled regions. While suspected Communists from France, Italy, and especially Britain fared somewhat better, they, too, were subjected to rigorous security checks. Canada's relationship with the International Refugee Organization (IRO) was also affected by RCMP complaints that the activities of the refugee organization were hampered by the "infiltration of communists and sympathizers." These complaints were repeated by Colonel Laval Fortier, associate commissioner of the Overseas Immigration Service, who warned Ottawa after his 1948 tour of Europe that Communist elements were trying to introduce "undesirables" into Canada. [75]

Bias against leftist refugees was evident in the high ratio rejected. It was also reflected in the support given anti-Communist refugees once they had arrived in Canada. [76] In the case of the 30,000 Ukrainian displaced persons, for instance, their arrival and saga helped expose the ULFTA's myths about the promise of Soviet life. Since many of these Ukrainian DPs were well educated and politically conscious, their arrival also "injected new life into and raised the morale of the nationalist camp." This, in turn, meant more frequent and violent conflict with the Ukrainian Communists. Although each side blamed the other for the violence, the RCMP had no difficulty identifying the culprits – the Communists. [77]

That the RCMP should have welcomed this support in their campaign against Ukrainian Communists is understandable. Yet surprisingly, Ukrainian anti-Communists received very little recognition or concessions from the government in return. This was most evident in the area of immigration. Throughout the years 1946-52 officials of the newly established Department of Citizenship and Immigration were generally hostile when the Ukrainian Canadian Committee lobbied on behalf of various "Ukrainian cultural workers and artists." The government rationale was simple and familiar: Ukrainian intellectuals would keep Old World cultures alive and thereby impede the further Canadianization of the Ukrainian community. Obviously, in the minds of many government officials, true loyalty was still equated – as it was in the 1914-19 period – with unhyphenated Canadianism. [78]

Conclusion

Canada had no real refugee policy during the Great Depression and World War Two. While the country did admit about 8,000 so-called refugees, this action was not in response to any broad international principle or specific national refugee program, such as evolved after 1945. On the contrary, those European refugees who slipped under and around the immigration gates did so only after overcoming formidable obstacles or because of their unique circumstances. Would Canada, for instance, have accepted 900 German and Austrian refugees in 1940 if they had not come as internees? Probably not, for during the war the government appeared more interested in looking after and using docile POWs than independent and assertive European refugees.

But was the policy restrictive primarily because so many of the refugees were Jews? The answer, on the whole, is yes. Less clear, however, is the extent to which the decisions of gatekeepers such as F.C. Blair of the Immigration Branch, W.T. Wood of the RCMP, and O.D. Skelton and Norman Robertson from External Affairs were motivated by anti-Semitism and xenophobia. During the war, Blair, for instance, was opposed to allowing any refugees into the country, whether they were Spaniards, Jews, Poles, Mennonites, or Czechs. In this regard, his position was similar to that of Breckenridge Long, who was in charge of the American State Department's Visa Division. Both saw refugees as creating administrative problems, a possible source of political controversy, and posing a threat to national security. And both found many powerful allies within the security agencies of their respective countries.[79]

It must be remembered, though, that these were desperate times. The men who staffed these agencies believed they had an awesome responsibility to protect their country from an unbelievably devious and ruthless Nazi adversary. In Canada, the leadership of the RCMP and the Immigration Branch assumed that in the national interest it would be better to reject all refugees rather than to allow a single Nazi or Soviet agent into the country. That this position was both morally wrong and often unnecessary, even from a security standpoint, does not change the fact that the arguments of Blair and Wood carried great weight in the War Committee of cabinet. Canada was at war, and its government was committed to military goals and humanitarian considerations. No doubt, the country's refugee policies were legalistic and cold, but these policies must be understood within the context of total war, which does not encourage fine distinctions.

After 1946, with the arrival of over 160,000 refugees and displaced persons into the country, it became difficult to administer the wartime security screening system. How to detect Communists, and for that matter former Nazis, severely tested the resources of all the Canadian security agencies. The advent of the Cold War did, however, provide further justification for keeping out the radicals.

CHAPTER 7

Altruism and Economic Self-Interest: Canada's Immigration Policy and European Displaced Persons, 1945-1952

In his autobiography, Hugh Keenleyside, a prominent public servant, reflected as follows on his years as co-ordinator of Canada's immigration policy between 1946 and 1950:

> Because each of its decisions involved the fate of at least one human being, the Immigration Service was the most difficult of all the branches with which I had to deal . . . the immediate impact of its rulings relating to admissions, exclusion or deportation [affected] . . . the future whole life of persons begging for admission to or permission to remain in Canada. Here the complex of fear, ambition, family welfare and other emotional factors, had to be measured against existing rules and plain human decency. [1]

In May, 1945, with the end of hostilities in Europe, the complex historical problems associated with Canada's policies toward refugees once again became a matter of concern to the Dominion government. At this stage, however, Canada's highest priorities were to carry out its alliance obligations in the war against Japan and to begin the repatriation and demobilization of its own armed forces in Europe. Nor did the country appear ready for a meaningful debate over post-war immigration policy. World War Two had exacerbated already serious economic and social problems at home, especially between English and French Canadians and between capital and labour. Fear of an impending return to the conditions of the Great Depression was also pervasive. There were many Canadians, therefore, who warned that the country could not afford the luxury of accepting "unproductive" immigrants or those who could not easily assimilate. [2]

On the other hand, Canada was no longer the quasi-isolationist nation of the 1930s that had been able to turn a blind eye to many aspects of international affairs. As a major military power, ranking third among the Western Allies in war production, and a founding member of the United Nations, Canada was, whether its people liked it or not, a player on the stage of world affairs. And in 1945 this meant, among other things, that the country was expected by its allies and indeed by many of its own people to respond positively to the immense problem of European refugees and displaced persons.[3] By September, 1945, the Western Allies were caring for nearly seven million people, and the Soviets claimed that they were looking after an equal number. Moreover, as fast as these refugees and displaced persons could be relocated within Germany or repatriated to their countries of origin, others took their places in the numerous DP camps that had been established.[4]

Endless processions of people trudged across the ruined Reich, sometimes with pathetic bundles of belongings, sometimes pushing handcarts, the ubiquitous refugees' conveyance, piled with household belongings. The roads . . . were like mountain torrents in the spring. Babel of people and languages. . . . Awe struck by the spectacle, Western observers feared a complete breakdown of public order in Central Europe, which was already facing acute shortages, the collapse of established authority, and severe deprivation.[5]

The Canadian government of William Lyon Mackenzie King was acutely aware of these dreadful conditions through the reports of its military and diplomatic officials; it also knew about them, perhaps more comprehensively, through the work of its representatives on the United Nations Relief and Rehabilitation Administration (UNRRA). Within Canada a wide range of ethnic organizations and the broadly based Canadian National Committee on Refugees appealed to the humanitarian instincts of the Canadian people and their elected representatives. When economic conditions remained buoyant after the war and the beneficial effects of the federal social security system had begun to be felt, Canadians became even more disposed to meet their humanitarian and international obligations. The familiar voice of the industrialists and the transportation companies exalting the advantages of a large-scale influx of immigrant workers was also heard. The result was that between 1946, when the movement of displaced persons began, until 1952, when the International Refugee Organization was phased out, over 100,000 DP workers came to Canada. These people, in turn, began sponsoring relatives from the IRO camps so that the total movement of displaced persons to Canada during these years is closer to 165,000. For its part, the United States, after the passage of the Displaced Persons Act of 1948, received about 329,000 refugees; at the same time Australia accepted 182,000 and the countries of western Europe about 170,000.[6]

So much for numbers. These tell part of the story, but the saga of displaced persons in Canada involves much more than statistics and immigration regulations. While the most contentious aspects of Canada's refugee policy are associated with the pre-1945 period, insightful studies by Gerald Dirks, Milda Danys, Reg Whitaker, and Irving Abella and Harold Troper have raised a number of important questions about post-war policies.[7] To what extent, for example, did Canadian immigration and foreign policy priorities coincide in these years? How were various groups of displaced persons affected by the occupational selection criteria and security screening methods employed by the government? Did the economic utilization of DP workers conform to the traditional role of "alien" labour in this country? And, were the victims of war accepted by Canadians and provided with the opportunity to rebuild their shattered lives?

Redefining Refugee Policy

Changes in Canada's immigration policies after World War Two were in response to important domestic and international developments. While Canadians remained wary about accepting large numbers of refugees, especially if they were Jewish, there were indications that the country was gradually discarding xenophobic and racist policies. This was reflected in the Ontario Racial Discrimination Act, passed in 1944, which began the process of enshrining human rights laws.[8] The 1947 repeal of the noxious Chinese Immigration Act and the enfranchisement of Canadian Chinese were also important steps in the right direction.[9] So, too, was the belated decision not to repatriate thousands of Japanese Canadians, although the government was swayed more by political arguments than humanitarian considerations.[10]

Canada's involvement in the work of the United Nations Relief and Rehabilitation Administration from its founding in Atlantic City in 1942 until its dissolution in 1947 also helped move the country away from its restrictionist immigration policies. Certainly the idealistic side of the Canadian character was very much in evidence when Lester Pearson, already one of Canada's most important diplomats, spoke as follows at Atlantic City:

> [if] UNRRA . . . should fail or falter in its tasks, much more will be lost than relief for the liberated lands. The cause of international collaboration itself would suffer. If UNRRA, which makes its appeal both to our highest feelings of human compassion and to our instinct of enlightened self interest, cannot prove by its actions that nations can work together, effectively and harmoniously, then, believe me, the outlook for international peace and progress is bleak indeed.[11]

Canadian policy toward UNRRA was not entirely based on altruism; it also sought to fulfil certain economic goals. The new organization, through its purchases in Canada, would stimulate production and prevent unemployment. The dimension of UNRRA was well understood by many economic interest groups within the country, including the Canadian Manufacturers' Association, the Retail Merchants Association, and various farm organizations. In a June, 1944, editorial *The Country Guide* had declared that "UNRRA was very important to Canada. . . . We're the country with the groceries." Not surprisingly, therefore, the UNRRA Agreement was unanimously endorsed by Parliament in June, 1943. M.J. Coldwell, leader of the Co-operative Commonwealth Federation, caught the mood of the House of Commons when he called UNRRA "a stepping stone to peace." Between 1943 and 1947 Canada contributed approximately $154 million for international relief; during the same period UNRRA purchased more than $254 million worth of Canadian goods. Canada was also an active participant in the three major sessions of UNRRA that formulated its policies and procedures; in fact, the second session was held in Montreal in June, 1944. At the third such meeting, held in London in August, 1945, the focus of the organization was the desperate situation in liberated Europe. On this occasion Lester Pearson left little doubt about the commitment of his government to extend help to the best of its ability:

As President Truman said on Thursday last: 'As the winter comes on the distress will be increased. Unless we do what we can to help, we may lose next winter what we won at terrible cost last spring. We must help to the very limits of our strength, and we will!' Speaking for my own country – Canada – may I repeat those words? We must help to the very limits of our strength, and we will. [12]

In keeping with these views, Canada endorsed UNRRA's decision to assume official responsibility for administering the needs of almost one million displaced persons in the fall of 1945. It was an awesome undertaking. [13] By June, 1947, UNRRA, through its 762 camps, provided food, clothing, shelter, and medical care to myriad desperate people. Equally challenging were the attempts to reunite families separated by war and exile. Messages, often accompanied by photographs, were placed in railway stations and in the camps: "This is my husband. I have had no word from him for four years. Does anyone know where he is now or whether he is still among the living." [14]

The original UNRRA mandate had assumed that the displaced would eventually return to their homelands. By 1946, however, it was clear that at least one million were either unwilling or unable to consider repatriation. [15] At this juncture two major issues came to divide the U.S.S.R. from the Western Allies. The first of these was whether the Soviet Union, as one of the countries devastated by the war, qualified for extensive UNRRA relief? The American Congress and public thought not. The other divisive issue was whether or not UNRRA should extend individual relief to those displaced persons who were refusing to return to their countries of origin, most of which were now under Soviet control. After subtle prodding from the United States, most members of the UNRRA council agreed that the displaced persons could remain wards of the United Nations until resettled. Undoubtedly, the revulsion felt over Russia's brutal treatment of persons forcibly repatriated under the Yalta Agreement was a factor in this decision.[16] Against this background of debate and division, UNRRA was scuttled in 1947, whereupon European refugees became the responsibility of a new body the Soviets did not join, the International Refugee Organization.[17]

Canada's transfer of allegiance from UNRRA and from the older Intergovernmental Committee on Refugees to the International Refugee Organization was achieved without difficulty administratively.[18] There was, however, some apprehension in Ottawa about the implications of the IRO's aggressive campaign to resettle most of the remaining 844,000 displaced persons in the Western democracies. But the IRO's emphasis on the economic utility of the DP worker and its emerging role as an "international employment agency" appealed to Canada's self-interest and was introduced at a moment when the country was reviewing its whole immigration policy. Of central importance was the exclusionist 1931 order-in-council that had confined eligibility to (a) British subjects and American citizens; (b) wives and unmarried children under 18 and fiancées of Canadian residents; (c) agriculturalists having sufficient means to farm in Canada.[19]

This review had already been launched in October, 1945, when a report submitted by J. Allison Glen, the Minister responsible for immigration, had recommended that the 3,500 refugees admitted during the war should be granted permanent residency.[20] In his report Glen particularly complimented 665 Polish engineers and technicians for having "rendered faithful and valuable service connected with the war effort" and, by implication, suggested that other such refugees would make good Canadian citizens.[21] Significantly, in 1946 another group of Polish refugees – 4,000 officers and men who had fought under General Anders with the British in the Italian campaign – became the first test case of Canadian post-war intentions.

Ottawa ultimately agreed to accept these men and their dependants for two reasons: one was that it would help to extricate the British government from a most awkward situation; the other was to fill a temporary gap in the agricultural labour force caused by the departure of POW agriculturalists.[22] Hume Wrong of External Affairs patiently explained all this to the Minister of Labour:

> It was suggested to the Prime Minister that by agreeing to take demobilized Polish soldiers in return for the German prisoners-of-war we would be getting a supply of heavy labour of a type which is in considerable demand, and that the movement, which might run to three or four thousand, would make an appreciable beginning on the very difficult task of

disposing of the large forces of Polish soldiers in Western Europe who, for understandable reasons, are unwilling to return to Poland. The fact that the Polish soldiers would be coming to Canada as agricultural labourers or lumber workers to take the place specifically of German prisoners-of-war who would be shipped back, would diminish or remove the danger of political controversy. In the ordinary course most of the Poles who are of the type from which a good part of our useful immigration has come, would probably settle here as valuable citizens.[23]

Canada proved less willing, though, when the British suggested that a number of Jewish refugees be admitted to the country to relieve some of the pressure of the Palestine problem.[24] Nor was Canada to be pushed along by the American president of UNRRA, Fiorello La Guardia. According to Pearson, he could be expected to argue "that countries such as Canada and the United States which have been so generous in forwarding food and supplies . . . should be at least a half or quarter as generous in receiving into their countries the persons who have been most tragically dealt with by the war."[25]

At this stage External Affairs officials were also concerned that they differentiate effectively between "the genuine refugee and the political agitator who may have laid himself open to the charge of treachery by collaborating with the enemy"; the groups most suspected in this latter regard were Ukrainians, Poles, and Yugoslavs. Members of these groups, it was argued, would be undesirable citizens, especially if they continued "their political activities in their new homes." For their part, Polish and Yugoslav diplomats in Ottawa charged that many, if not most, of their nationals who now sought sanctuary in Canada had either served in the Waffen SS or in concentration camps. These spokesmen also took exception to the idea that Canada should regard their former nationals "as a human reservoir upon which [it] could draw . . . without approval."[26]

By the fall of 1946, however, the Canadian government was no longer listening to such criticism as public opinion swung sharply in favour of a more generous refugee policy. This trend was clearly evident in newspaper editorials across the country. On July 26, the Winnipeg *Tribune* argued that "Agricultural workers are still short in Canada, so short that German prisoners of war continue to be used. The coming of the Poles will do nothing to take scarce jobs from Canadians, and they will not undercut prevailing wage rates, at least not for two years that they must serve as agricultural workers." The Toronto *Globe and Mail* likewise approved of the arrival of the Poles, but questioned the motives of the Canadian government:

We have no reason to doubt . . . that the decision was arrived at because of the need for a quick labour force, rather than through any desire to assist these refugee troops in their political predicament. There can be no quarrel with the conditions under which these men may achieve eventual citizenship. But neither can it be supposed that this is even [a] beginning of an intelligent program of immigration.

But perhaps the most telling comment came from the Owen Sound *Sun Times*, which set forth the traditional Anglo-Canadian view that European immigrants should begin their Canadian odyssey on the bottom rungs of the occupational ladder: "If . . . we find these hard-working immigrants accepting employment at wages or under conditions which Canadian-born citizens are reluctant to accept, there should be no outcry against these immigrants for accepting a lower standard of living. . . . They are being brought to this country on the condition that they do exactly this."[27]

Thus it was that in 1946, after a hiatus of sixteen years, Canada once again began to accept large numbers of European immigrant workers.[28] In August of that year, the cabinet recommended that an independent inquiry should be made into the possibilities "of extending to other groups the policy adopted in admitting 4,000 selected Poles for agricultural labour." The Senate Immigration and Labour Committee carried out this work, and by the middle of October, 1946, it had held ten meetings, examined thirty-four witnesses, and considered twenty-four briefs. Traditional immigration boosters such as the Canadian Pacific Railway and the Canadian National Railways lauded the advantages of larger-scale immigration.[29] Organized labour was more cautious but came out in favour of "selective immigration designed to . . . increase employment and . . . to solve the refugee problem." Representatives of the Canadian Congress of Labour did, however, warn that the level of intake should correspond with job opportunities and that Canadian workers should not be displaced. Trades and Labour president Percy Benough was even more blunt: post-war immigration policy should exclude "certain nationals who have in the past been admitted into Canada [who] remain as a distinct race and will remain a problem for future generations."[30]

The most bitter comments came from rival Ukrainian, Polish, and Yugoslav organizations who presented diametrically opposed views of both the character of the potential refugees and their likely value to Canadian society.[31] In contrast, the message of the Canadian National Committee on Refugees was an unqualified endorsement of a generous refugee policy.[32] Both in its appearances before the Senate Committee and in direct submissions to Prime Minister King the CNCR mixed arguments based on altruism with those stressing economic self-interest and the diverse skills and strong backs of the DP workers. Canada, it was held, should move into the displaced persons market first and therefore get the "cream of the crop":

Eventually these Displaced Persons must be settled somewhere and presumably it will be an international responsibility for which Canada will have a share. If this resettlement on an international basis is postponed for some time, the most desirable persons will have been selected by other nations and those who are left will have been so long in camps that it will be difficult for them to adjust to normal life. It seems, therefore, that it would be to Canada's advantage to take some initiative in selecting future immigrants from this group promptly.[33]

By the fall of 1946 the Canadian government was aware of both the humanitarianism and self-interest of the British, Australian, and American governments toward displaced persons. Not surprisingly, given its location and its post-war priorities, Britain had taken the lead in tapping this diverse source of labour. In 1946, under the European Volunteer Worker Program, some 77,000 displaced persons, 88,000 Polish veterans, and 8,000 Ukrainian former POWs were admitted after medical and security screening. Preference was given to "men of labouring type who are hardy and of good physical standard" who signed a labour contract stipulating that they would accept jobs arranged for them by the British Ministry of Labour.[34] This contract system for DPs greatly impressed Australian immigration authorities, who had decided that large-scale European immigration was the key to future industrial development.[35] The rationale for this bold change in policy was provided by Australian Minister of Immigration Arthur Calwell in an urgent July, 1947, letter from London:

Other countries are keen competitors for best migrant types and unless we act quickly we may lose our opportunities of securing migrants on selection basis . . . we would select types specially suitable for rural work, nursing and domestic work in hospitals, labour for our reconstruction . . . developmental projects. Selection will be on general suitability for work to be performed, after IRO and British security have satisfied our medical and security requirements.[36]

The advantages of obtaining the best DP workers also impressed Canadians.[37] Within the cabinet a diverse pro-immigration lobby had emerged. The key player was Clarence Decatur Howe, the Minister of Reconstruction, who had "long been bullish on the economy" and who agreed with his corporate friends that immigrant workers were good for Canada. At the same time, officials of External Affairs, concerned with Canada's international image and the enormity of the refugee problem, pressured the Prime Minister from another direction. Jimmy Gardiner, Minister of Agriculture, conveyed the message that western farmers wanted immigrant labour and lots of it. The appointment of Hugh Keenleyside as deputy minister of mines and resources was another important factor; his instincts were liberal and humanitarian, and under his direction the Immigration Branch of his department would soon emphasize recruitment rather than exclusion.[38] In October, 1946, the Department of Labour, which had grown in importance during the war, provided cabinet with a lengthy report, "Occupational Needs That Might Be Met By Immigration." This strongly endorsed the recruitment of immigrant workers to meet the needs of Canada's staple industries:

> agriculture as a field of employment has several disadvantages which make it unattractive when alternative opportunities are available. Much of the employment is seasonal. Agricultural wages also have in the past been lower than in many other occupations. . . . It seems doubtful therefore whether all those Canadians who left agriculture since 1930 will be willing to return.

The forest industry in the country could also be helped in this way: "French Canadians and various immigrant groups have made up a large proportion of Canadian loggers in the past. If the industry cannot be made more attractive and if high employment is to be maintained throughout the Canadian economy, it may be that the deficit of loggers can most easily be made up by immigration." Yet another industry starved for labour was mining. In both coal and metalliferous mines employment was well below the 1939 level despite vastly increased output, relatively high wages, and good opportunities for steady work. The problem was that this "hard, dirty, dangerous work" was not attractive to most Anglo-Canadians; the immigration of DP workers seemed "the logical solution."[39]

Despite all these pressures to open the immigration gates wider, Mackenzie King remained cautious. This was evident in a statement on refugees he made in the House of Commons on May 1, 1947: "The policy of the government is to foster the growth of the population of Canada by the encouragement of immigration. The government will seek by legislation, regulation and vigorous administration to ensure the careful selection and permanent settlement of immigrants as can be advantageously absorbed by our national economy." King also emphasized on this occasion, sending a pointed message to the persistent IRO, that immigration remained above all a matter of domestic policy and subject to the control of Parliament: "An alien has no fundamental right to enter Canada. This is a privilege. The people of Canada do not wish to make a fundamental alteration in the character of their population through mass immigration."[40] As a master political tactician, King's careful approach no doubt took account of an underlying fear among many Canadians that their country might become "a dumping ground for dissatisfied people."[41] He might have been influenced by negative comments of French-Canadian politicians such as Liguori Lacombe, the independent member for Laval-Two Mountains who charged that "when 200,000 people are unemployed our duty is to solve this distressing problem rather than make it worse through immigration."[42] King had to consider as well the ramifications of Premier George Drew's dramatic airlift of over 7,000 British immigrants to Ontario, which the *Globe and Mail* had hailed as a "conquest of the lethargy and defeatism of the Dominion Government."[43]

In keeping with the Prime Minister's desire to reassure the public, the government admitted the displaced persons by orders-in-council with an eye to particular employment conditions.[44] No major change was made in the regulations of the Immigration Act except for the deletion of PC 695, which had prohibited the entry of contract labour. The tap had been opened, but clearly it could just as quickly be closed. The administrative vehicle for carrying out government policy was the interdepartmental Immigration-Labour Committee, established on March 27, 1947. Its purpose was to advise the cabinet Committee on Immigration and to maintain an effective liaison with the major sectors of the Canadian economy.[45]

Between 1947 and 1952 representatives of the joint Immigration-Labour Committee consulted with various economic organizations. Groups heard from included the Canadian Manufacturers' Association, the Canadian Forestry Association, the Canadian Metal Mining Association, the Canadian Dressmakers Association, and the Canadian Sugar Beet Growers Association. Most of the displaced persons destined for agricultural jobs were handled by the Dominion-Provincial Farm Labour Administration, which came under the Department of Labour. In March, 1947, a report was submitted to cabinet by the Immigration-Labour Committee proposing an elaborate Bulk Labour Program that would facilitate the movement of displaced persons from the European camps to the Canadian workplace. This would involve the IRO, the federal government, and major trade associations in the country. Under the system the refugees would commit themselves to a specific Canadian employer for two years. In return they would receive free transportation (paid jointly by the IRO and the employer) and would be guaranteed employment and the possibility of permanent residence. If they fulfilled their contractual obligations they could sponsor their dependants. The Committee was aware, however, that this whole scheme might be subject to public criticism for the following reasons:

1. Restricts the freedom of the immigrant accepting any employment he wishes.
2. Would require an expensive administrative organization for handling placements and follow-up of the immigrants.
3. Would be difficult to enforce.
4. Canada has not required such undertakings, with the exception of the Polish veterans, in the past.

Yet in the Committee's view the advantages of the new plan far exceeded any of the problems it might entail.

1. The administration problem could be overcome by using the National Employment Service . . . this agency does much of its work, particularly farm placement, in cooperation with the provinces. . . .

2. In respect to the immigrant not fulfilling his obligations, when it is recalled that the new arrivals would look upon the obligation as a contract with the Government, it is very doubtful if there would be very much difficulty in bringing about fulfilment of the obligation. In any event, the National Employment Service could make it very difficult for the men to obtain a position in an urban community.

3. The undertaking should appeal to organized labour which has a direct interest in workers entering Canada especially for employment in those industries where unions are well developed.

4. . . . the undertaking would enable all such additions to the national working force to be dealt with more systematically. This could be done positively, through the initial placements and through subsequent transfers, during the initial two-year period, to the employment within the industry where the services of the immigrants were most required; and, negatively, through preventing the immigrants from entering areas or other industries where there is actual or potential unemployment.[46]

These arguments prevailed and the Bulk Labour Program was endorsed by cabinet. The system was the administrative responsibility of the Department of Labour, which was to work closely with the Immigration Branch. Unfortunately, as matters developed, this departmental interaction was often marred by bitter jurisdictional disputes, complicated by personality conflict at the deputy minister level. At issue were both the selection and placement processes. In his memoirs Hugh Keenleyside gave his version of what happened:

> The Department of Labour, which under its leadership at that time was sometimes more reluctant than the labour unions to agree to the admission of persons whose placement might prove difficult, was at first officially hesitant and unofficially strongly critical. . . . In contrast, it is interesting how little general opposition there was to the expanded movement of immigrants to Canada.[47]

But hindsight can be misleading. Certainly the historical evidence does not warrant such a cursory dismissal of the role assumed by the Department of Labour. In negotiations with the various trade associations that department proved quite adept at reconciling the requirements of both employers and displaced persons. A case in point is to be found in the interaction with the Canadian Metal Mining Association (CMMA). Under a September, 1947, agreement with the Immigration-Labour Committee the CMMA became in effect a clearinghouse for requests from its constituent corporate members for immigrant labour. The Association also now assumed responsibility for sending selection teams to

Europe in order to maintain industry standards of skill and strength. When the DPs arrived in Canada, CMMA representatives directed them toward "the mine to which they had been assigned."[48]

From the point of view of the Canadian mining industry this system seems to have worked very well.[49] On the other hand, there were periodic complaints that some of the selection teams sent to the DP camps tended to be preoccupied with the skill and strength of the DP rather than with his human dignity. In September, 1948, an IRO camp director gave this account of one such incident:

> On Friday afternoon on 24th September 1947, Mr. Sharrer (representative of the Dept. of Labour and Mr. Bennett from the CMMA) arrived at Trofaiach Camp Steiermark to pre-select Metal Miners for Canada. The persons to be interviewed had been waiting for some considerable time and were standing around in small groups talking and smoking. . . . Mr. Sharrer told them to line up on the open road in open file . . . then walked down the centre looking persons up and down and in some cases feeling their muscles and finally selected three persons out of a total of twenty-eight applicants.

The following day the national group leaders from the camp came and laid complaints to the resettlement officer about this incident and asked if it was essential that their fellow men be treated like so many cattle. This report was forwarded by IRO headquarters to the Canadian government with a strong plea for remedial action:

> We feel sure . . . the Canadian representatives will realize the most unfortunate effect such a display has on the refugees and on the IRO resettlement programmes generally, but in particular on the Canadian Government's representatives, who so far enjoy such a high reputation among the refugees. Finally, you will no doubt appreciate the forceful propaganda which could be circulated detrimental both to IRO and the Canadian Government if such incidents were to come to the notice of certain antagonistic powers.[50]

Canada was also accused of having a refugee policy that was in practice anti-Semitic, especially in the design and application of the selection standards. Representatives of the Canadian Jewish Congress were dismayed that neither the Close Relative Scheme nor the Bulk Labour Program would assist many European Jews in gaining entry to Canada.[51] Specifically, the Congress complained that Jewish candidates for positions as domestics, farmers, and lumber workers were being passed over in favour of other ethnic groups. Irving Abella and Harold Troper's *None Is Too Many* gives this account of how the anti-Jewish bias worked:

Refugee officials had brought many Jewish woodworkers forward for interviews, and the Canadian government had advised its team to accept a few Jews in order to maintain the fiction of non-discrimination. One had to give a little to get a lot. Forest-industry representatives, whose labour needs the teams were filling, disagreed, however, and they stalled selections. . . . Immigration and Labour Department authorities . . . fell in line behind the industry. A solicitous commissioner of immigration assured industry leaders that any effort to force Jews on the industry would be investigated fully and nipped at the bud.[52]

But were these rejections solely because the applicants were Jewish? Abella and Troper say yes, and claim that the occupational arguments were merely a screen, part of an elaborate system used by the immigration gatekeepers since the 1930s. They also indicate, however, that in 1947 Canadian public opinion, as revealed in a Gallup poll, was still sharply divided as to whether the country should accept any immigrants at all except from Great Britain. Moreover, they quote a confidential UNRRA report on Canadian attitudes that claimed "that Jewish D.P.'s . . . rated lower than the Japanese in public fancy."[53]

Their points are well taken. But it could also be argued that Canadian immigration policy, as applied to white immigrants, was based on more complex selection criteria than the Jew-Gentile dichotomy. The elaborate ranking of preferred and non-preferred immigrants, which was the fundamental administrative blueprint prior to 1930, was based on both cultural background and occupational orientation. Jews, along with Armenians, Italians, and Greeks, had previously, in varying degrees, been categorized as non-preferred immigrants for these reasons and they tended to retain that status after 1945. No doubt this was based on negative cultural stereotypes, but it also related to the exacting occupational and physical standards that Canadian employers had traditionally applied to their "foreign workers."[54] The *Northern Miner*, the organ of the Ontario mining industry, described the attributes of the new "crop" of DP miners in the following editorial:

The 2300 displaced persons coming to Canadian mines are a husky lot who should make good miners and citizens. . . . The men were first selected on the basis of physical appearances with broad shoulders and chests a requisite. The next stop was an x-ray test. This was followed by Canadian security officers thoroughly checking the men for political beliefs, past records and so on. Any suspected of communist leanings were disbarred. . . . All the men are between 18 and 35 years of age. They are Baltic, Ukrainian and Polish nationalities. To qualify for entry all d.p.'s must be literate. . . .[55]

As this passage reveals, there were three major reasons for rejection at either the German DP camp or the Canadian mine site. High on the list were lack of good health and insufficient physical stamina. In 1948, for example, it was reported that out of 200 DP miners seeking jobs at Timmins, Ontario, only twenty-two passed the company medicals. Angry that so many of its candidates were rejected, the Canadian Metal Mining Association demanded to know how "so many men with obvious defects got by the Immigration doctors."[56]

Michael Marrus's study, *The Unwanted: European Refugees in the Twentieth Century*, provides at least a partial explanation of why so many Jewish applicants were vulnerable to medical screening: "In reality, the experiences of these Jews made it impossible for them to think and behave like other displaced persons. A vast gulf of agony and humiliation yawned between them and the rest of humanity. Prematurely aged, weak, and suffering from extreme malnutrition, many presented a ghastly appearance. . . . (Allied) Soldiers sometimes contrast the Jews – demoralized, brutalized, and half starved – with the healthier, well-scrubbed, or better organized Balts or other groups."[57]

There was also a tendency within the Canadian Immigration-Labour bureaucracy to equate certain types of jobs with certain types of immigrants. For instance, "Balts" – Estonians, Latvians, and Lithuanians – were regarded as excellent lumber workers and domestics while Ukrainians and Poles, the "stalwart peasants" of yesterday, were still thought of as people who would till the soil and work in the mines, despite their high degree of education.[58] Italians, it was believed, would make poor farmers but good construction workers. Jews were viewed as essentially urban and not used to hard labour; they would probably only be successful in Canada as "garment workers, furriers, dressmakers and milliners."[59]

Another factor in the Canadian selection process, arising out of King's 1947 parliamentary statement, was the attempt to reassure various patriotic and nativist groups that post-war immigration would not effect major changes "in the existing ratios of the Canadian population." Hugh Keenleyside told the interdepartmental Immigration-Labour Committee that "in view of . . . the recent admission to Canada of considerable numbers of persons of Polish and Jewish race, and of Catholic faith, it would be desirable in the present instance to give priority to persons who do not fall within these categories." Similar instructions were given to the Department of Labour selection team dispatched to Germany:

It is essential that in selecting Displaced Persons, great care be exercised to insure a reasonable division of nationalities. No doubt the great majority of the persons selected for woods labour operations will be Balts and Estonians and this group should be particularly suitable from the point of view of assimilation. It is felt advisable, however, to include in this a number of Ukrainians, as such action will be favourably received in some quarters here.[60]

Mine managers and lumber company executives were also anxious that in the interests of industrial and community harmony the selection teams should recruit "immigrants of the same nationality and political outlook . . . as the men now in the various areas." What they really meant was that they did not want Communists.[61] By contrast, despite a cabinet directive of 1946 that no former Nazis or Nazi collaborators would ever be admitted to Canada, members of this group did find their way into Canadian jobs.[62]

Until 1950 it was difficult for German nationals (*reichsdeutsche*) to gain entry, despite the lobbying efforts of various religious and humanitarian organizations. The problem was twofold: their exclusion from Canada because of their enemy alien status; their exclusion from IRO consideration because they were not classified as statutory refugees. Canadian public opinion also remained hostile toward German immigrants. This, however, was gradually changing. A Gallup poll of October, 1946, showed that only 34 per cent of Canadians regarded them as "undesirable," well below the 60 per cent and 49 per cent hostility toward possible Japanese and Jewish immigrants.[63] By 1948 German immigrants were being described in the press and in the House of Commons as "responsible, hard-working and industrious" and as "good agriculturalists." Senator Horner of Alberta went so far as to claim that Alberta sugar-beet growers "would prefer one German worker . . . to ten . . . Poles."[64]

In 1946 the most pressing problem was to find ways of assisting the nearly ten million ethnic Germans, or *volksdeutsche*, who had been expelled from eastern Europe. Since neither the IRO nor the Canadian government was willing to become officially involved in this rescue mission, responsibility shifted to voluntary organizations. In Canada this meant the Canadian Christian Council for the Resettlement of Refugees (CCCRR), a coalition of churches and transportation interests.[65] By 1950 the CCCRR managed to transport and place about 21,000 *volksdeutsche* with the unofficial blessing of the Immigration Branch.[66]

The February, 1948, Communist coup in Czechoslovakia created another dilemma for Canadian policy-makers: what to do about self-proclaimed democratic anti-Communists who wanted to enter Canada. The government was sharply divided on the nature of Canada's response. The mandarins of External Affairs called for a major effort to assist "democratic anti-communist refugees," especially the diplomats and intellectuals among them who, despite their many talents, did not qualify for admission under existing immigration regulations. But Hugh Keenleyside, while deeply moved by the plight of the displaced intellectuals and anxious to co-operate with his former colleagues at External Affairs, had many reservations about bringing such people into the country:

Most of the people in question are without financial resources, or very thinly supplied. They are, moreover, not of the type that can be relied upon to rustle for themselves. Professional men, and particularly ex-diplomats, do not readily find or easily accept the kind of jobs that are commonly available for immigrants. As you know we have had already a number of cases of foreign diplomats who have been rather serious problems here in Ottawa. As an ex-member of the profession, I may perhaps be forgiven if I suggest that the average diplomat is not likely to be very much use at anything else – particularly at the kind of initial jobs that are commonly available for immigrants. [67]

The attitude of Canadian immigration authorities toward the entry of large numbers of religious and clerical personnel was also unfavourable. This reflected a long-standing sense in government that such people, by helping to keep Old World cultures alive, were impeding Canadianization. In 1948, strong representation was made by the Ukrainian Canadian Committee, one of the few ethnic organizations with official status with the Immigration Branch in regard to its distribution of displaced persons within Canada, on behalf of the admission of a certain number of Ukrainian intellectuals:

> We feel that by the admittance of Ukrainian cultural workers and artists, their activities will be leading to the creating of the mosaic of Canadian culture which we all hope that Canada will have some day. . . . It must be pointed out that in the near future most of the intellectuals and specialists will be given an opportunity to emigrate. It would be a pity if Canada would not be able to get her share. [68]

The UCC also pressed hard for the admission of a group of Ukrainian DPs who had been consistently rejected by Canadian immigration officials – 8,000 members of the Halychyna Division who had been captured in Italy in German uniforms. According to the UCC brief, these "unfortunate men" had served in the German army "in order to free the Ukraine from Russian Communist domination," and when they had been transferred to the Western Front "they had surrendered almost en masse." This argument was not well received by the government; Keenleyside replied that Canada only accepted those who had not taken "an active part in the war against us." Despite the continual lobbying on this issue by the UCC and several Ukrainian MPs, members of the Halychyna Division were excluded until the spring of 1950, when Canada reversed its position on the matter of enemy aliens. [69]

Under the terms of orders-in-council PC 1606 and PC 1608 of March, 1950, and PC 4364 of September of the same year German immigrants could no longer be automatically excluded as enemy aliens. It also legalized the status of those

Germans who were already in the country, most notably the sponsored relatives and the 21,000 *volksdeutsche*. What was more contentious was that now "mere service in the German Army" no longer was the basis for exclusion. Nor, for that matter, was "nominal" connection with the Nazi Party the basis for exclusion. Left in a separate category were persons who had been in the elite military and security apparatus of the Third Reich. Within this group were former members of the Gestapo and the Schutzstaffel (SS), as well as concentration camp guards and other "important and dangerous Nazis." On the other hand, those who had been associated with the Abwehr, German military intelligence, were acceptable. In contrast, the Waffen SS was arbitrarily divided into two categories: those who had joined before January 1, 1943, were regarded as Nazi volunteers and therefore excluded; those who joined after January 1, 1943, were assumed to be conscripts and therefore theoretically admissible to Canada.[70] This reassessment had several important ramifications. Within a year over 35 per cent of the prospective immigrants who had been rejected by the RCMP on the grounds of their involvement in the German military had successfully appealed to the Minister of Citizenship and Immigration and had the door to Canada open to them. This happened despite the bitter opposition of the RCMP and the Canadian Jewish Congress.[71]

Professional Refugees: 1946-1952

The special problems facing displaced persons who were intellectuals and professionals were a matter of great concern for the IRO, and in September, 1947, it called a special meeting to consider new strategies. For specialists such as doctors, dentists, and engineers, whose skills were less affected by cultural factors, it was recommended that special qualification boards be established by the IRO to facilitate placement. For others, the solution was vocational re-training. IRO officials did, however, recognize that in some industrialized nations they would encounter "very strong opposition in professional circles" to the placement of "the white collars."[72] In Canada, organizations such as the CNCR made a determined effort to champion the cause of the DP professional; its success rate was not high.

This exclusionist impulse was not unique to Canadian professional associations. In Australia and the United States, DP professionals also encountered great difficulty in resuming their careers. One study estimates that while both countries received about the same percentage of DP professionals (6 per cent of the total), the rate of acceptance varied. "By the end of the first year in America one graduate in three was employed in a professional or semi-professional capacity, while in Australia only one in seven was so fortunate." The Canadian situation appears to parallel the Australian.[73]

Circumstances were particularly dismal for European medical doctors, whose credentials and training were usually judged inadequate by organizations such as the Ontario College of Physicians and Surgeons (OCPS) and the Canadian Medical Association (CMA). In his memoirs Keenleyside described this situation: "Perhaps the most adamant trade union official in opposition to the admission of competitive displaced persons was the medical association."[74] Not surprisingly, DP doctors were aggrieved about attitudes and practices they felt were ungenerous and unfair.

Officials of the OCPS and CMA emphasized their sacred trust to protect the public from unqualified and incompetent medical practitioners. And this task, they argued, was difficult to fulfil given the myriad professional degrees and references the newcomers presented. That is not to say that they were unaware of the commitments that organizations such as the World Medical Association (WMA) and the British Commonwealth Medical Association had made on behalf of DP doctors. Indeed, in September, 1948, CMA secretary Dr. T.A. Routley had participated in a WMA conference where Dr. R.L. Coigney of the IRO had appealed for all countries "to allow the refugee physician to practise his art after passing new examinations and obtaining his naturalization."[75] While these arguments were appreciated, others within the CMA, most notably its assistant secretary, wondered why "the government of Canada will so disregard its international obligations that refugee physicians will be admitted to Canada, when all indications point to the wisdom of settling them in the needy areas of the globe."[76] Canada's medical establishment, however, like its Australian counterpart, was prepared to see DP doctors practise in the frontier regions. For those unwilling to take jobs Canadian medical practitioners didn't want, there was a lengthy obstacle course "designed not so much to test the applicants' knowledge as to try their nerve and endurance."[77]

The movement and placement of DP professionals to Canada improved after February, 1949, when the Canadian government agreed to accept some of the 25,000 who still remained in the German and Austrian camps and arrangements were made for an interdepartmental committee to administer the program.[78] Among the professionals, the following groups[79] were represented:

university professors	5,213
engineers	2,998
lawyers	1,414
clergymen	1,140
agronomists	1,238
doctors (physicians and surgeons)	605
dentists	539
pharmacists	550

One motive for this more enlightened policy was altruism; another was self-interest. By 1949 many more Canadians believed that their country would "greatly benefit by the admission of 'brains', to balance an immigration consisting almost exclusively of manual labour." Or put another way, "It would be easier to explain this apparent ban on brains if the world had no more bridges to be designed and built by engineers, no more sick people to be healed, no more work for agronomists and soil chemists."[80]

With the active support of a variety of voluntary organizations the federal government established a new sponsorship system whereby individual displaced persons would be supported until they became established in Canadian society.[81] Although the initial number of candidates was only 500, there was a promise of additional places if the original contingent could find jobs.[82] This, however, remained difficult, as Keenleyside explained to the Immigration-Labour Committee at its July, 1949, meeting. "Lawyers would have to become . . . law clerks. . . . Teachers could only be absorbed as clerical workers," and medical professionals could only practise "in rural districts where doctors and dentists were badly needed." The future was deemed even more dismal for university professors, since Canadian universities, "which had formerly been willing, and in some cases eager, to recruit staff from among the displaced intellectuals, were now faced with the necessity of reducing their staffs."[83]

German Scientists

While DP professionals waited anxiously to discover whether they could come to Canada, another group of European professionals had already been granted both access and jobs. Although relatively small in number – only forty-four by October, 1950 – the recruitment of these German scientists and technicians tends to reinforce the thesis that Canada's immigration policy in these years had a definite double standard.[84]

The possibility of accepting German scientists had been given only cursory consideration during the late 1930s when most of the applicants were Jewish. Nor was the response any more enlightened during the war years. By September, 1946, a different view prevailed. This was evident when the NRC president, C.J. Mackenzie, informed C.D. Howe that his organization "would now favour the bringing to Canada of a few well vetted scientists for specific work for which there are no Canadian specialists available." Mackenzie also indicated that one of the reasons for his endorsing this policy was the success that the British and Americans had experienced in employing "specialized German scientists who were unsympathetic to the Nazi philosophy."

But if Canada was prepared to recruit German scientists and technicians, how would they be selected? Obviously the first criterion was outstanding ability and the personal recommendation of Canada's scientific elite for jobs either with the NRC or with Canadian universities.[85] Another consideration was meeting the needs of the private sector. In November, 1946, for example, G.D. Mallory of Trade and Commerce informed A.L. Jolliffe, superintendent of immigration, that "as the result of the visits of technical investigators from Canadian firms, it was found that in order to establish new industries in Canada, a limited number of German technicians were needed to design and build machinery for general technical purposes."[86] Another prominent advocate was Dr. Omond Solandt, director-general of the newly established Defence Research Board, who pointed out that certain high-ranking British military and government officials "were anxious to help Canada arrange to bring technicians and scientists to this country."[87]

This British incentive was explained by Norman Robertson, Canadian High Commissioner in London, in a November, 1946, memorandum.

> Until the present, the motive . . . has been . . . to make use of the knowledge and *expertise* of some German scientists and technicians which is not otherwise available. But as a result of apprehensions raised by the recent deportation into the Soviet Zone of German scientists resident in Berlin, the [British] Chiefs of Staff here and their counterparts in the United States have recommended that a number of German scientists should be brought from Germany; not because their services are required, but to deny their services to the Soviet Union.

Robertson went on to explain that the number of German scientists "might be of the order of 2000, of which approximately 600 are believed to live in the British Zone." Could the Canadian government "find employment for some of these scientists?"[88]

That the British would make such a request was not unexpected since Canada had already helped bail them out of awkward situations in 1938 with the Sudeten Germans and in 1946 with the Polish veterans. The movement of German scientists, however, was unique in several ways: they would come into the country as highly skilled professionals, not as farmers or unskilled labour, and they were classified as enemy aliens.

Although there were misgivings about the scheme, on November 27, 1946, the cabinet approved the entry of a limited number of German scientists and technicians "both for technical and for educational purposes." Mackenzie and Solandt would jointly supervise the selection and placement. The German scientists were not granted immigrant status; instead, they came into the country as temporary migrants for an initial period of one year under the Immigration Minister's permit.[89] Provision was also made for the RCMP to ferret out Nazis and Communists, but in reality two British panels, one civilian and one military, determined suitability.[90] British authorities also gave instructions that under no circumstances should Canada offer German scientists and technicians "higher rates of pay than those currently being tendered by United Kingdom and other Commonwealth countries," and insisted as well that they should be "on the preferred lists of either the British or the Americans."[91]

The contract system adopted by Canada's allies was duplicated in Canada for a number of reasons: it would enable the government to monitor the activities of the German scientists; it would reduce the criticism of Canadian professional organizations and trade unions;[92] and it would provide a way of repatriating these men to Europe, if necessary.[93] This last consideration seemed more attractive after December, 1946, when a controversy erupted in the United States over the U.S. Army's use of large numbers of German scientists who were given only "very perfunctory screening." According to the Canadian ambassador in Washington "this question has already become a very 'hot' political issue and numerous vehement protests from veteran and patriotic associations are pouring into the State Department." He also indicated that the controversy had created a serious rift between the military and various government departments. "The immigration authorities which are more sensitive to Congressional opinion than the Army and Navy Departments, will be unsparingly thorough in their screening of those German scientists already in the country. It is fully expected that a great many of them will be refused a visa and will have to be deported over the strong protestations of the military authorities."[94]

This struggle continued for the next three years. On balance the arguments of the American military, buttressed by the support of the FBI and greatly enhanced by external developments such as the 1948 Czech coup and the Korean War, carried the day. By 1950, it was estimated that over 500 German scientists had been located in various defence-related industries in the United States.[95]

No such controversy occurred in Canada, in part because the numbers were so small and those who were selected did not arrive until after May, 1947, by which time Canadians were more concerned about Soviet subversion and expansionism than they were about excluding war criminals.[96] Yet another consideration was that unlike the United States and Great Britain, Canada had few German scientists directly involved with military-related research.[97] As a result, Canada escaped the moral dilemma that has haunted American liberals:

> Paperclip and the use of German scientists by the other allies was profitable because it gave an invaluable boost to their scientific and technical expertise. Without it, the American space programme would have been greatly delayed. But the question remains – at what price? Should the military be . . . praised or criticized for their single-mindedness of purpose? And can there be any justification for their determination to employ men who had committed crimes against humanity, or for the web of conspiracy and deceptions which Paperclip inspired?[98]

Labourers and Domestics

At the other end of the occupational ladder, DP workers had assumed an important role in the economic boom of the post-war years. This contribution was notable in many different sectors of the economy, but in the fields of agriculture and domestic service the dichotomy between the goals of Canadian employers and the aspirations of DP workers was most pronounced.

Polish veterans were the original group destined for Ontario and western Canadian farms.[99] Initially, the scheme appeared to be a great success. By December, 1947, the Calgary *Albertan* provided another version when it complained that these workers "come and go when they feel like it . . . [and] pick up city jobs by the dozen at somewhat higher wages." As a result, the paper charged, provincial farmers "don't want to have anything to do with Polish immigrants, whereas 10 months ago they were in hearty praise of these people."[100] Stung by this criticism, the Department of Labour and the federal-provincial Farm Labour Conference recommended that Polish veterans and DP agricultural workers be forcibly reminded of their contractual obligations and, if necessary, deported. Threats of this sort made little impression on men who had fought the Nazis and who reminded Canadian officials that they had come not "to . . . beg for bread . . . but . . . as political prisoners." After coercion failed, an attempt was made to select only "real farm workers from DP camps," who were "likely to remain in farm employment." And when in turn this failed to materialize, attempts were made to recruit Dutch and German agricultural workers.[101]

High job turnover also typified Canada's experience with DP domestics. Most of these 10,499 women were Balts, Poles, and Ukrainians who were moved from the camps once they had passed rigorous medical and occupational tests designed to weed out the educated and effete. "We had already learned from the men," one DP domestic related, "they had made themselves into specialists who had worked for years and years in the woods." These women arrived in Canada under a contract system that required one year of service in pre-selected jobs at a wage of $35-$40 per month. The lucky ones found day jobs in hospitals or nursing homes; the others worked in private homes, often from dawn to dusk. In addition to demanding employers, DP domestics had to cope with Department of Labour officials whose views of European household life were ill-informed and patronizing. For instance, Arthur MacNamara proposed setting up an orientation program so that "if a girl on first trial of a vacuum cleaner ran out of the front door screaming 'blue murder' we shall have a place to send her where the intricacies of Canadian housekeeping could be explained."[102]

From Displaced Person to Citizen

The thousands of refugees and displaced persons who came to Canada between 1946 and 1952 had many common experiences. The greatest of these was the trauma associated with the Second World War, with "varying periods in the soul-destroying geographical, temporal and psychological 'midway to nowhere' of POW camps, deportation, refugee camps and exile."[103] Another characteristic of this latest generation of immigrants was the tendency to view their departure from Europe as the beginning of a new life. The following motives were given by a DP who chose Australia: "I left from desperation. After the experience of the life in the camp any place looked better than Austria. Australia seemed a good country (of what I knew of it) . . . and seemed at the other end of the world, far away from Communism and Europe war upheavals."[104] But for those who came to Canada under the Bulk Labour Program or its related initiatives, it meant leaving dependants for two years either in European DP camps or with relatives in war-ravaged Germany. This was invariably a painful experience, particularly when desperate letters followed them from family members. A graphic example of this difficulty can be seen in a January, 1952, incident when a group of DP workers in northern Quebec submitted a petition to the Department of Labour for the immediate admission of their wives and children. The petition was accompanied by letters from their wives describing conditions in the DP camps:

Mrs. Gisela Krol (December 23, 1951)

"We feel as if we were in jail. If it would last only a few days it would not be as bad, but we do not know how long we have to stay here. If we should have to remain for another few months we will have lost our minds. . . . And tomorrow is Christmas Eve."

Mrs. Annemarie Scharpajew (December 26, 1951)

"My shoes are completely worn out and so I am going around on my stocking feet. . . . There is no privacy in the toilets and washrooms. Every building is overcrowded . . . and the people sleep like animals. They are also treated like animals. I am really driven to desperation."[105]

The separation of families was but one of many adjustment problems experienced by European displaced persons in Canada. By 1948, however, a variety of ethnic and humanitarian organizations had rallied to their cause. Not surprisingly, given both its high profile and its long-term commitment to destitute immigrants, the Canadian National Committee on Refugees demanded that the Canadian government provide additional services to the newcomers. In June, 1948, for example, the CNCR informed Paul Martin, federal Minister of Health and Welfare, that many refugee families were "without the necessities of life and entirely dependent on their earnings," which were minimal "until they became established." The CNCR suggested, therefore, that Ottawa should immediately make arrangements so that destitute DPs could receive family allowances and free medical and hospital care.[106] Citizenship training was the other high priority for the CNCR, and it warmly applauded the creation in 1950 of the new Department of Citizenship and Immigration. Not only would this new agency help displaced persons adjust to Canadian society, but it would also help Canadian society adjust to the DPs "by encouraging a sympathetic attitude" for the post-war dispossessed.[107]

By 1950 this form of public education was clearly needed, as the term "DP" increasingly assumed a pejorative character in Canada.[108] Many Anglo-Canadians tended to underestimate the abilities of displaced persons because of the latter group's unfamiliarity with the English language. Accordingly, there was growing resentment when DP workers sought to move up the job ladder and to find employment more in keeping with their ability and training. In some ways the most disturbed occupational groups were not Canadian blue-collar workers but Canadian professional organizations.

Conclusion

The influx of 160,000 displaced persons into Canada between 1946 and 1952 stands in sharp contrast to Canada's pitiful response to European refugees in the 1930s. Increasingly, Canadians once again viewed immigrants as an asset rather than a liability. This positive reaction was reinforced by good economic conditions and low unemployment. From the corporate outlook, the post-war refugee policy was a success in that it provided a badly needed supply of malleable labour, at least on a temporary basis. But as more and more DP workers moved out of low-status and arduous jobs Canadian employers had to find new immigrants to take their places. Since the IRO camps in Europe were about to close and the only people left were the aged and the infirm, needy Canadian employers had to look elsewhere. After 1952, immigration recruitment focused on Holland, Germany, Italy, Greece, and Portugal. During the 1950s thousands of immigrants from these countries sought jobs in Canada, especially after 1952 when the United States reimposed its immigration quota system. But these workers were not contract labourers or *Gastarbeiter*. Instead, they were independent immigrants who could pick and choose their place of employment, and most, as might be expected, chose the metropolitan centres of central Canada rather than the frontier work world of the displaced person.[109]

During the period when displaced persons had dominated the Canadian immigration scene, the priorities of Ottawa's manpower and foreign policies had coincided. Despite their sharp differences in educational background and occupational requirements, immigration officers and External Affairs officials found themselves grappling with the same "refugee problem." Together they had to reconcile Canadian economic and social needs with the international obligation arising out of the country's membership in the United Nations Relief and Rehabilitation Administration and the International Refugee Organization. Moreover, as the Cold War developed the Immigration Branch and External Affairs joined forces to keep suspected Communists from Canadian shores. Non-whites were also rigorously excluded. Even so, Canadian immigration policy in 1952 was much more generous than it had been in 1930. And it would get better.[110]

PART TWO

Immigration Policy and Social Trends Since 1952

Departmental Affiliation
Ministry of Citizenship and Immigration, 1949-66
Ministry of Manpower and Immigration, 1966-77
Employment and Immigration Commission, 1977-93
Public Security Department, 1993
Citizenship and Immigration, 1993-95

Ministers responsible for immigration
Liberal government of Louis St. Laurent, 1950-56
Walter Harris
John W. Pickersgill

Conservative government of John G. Diefenbaker, 1957-63
Edmund David Fulton
Ellen L. Fairclough
Richard A. Bell

Liberal government of Lester B. Pearson, 1963-68
Guy Favreau
René Tremblay
John R. Nicholson
Jean Marchand

Liberal government of Pierre Elliott Trudeau, 1968-79
Allan MacEachen
Otto Lang
Bryce Mackasey
Robert Andras
Bud Cullen

Conservative government of Joe Clark, 1979-80
Ron Atkey

Liberal government of Pierre Elliott Trudeau/John Turner, 1980-84
Lloyd Axworthy
John Roberts

Conservative government of Brian Mulroney/Kim Campbell, 1984-93
Flora Macdonald
Benoit Bouchard
Barbara McDougall
Bernard Valcourt

Liberal government of Jean Chrétien, 1993-
Sergio Marchi

CHAPTER 8

Immigrant Workers and Canada's Changing Immigration Policy, 1952-1980

Canadian immigration policy in the thirty years after 1950 went through a number of significant changes associated with fundamental shifts in the source of immigrants. In the first stage, Britain and Europe resumed their role as the primary target areas for new labour recruits; immigrants from other regions faced formidable legal and administrative barriers. Most of those who came from Europe prior to 1966 were unskilled or semi-skilled workers, male and female; their entry greatly expanded through the use of the government's family sponsorship system. The second stage was the 1966-67 attempt by the hierarchy of the newly created Department of Manpower and Immigration to create a more selective recruitment system, based more on occupation and education than on ethnic background or family connection. At the same time, there was an attempt to bring Canada's refugee policies into line with the guidelines of the United Nations High Commissioner for Refugees. The third stage, which lasted until the 1980s, featured a debate between the advocates of a more occupationally selective approach and those who argued for a more generous response to both immigrants and refugees. In general, the views of the latter group prevailed. The substantial amendments to the Immigration Act in 1976 embodied these changes and provided for a broad basis of selection, eliminated residual racist barriers, and established an elaborate appeal procedure. While most Canadians applauded this legislation, there were still those who expressed concern that more and more immigrants to Canada were coming from non-traditional regions and were immigrants of colour.

Table 4
Changes in Backgrounds of Immigrants, 1968-1988

	1968			*1988*	
Rank	*Country*	*%*	*Rank*	*Country*	*%*
1.	Britain	20.3	1.	Hong Kong	14.4
2.	U.S.A.	12.1	2.	India	6.4
3.	Italy	9.5	3.	Poland	5.7
4.	Hong Kong	4.5	4.	Britain	5.7
5.	Germany	4.6	5.	Philippines	5.1
6.	Greece	4.3	6.	U.S.A.	4.0
7.	France	4.2	7.	Portugal	4.0
8.	Australia	1.9	8.	Vietnam	3.8
9.	India	1.9	9.	Jamaica	2.4
10.	Trinidad	1.7	10.	Iran	2.3

SOURCE: Employment and Immigration Canada, *Immigration Statistics*, 1968, 1978, 1988.

Immigration Policy During the 1950s

Canadian immigration policy between 1950 and 1966 was strongly influenced by Mackenzie King's 1947 dictum that immigration must be directly related to the country's "absorptive capacity." In part, this meant that the flow of immigrants would be determined by domestic economic conditions, which would, of course, vary from year to year. Closely related was his view that the "serious loss of population in the past through emigration – particularly of young people educated and trained in Canada – [was] a warning that absorptive capacity should not be exceeded." King also set forth the creed that Canadians did "not wish to make a fundamental alteration in the character of their population through mass migration . . . from the Orient." But the most important legacy was King's prewar insistence that immigration was "a matter of domestic policy . . . subject to the control of Parliament." For King, Canada was "perfectly within her rights in selecting the immigrants she wants. An alien has no 'fundamental human right' to enter Canada. This is a privilege." [1]

Most of these principles were embodied in the terms of reference of the new Department of Citizenship and Immigration (DCI) created in 1950. This reorganization was largely in response to the anomaly of having the Immigration Branch lodged in the Department of Northern Development and out of touch with the needs of the post-war Canadian economy. It was also an attempt to put all human resources in one department. In the words of Prime Minister Louis St. Laurent, "having citizenship, immigration and Indian affairs in the one department would . . . make Canadian citizens of those who were born here, of the original inhabitants of the territory, and of those who migrated to this country." Unfortunately, as the next sixteen years would show, the fusion of two quite different agencies was not a success. Part of the problem was that veteran Immigration Branch officers viewed the Citizenship Branch as an upstart with little experience or knowledge about the complexities of the immigration process.[2]

On the positive side, DCI was launched at a time when some of the more draconian disabilities had been removed from the Immigration Act. This included repeal of the 1923 Chinese Immigration Act and the removal of barriers against all former enemy aliens, including Japanese Canadians.[3] In addition, by an order-in-council of June 9, 1950 (PC 2856), admissible classes for European immigrants were expanded to include any immigrant "who satisfies the Minister that he is a suitable immigrant having regard to the climatic, the social, educational, industrial, labour or other conditions or requirements of Canada; and that he is not undesirable owing to his probable inability to become readily adapted and integrated into the life of the Canadian community and to assume the duties of Canadian citizenship within a reasonable time after his entry." Arrangements were also made for the limited entry of immigrants from India, Pakistan, and Ceylon (Sri Lanka) as a gesture of Canada's good will to the Commonwealth.[4]

On the negative side, many of the senior officers of the Immigration Branch had been conditioned by the restrictionist policies of the war and the depression[5] and these heirs of the F.C. Blair tradition "set a stamp on the new Service," particularly their commitment to control what they perceived to be a horde of eager immigrants.[6] Although on occasion this bureaucratic impulse was offset by the direct intervention of the Minister of Immigration, this was atypical. To make matters worse, DCI was a deprived department with weak political support, despite having two strong ministers in the Liberal government of the day – Walter Harris (1950-54) and J.W. Pickersgill (1954-57).[7]

Harris's major contribution was the revision of the Immigration Act in June, 1952. Unfortunately, more emphasis was devoted to speedy passage than for adequate consultation and review. Indeed, during the four days the House of Commons Committee allowed for public hearings only a handful of national organizations were represented, the four major transportation companies (CPR, CNR, Trans-Canada Airlines, and Cunard Steamship Lines) being in the forefront. Conspicuous by their absence were the Trades and Labour Congress, the Canadian Congress of Labour, the leading welfare and civil liberties bodies, and ethnic and religious organizations.[8]

The new Act reflected this narrow and conservative approach. For example, provision was made for the delegation of very broad powers to the cabinet and the officers of the Immigration Branch. Under section 61 the cabinet could, through orders-in-council, make regulations concerning assisted passage, levels of literacy, means of support, and continuous journey, and could prohibit the admission of immigrants on the basis of:

(i) nationality, citizenship, ethnic group, occupation, class or geographical area of origin;

(ii) peculiar customs, habits, modes of life or methods of holding property;

(iii) unsuitability having regard to the climatic, economic, social, industrial, educational, labour, health or other conditions or requirements existing temporarily or otherwise, in Canada or in the area or country from or through which such persons come to Canada . . .;

(iv) probable inability to become readily assimilated or to assume the duties and responsibilities of Canadian citizenship within a reasonable time after their admission.[9]

The Canadian Bar Association and other advocates of immigration reform denounced the sweeping basis for exclusion, as well as the quasi-judicial powers granted immigration officials. Of particular concern was the discretionary authority of the Minister of Immigration to "confirm or quash . . . or substitute his decision." Walter Harris, however, viewed these complaints as vexatious and trivial, and he assured the House of Commons that administrative justice was much better than continuous immigration litigation.[10] Canadians did not want, he argued, the type of system existing in other countries "whereby we would try to define in a law those persons who could be admitted to Canada, so that one could approach the Courts in this country and have a Judge decide in an action at law whereby an application came within the terms of the law."[11]

Significantly, the most strident criticism of the 1952 Act came not from the opposition parties, the Progressive Conservatives and CCF, but rather from those MPs who had large numbers of immigrants in their ridings or who had "for some reason, perhaps their own ethnic origin, a special interest in immigration."[12] This particularist and self-interested involvement was in many ways preferable to an ideological or racist agenda. It meant, however, that ethnic lobbying had become an increasingly important factor in the debate over immigration policy, and it would increase during future attempts to revise the Immigration Act and its regulations.

The 1952 Immigration Act reinforced Canada's Eurocentric immigration policy and the dictum that entry into Canada was a privilege, not a right. This maintenance of the status quo did not concern J.W. Pickersgill, who became Minister of Immigration in 1954. Nor was he prepared to modify the exclusionary powers of immigration officials or to expand the scope of the Immigration Appeal Board. In February, 1955, Pickersgill provided this defence of existing immigration procedures:

It seems to have entered into the minds of many of the decent people of this country that in some way or other we are conducting a trial of an applicant for admission. We are not doing anything of the kind. The person concerned is trying to be given a chance to become a citizen of Canada and parliament has enacted that somebody has got to decide whether he is the kind of person we want. It is much more like an applicant for a job. If an employer . . . had to explain to every unsuccessful applicant for a job why he was refused a post . . . it would be perfectly impossible to get anything done at all. [13]

Pickersgill was also not prepared to expand Canada's international commitment to refugees since the 1952 Immigration Act had been singularly quiet in its references to refugees, in general, and the United Nations Refugee Convention (1951), in particular. According to Howard Adelman there were four major reasons for this omission: "refugees were viewed as individuals fleeing persecution to whom a country gave temporary asylum . . . (while) Canada saw itself as a country of permanent resettlement of immigrants. . . . Canada wanted to control who came into the country . . . the key that unlocked the door to Canada was self interest. . . . Racism, too, was a factor." [14]

Yet despite any official commitment, Canada's response to Hungarian refugees fleeing Soviet repression in 1956 was one of the most generous of all Western countries. Over 37,000 were admitted, or 20 per cent of the total; in contrast, the United States, with ten times Canada's population, accepted 38,000. [15] What made the difference was not a new refugee policy but a vigorous minister. Pickersgill personally directed the rescue and mobilized support in the House of Commons and from the Canadian public. [16] On this occasion, he also did not allow the usual anti-Communist barriers, erected by his department and the RCMP, to impede the flow of Hungarian freedom fighters. This resolve was evident when he warned his departmental security officers that unless there was "serious reason to believe the applicant is a security risk, we would expect him to issue a security clearance." [17] In his memoirs, Pickersgill claimed that his involvement in the movement of Hungarian refugees was his proudest moment as Minister, especially since so many "achieved eminence in Canadian life." [18]

This enlightened approach was short-lived, however, and the Department of Citizenship and Immigration soon returned to its previous obsession with excluding subversives. During the 1950s, with the Cold War in full force, even Pickersgill was wary about rejecting the advice of the RCMP or circumventing the security provisions in the 1952 Act. [19] Immigrants from eastern Europe were particularly suspect, a situation that enraged Polish, Ukrainian, and Yugoslav organizations that claimed "that Chinese immigrants were admitted to Canada more easily than their relatives." [20] The RCMP and Security Panel were also vigilant in excluding prominent Communists and fellow travellers. For example, in 1947 Paul Robeson, the renowned African-American singer, was denied entry; five years later the eminent civil rights leader W.E.B. Du Bois had a similar experience. Both were accused of being Communist sympathizers.[21] Homosexuals were another target group since the RCMP assumed they were susceptible to blackmail by hostile powers. In December, 1950, a government committee considering amendments to the Immigration Act added "homosexuals, lesbians, and persons coming to Canada for any immoral purposes" to the list of prohibited classes.[22] In contrast, convicted felon and union gangster Hal Banks was allowed to remain in the country because of his role in smashing the pro-Communist Canadian Seamen's Union.[23]

Exclusion on racial grounds also remained the order of the day. Although the Chinese Immigration Act of 1923 had been repealed, very few Chinese immigrants were legally admitted. As a result, there was a growing traffic in illegals organized primarily by shadowy Hong Kong companies that "existed for the sale and purchase of false identities."[24] Life for most Chinese illegals was harsh since they became both indentured servants and fugitives.[25] It became worse when the RCMP, responding to public pressure and its own sense of propriety, increased its efforts to deport them during the late 1950s.[26]

The Sponsorship Debate

Although the recruitment of Italian, Greek, and Portuguese workers through the Bulk Labour Program was important, most immigrants during the 1950s were sponsored by relatives. In the case of Italians, for instance, more than 90 per cent were sponsored. From their perspective, this formally endorsed chain migration system had many advantages, particularly since it helped to widen reciprocal kin relations "to include a host of distant relatives and co-villagers who might never have formed part of an individual's support network in Italy. This strong and sustained contact between the home villages and Toronto, for example, could result in the relocation of almost the entire population."[27]

But for Canadian immigration officials the sponsorship system meant enormous backlogs, fraudulent claimants, and an alarming concentration of unskilled immigrants in the metropolitan centres.[28] By the late 1950s departmental statistics showed that less than 8 per cent of those admitted would have qualified as unsponsored immigrants.[29] With the advent of the 1957-58 economic recession, the sponsorship system was increasingly criticized by immigration officials for flooding the semi-skilled labour market. The new Minister, Ellen Fairclough, was impressed by these arguments, and she was determined to bring immigration intake under control.

In March, 1959, Fairclough convinced her cabinet colleagues to endorse order-in-council PC 1959/310, which restricted the entry of non-dependent relatives.[30] This change in immigration procedures brought an immediate and angry response from Italian, Portuguese, and Greek organizations, who deluged the government with protests and threats of political retaliation. Jack Pickersgill, Liberal immigration critic and political strategist par excellence, added his voice to the chorus of protest.[31] The Conservative immigration policy, he told the House of Commons, was "an unnecessary and inhumane restriction . . . aimed at one community in this country."[32] Although Fairclough tried to defend her policy by pointing out that the sponsorship system was itself discriminatory since "well qualified Italians who wished to migrate to this country had little or no chance of having their applications considered unless they were in the sponsored categories," these arguments were to no avail.[33] Concerned about alienating the ever more powerful ethnic vote, Prime Minister John Diefenbaker decided to leave the sponsorship system intact.

Ellen Fairclough's term as Minister of Immigration, while controversial, was also characterized by important changes in the selection criteria for immigrants. There was, for instance, a new effort to place occupational skill and education ahead of ethnic background in determining eligibility. Moreover, in keeping with the principles of the 1960 Bill of Rights, there was an attempt to remove the most discriminatory features of immigration policy in the January, 1962, regulations, which promised "to eliminate all discrimination based on colour, race or creed." More specifically, the regulations stipulated that if the Canadian government continued "to allow Greeks, Poles, Italians, Portuguese and other Europeans to bring in the wide range of relatives presently admissible, we will have to do the same for Japanese, Chinese, Indians, Pakistanis, Africans, persons from the Arab world, the West Indies and so forth."[34]

The immigration controversies and changes between 1959 and 1962 had several ramifications. One was the continuing success of unskilled southern European immigrants to circumvent attempts by immigration officials to control their numbers by means of the sponsorship system. And when this system was threatened, Italian, Greek, and Portuguese organizations used their political muscle to force the Conservative government of the day to back down. Nor was this lesson lost on political organizers, especially after Ellen Fairclough lost her Hamilton West riding in 1963 to an Italian-Canadian Liberal, Joseph Macaluso.[35]

Immigration Policy Review: Skill Over Ethnicity

Between 1960 and 1966 Canadian immigration officials, federal politicians, and various pressure groups considered the prospects of increasing the ratio of skilled and professional immigrants. In part, this response was related to growing concern over the level of structural unemployment as the Canadian economy became more dependent on technology and less committed to the primary sectors. There was also the reality that most immigrants gravitated to the large urban centres, especially Toronto, Montreal, and Vancouver. In addition, there were charges that Canada was experiencing a serious "brain drain" as large numbers of Canadian-born professionals sought jobs in the United States.

This latter subject was the focus of a number of reports prepared by the Department of Labour. The most sweeping of these, *The Migration of Professional Workers Into and Out of Canada, 1946-1960*, examined the backgrounds of nearly 92,000 professional people who entered the country during these years. The largest group was comprised of engineers, who numbered 16,000, or 18 per cent, of the total, followed by graduate nurses (13,713 or 14.9 per cent), teachers and professors (11,766 or 12.8 per cent), draughtsmen and designers (9,529 or 10.4 per cent), and physicians and surgeons (4,207 or 4.6 per cent).[36] In general, the influx of professionals was quite steady, with an average annual intake of about 7,000. Another constant was the importance of British professionals, who represented 53.1 per cent of the total, with even higher ratios for graduate nurses (67 per cent), draughtsmen (65 per cent), teachers and professors (64 per cent), engineers (59 per cent), accountants (59 per cent), architects (57 per cent), chemists (54 per cent), and physicians and surgeons (48 per cent). Immigrant professionals from the United States were next in line with 14 per cent, followed by those from Germany (5 per cent), Poland (4 per cent), and Hungary (3 per cent). Those of French and Jewish background represented about 2 per cent each.[37]

All of these reports stressed that immigrant professionals had been an asset to the Canadian economy during the immediate post-war years,[38] particularly since they came "already fully trained and, frequently, with considerable work experience behind them." In many instances, it was argued, these professionals "also brought along new ideas as well as fresh approaches to the solution of our problems." Another advantage of this source of manpower supply was that it could "be adjusted to changes in the labour market through government policy."[39] There was, however, some concern that licensing procedures of Canadian professional associations could reduce the number of immigrant professionals admitted to specific fields since the newcomers might not be permitted "to start even at the lowest level of the profession." A 1959 Immigration Branch report was particularly critical of the certification procedures of the Canadian medical profession; in contrast, it applauded engineering associations for having "developed very fair procedures of professional recognition, due largely to the great demand for these professional skills."[40]

The search for immigrant professionals was intensified by the need to replace those Canadians who had accepted high-paying professional jobs in the United States. Immigration statistics showed that between 1950 and 1960 over 10 per cent of those heading south were professionals, with graduate nurses, mechanical and aeronautical engineers, architects/draughtsmen, and physicians and surgeons leading the way. Indeed, during this decade Canadian professionals represented about 27 per cent of the total immigration of foreign-born professionals to the United States, a trend the Department of Labour attributed to various factors, including:

> The similarities of United States and Canadian cultures, standards of living, and educational systems. . . . Operating along the same lines are the relatively high educational standards of Canadian universities and colleges and the high professional standards which place the Canadian immigrant in a privileged position with respect to other immigrants. Graduates from Canadian professional training institutions, generally speaking, have a good reputation and are sought after in the United States.[41]

The Department of Labour put on a brave face by claiming that this brain drain was offset by the arrival of American professionals and the management and administrative employees of "subsidiaries of United States parent companies."[42] But, in general, labour and immigration officials regarded this exodus as a severe loss of Canadian talent and did not believe that "the loss of a Canadian professional is . . . necessarily offset by the gain of a qualified immigrant professional from Europe or elsewhere, since, on the one hand, we are losing a worker who is acclimatized to this country and who is familiar with Canadian industrial techniques and ways of doing things, while on the other hand, the immigrant is not."[43] Nor were the bureaucrats confident that the necessary numbers of immigrant professionals could be recruited during the 1960s, given "the high degree of prosperity in Europe and in the United Kingdom and the relatively low level of unemployment."[44]

These dire predictions proved unwarranted. During the 1960s the number of immigrant professionals made up nearly one-quarter of the total number of foreign-born workers destined for the Canadian labour force.[45] Although Britain remained the single most important source of professionals, its percentage of the total declined from two-thirds to one-third; in contrast, the U.S. numbers expanded from 1,643 in 1962 to 5,200 in 1969. Even more dramatic was the increase of Asian professionals, as Canada moved "from an ethnic-based immigration policy to a skill-based, universalistic one."[46]

Changing the Policy: 1965-67

In its 1964 report, the Economic Council of Canada went on record with the message that "during the post-war years it has become increasingly apparent that the future prosperity of a nation will depend on an adequate supply of professional, technical, managerial, and other highly skilled manpower."[47] This message came as no surprise to Tom Kent, the British-born journalist and technocrat who became deputy minister of the new Department of Manpower and Immigration in 1966. Kent was well placed, having been part of the inner circle of policy advisers who helped reshape Liberal Party social policies during its six years in opposition. For this reason he was hand-picked by Jean Marchand, Minister of Manpower and Immigration, to integrate the activities of the National Employment Service, the Unemployment Insurance Commission, and the Immigration Branch.[48] It was not an easy task, as Kent confirms in his memoirs:

> Politicians were understandably chary of defining immigration policy at all precisely. On one hand, there was a broad public sentiment in favour of easy immigration; so many Canadians, if not immigrants themselves, had known parents or grandparents who were. There was also strong humanitarian sentiment on behalf of the oppressed and the deprived. And behind these general attitudes were powerful special interests: businesses wanting both skilled professionals and cheaper labour; expanding universities wanting professors with doctorates not available in Canada; richer people wanting domestic servants. And, of course, recent immigrants wanted their relatives and friends to join them, and ethnic organizations had strong interests in the growth of their particular communities.

Kent was also aware that many Canadians were still concerned "about immigrants taking jobs from Canadians and undercutting union wages," and "challenging the values of Anglo-Canadians"; in Quebec there was also the refrain that immigrants were "shifting the linguistic balance by sending their children to English-language schools."[49]

In devising a new immigration policy for Canada, Kent differentiated between the two major categories of immigrants – the independent and the sponsored. He, like his predecessors, was particularly wary of the sponsorship system, with its "potential for explosive growth in the unskilled labour force." But how to change the system without inviting the same political controversy that plagued Ellen Fairclough?[50] One of his strategies was to sound out public opinion through the White Paper on Immigration Policy, which was issued in the fall of 1966. While this document reaffirmed the importance of immigration to Canada's economic growth, it refuted "the theory that to fill up our empty spaces as rapidly as possible with any and all immigrants willing to cast their lot with us would serve not only the humanitarian purpose of helping to redress the world's population imbalance but also the national economic goal of providing an enlarged market for domestic production."[51] Instead, the White Paper called for the recruitment of "workers with a relatively high level of education and training," regardless of "of race, colour or religion." This strategy, it argued, would mean a decreased need "for the unskilled or semi-skilled . . . in the foreseeable future."[52] While the sponsorship system was praised for helping over 900,000 immigrants adapt to Canadian society, its "potential for explosive growth" of unskilled dependants was emphasized; it was also associated with the emergence of "ghetto-like slums," especially in Toronto, Montreal, and Vancouver.[53]

Keeping certain people out of Canada was another priority of the White Paper. Transportation companies were warned that they would have the responsibility of returning any "misfits" excluded by Canadian immigration officers.[54] There were also additional measures to exclude or deport certain prohibited classes, especially those suspected of being involved with organized crime or subversive organizations.[55] At the same time, the White Paper announced the government's intention to accede to the 1951 International Convention on the Status of Refugees and establish a Refugee Eligibility Commission "with authority to decide whether an individual applying for asylum is entitled to refugee status."[56] There was also to be a more independent Immigration Appeal Board for those excluded or subject to deportation, whose jurisdiction would be limited only by the right to appeal its decisions on question of law to the Supreme Court of Canada with leave of that court."[57]

On November 10, 1966, the Special Joint Committee of the Senate and House of Commons on Immigration commenced its public hearings on the White Paper. The first witness was Marchand, who praised the new policy for its commitment to cultural pluralism and economic efficiency. Citing his twenty years' experience in the Quebec labour movement, the Minister reminded his critics that when he started out "30 per cent of the working force of the plant was unskilled . . . today it is 5 per cent."[58] He also stressed that Quebec was just as supportive of immigration as the other provinces.[59]

This new attitude in Quebec was reflected in the brief of the Confederation of National Trade Unions (CNTU), which emphasized a commitment to the principle "that every person has a right to immigration." It stressed, however, that immigrant workers in Quebec faced special problems "of not knowing our way of life, of thought, of action," as well as being exploited by unscrupulous employers. To deal with the latter problem, the CNTU proposed "that employers who request or who employ immigrants guarantee them a minimum term of one year's employment; that they make the necessary arrangements for their training, their accommodation, and for ensuring them a certain well-being." Significantly, the CNTU was not enthusiastic about the White Paper's emphasis on skilled immigrants, which it categorized as both a subtle form of bias in favour of British and western European immigrants and an exploitative policy toward Third World countries by "skimming" off their specialized workers and professionals.[60]

The Canadian Labour Congress, long an opponent of unregulated immigration and corporate recruitment of skilled immigrants, endorsed many of the CNTU arguments. Its brief also took exception to the proposal that a higher ratio of immigrants should be skilled workers. This, it claimed, was ludicrous when there were "literally thousands of men and women . . . who . . . should be retrained rather than leave them unemployed and bring in immigrants." Canadian workers, it argued, were "entitled to priority" not only as citizens but because they were "more easily assimilated into industry than people who come from abroad."[61] In keeping with the traditional priorities of Canadian organized labour, the CLC was less concerned about the entry of large numbers of unskilled workers. Indeed, Claude Jodoin, president of the CLC, conceded that certain sectors of the Canadian economy required immigrant workers "to carry out . . . tasks which native born or already established immigrants refuse to perform because of their better training." CLC representatives did, however, chide Canadian employers, especially in the mining industry, for their unwillingness "to pay the rate for the job high enough to attract native Canadians and naturalized Canadians . . . to work in isolated areas, particularly in the far north."[62]

The most passionate appeal for cheap immigrant labour came from the Mining Association of Canada (MAC).[63] In its appearance before the Special Joint Committee, the MAC stressed its important contribution to the Canadian economy with "an annual production of some $3 billion of new wealth annually . . . 30 per cent of Canada's exports." But, the MAC warned, the industry productivity could only be maintained if it obtained a minimum of 4,000 immigrant miners immediately and a guarantee of a steady flow in the future. "The type of immigrant we have in mind has been the backbone of the labour force of the mining industry in the past . . . a man has to be physically fit; but his education is not too important, so long as he can read and write."[64] In response to the CLC criticism, the mining association claimed that its members had made a concerted effort to recruit miners from among the country's unemployed, especially from the coal-mining regions of Atlantic Canada, but had been singularly unsuccessful.[65] According to J.C. Byrne, president of Discovery Mines in the Northwest Territories, there were six reasons why Canadian workers refused to work for his company: "There are no roads, no TV's, no cars, few girls, little or no liquor and most people recoil from the idea of working underground."[66] In its summary, the MAC branded the White Paper an abomination that threatened the future of the Canadian mining industry.[67]

A similar indictment was forthcoming from the Canadian Federation of Agriculture, especially the sugar-beet producers of southern Alberta. They, too, demanded an immigrant manpower reservoir that would, in time, produce the "field worker–share crop producer–tenant operator–owner cycle." Reference was made to the region's successful use of post-war Polish veterans, displaced persons, and Dutch immigrants, and it called on the government to provide, at the very least, temporary agricultural workers, either "people originating from peasant stock of Europe" or "Mexican workers in family groups . . . because of their adaptability and experience as field labour in speciality crops production."[68]

However, the most strident demand for "stalwart" European workers came not from Canadian industrialists but from Sydney Spivak, Manitoba Minister of Industry and Commerce. In his brief Spivak criticized the Special Joint Committee for endorsing an immigration policy aimed "against the very people who built this country." Manitoba's future, Spivak claimed, was primarily "based on her northern frontier," and the province was receiving too few, not too many unskilled immigrants. What the White Paper ignored, Spivak charged, was that each region had its own particular labour requirements and priorities. "Without immigrants . . . cutting timber, mining, building hydro projects and transportation facilities, and carrying out work essential to the exploitation of remote resources . . . developments will be slow and costly."[69] Although the Committee generally applauded Spivak's frontier soliloquy, several members challenged his premise that immigrant workers would remain in these resource jobs. One of the more biting comments came from John Munro, who drew on his personal experience as MP for Hamilton East to suggest there was little evidence that European immigrant workers would choose "to go to the north country" rather than "join their relatives and make a life in the urban areas."[70]

Among the corporate immigration boosters, the Canadian Manufacturers' Association brief was the most supportive of the White Paper's preference for well-educated and technologically adept immigrants.[71] It was, however, insistent that the DMI adopt a long-range approach to immigration recruitment rather than the tap-on and tap-off approach: "In the light of the growth requirements of the Canadian economy through the next several years and the stimulus to real income per capita provided by population and skill additions, a wise policy for Canada would be to continue encouraging immigration, giving special emphasis to the selection of immigrants with technical and professional qualifications and experience." Nor, it suggested, should the initiative only rest with immigration officials, since a much better approach would be "aggressive recruiting programs" that combined corporate guarantees of employment and the government's Assisted Passage Loan Scheme.[72]

The Canadian Medical Association also put itself on record as endorsing the recruitment of the highly skilled. It paid special tribute to the "vital part played by immigration in maintaining a reasonable ratio of doctors to population in recent years." But it questioned whether this source of medical manpower, "comprising 35-40% of our total licensees," would continue in the future.[73] And if British and American doctors stopped coming, what then? Should Canada relax its immigration regulations so that more doctors from Europe, Asia, and Latin America could help meet the shortfall? The CMA representatives did not have answers to all these questions. But on the subject of medical workers from Third World countries they were adamant: unqualified doctors must be excluded, especially from countries such as India, Pakistan, and the Philippines, where medical graduates were "trained to do a job in these vastly populated countries of very different cultural and economic standards from our own." In fact, the CMA made a strong case that Canada should rob Third World countries of their best and brightest medical workers either through immigration recruitment or by allowing those who came to study in Canada under international assistance programs to remain in the country after they had graduated.[74] Dr. Roy of the Collège des Médecins et Chirurgiens de la province du Québec was particularly cynical when he claimed that many of these foreign-born medical students not only manipulated their way into Canada, but then migrated to the United States once they had passed the Medical Council of Canada examinations.[75]

The Select Committee also heard briefs presented by the various ethnic organizations. Some, like the Canadian Jewish Congress, the Polish Canadian Congress, the Trans-Canada Alliance of German Canadians, and the Italian Immigration Aid Society, were seasoned lobbyists. Others, representing Canada's expanding Chinese and West Indian communities, were more tentative and deferential. All groups, however, shared one common goal: they wanted a generous and accessible immigration policy.

Representatives from the Canadian Jewish Congress (CJC) and the Jewish Immigration Aid Services of Canada, given their long involvement in refugee matters, were the most insistent that the White Paper properly acknowledge Canada's humanitarian commitments. These Jewish organizations pointed out that the 1960s had shown "the need for people to find asylum . . . so radically different from heretofore, that a new look has to be taken of refugees and not the rather . . . facile one, of merely accepting an international convention."[76] Given its own active role in caring for Jewish immigrants, the CJC urged the Committee to acknowledge the important role non-government organizations could provide in helping newcomers adjust to Canadian society. The CJC was also concerned that Canadian security screening procedures would be used to exclude bona fide refugees and particularly opposed to suggestions that immigrants be required to carry identity cards.[77] If federal authorities wanted to ferret out criminals, the CJC suggested that they might begin with the arrest of "war criminals who entered this country illegally," those who had been "part of the death machine – the final solution of Hitler." This, it suggested, could be done "without any kangaroo courts . . . with all procedures open and above board."[78]

Polish and Italian organizations, in their appearances before the Committee, spent much of their time talking about the importance of assisting newcomers to adjust to Canadian society and in praising the sponsorship system.[79] For the Polish groups, sponsorship was a way of drawing skilled and professional immigrants from Poland without making them subject to unreasonable Canadian security checks.[80] In contrast, Italian organizations praised "the time tested device of sponsorship" as the vehicle whereby "persons who might otherwise have been judged to be unsuitable or unadaptable, have managed readily the transition into Canadian society."[81] One such success story was Nick di Lorenzo, a Hamilton-based contractor who impressed the Committee with his spirited defence of his company's employment practices toward Italian workers: "We teach them how to work. . . . Our men walk with their heads straight up, being very proud. . . ."[82]

Canada's oldest and largest ethnic group was represented by the Trans-Canada Alliance of German Canadians.[83] Their brief was one of the few coming from an ethnocultural organization that endorsed the new emphasis "on education, skills and occupational competence rather than on the criteria of race and ethnicity"; and it applauded the fusion of immigration and manpower policies.[84] Similar accolades were forthcoming from the Chinese-Canadian delegation, which also applauded the removal of the racist immigration regulations; this change, they argued, would now make it possible for Canada to draw immigrants from the "large pool of qualified, adaptable and industrious Chinese in Hong Kong and Formosa." The Chinese delegation also reminded the Committee of the pervasive discrimination their community had endured in the past.[85]

Groups representing West Indian immigrants likewise welcomed the opportunity to explain their aspirations and grievances, especially at a time when Britain's rigid immigration laws had curtailed traditional opportunities in that country.[86] While they endorsed the removal of racial, ethnic, and geographical discrimination, they were concerned that the new emphasis on education and skill would, as in the past, be more stringently "applied to the West-Indian than to the European immigrant."[87] In general, though, these groups were optimistic that the White Paper would make it possible for more Caribbean skilled and unskilled immigrants to come to Canada, since they were "a very robust people and they would be prepared to work any place where employment is offered."[88]

Questions about immigrant adaptability were a constant theme throughout the hearings. One of the most comprehensive assessments came from the International Institute of Metropolitan Toronto (IIMT), which had been founded in 1952 "by native born Canadians who recognized the value of immigrants to Canada and the problems that they encountered."[89] Although the IIMT endorsed the skill criterion of the White Paper, it insisted that the federal government had an obligation to provide vocational training, social services, and citizenship programs for the newcomers, many of whom were rural immigrants. Such an immigrant, the IIMT said, experienced "special difficulties just to equip himself to deal with our rather complicated society." Effective citizenship programs, it suggested, could also be linked to the major ethnic organizations, which supported "more integration, a feeling of harmony . . . as Canadians."[90] Similar messages were forthcoming from organizations such as the Canadian Welfare Council, the Ontario Welfare Council, the United Council for Human Rights, the Inter-Ethnic Council of Toronto, and representatives from the Anglican Church of Canada and Catholic Immigrant Services.[91]

Faced with formidable opposition to its policies on the sponsorship question, including many members of the Special Joint Committee, the Immigration Branch was forced to compromise. But how to reconcile long-term immigration planning with chain migration? The answer: an artificial points system which rewarded potential immigrants for a variety of assets. In his memoirs Kent describes the genesis of a system designed more for political expediency than for administrative efficiency:

> If we could identify and define the various factors affecting a person's ability to settle successfully in Canada, and attach relative weights to them, then immigration officers would have a consistent basis on which to assess potential immigrants. . . . Education was . . . one unit of assessment (out of a hundred total) for each year successfully completed . . . to a maximum of twenty. . . . From zero to fifteen units were assigned according to employment opportunities in the occupation that the applicant was likely to follow in Canada . . . his or her present occupation . . . was given a weight between one (for the unskilled) and ten (for the professional) . . . ten units of assessment to applicants between eighteen and thirty-five . . . a maximum weight of fifteen was assigned for the immigration officer's assessment of the applicant's relevant personal qualities of adaptability, initiative and resourcefulness.[92]

The Select Committee enthusiastically endorsed the points system, as did cabinet, which approved the new policy in August, 1967. It came into effect on October 1, 1967. Although Kent could congratulate himself in having "civilized" the immigration process, he was well aware that he had achieved only "partial reform of the policy."[93]

The 1966-67 hearings on the White Paper reveal much about the key immigration issues of that period and how various economic and ethnic groups sought to articulate and protect their interests. It also demonstrated that Kent's rational and comprehensive – and perhaps naive – approach to immigration reform seriously underestimated opposition to change. This was particularly the case when he tried to change the sponsorship system and to select many more educated and skilled immigrants. In the end these initiatives were defeated by a strange alliance of corporate, trade union, and ethnic groups. In contrast, the lobby for highly skilled immigrants lacked resolve and political muscle.

One area of unfinished business was the security dimension of immigration policy. While the Select Committee had considered the testimony of both security hardliners and civil libertarians, it was reluctant to take a stand. Part of the reason was that Canada's entire security system was under review by the Royal Commission on Security. Appointed in November, 1966, "to make a full and confidential inquiry into the operation of Canadian security methods and procedures," the Commission devoted considerable attention to the screening procedures of prospective immigrants and citizenship applicants. While it was generally satisfied with the existing system, the Commission emphasized that continued vigilance was essential both for internal security and in carrying out "Canadian responsibilities to her allies for security measures."[94]

In keeping with this mandate, the Commission recommended a number of changes in the Immigration Act and its regulations. These included extending security vetting to all immigrants, improvement in the DMI's enforcement abilities, and special screening of immigrants from East Bloc countries.[95] To do otherwise, the Commission warned, "would encourage communist governments to make use of an obvious opportunity to infiltrate persons into North America . . . ."[96] Chinese immigrants were also viewed as a special security problem, and the Commission recommended that intensive screening of applicants should be accompanied by fingerprinting as "the only sure method of establishing identity and facilitating criminal traces, particularly in Hong Kong."[97]

Immigration Trends After 1965

The Immigration Regulations of October, 1967, were an important step in altering Canada's traditional Eurocentric and "white" immigration law and policy. Equally significant was the creation of the Immigration Appeal Board in November, 1967, with a mandate to review deportation and exclusion cases and the power to recommend reinstatement. Provision was also made under the Canada Manpower and Immigration Council Act for the creation of an advisory board on the adjustment of immigrants.[98] Unfortunately, the flawed 1952 Immigration Act remained the guiding statute and it still contained many of the racist and ethnocentric biases of the early twentieth century, including prohibitions against the entry of a wide range of perceived mental and moral defectives. Clearly, if Canada was serious about immigration reform a new Immigration Act was necessary.

Much of the energy and imagination for this initiative came from the new Minister, Robert Andras, and his deputy minister, Alan Gotlieb, formerly a high-ranking External Affairs official. An energetic politician, Andras was determined to implement new immigration principles and guidelines, and to carry out a review of population issues that the Trudeau government had promised when it assumed office in 1968. During the next five years the problem of reconciling Canada's demographic and labour force requirements with the country's immigration policy was given much attention.

As soon as he took on the Manpower and Immigration portfolio in late 1972, Andras was forced to respond to an immediate crisis caused by thousands of immigrants who took advantage of section 34 of the 1967 Immigration

Table 5
Percentage of Employment Authorizations:
Ten Leading Countries, 1978, 1984

| *1978* | | *1984* | |
Country	%	Country	%
U.S.A.	45.7	U.S.A.	42.2
Britain	7.9	Jamaica	5.0
Jamaica	6.8	Britain	4.4
France	2.8	India	3.8
Trinidad/Tobago	2.2	Guyana	3.7
Japan	2.0	Philippines	3.1
India	2.0	Sri Lanka	2.8
Germany	1.7	France	1.9
Barbados	1.7	Germany	1.8
Hong Kong	1.6	Iran	1.7
	74.4		70.4

SOURCE: Employment and Immigration Canada, *Immigration Statistics, 1984*.

Regulations. Under this system visitors could apply for landed immigrant status from within Canada, and, if rejected, they could then apply to the Immigration Appeal Board on either compassionate or humanitarian grounds.[99] The problem was remedied by regulations limiting the right of visitors to apply for landed immigrant status; these required all visitors in Canada for more than three months to register and all visitors seeking work to obtain an employment visa. To soften the blow, as well as to cope with the enormous backlog of cases before the Immigration Appeal Board, a thinly disguised amnesty program – called the Adjustment of Status Program – was established.[100]

But it was one thing to try to curb illegal immigration; it was quite another to deprive Canadian employers of cheap labour. As a result, in January, 1973, the Department of Manpower and Immigration began issuing employment visas for migrant workers to pursue temporary employment in Canada "to solve the labour market conditions . . . without a recourse to immigration." Although these guest workers could only stay in Canada for twelve months, a variety of employers sought their services. By the end of 1973 over 80,000 visas were issued, many to the growing number of seasonal workers coming from the Caribbean and Mexico (see Table 5).[101]

In September, 1973, Andras told the House of Commons that plans were under way "to create a long-term basis for Canada's immigration and population policy." This, he proposed, would be in the form of a Green Paper prepared by departmental officials and academic consultants and that would then be submitted to public scrutiny. He made it clear that the immigration dialogue would also involve the provinces and, if possible, arrive at a common set of national guidelines. The Green Paper and the national debate that followed were viewed as a means of obtaining public feedback and "as a means of *educating* the provinces and general public about critical immigration and population issues."[102]

The published version of the Green Paper consisted of four separate volumes dealing with various aspects of immigration policy – past, present, and future. The essential component, however, was the move away from the principles and precedents of the 1952 Act, which was "itself an outgrowth of legislation dating back to the turn of the century . . . and many of its provisions betray approaches rooted in the circumstances, conditions and attitudes of an earlier era." Much emphasis was also placed on the need for new immigration principles reflecting the needs of the 1970s "because the Act underpins the entire legal system for the conduct of policy, [and] the question of how it should be shaped."[103]

On tabling the Green Paper in the House of Commons on February 3, 1975, Andras provided an explanatory statement emphasizing that immigration was more than regulations and statistics. "At issue," he declared, was "nothing less than the future of Canada's population, its size, rate of growth, distribution and composition – and the basic principles that should govern our decisions to augment the nation's human resources through the admission of migrants from abroad." Andras also made a point of reaffirming his commitment to family reunion and his concern for the welfare of refugees, as well as stressing the relationship between immigration and the government's social and economic policies.[104]

These broad concerns were highlighted in volume one of the Green Paper – *Immigration Policy Perspectives.* It emphasized the importance of relating immigration to national manpower problems, particularly since only a minority of those entering Canada in the previous decade had prearranged employment. But in sharp contrast to the 1966 White Paper's emphasis on the need to recruit skilled immigrants, arguments were now advanced that the most difficult problems were at the opposite end of the labour market spectrum. Most needed, the report argued, were hard-working immigrants "willing to remain in unskilled or semi-skilled occupations, especially if they involve geographical remoteness, unattractive working conditions, low wages . . . ."[105] The report also observed that while no attempt had been made in the past to encourage or require sponsored, nominated, or independent immigrants to settle and remain in regions of labour shortage, this policy might be considered. In addition, the goals and practices of the Employment Authorization Program were endorsed since it allowed Canada "to respond to the urgent search by employers for people to fill jobs that cannot be filled domestically . . . [and] which, if left unattended, might impair Canada's agricultural or industrial productivity."[106]

The second major concern of the Green Paper was the dramatic change in the ethnic and geographical background of immigrants. In 1966, 76 per cent came from Europe and only 6 per cent from Asia; by 1973 European countries contributed 39 per cent of all immigrants, while the flow from Asia was 23 per cent. Most of the Asian immigrants were from India, Hong Kong, and Pakistan, who took advantage of the educational and family provisions of the points system. Although the Green Paper welcomed this ethnic diversity, it did warn that excessive immigration to Canada's metropolitan centres would intensify demands "for housing, transit facilities, community services," and could produce "a high degree of social tension." Overall, however, the authors of the Green Paper were impressed with "the resilience Canadian society has demonstrated in accommodating so many foreign migrants during this period with so little social stress."[107]

A third consideration was how to improve the actual operation of Canada's immigration system. This included the division of responsibility between the federal government and the provinces, the terms of admission to Canada, the powers and responsibilities of immigration officers, the justification for exclusion and deportation, the function of the Immigration Appeal Board, and the commitment to refugees.[108] On this last point, it was noted that since 1945 one out of ten immigrants had been a refugee and that Canadian public opinion had demonstrated "time and time again – by individuals, voluntary agencies, churches, and provincial authorities ... the extraordinary assistance the successful resettlement of refugees normally requires."[109]

Public reaction to the Green Paper varied. The most vigorous criticism occurred at the twenty-one special public hearings the Joint Committee of the Senate and House of Commons on Immigration Policy held across the country, with the most raucous meetings in Toronto, Vancouver, and Montreal, where competing groups of left-wing and right-wing extremists disrupted proceedings. Shouting matches often erupted between members of the Marxist-Leninist Committee, which denounced the Green Paper as a racist document, and the neo-Nazi Western Guard, which claimed that it encouraged the further disruption of the "Canadian way of life."[110] Fortunately, the Committee members maintained their composure and did much to prevent the public hearings from becoming an exercise in hate mongering.[111]

On July 31, 1975, the Committee had submitted its report, replete with a set of imaginative recommendations. Most of these were subsequently incorporated into the Immigration Act of 1976 (passed August 5, 1977) under the objectives section. This stipulated that the major principles behind Canada's immigration policy should be:

(a) to support the attainment of such demographic goals as may be established by the Government of Canada in respect of the size, rate of growth, structure and geographic distribution of the Canadian population;

(b) to enrich and strengthen the cultural and social fabric of Canada, taking into account the federal and bilingual character of Canada;

(c) to facilitate the reunion in Canada of Canadian citizens and permanent residents with their close relatives from abroad;

(d) to encourage and facilitate the adaptation of persons who have been granted admission as permanent residents to Canadian society by promoting cooperation between the Government of Canada and other levels of government and non-governmental agencies . . . ;[112]

(e) to facilitate the entry of visitors into Canada for the purpose of fostering trade and commerce, tourism, cultural and scientific activities and international understanding;

(f) to ensure that any person who seeks admission to Canada on either a permanent or temporary basis is subject to standards of admission that do not discriminate on grounds of race, national or ethnic origin, colour, religion or sex;

(g) to fulfil Canada's international legal obligations with respect to refugees and to uphold its humanitarian tradition with respect to the displaced and the persecuted;

(h) to foster the development of a strong and viable economy and the prosperity of all regions in Canada;

(i) to maintain and protect the health, safety and good order of Canadian society; and

(j) to promote international order and justice by denying the use of Canadian territory to persons who are likely to engage in criminal activity.[113]

The 1976-77 Immigration Act, along with the 1978 Immigration Regulations, defined not only Canada's immigration policy but also its planning and management, the priorities in admission, the basis for exclusion and deportation, the system of control and enforcement, and the criteria for refugee status. As was the case in 1967, there were also links with the Canadian security state for excluding those guilty of serious crimes or suspected of political threats through acts of espionage, subversion, or terrorism. In 1984 the newly created Canadian Security Intelligence Service was entrusted with this responsibility.[114]

The Act specified three classes of immigrants who would be admitted to Canada: family class, including immediate family and dependants; refugees, including Convention and specially designated displaced persons; and a combined third category of independent and assisted family, who would be subject in varying degrees to the points system.[115] Another important measure was the plan to establish annual immigration quotas, after consideration of economic and social conditions and consultation with the provinces. The shift away from

Table 6
Immigrants to Canada by Category, 1981-1991

		Family	*Refugee*	*Designated*	*Independent*	*Total*
1981	No.	68,607	810	14,169	45,032	128,618
	%	53.4	0.6	11.0	35.0	100
1982		61,928	1,791	15,134	42,294	121,147
		51.2	1.5	12.4	34.9	100
1983		53,695	4,100	9,867	21,495	89,157
		60.2	4.6	11.1	24.1	100
1984		51,981	5,625	9,717	20,916	88,239
		59.0	6.3	11.0	23.7	100
1985		45,910	6,080	10,680	21,632	84,302
		54.5	7.2	12.7	25.4	100
1986		48,087	6,490	12,657	31,985	99,219
		48.4	6.5	12.8	32.3	100
1987		65,881	7,473	14,092	64,652	152,098
		43.3	4.9	9.3	42.5	100
1988		66,898	8,741	18,095	68,195	161,929
		41.3	5.4	11.2	42.1	100
1989		82,294	10,210	26,794	72,703	192,001
		42.9	5.2	14.0	37.9	100
1990		96,850	11,398	28,291	77,691	214,230
		45.2	5.3	13.2	36.3	100
1991		107,718	18,178	34,553	68,108	228,557
		47.1	8.0	15.1	29.8	100

SOURCE: Employment and Immigration Canada, *Immigration Statistics*, annual publication; Jean Dumas, *Report on the Demographic Situation in Canada 1992* (Ottawa, 1992), 77.

occupational and educational criteria, which were essential in the 1966-67 legislation, back toward a family sponsorship system would have many long-term implications.[116] This trend is evident in Table 6.

But the most sweeping changes dealt with the statutory commitment to accept a wide range of refugees, admitted separately from immigrants; this included not only refugees defined by the Geneva Convention and the Protocol of the Office of the United Nations High Commissioner for Refugees, but also "designated-class" refugees admitted for humanitarian reasons.[117] In addition, provision was made for the creation of a Refugee Status Advisory Committee and for a special Refugee Sponsorship Plan, which allowed individuals and groups to sponsor "the displaced and persecuted." Many of the thousands of Vietnamese refugees who came to Canada between 1979 and 1984 benefited from this plan. [118] This generous system, with its elaborate process for determining and appealing refugee status, proved vulnerable to abuse. By 1982 the backlog of status determination cases had reached unmanageable proportions, and many of the applicants were economic migrants, not bona fide refugees. [119]

The Immigration Policy Debate, 1976-80

The 1976-78 immigration debate and the creation of the Employment and Immigration Commission did not attract wide public attention, in part because the major political parties did not make it a major policy issue and also because the changes were generally applauded. Most Canadians welcomed the removal of outdated clauses excluding immigrants on the grounds of medical deficiencies or moral turpitude; in addition, they supported the commitment to refugees. There was also support for the new emphasis on federal-provincial consultation and for the appearance of effective long-term immigration planning.

Just prior to the passage of the Act, the House of Commons Standing Committee on Labour, Manpower and Immigration provided the opportunity for many of the country's leading economic and social organizations to assess the merits and defects of the new legislation. Significantly, those calling for a steady flow of unskilled and skilled labour were not as well represented as they had been in 1966-67, but they were still a powerful lobby. [120] The most persuasive "booster" brief was presented by the Canadian Chamber of Commerce, which, predictably, repeated most of the hallowed arguments for an expanded flow of immigrants: larger domestic markets, a shortage of willing workers, and regional underdevelopment. The Chamber also gave cautious endorsement to the Green Paper proposal that recent immigrant workers locate "in a designated community for a prescribed period," although it wondered about enforcement. It was even more sceptical about the merits of importing non-immigrant workers, "those who might be categorized as 'guest' workers admitted to Canada to fulfil employment requirements for temporary periods of relatively short duration." [121] Here, the Chamber differed from the Canadian mining industry, which continued to press for more cheap and willing labour. [122] Representatives of the Canadian garment industry and sugar-beet growers joined this chorus. [123]

The Canadian Labour Congress did not reject the migrant worker scheme out of hand, but it warned that "temporary workers cannot be used to undercut the position of Canadian workers nor should workers from other countries be expected to fill jobs which are unsuitable for Canadians." It also urged Manpower and Immigration, in its administration of the Seasonal Workers' Program,

Table 7
Convention Refugees and Members of
Designated Classes: Type of Sponsorship

	1980	*1983*	*1987*
Convention Refugees			
Government	864	3,260	5,952
Family	53	159	197
Group	35	534	1,016
Self-supporting		148	195
Sub-total	952	4,101	7,473
Designated Classes			
Government	18,373	6,495	8,155
Family	1,414	1,002	1,016
Group	19,281	2,090	4,802
Self-supporting	328	281	119
Sub-total	39,396	9,868	14,092
Total	40,348	13,969	21,565

SOURCE: Employment and Immigration Canada, *Immigration Statistics, 1989.*

to establish effective consultation with "organizations such as ours to ensure the system will work." [124] In contrast, the CLC seemed pleased that the 1966 "obsession" with recruiting skilled and professional immigrants had been discarded.

Both the CLC and the Canadian Civil Liberties Association, however, were not happy with the refugee determination system outlined in the Green Paper, and they insisted that an independent assessment be carried out prior to the case being forwarded to the Refugee Status Advisory Committee. Even more serious, to the CLC, was the government's intention to subject Convention refugees to the same selection criteria as independent immigrants: "a Convention refugee may well have committed an offence in such a place as Chile for example.... It is possible that some of the activities of the Convention refugees could be interpreted to constitute actions for the purpose of 'instigating subversion by force of any government,' particularly if that government were a repressive one ...." [125]

The most extensive discussion of immigration and race relations in Canada was provided by the Toronto-based Urban Alliance on Race Relations. Its brief was a hard-hitting indictment of bias on the part of immigration officials and spoke of the need to ensure "that the prospective immigrant or the prospective visitor to Canada who is black or brown or yellow gets the same kind of treatment that . . . any country which is primarily white in orientation gets." In the opinion of the Alliance, the proposed legislation, rather than removing this bias, left immigration officials "to operate from a racist perspective if they choose to do so." [126] Nor were they confident that bureaucrats had come to grips with the fact that "Canada has become now a multicultural and multiracial society." [127] While the Alliance conceded that Canada's response to visible minorities was more enlightened than that of many other nations, this was no excuse for complacency. [128] Nor were they satisfied that white society had responded very effectively to recent incidents of racial violence in Toronto: "we have been disappointed in the lack of response from clergymen, from business leaders, from professional people . . . like university professors and . . . labour." The Alliance was particularly grieved that organized labour had "said practically nothing about . . . these overt attacks." [129]

What the Standing Committee did not discuss, however, was the extent that effective decision-making within the small Employment and Immigration Commission had been reduced by the 1976-78 changes. [130] In addition, many immigration officials were concerned about the decrease in the number and percentage of independent immigrants selected under the modified points system and the corresponding increase in the number of "less qualified" family-class immigrants. [131] Although the Canada Employment and Immigration Advisory Council in 1980 recommended that family reunion be confined to close, dependent relatives and that sponsors fulfil contractual obligations for their relatives, the Minister, Lloyd Axworthy, did not act. [132] By 1986 there were complaints that family-class immigrants and refugees were being favoured at the expense of more highly skilled independent immigrants. [133]

On the other hand, various studies sponsored by the department indicated that most immigrants who had entered the country after the liberalization of the system in 1967 had adjusted effectively to Canadian society. For example, a 1974 study had demonstrated that of the 161,531 immigrants who had entered the country in 1969, half of these entered the labour market immediately – 65 per cent in the independent category and 26 per cent in the nominated group. The most successful, in economic terms, were those in the managerial, professional, or technical fields; those in crafts and clerical and sales occupations also did rather well. [134] The report also showed that most of these immigrants were able "to realize the occupational intentions they held prior to arrival in Canada" [135] and that a high ratio of immigrant wives entered the labour force, especially in Ontario and Quebec. In cultural terms, special note was taken in another, more recent departmental study of the "increasing tendency to marry across ethnic lines with the passage of time, with the young, the independent immigrants, and the immigrants from English-speaking countries leading the way." [136] Adaptation to Canadian society was demonstrated by the fact that 31 per cent of the

Table 8
Entrepreneurs: Top Ten Countries of
Last Permanent Residence

| | 1984 | | | 1992 | |
Rank	Country	Number	Rank	Country	Number
1.	Hong Kong	474	1.	Hong Kong	8,080
2.	Germany	100	2.	S. Korea	1,899
3.	China	59	3.	Taiwan	1,418
4.	U.S.A.	27	4.	Egypt	456
5.	Taiwan	25	5.	Britain	259
6.	Britain	24	6.	Kuwait	257
7.	Philippines	24	7.	Saudi Arabia	240
8.	Israel	21	8.	Philippines	214
9.	Italy	17	9.	Jordan	188
10.	Malaysia	17	10.	Arab Emirates	175
	Others	226		Others	2,511
Total		1,014		Total	15,697

SOURCES: Employment and Immigration, *Immigration Statistics, 1984*; Citizenship and Immigration Canada, *Immigration Statistics, 1992*.

sample had become involved with broadly based voluntary organizations and that over 50 per cent "reported that they felt at home or *chez soi* in Canada."[137]

A somewhat less flattering profile had emerged from an earlier study, *Immigration and the Canadian Labour Market*, which sought to determine the relative merits of importing professional, skilled, and unskilled immigrant workers as compared with the experience of other countries. According to this report post-war immigrants to Canada had "a disproportionately large impact on the highly-skilled professional-technical labour force," with about 20 per cent of recent immigrants so situated by the 1971 census.[138] In contrast, Sweden had 12 per cent of foreign workers in white-collar jobs, West Germany had 8 per cent, and the United States had 20 per cent.[139] The report also noted that while 7 per cent of professionals in Canada were foreign-born, in the United States the level was only 1 per cent. Did this mean, the authors asked, that Canada's immigration policies were limiting chances for native-born Canadians to gain "access to the generally more desirable professional-technical occupations"?[140]

The timing of the above study coincided with the renewal of the debate over Canada's brain drain to the United States.[141] Throughout the 1970s the Canadian Medical Association kept the issue in the forefront both in its brief to the Standing Committee and in editorials in the *CMA Journal*.[142] In May, 1977, for example, the CMA deputy president, Dr. E.W. Barootes, warned that many Canadian doctors were attracted by U.S. positions offering "considerably higher earnings, lower income taxes, respectable professional status, professional freedom and protection from the harassment and criticism that Canadian physicians have experienced in recent months."[143] What made the situation worse, Barootes claimed, was the recruitment activity of U.S. private hospital corporations such as the giant American Medical International Inc., which in 1977 alone had made contact with over 700 Canadian doctors offering them jobs, high incomes, and speedy licensing.[144] In addition, there was the promise of "instant Americanization," a prospect directly related to changes in both the U.S. Immigration and Naturalization Act and the U.S. Department of Health, Education and Welfare's regulations toward Canadian health workers.[145] This meant that after 1977 Canadian medical school graduates were exempted from U.S. immigration regulations aimed at reducing the influx of foreign medical graduates, and they were likewise excused from taking national medical examinations since their training was considered "equivalent to U.S. graduates." According to the CMA these measures further encouraged American "head hunters," and it complained about the presence of recruiting teams at Canadian medical conventions whose main target were "physicians mainly in the 35-50 range who have reached or are approaching the peak of their professional life productivity."[146]

Another immigration issue was whether Canada was receiving a sufficient number of professional and business immigrants, especially after a 1980 freeze on the independent category of immigrants "unless they had a validated job offer from a Canadian employer."[147] This meant a decline of independent immigrants from 45,032 in 1981 to only 20,495 in 1984; the ratio also went down to 23.7 per cent of all immigrants. The situation improved somewhat after the Conservatives came to power, especially in 1988 when the number of independents reached 68,195 or 42.1 per cent of the total. There was, however, residual concern that independent class applications "are processed after other Classes, and applicants must wait, sometimes for long periods, to let applicants in the other Classes go through."[148]

During the mid-1980s the Mulroney government, given its view "that business is the engine which drives the Canadian economy," made a determined attempt to recruit foreign entrepreneurs and investors. Provision was made for the fast-track entry of businessmen who had "a net personal worth of $500,000 or more, were prepared to sink a minimum of $250,000 in a provincially approved project for three years, and had demonstrated success in the business they were in."[149] The program appeared to be a great success: in 1984 there were 1,014 entrepreneurs; by 1992 there were 15,697.

Conclusion

Canadian immigration policy changed dramatically between 1952 and 1980. Gone were the racist and Eurocentric provisions that excluded immigrants from Asia, the Caribbean, Latin America, and Africa. The dramatic increase in immigrants from these regions gave notice that Canadian society had become more pluralistic. The economic and cultural contribution of these newcomers enriched Canadian society in a variety of ways. There were, however, those who were not comfortable with these changes, especially since such a high percentage of immigrants of colour located in large cities, and there were periodic demands that immigration levels should be reduced.

But most Canadians in 1980, as they had in 1952, equated immigration with economic growth. Canada needed skilled workers and professionals; it also required immigrants for the jobs Canadians didn't want. Until the 1970s British, American, and western European immigrants, with their higher level of education, had a decided edge over other immigrants in obtaining professional and managerial jobs. They were also more readily accepted by Anglo-Canadians. In contrast, immigrants from Italy, Greece, and Portugal usually started as unskilled and semi-skilled workers and encountered various forms of prejudice. But the level of economic achievement and social adjustment by these European men and women was quite impressive. This sense of struggle is captured in the recollections of a southern Italian immigrant to Toronto: "I didn't mind coming to Canada because it was an immigration country. I feel I'm one among other immigrants. Our lives were difficult, and we didn't always get the respect we deserved. But we made something of ourselves too."[150]

There are, however, several questions about Canada's immigration policy in these years that require further explanation. How influential, for example, were Immigration Branch bureaucrats in determining the numbers and ethnic composition of the newcomers? To what extent did resource companies and urban-based manufacturing companies, the traditional immigration boosters, influence policy? Did the growing percentage of family-class immigrants, especially after 1976, indicate that immigration policy was being shaped more and more by the ethnic lobby and their allies? Do the arguments favouring large-scale immigration for long-term population reasons justify short-term unemployment problems? Do immigrants take jobs from Canadians? The answers to these questions remained outstanding during the 1980s and even in the 1990s.

CHAPTER 9

Immigrant Workers and the Canadian Vertical Mosaic

Canadians generally applauded the federal government's commitment to democratic ideals and cultural pluralism reflected in the Immigration Act of 1976-77. At long last, nineteenth-century racist assumptions about racial and ethnic hierarchy had been removed from this statute, as had most of the puerile medical and moral reasons for excluding and deporting. Security screening even seemed less onerous under the new Act, although it still remained an integral part of Canadian immigration policy. But at least there was now an elaborate appeal system that, on paper at least, offered protection for those immigrants and refugees once deemed dangerous.

These changes reflected a changing consensus in Canadian society toward multiculturalism and the importance of confronting racism. The 1971 Multiculturalism Act, with its emphasis on the "equality of status of all cultural and ethnic groups within the framework of our officially bilingual country," provided the statutory justification and administrative machinery.[1] Even more important was the 1982 enactment of the Canadian Charter of Rights and Freedoms, which gave all Canadians constitutional protection of basic civil liberties.[2] But in the immediate post-war years immigrant workers in Canada did not have these cultural and human rights guarantees. Nor did they have the protection of a comprehensive welfare system. It was not until the late 1960s that Canada adopted a national medical health insurance plan, as well as expanded welfare services through the Canada Pension Plan and the Canada Assistance Plan.

Throughout the post-war years there was considerable debate about the relative importance of immigration to Canada's population growth and economic and social progress, and how the various groups of immigrants should be ranked.[3] And the influx was impressive. Between 1946 and 1968, 807,549 British, 253,510 Germans, 444,739 Italians, 164,388 Dutch, 136,420 Poles, 90,520 Greeks, and 67,413 Portuguese had entered the country.[4] Their motives for coming were essentially economic – to improve their standard of living – although some European immigrants still came for political reasons.[5] Return migration was highest among British, Commonwealth, and American immigrants. But good economic times and abundant opportunities provided strong incentives to remain. Once the initial period of adjustment had passed, most post-war immigrants were able to earn about the same as other Canadians of similar age and occupation.[6]

Immigrant Workers, 1950-66

Traditionally, the British-born were the most fortunate group of immigrant workers in Canadian society. This did not change in the post-war years. The high status for British immigrants can be explained by a number of factors. One of the most important was their higher educational and occupational standing, with half of them coming from white-collar occupations and another 30 per cent from the skilled worker category.[7] They also had the advantages of language fluency and social acceptability, important attributes for those immigrants seeking entry into Canadian professions.[8] "Whereas 77 per cent of the British immigrants who were formerly in white-collar occupations retained their status in their first job in Canada, only 32 per cent of the immigrants from other countries did so."[9]

The number of British immigrants relative to those coming from Europe remained a political issue. Under former Ontario Premier George Drew, the Conservative Party periodically charged the Liberals with ignoring British immigration and thereby "upsetting the racial balance in Canada."[10] In rebuttal, Pickersgill reaffirmed his government's preference for British immigrants because they "had the same kind of political institutions . . . the same social customs, [and] found it easier to adapt themselves quickly and readily to this country."[11] After the Suez Crisis of 1956, when thousands of British citizens displayed their dissatisfaction with their government's policy with their feet, the Department of Citizenship and Immigration (DCI) arranged a special airlift for thousands of British immigrants "to forestall the anticipated criticism that the government was more concerned about Hungarians than British immigrants!"[12]

These concerns reflected the extent that Canada had reverted to the 1929 practice of importing large numbers of European workers. An expanding economy, low unemployment, and a shortage of workers to do the jobs Canadians didn't want meant that Canadian immigration officials had to find alternative supplies of unskilled workers. During the early 1950s Canada's manpower

Table 9
Intended Occupational Groups of Post-War Immigrants, 1946-1968

	1946-55	1956-68
Managerial	4,213	18,606
Professional	44,526	184,232
Clerical	46,788	120,046
Transportation	14,331	14,694
Communication	1,001	4,912
Commercial/Sales	25,257	32,412
Financial/Sales	474	2,927
Service	69,447	122,526
Farmers	138,195	54,473
Construction	52,516	87,416
Fishers/Loggers	12,928	2,979
Miners	10,029	5,955
Manufacturing	148,095	217,596
Labourers	58,743	100,364
Others	9,255	5,617
Sub-total	635,798	974,755
Non-workers/dependants	586,521	908,539
Total	1,222,319	1,883,294

SOURCE: Department of Manpower and Immigration, *Immigration Statistics, 1970*, 25.

needs coincided with powerful push factors in Europe; indeed, a number of countries, facing severe economic and social problems, viewed emigration as one way of coping with their problems. In the case of Italy and Greece the causes were economic and political: both countries had suffered greatly during the war and experienced considerable social unrest during post-war reconstruction. In Greece there was the added horror of a ferocious civil war (1946-49). In contrast, the Portuguese were almost exclusively economic immigrants from the depressed regions of the north and the Azores.

The first post-war bilateral immigration agreement was with the government of the Netherlands. Under this scheme, 94,000 Dutch immigrants came to Canada between 1947 and 1954, 80 per cent of whom were agriculturalists.[13] From the point of view of the Dutch government, which selected and screened the immigrants, the experiment was a great success.[14] A high percentage of Dutch agriculturalists quickly adapted to Canadian farming conditions and soon acquired their own farms, especially in the southern regions of Ontario and

Alberta. While Canadian immigration officials also applauded this, their enthusiasm was dampened by the realization that they had to find farm workers to replace the upwardly mobile Dutch.

Pressure for the admission of other groups of European workers, especially Italians, had been under way before the Dutch agreement and the DP Bulk Labour Program had been adopted. Resource companies, railway interests, and Italian-Canadian groups urged Ottawa to discard the enemy alien barrier and allow relatives and "husky" workers into the country. The Italian government, overwhelmed by post-war reconstruction, added its voice to the immigration chorus.[15]

Although immigration officials strongly endorsed the return of an active recruitment policy, they did not regard large-scale Italian immigration favourably. This bias, especially against southern Italians, was reflected in deputy minister Laval Fortier's October 4, 1949, memorandum: "The Italian South peasant is not the type we are looking for in Canada. His standard of living, his way of life, even his civilization seems so different that I doubt if he could ever become an asset to our country." In contrast, Fortier regarded immigrants from the industrialized northern regions as having considerable potential, an impression reinforced during his 1949 visit to Italy. On this occasion, Fortier signed a bilateral agreement under which the Italian labour ministry screened those coming under family sponsorship arrangements, as well as those entering under bulk labour orders.[16] The latter group were expected to fulfil contractual obligations similar to those experienced by DP workers, with the reward of a job, future occupational mobility, and eventual citizenship.[17]

Urgent demands for Italian railway workers and miners also expedited the movement, and by the summer of 1951 there was heavy traffic between Canada and the ports of Naples, Milan, and Genoa. Most of the recruits were unskilled.[18] There were, however, notable exceptions: the transfer of 500 experienced miners from the Rome-based mining association La Societa Finanziaria (Finsider) to the Canadian Metals Mining Association; and skilled workers forwarded by the powerful Societa per L'Industria e L'Elettricita. Although Canadian immigration officials were concerned about the high percentage of southern Italians among the arrivals,[19] Department of Labour screening officers were more optimistic, reporting that they were "genuine farmers, hard working men, used to tilling the soil," with "no lawyers, philosophers, or other such professions among them."[20] Labour officials were less enthusiastic toward Italian skilled workers, largely because of complaints from Canadian trade unions that the newcomers were taking scarce jobs and undermining industrial relations.[21] Another complaint was that a high percentage of unskilled Italian workers were leaving their frontier jobs and "flocking to the cities and becoming 'unnecessary competitors of Canadians for existing jobs.'"[22]

By the mid-1950s immigrant workers from Greece and Portugal were also arriving in large numbers. They, too, came under labour migration schemes negotiated by their governments as a way of coping with high unemployment and reducing social tension. In 1951 the Greek government took the initiative when it informed the DCI that there were over 50,000 Greek farm labourers, industrial workers, and female domestics available for employment in Canada. Although Canadian immigration officials were intrigued with the proposal, they decided to proceed cautiously. An initial trial group of 1,100 were admitted, consisting of 500 domestics, 200 restaurant workers, and 400 agriculturalists and miners. Pleased with the results, the DCI authorized the entry of other occupational groups. By 1957 total immigration from Greece was 17,747.[23]

At this stage the Immigration Branch hierarchy called for a reassessment of the program. They were particularly interested in the occupational patterns of Greek immigrant workers, more specifically, how many remained in the extractive industries. The results were disappointing. Most Greek workers had left the frontier regions at the earliest opportunity, gravitating to the major urban centres of central Canada to seek jobs in restaurants and factories. As a result of this study, in December, 1957, the acting deputy minister, C.S. Smith, advised his Minister, Jack Pickersgill, that the movement of Greek farm labourers be curtailed:

> Throughout the past decade we have had a sympathetic attitude toward immigration from Greece, mainly because Greece is a member state of NATO and also because of the economic situation there. . . . But invariably those workers who came from Greece would not be considered suitable due to their unwillingness to live in rural areas and the difficulties of learning English or French. . . . Greek immigrants have a strong tendency to move to the Greek communities, accept employment with Greek Canadians, usually in non-productive industries at depressed wages and thereby never really contribute very much to Canada.[24]

If Smith have ever experienced the rigours of life in a frontier rail or bush camp he might have been more sympathetic. He might also have reflected on the anguished appeal that twenty Greek workers, stranded in an Abitibi Pulp and Paper Company lumber camp in northern Ontario, sent to the Greek consul-general in Toronto:

> . . . we have suffered owing to our lack of knowing the work of a lumberjack. . . . Thousands of mosquitos await us every morning . . . so they can get their fill with our blood. . . . We have no clothes left and we are forced to get some from the supply house signing and paying for them with our future earnings. . . . We are poor people who came here to work. . . . However, we do not want to die under these conditions.[25]

Greek domestics seem to have had an easier time – if working twelve hours a day, six days a week for middle-class Anglo-Canadian homemakers in Toronto was easier. But at least there were no swarms of mosquitoes. There was also the prospect of gaining landed immigrant status and sponsoring fiancés and family members, as this example of chain migration shows:

> In 1953 Mariana left her village in southern Greece at the age of 17 and came to Canada to work as a domestic. Upon her arrival in London, Ontario, she was able to obtain a job in a factory and thus avoid the degrading job of a domestic servant. Two years later she sponsored her oldest brother Nikos who came and started as a dishwasher in a Greek-owned restaurant. A few months later Mariana sponsored her parents, two brothers and a sister. The following year (1956) Mariana sponsored her fiancé George, a young man from a nearby village whom she married as soon as he arrived in Canada. The same year George sponsored his sister Dena who came to London and started her first job in a dry cleaning store. A year later (1957) Dena sponsored her fiancé John. . . . That same year John sponsored his sister Eleni who got a job in a dry cleaning store. In 1958 Eleni sponsored her fiancé Petros who obtained a job as a dishwasher in a Greek-owned restaurant.[26]

As this account demonstrates, Greek immigrants showed a strong proclivity for urban jobs, usually in the service industry where they were often hired by other Greeks. This ethnic employment chain had obvious advantages for recent arrivals since they got jobs quickly and they could work and live in a Greek cultural environment. There was, of course, the distinct possibility that their Greek benefactor might pay low wages for gruelling and monotonous work. But for many, a lowly apprenticeship in a compatriot's restaurant carried with it the promise of their own business opportunity sometime in the future.[27]

Opportunities in ethnic enterprise were also familiar to thousands of Portuguese immigrants who chose central Canadian cities after their frontier apprenticeship.[28] They, too, had come to Canada under bilateral immigration arrangements. The most important of these was a 1954 pilot project whereby 200 Portuguese track workers were sent to the R.L. Welch Company in Port Arthur, Ontario; there were also 700 agricultural workers and fifty tradesmen. All came from the Azores. While these men proved willing workers, they often found their jobs arduous and difficult, especially the farm labourers.[29]

Caribbean migrant workers entered Canada during the 1950s as a replacement for the departing DP and European workers, especially in the agricultural sector.[30] The Ontario agricultural lobby was impressed with the success American growers had enjoyed with Caribbean and Mexican workers and wanted their own supply of cheap and malleable labour. But they faced formidable problems:

there were no Canadian-Caribbean guest worker programs to build on, and they had only limited political clout. On the other hand, their recruitment efforts were strongly encouraged by several of the West Indian governments, most notably Barbados, whose House of Assembly passed a resolution in June, 1954, calling for a bilateral agreement with Canada on the grounds that acute agricultural labour shortages in Ontario and western Canada presented "definite prospects for temporary emigration of appreciable numbers of both men and women . . . during the summer and early autumn." Nothing came of this initiative, largely because Canadian immigration and labour officials were not interested in encouraging West Indian immigration. Their rationale was, however, more devious: Caribbean workers, they argued, were unfit for these jobs because of their lack of "previous experience in the types of agriculture practised in Canada."[31]

The Immigration Branch's bias against Caribbean workers was of long standing. In 1952, Walter Harris had made the celebrated remark that "persons from tropical countries or sub-tropical countries find it more difficult to succeed in the highly competitive Canadian economy." A 1958 policy statement by the director of the Immigration Branch reinforced the exclusionist policy: "it has been our long standing practice to deal favourably with British subjects of the white race from the British West Indies. . . . On the other hand, apart from a limited domestic movement, no encouragement is given to persons of coloured race unless they have close relatives in Canada or their visas have exceptional merit, such as graduate nurses, qualified stenographers, etc."[32] The controversy in Britain over West Indian labour did not improve the situation. In January, 1966, for example, Tom Kent, the newly appointed deputy minister, was informed about "the long range wisdom" of preventing "a substantial increase in negro immigration to Canada," particularly given the current "racial problems of Britain and the United States." Another brief warned that Canadians, who "in normal circumstances would not have any prejudice in respect to race, colour or creed, have shown concern that through rapid increases in the intake of under-educated and un-skilled immigrants, especially if multi-racial, we could end up with situations [race riots] similar to those in the United Kingdom."[33]

Migration between the Caribbean and Canada was therefore not possible until the discriminatory immigration policy was changed. This was partially achieved by the White Paper reforms of 1966-67, and the changes were immediately evident. In a dramatic turnabout, immigration officials now supported – although not for the noblest of motives – Canadian growers' demands for temporary Caribbean workers: "By admitting West Indian workers on a seasonal basis, it might be possible to reduce greatly the pressure on Canada to accept unskilled workers from the West Indies as immigrants. Moreover, seasonal farm workers would not have the privilege of sponsoring innumerable close relatives."[34]

By mid-1966, the Immigration Branch tried to work out a deal for Caribbean temporary workers.[35] At the March meeting of the Federal-Provincial Manpower Committee the following arrangement was recommended: (1) growers should offer a wage rate of $1.50 per hour; (2) they should guarantee a weekly wage of $50 per worker; (3) workers should be provided with satisfactory meals and lodging, not to exceed $20 per week; (4) the term of employment should range between eight and twelve weeks; (5) daily work hours should not exceed local standards; (6) growers should pay the return transportation costs of the workers.[36] Between 1966 and 1973 the annual number of Jamaican temporary agricultural workers ranged between 264 and 3,048.[37] In the early stages, the system seemed to operate effectively with little opposition. Even the *Toronto Sun*'s 1972 complaint, during the federal election, that Ottawa was importing 1,500 West Indians "to work in Ontario at a time when 146,000 Ontarians are out of jobs," caused only a minor political ripple.[38] More serious were July, 1973, reports that some Ontario growers were exploiting their Caribbean and Mexican workers. Stung by these charges, Robert Andras assured the House of Commons that under no circumstances would his department "bring foreign workers in if working conditions, including but not limited to wages, are sub-standard."[39] He also ordered a full investigation.

Two reports on seasonal farm labour in southwestern Ontario were submitted in the fall of 1973. One of these was an official account by the Department of Manpower and Immigration that exonerated the industry of any wrongdoing.[40] The problem, it suggested, was not with the Caribbean Seasonal Workers and Canada-U.S. Tobacco Workers programs but with the movement of illegal migrant workers, most of whom were Mennonite families from Mexico with "a Canadian connection." Unsanitary living conditions, the report concluded, could not be blamed on the growers since "the pickers had, through indifference or malice, turned these quarters into uninhabitable accommodation."[41]

Quite a different profile emerged from an internal DMI report. The Ontario cash crop industry was guilty of "intolerable and inhumane conditions involving workers and their families living in hovels, literally and where child labour and other forms of exploitation were evident."[42] It was particularly critical of the treatment of Mexican Mennonites and Portuguese workers, neither of whom were covered by the Caribbean Seasonal Workers Program.[43] On the positive side,[44] the report noted that many Ontario growers were bitterly opposed to the employment of illegals because it undermined the local wage structure and gave the industry a bad reputation.[45]

Canada's dependence on immigrant workers for low-paying, low-status jobs attracted the attention of many commentators during the 1970s review of Canadian immigration policy. The Green Paper on Immigration Policy, for example, considered the European guest worker model as one way of meeting shortfalls in the Canadian labour supply.[46] It pointed out that during the economic boom of the 1960s, France, Sweden, Switzerland, and West Germany had all depended on a constant flow of migrant workers from the economically deprived periphery – southern Italy, Spain, Portugal, Greece, Yugoslavia, Turkey, and North Africa.[47] But the West German experience attracted the greatest attention because of the scale of the influx and the institutional structures and policies it required.[48] Yet despite efforts by German authorities to avoid confrontation between guest workers and German communities, tension between the two groups mounted during the 1970s. This was particularly the case in centres such as Frankfurt and Berlin, which attracted large numbers of Turkish workers who became the special target of fascist and racist organizations.[49]

Another important international development influencing the Canadian debate was the British government's decision during the 1960s to exclude migrant workers from the Caribbean, Africa, and the Indian subcontinent. This dramatic change in Britain's traditional liberal immigration laws was a response to the massive movement of migrant workers from former British colonies who took advantage of rights of entry conferred by the British Nationality Act of 1948 and of abundant employment opportunities.[50] Impetus for change came primarily from Conservative backbenchers in the government of Edward Heath, who responded to their own prejudices and their constituents' concern that the rising tide of "coloured" immigration threatened "traditional" British values and social stability. Indeed, when Home Secretary R.A. Butler introduced the legislation he claimed that coloured immigrants were difficult "to integrate" into British life because of their large numbers and their tendency "to settle in communities of their own . . . in big cities."[51] The situation became more tense when demagogues such as Conservative MP Enoch Powell demanded total exclusion of all coloured immigrants and the repatriation of those already in the country.[52] This nativist appeal surfaced during the 1971 election and was one factor in the Conservatives return to power. In quick order the Heath government passed the Immigration Act of 1971, which further excluded non-white Commonwealth immigrants through the device of patriality, whereby only those persons "whose parents or grandparents had been born in the United Kingdom could enter freely."[53]

But the domestic labour market and the role of migrant/guest workers had the greatest impact on the Canadian immigration debate. In 1976, for instance, the Department of Employment and Immigration commissioned a study, *Immigration and the Canadian Labour Market*, to assess the extent that Canadian employers used the Temporary Worker Authorization Program (TWAP), especially for agricultural labour, service sector and product fabricating jobs, and domestic and garment workers. By way of comparison, reference was made to the European experiences with guest workers:

In a situation [in Europe] where demand for labour was strong in all sectors, filling the unwanted "bottom" jobs would have required substantial pay hikes; and employers plus large segments of the public, preferred to hold the line. Foreign workers offered a solution in which historic wage differentials could be preserved while still getting the work done in service and other low-pay sectors. . . . without the foreign workers, it would have been necessary to raise wages in low-wage jobs, and this of course would have reduced the share to other sectors. Forestalling those wage increases preserved the privileged income position of most nationals.[54]

While the annual movement of migrant workers was of much smaller scale than in western Europe and confined to specific jobs, there is little doubt that it was a version of the European guest worker system. This was confirmed in an article by sociologist Lloyd Wong, who noted that between 1978 and 1982 the number of employment visas increased from 94,413 to 124,114, and that many of these entrants were "similar to guest workers elsewhere." Although many of Wong's conclusions were challenged, even his critics were prepared to admit that employment authorizations for jobs in domestic service and farm labour did share many characteristics with the situation of European guest workers since "both occupations are considered to be low skill and the steady demand for workers in these occupations indicates that the work is a permanent part of the Canadian economy."[55]

In 1974 Mexico signed a seasonal labour agreement with Canada, and throughout the remainder of the seventies and early eighties there were periodic newspaper reports and parliamentary questions about the treatment of foreign-born agricultural workers. One of the most revealing was a July, 1982, article in *Canadian Forum*, "Racism and Labour: The Struggle of British Columbia's Farmworkers." Here the focus was not on Caribbean or Mexican migrants but on East Indians, who made up 90 per cent of the province's 12,000 farm workers. The exposé was particularly critical of the *padrone* or brokerage system:

This legal pimping is often undertaken by East Indians who have lived in Canada for several years and become enamoured with this country's potential for exploitation. Farmworker contractors have been known to withhold as much as 40 per cent of the piece-meal rate for their services in driving the pickers to and from the farms – often crowding 20 to 30 workers in one small van. Some neglected to pay their workers altogether. . . . Farmworkers' dependence on labour contractors is heightened by the fact that in many cases the contractor is the only link between workers and the linguistically and culturally alien Canadian society. In some instances the contractor actually sponsors their immigration to Canada, thus holding the threat of deportation over his labour force.[56]

Provincial and federal authorities also came under fire for their refusal to extend the minimum wage to the agricultural sector and for a discriminatory unemployment insurance clause that penalized those engaged in seasonal and fluctuating work patterns. Even worse was the lack of inspection of worker accommodations, often "converted barnstalls and dilapidated outbuildings . . . somewhere between a slum and a gutter." The greatest menace, however, was in the fields, where dangerous machinery and toxic pesticides were often the rule rather than the exception.[57] Nor were injured or contaminated workers eligible for full coverage under the province's Workers' Compensation Act.[58]

In contrast to migrant workers in Ontario, these B.C. East Indian migrant farm workers were more successful in forcing the agricultural interests to deal with their complaints through a variety of collective measures. Their ability to organize was enhanced by being able to draw on their ethnocultural and class unity; in fact, they created their own trade union in 1979. The Canadian Farmworkers Union soon had a membership of over 1,200 workers. It fought several strikes and negotiated three separate contracts guaranteeing better wages and working conditions.[59] Attempts during the 1980s to expand its operation into Ontario, with its ethnically diverse farm labour force, however, proved a difficult challenge for the CFU. Part of the problem was that many of the Caribbean and Mexican offshore workers were sojourners who put their personal lives "on hold" while enduring "long working hours . . . [that] confine them to the farms for most of their times . . . within a somewhat culturally irrelevant, sometimes unfriendly, [Ontario] farming community system."[60]

Immigrant Women Workers

The demand for domestic workers, an integral part of immigration prior to World War Two, remained high during the 1950s and 1960s despite the ever-increasing use of household technology. Great Britain remained the most important source, particularly during the early 1950s when many British domestics were attracted by the assisted passage loan scheme and the long-term prospects of better jobs in Canada. Since many of these women soon left domestic service, DCI officials were under constant pressure to find suitable replacements from both Britain and Europe.[61] One of the most ambitious schemes was the 1950 movement of 500 Italian domestics who received assisted passage and guaranteed employment under the Bulk Labour Program. This venture floundered largely because of religious, cultural, and linguistic differences between the domestics and their employers.[62] More successful was the recruitment of 7,000 Greek domestics, who represented about 25 per cent of total Greek immigration during the 1950s.[63]

Because of the difficulty in obtaining a stable domestic service labour force from Britain and Europe, DCI officials decided to explore the British Caribbean market. In 1955, with much fanfare about Commonwealth unity, the Canadian government made arrangements for admitting 100 domestics from the West Indies. As usual, however, immigration officials drove a hard bargain: the candidates had to be single, between the ages of eighteen and thirty-five, and in good health. While the occupational and personal screening was carried out by Jamaican or Barbadian authorities, the mandatory medical examination remained in Canadian hands.[64] In the short term, the scheme was regarded as a success since a high proportion of the immigrants remained in domestic service, not necessarily because they liked the work but because racism excluded them from other jobs.

In 1960, DCI officials considered cancelling the program despite the generally good performance of West Indian domestics. The reasons for this decision were set forth in a May, 1960, memorandum from the director of immigration, who noted, with some concern, that "these girls, as soon as they are established, are free to apply for the admission of their relatives and fiancés . . . [who] are likely to be unskilled workers."[65] He also claimed, without a shred of evidence, that most of these Caribbean fiancés were frauds since illegitimacy was "a fact of life . . . [and] it is not uncommon for a single girl to have children by 2, 3, or 4 different men."[66] These ethnocentric and biased attitudes, combined with the department's new emphasis on recruiting highly educated workers, meant a curtailment of the program in 1966.[67] When the movement was reinstated in 1973, it was quite different. Caribbean domestics now entered under the temporary employment authorization program, which meant they could only remain in the country if they kept their positions; changing occupations or employers could result in deportation.[68]

Controversy over Canada's treatment of immigrant domestic workers was of long standing. Study after study had shown that few Canadian women were prepared "to take and keep jobs as live-in domestics, regardless of labour market conditions." Most domestics, recruited from Great Britain, the Philippines, and the Caribbean, entered under a variety of contractual arrangements.[69] In the case of Jamaicans, the preferred applicants were to be "single, widowed, divorced, without minor children or the encumbrance of common law relationships . . . prepared to work in domestic employment for at least a year." These working conditions made the foreign domestic vulnerable to employer control:

> She usually works by herself in a private home, often with few opportunities to socialize. This isolation and her temporary status offer virtually no opportunities for collective action with others similarly situated. She depends on her employer not only for her wage, but also for her dwelling place and continued stay in the country . . . the employment authorization device serves to maintain the supply of domestics by restricting their mobility. As presently administered, however, it also serves to inhibit the

type of improvement in wages and working conditions which might ultimately attract Canadians to these jobs and reduce the need for foreign
workers. [70]

During the early 1980s there was considerable discussion about the future of
the domestic authorization scheme. Some critics questioned why affluent Canadian professionals should be supplied with a steady supply of cheap, malleable
immigrant labour when Canadian workers would undertake these jobs if the
wages and working conditions were improved. The Minister, Lloyd Axworthy,
acknowledged this argument when he addressed the National Conference on
Immigrant Women in Canada, held in Toronto on March 21, 1981:

> Domestic work encompasses a wide assortment of duties with a corre-
> sponding array of skill requirements. Some domestic responsibilities such
> as child rearing and the management of a household require professional
> skills which are only now becoming recognized and respected in our soci-
> ety. Individuals with such skills are people who can make a positive and
> enduring contribution to Canada. I have therefore asked my officials to
> look at ways of encouraging domestic workers to come to Canada as
> landed immigrants rather than transient workers. [71]

The only problem with this scheme, as Sheila Arnopoulos pointed out in her
1979 report, *Problems of Immigrant Women in the Canadian Labour Force*, was
that allowing domestics to enter as landed immigrants would not solve the shortage of domestics, since on arrival these women would "soon discover that factory work pays better." [72] To make domestic service more attractive, the DEI task
force recommended that domestics who remained in their jobs for one year
"should be 'grandmothered' – permitted to seek landing from within Canada
under the revised point system and allowed to remain in Canada working as
domestics until their applications are processed." [73]

Although attempts were made to improve the system during the early 1980s,
there were still many reasons for immigrant women to be apprehensive. [74] Using
data from the 1973 Canadian Mobility Study Monica Boyd found that in large
cities, where upwards of 80 per cent of foreign-born women were located,
"immigrant women have on the average an occupational status which is nearly
four points below that of foreign born males and native born females . . . immigrant women in Canada are indeed disadvantaged by the combination of their
sex and foreign born status." Most found jobs in the service, production, fabrica-
tion, and assembly occupations, either because of their lack of marketable skills
or because other mechanisms "either devalue their labor market capabilities or
restrict their employment opportunities to certain job ghettos." In addition to the
restrictions and burdens of a sex-segregated occupational structure, full-time

work was often accompanied by onerous family duties, "the double duty/double burden syndrome."[75]

The burden of racism was an additional obstacle that immigrant women of colour had to overcome. Caribbean immigrants spoke about being relegated to black women's work: "cleaning white people's houses, bathrooms and hotel rooms; serving white people breakfast, lunch and dinner in private homes, in office cafeterias, hospitals; lifting, feeding, mending, washing white people's children and older white people; sweeping, boxing, scouring, washing, cooking."[76] There was also the difficulty of obtaining full-time jobs. For instance, of the 1,500 workers in CUPE Local 79 in Toronto who were temporary, 90 per cent were women and over half were "black, Asian or Native people."[77] Local 79 thus demonstrated a willingness to develop effective labour strategies "for representing and defending women of colour."[78] On a broader level, the activities of the Ontario Coalition of Black Trade Unionists, founded in 1986, helped to focus on racism in the workplace.

Immigrant women workers were also susceptible to harassment by immigration officials and exploitation by unscrupulous employment agencies. In 1976, for example, a special immigration inquiry documented cases of DEI officers in Montreal extracting sexual favours from women immigrants in return for approving their applications. This report also described how hundreds of visitors to Canada used fraudulent means to obtain landed immigrant status: "These visitors had usually left families at home, and had paid an equivalent of two or three years income . . . to travel to Canada . . . [where] the 'visitor' sometimes produced suspect school certificates and letters testifying to previous employment, and doubtful letters offering jobs in Canada."[79]

By 1981 the number of illegal immigrants, many enticed by family members and travel brokers, had reached alarming proportions. This, in turn, produced strong public concern about "the deleterious effect of illegals on the economy, and, particularly, in relation to unemployment, the burden on welfare and the failure to pay taxes." These and related problems were the focus of two special studies commissioned by DEI.[80] *Illegal Immigrants in Canada* (1983) began its analysis by suggesting that any country such as Canada that committed itself to immigration was "bound to experience a certain level of illegal migration." It observed, for instance, that West Germany had apprehended over 25,000 illegals in 1981 and that there were as many as six million illegals in the United States.[81] In these countries, as well as in Canada, there was an appreciation that if employers could be deterred from hiring illegals the traffic could be controlled.

Although the 1976 Canadian Immigration Act had provided sanctions for those who "knowingly" hired illegals, many employers succumbed to the temptation of getting cheap and exploitable workers.[82] Adding to the problem was the difficulty of detecting illegals since DEI had to rely on an anonymous tip, a police referral, or chance – such as the illegal who "was detected after winning a $100,000 lottery prize."[83] The 1983 DEI report also provided a composite profile of the illegal: "most were between the ages of 20 and 35, were single and were employed; arrived by air, entered legally and overstayed their lawful visits."[84] While family members and friends could provide jobs, shelter, and anonymity,[85] the subculture of the illegal was full of pitfalls. Some of these were described in an interview with the rector of an inner-city Toronto church:

> the children of illegal immigrants . . . find it difficult to register for school for fear that their parents will be found out and shipped back . . . ; there is a fear of being denounced . . . by fellow countrymen who know their secret; some of them have been misused by their employers . . . others have . . . been misused by unscrupulous lawyers who charge them high fees, with promises of shortcuts to legality but who know that nothing can be accomplished.[86]

Although the DEI report rejected a general amnesty for all illegals because it would further undermine Canada's immigration laws and procedures, it did suggest greater use of the Minister's discretionary authority on a case-by-case basis, taking into account the individual's employment record, family ties, criminal record, and whether he/she qualified for refugee protection. Greater use of visitor visas, especially against those countries with a high ratio of illegals, was also proposed. Tougher legislation against immigration consultants was another major recommendation.

This latter topic had, in fact, been the focus of a special report to the Minister in April, 1981, in response to a number of incidents where unwary and naive immigrants had been bilked. In its analysis of the problem, this report sought to explain why so many immigrants showed "a willingness to place special trust in an adviser simply because of a shared language or cultural background." It found that motives ranged from "a feeling that to succeed in an application, something more than mere compliance is necessary – something in the nature of an 'inside track' or special advantage over other applicants," to a general feeling of distrust "of government officials (perhaps based on experience in the country of origin) or the belief that the payment of a bribe is the ordinary manner of transacting business with officialdom." There was also a tendency "not to report an incident where one has been victimized . . . to avoid 'making waves' for fear of being viewed as a 'troublemaker' and thereby jeopardizing the potential success of an application."[87] The fact that few of these queue jumpers were deported did not help public perceptions of the system or morale within the Department of Employment and Immigration. One immigration officer expressed his frustration as follows:

We are told to uphold the Immigration Act. That's our job. So we get a tip and apprehend an illegal. We set in motion the work to remove the person from the country. After all, he has broken the law. But while the procedure is in motion, this guy either through his lawyer or some leader in his community, gets the support of the local member of Parliament who in turn lobbies the Minister of Immigration. Before you know it, the guy – who knowingly came here illegally . . . is rewarded by being given landed immigrant status. [88]

Visible Minorities and Canada's Vertical Mosaic

Immigrant workers of colour have often experienced more difficulty in adjusting to Canadian society than their European counterparts. In part, this can be attributed to the legacy of racism, which was more pronounced during the 1950s and 1960s than it is today. Those arriving in subsequent decades were more fortunate in having some human rights protection, but they had additional economic problems in gaining access to permanent full-time jobs. Clearly, there were more unskilled and semi-skilled jobs in Canada during the earlier period, and competition for professional positions became more intense by the late 1970s. Some immigrants of colour have also been forced to accept jobs below their educational level because of discrimination and because of the difficulty of having their qualifications accepted by Canadian professional organizations. In recent years, Canada's commitment to multiculturalism and human rights has helped reduce the level of overtly racist employment practices, but more subtle discrimination still remains. Canadian society has also remained susceptible to negative stereotypes of certain ethnic groups, and in some instances these stereotypes have been reinforced by the police and the media.

One of the most celebrated instances of state harassment of a visible minority was the May 24, 1960, RCMP raid on Chinatowns across the country in "one of the biggest searches in Canadian history." In their attempt to accumulate incriminating evidence, police teams barged into private homes and business offices, often intimidating the occupants. The popular press fanned public hysteria with headlines such as "RCMP Squads Crack Huge Chinese Immigration Racket." Nor did RCMP Commissioner Harvison help the situation when he announced that "11,000 Chinese of the 23,000 that have come to Canada since 1946 have entered the country illegally." [89]

This allegation was immediately challenged by Chinese organizations, especially the Chinese Benevolent Association, and by Liberal MP Jack Pickersgill, who challenged the Conservative government to prove wrongdoing by a community "which has a record of obeying the law that most of us might envy." With public opinion swinging toward the victims, Immigration Minister Ellen Fairclough announced a policy of clemency in the House of Commons. She did not, however, apologize for the government's harsh measures: "I feel sure that many of the Chinese themselves are most anxious to regularize their status in Canada and to relieve themselves once and for all from the feeling of insecurity . . . knowing as they do, that they have entered Canada through illegal means and are constantly subject to the dangers of exposure."[90] While the promise of amnesty, however vague, was reassuring to the Chinese communities, they felt it imperative to present their concern about individual and collective civil rights directly to Prime Minister John Diefenbaker. They were particularly upset that some police forces "freely arrest and detain Chinese under suspicion. . . . The situation resembles a country under martial law." In the end, the Crown prosecuted only twenty-eight people, and no sentence was greater than six months. For Chinese Canadians this incident remains "the 907 days of fear."[91]

During the 1980s Chinese immigrants once again became the centre of controversy. In part, the issues were closely related to past allegations about criminal activity and the traffic in illegal immigrants. Periodically, there were sensationalist news reports about Chinese-Canadian gangs and triads carrying out extortion and narcotic operations in the Chinatowns of Toronto and Vancouver.[92] In June, 1988, the *Globe and Mail* revealed that a partner of a prestigious Toronto law firm "was helping Hong Kong clients to fake Canadian residence and investment requirements in order to fraudulently obtain citizenship."[93] At the popular level, middle-class homeowners in Toronto and Vancouver often resented wealthy Hong Kong businessmen buying up choice residential property and building vast houses, or "monster homes." "Bad taste," journalist Margaret Cannon wrote, "was only one part of the problem; the newcomers were also unwilling to accommodate themselves to the culture around them."[94]

There are many reasons why so many Hong Kong residents have come to Canada in recent years. The most important is that Hong Kong will revert to the control of the Chinese government in 1997; this is "a form of pre-emptive migration, a rare instance in which people have known for a long while what the future holds for them, in general terms." Some among these immigrants have sought Canadian citizenship as "an act of insurance . . . they seek only the protection of a foreign passport so they can live in Hong Kong with greater security than they would if they were Chinese citizens."[95] Another important factor was the concerted effort by the Conservative government of Brian Mulroney to attract Hong Kong businessmen through its Immigrant Investor Program, which came into full force during the late 1980s.[96] Indeed, in 1989 among the 23,000 immigrants from Hong Kong, 5,300 (23 per cent) came as investors; they brought $3.1 billion of assets to Canada. Most of these people – 42 per cent of all investor immigrants and another 25 per cent of all business immigrants – gravitated to British Columbia. Peter Li describes their impact on the Vancouver region:

Among the new middle class Chinese of Richmond are recent immigrants from Hong Kong, many of whom came as retirees or investors who maintain regular financial and business contacts with their country of origin. A segment of Chinese business people comes to be known as "astronauts" among the Chinese because they shuttle between their business in Hong Kong and their families in Canada after becoming landed immigrants in Canada. . . . the lower real estate price of Richmond relative to the west side of Vancouver is another feature which attracts middle class immigrants. Many of these affluent newcomers brought with them the cosmopolitan consumer culture of Hong Kong.[97]

Immigrants from the West Indies are another group subject to negative stereotypes. This negative bias has increased as the West Indian population of Canada increased from about 12,000 in 1961 to 68,000 in 1971, to 211,000 in 1981, with largest numbers coming from Jamaica (77,950), Trinidad (38,465), Haiti (26,755), and Guyana (37,975).[98] There were many reasons for this movement. Unsatisfactory political and social conditions in their homelands certainly motivated most Haitians fleeing from the tyranny of the Duvalier regimes;[99] it was also cited as a reason by some Jamaicans, although better job prospects were the major incentive.[100] In addition, Britain's racially selective immigration policy virtually excluded all unskilled and semi-skilled migrant workers from Caribbean countries.[101] Those who could not gain entry to Canada as immigrants had an alternative: the temporary employment visa program.

Although Caribbean immigrants were often divided by ethnicity, they also shared a number of social characteristics and over 80 per cent spoke English, with only the Haitians being predominantly Francophone (11 per cent). On arrival, they gravitated to metropolitan centres, most notably Toronto and Montreal. And, contrary to popular stereotypes, they had a relatively high level of education.[102] Job opportunities in Canada did not, however, correlate with educational or skill attainment.[103] As a result, there was a "relative concentration of male and female Caribbean immigrants in processing and fabricating industries, and, to a lesser degree, in professional and technical occupations, but only among the pre-1970 arrivals."[104] They were also subject to prejudice and racism.[105]

The problem of racism in Toronto was the focus of a special 1976 task force in Metropolitan Toronto headed by former provincial NDP leader Walter Pitman. The catalyst for this inquiry was a rash of racially motivated attacks during the winter months of 1976-77, which convinced many observers that Toronto "was a time-bomb of potential conflict that could explode in the not-too-distant future."[106] The task force report suggested several explanations for this phenomenon. One was to view the assaults "as part of a 'rite of entry' – that every immigrant minority must undergo initial abuse and discrimination which will dissipate for that group as time goes on." Closely related was the argument that certain ethnic groups, because of their cultural traits and racial characteristics, became more likely targets. Using these arguments it was possible, therefore, to explain why South Asians had replaced blacks as primary victims of random violence:

> The present victim – the brown skinned citizen – is less able to cope with this aggression. . . . First, most South Asians come from a non-violent tradition and do not normally react with the physical force which might impress the "bully" belligerent. Often, the South Asian is of slight physical build and does not easily impress the individual bent on abusing him. Further, the South Asian community, still relatively small, and with little of the cohesion which other ethnic communities have achieved, cannot organize easily. . . . It must be obvious too, that the South Asian has a cultural tradition which is unfamiliar and threatening to some people. The turban, the sari, the spiced food, the articulation . . . are all aspects of high visibility. . . .[107]

The task force was impressed by the fact that "probably no group of immigrants has ever come to Canada with more skills and more advanced educational background" and yet encountered so many obstacles. This included not only verbal and physical assaults and the iniquitous "Paki" jokes, but also strained relations with the metro Toronto police. All too often, they noted, South Asian communities had come to regard the police as biased and unfair. In return, many police officers saw the Asian newcomer "as an aggressive queue jumper, who is arrogant, extremely excitable and has a tendency to lie and bribe."[108] While the task force felt that both groups had erred, the police were most to blame. This was attributed, in part, to the failure of the Toronto police force to hire more visible minority officers; there was also a deplorable tendency by some officers not just "to investigate the crime, but to act as judges and jury."[109] Although the task force acknowledged that Toronto had dramatically altered from 1951, when the foreign-born were only 19 per cent of the population, to 1971, when they represented 37 per cent, it was adamant that pervasive racism was unacceptable.

While the Pitman report was well received, developments during the 1980s showed that Toronto and other Canadian cities were still plagued by racism and ethnic bigotry. One of the most comprehensive analyses of this problem was the survey conducted by the parliamentary Special Committee on Participation of Visible Minorities in Canadian Society. Commissioned in December, 1983, "to seek positive and constructive ideas and models pertaining explicitly to ameliorating relations within Canada between visible minorities and other Canadians," the Committee heard testimony from over 200 organizations and individuals and considered a like number of briefs. Its major observations and recommendations were published and distributed in 1984 under the title *Equality Now*.[110]

The Committee left little doubt that they believed Canada was "a flawed society." One of the reasons for this indictment was evidence that "as many as 15 per cent of the population exhibit blatantly racist attitudes, while another 20-25 per cent have some racist tendencies." Visible minorities were the most likely to be victimized because they were "frequently believed to be from a different culture and . . . will not 'fit' the structures of public and private institutions in Canada."[111] Employment discrimination was regarded as one of the major problems not only in the private sector but with "police departments, fire departments, government services, [and] universities."[112] Failure to hire qualified visible minorities was also viewed as a problem "because the absence of any positive role models affects the image which visible minorities have of themselves."[113]

The Committee's recommendations included a five-year affirmative action program sponsored by the federal government, special assistance to visible minority businessmen and youth, improved media coverage of visible minority communities, and better access to English and French classes. There was also a call for increased co-operation between federal and provincial authorities for the validation of "non-Canadian degrees and credentials, and the licensing of professions, trades and apprenticeships." The specific needs of visible minority women were another concern: both those "isolated in their homes by the restraints of culture" and those who found themselves in exploitive work environments because of "language and skill deficiencies and discrimination."[114] More effective laws against those involved in the "public incitement of hatred" were also deemed essential. The report concluded with an appeal that Canadian society must change from being "a 'vertical mosaic' with some pieces raised above the others."[115]

Strained relations between visible minorities and the police had been extensively discussed in *Now Is Not Too Late*. But on that occasion most of the complaints were about the lack of police protection, not police harassment. Allegations of police racism and excessive use of force were the focus of three separate Ontario studies in 1979 and 1980: *Report to the Civic Authorities of Metropolitan Toronto and its Citizens* (1979) by G. Emmett Cardinal Carter, Archbishop of Toronto; *Report of the Task Force on the Racial and Ethnic Implications of Police Hiring, Training, Promotion and Career Development* (1980) chaired by Dr. Reva Gerstein for the Ministry of the Solicitor General; and *Report of the Task Force on the Use of Firearms by Police Officers* (1980) by Judge John Greenwood for the Ministry of the Solicitor General. In December, 1988, the Ontario Solicitor General, Joan Smith, in the wake of more incidents involving Toronto police and the city's black community, ordered a new investigation by the Race Relations and Policing Task Force.[116] Its mandate was "to address promptly the serious concerns of visible minorities respecting the interaction of the police community with their own," as well as to inquire "into police training, policies, practices and attitudes as they relate to the visible minorities within the Province of Ontario."[117]

Although conceding that the police forces of Ontario faced shortages of manpower and funding, the Task Force concluded that there was "an actual and serious problem in race relations and policing."[118] Black youths, it was charged, were particularly vulnerable to police "using racial slurs and exercising their right to use force in excessive and humiliating ways."[119] Visible minority women also claimed discriminatory treatment.[120]

While the Task Force acknowledged that no easy solutions were readily available, it did propose a number of recommendations. One was the creation of an Ontario Race Relations and Policing Review Board to monitor the interaction between visible minorities and police and provide "an on-going review of change processes in Ontario police forces."[121] Another proposal was for immediate changes so that the province's police forces "reflect the diversity of the population at all ranks."[122] Restraint and accountability in the use of firearms also concerned the Task Force, and it recommended a wide range of improvements, most notably the filing of use-of-force reports and independent postshooting investigations.[123] While it is not clear whether the Task Force recommendations will all be implemented, there has been an increase in the number of officers of colour, and there now is greater police accountability than had been the case. On the negative side, fear and distrust of the police by young blacks remains a serious problem, as was evident during the riot of May 4, 1992, sparked in part by the jury verdict in California in the Rodney King beating trial.[124] Austin Clarke, the Barbados-born Canadian author, provided a vivid and controversial explanation of this incident in a pamphlet, *Public Enemies: Police Violence and Black Youth*:

> It was not the first time that American racism had taken root in Canada in the minds of black Canadians. It was not the first time that black Canadians assumed an African brotherhood and sisterhood as the basis of their sympathy with the brothers and sisters below the border, negating any differences between American racism and Canadian racism. It was not the first time . . . of police brutality. . . . It was, on the night of May 4th, as if war had been declared. It was as if the first hundred years of patience, caution, dialogue, fear, fear of reprisals, and negotiation had been thrown out with no existing possibility of understanding; and a new slate produced on which would be written the new creed: 'all cops are racists.'[125]

CHAPTER 10

Immigration Since 1980:
Contemporary Debates

Once the principles and procedures of the 1976-77 Immigration Act had become operative, officials of the Department of Employment and Immigration were faced with a new set of challenges. How many immigrants should be admitted annually? What should be the ratio among the family, refugee, and independent categories? Were the highly publicized incidents of illegal immigration and the difficulty of deporting foreign-born criminals symptomatic of serious problems with the 1976 Immigration Act and the role of the DEI, or atypical events associated with a highly complex legal and administrative system?

How to deal with cycles of unemployment while maintaining a reasonable level of immigration was another problem the Trudeau and Mulroney governments had to confront during the 1980s. As a result, the number of arrivals fluctuated between a low of 84,000 in 1984 and a high of 260,000 in 1990. There was also a problem of trying to reconcile domestic priorities with Canada's international obligation to take its share of the millions of refugees and asylum seekers desperately searching for new homes.

Responsibility for immigration has been under three different titles since 1980: the Department of Employment and Immigration retained control until the spring of 1993; then there was the short-lived Public Security Department, established by the Conservative government of Kim Campbell; and, at present, immigration matters are handled by the Department of Citizenship and Immigration, created by the Liberal government of Jean Chrétien after its October, 1993, electoral triumph. During the past fourteen years, there has also been an increase in the degree of co-operation with the provinces. This was particularly true after 1990 when the federal government introduced its five-year planning cycle, with annual quotas of between 220,000 and 250,000 immigrants.[1] Quebec had been in a special category since 1968 when it established its own immigration service; Quebec's right to select its own independent immigrants had been established in 1978 by the Couture-Cullen Agreement and later expanded by Conservative Immigration Ministers Monique Gagnon-Tremblay and Barbara McDougall. But French-Canadian nationalists, such as members of the Bloc Québécois, were determined to place "immigration policy under Quebec's exclusive jurisdiction. . . . We . . . want them to be French-speaking as much as possible or at least to join the French-speaking community."[2]

On February 2, 1994, the new Minister of Citizenship and Immigration, Sergio Marchi, outlined his government's principles and priorities in creating "an open and progressive immigration policy that does not close the door to those who need our help or plan to contribute to the growth of our country." Emphasis was placed on maintaining a positive stance toward large-scale planned immigration, the importance of long-term planning, the need for more extensive consultation with Canadians, the expansion of partnerships with the private sector, and the commitment to refugees. The quota for 1994, Marchi announced, would be 250,000 immigrants, or about 1 per cent of the country's population. Despite criticism from the Reform Party, which claimed that this quota was too high, the Minister remained resolute:

> Many new groups of people have come to Canada over the years, each of them justifying its faith in our country. . . . Why should we believe now at this juncture of Canada's history and development that such nation-building will all of a sudden come to a halt? Why should we contemplate now . . . that today's immigrants, today's newcomers cannot be tomorrow's leaders?[3]

Refugees and the Canadian Immigration Act: The Debate, 1980-1992

Throughout the late 1980s, debate over the scope and composition of Canada's refugee policies attracted national and international attention. It was characterized by a sharp division of opinion between those who believed that a country's refugee policy was "the litmus test of the concept of justice in a society" and those who were primarily concerned "with controlling the destabilizing forces of an influx of refugees . . . guiding and managing the process." In their war of words the two sides made ample use of competing metaphors: closed vs. open doors; gatekeepers vs. immigration managers; unwanted victims vs. refugee frauds.[4]

For Canadian immigration officials one thing was clear: the number who could reach Canada was "many times greater than the number of refugees we can finance." Rigorous offshore selection, they argued, was imperative not only to prevent a flood of refugee claimants but also to ferret out the frauds.[5] In their exclusionist campaign DEI authorities made ample use of incidents such as the 1987 arrival of 155 Tamils from Sri Lanka who, it was later found, were part of an illegal smuggling system based in Hamburg, West Germany. They also alleged that other smuggling syndicates were adjuncts of international criminal and subversive organizations.

But for refugee supporters, many of these arguments were spurious, part of a bureaucratic conspiracy to stem the flow of refugees from Third World countries. They claimed that overseas immigration officials, through intimidation and red tape, tried to prevent both Convention refugees and those in the three designated categories from proving they had "well-founded fear of being persecuted." It was alleged that "away from the watchful eyes of the Canadian judiciary or any domestic adversarial review process," refugee claimants often found themselves subject to "'despotic consular absolutism.'"[6] Claimants who sought refugee status in Canada also encountered a maze of regulations and devices.[7]

Canadian immigration policy did not exist in a vacuum. During the 1980s western Europe experienced a 600 per cent increase in asylum seekers, most of whom had "left conditions of generalized violence rather than individual persecution." Not only did this movement test the traditional interpretation of "refugee"; it also gave rise to allegations that many of these displaced persons were economic migrants rather than bona fide refugees. Public reaction was particularly hostile in France and Germany, where neo-fascist groups demanded an immediate repeal of liberal asylum laws.[8]

Developments in the United States also influenced Canada's immigration policy. During the eighties the U.S. accepted more refugees than any other country. Most came directly from their country of origin – Vietnam, the Soviet Union, and Cuba.[9] Although the bias against suspected leftist refugees was altered somewhat in the 1980 Refugee Act, asylum seekers from El Salvador, Guatemala, and Chile still found it difficult to gain sanctuary.[10] The most compelling issue for Congress, however, was not refugees but control over illegal Mexican immigration.[11] The battle began with the Immigration Reform and Control Bill, which in August, 1982, was overwhelmingly endorsed by the U.S. Senate.[12] But only after four years of acrimonious debate did a version of this bill became law in November, 1986.[13] What ensured its passage was the creation of a new category of immigrant worker – the temporary resident alien – who could, after two years of employment, apply to become a lawful permanent resident alien and, after another five years, become an American citizen.[14]

American attempts to curtail illegal migrant workers and German efforts to exclude asylum seekers were often cited by Canadian immigration officials as they sought to strengthen immigration enforcement. This was particularly pronounced during the spring of 1987 when the Mulroney government submitted Bill C-84 and Bill C-55 to the House of Commons. These measures provided for changes in Canada's refugee determination system and tougher penalties for illegal immigration brokers; despite bitter opposition both bills passed on July 21, 1988. Significantly, the acrimonious parliamentary and public debate[15] over the increase in the enforcement powers of immigration officials did not spill over to the 1988 federal election campaign. In part, this could be explained by the Mulroney government's last-minute concession that refugee claimants would not be forcibly repatriated to "safe" third countries.[16] It was also apparent that none of the country's political parties wanted to alienate the powerful ethnic vote, especially in the metropolitan centres. Another reason is that the policies of the Conservative and Liberal parties on immigration issues had remained remarkably consistent since World War Two. As well, no party wanted to encourage neo-Nazi racist organizations such as the Heritage Front.

Demands for reduced immigration, however, were not just the preserve of the lunatic fringe. During the late 1980s some middle-class Canadians also began to question publicly whether Canada should accept large numbers of visible minority immigrants and refugees. An example of this genre of "respectable" exclusionism was Doug Collins's *Immigration: Parliament Versus The People* (1987), which alleged that all of the major political parties were involved in a conspiracy to ensure "that we must not be selective about whom we let into Canada . . . [that] the alien masses will continue to pour in, while traditional immigrants from Europe, the UK, etc. will be kept out." Collins had particularly harsh words for former Prime Minister Pierre Elliott Trudeau, who, he claimed, had only disdain for "the problems of ordinary people," an attitude reflected in Trudeau's determination "to break this country's traditional immigration pattern and replace it with 'multiculturalism.' "[17] Collins also cited various public opinion polls indicating that most Canadians opposed non-white immigration and wanted strict quotas "so that new immigrants will not upset our present ethnic balance."[18]

Attacks on Canada's pluralistic immigration policy and commitment to multiculturalism did not diminish as the country reached the last decade of the century. In 1990, for example, a spate of publications questioned federal cultural policies: *Mosaic Madness*, by sociologist Reginald Bibby, was one of the more popular. A scholarly work based on extensive surveys, the book attacked both the concept of pluralism and its negative implications for Canada: "In this country, there will be no pressure, as there is in some other countries, notably the United States – to discard one's cultural past, and conform to the dominant culture. . . . In its zeal to promote coexistence, Canada may find itself a world leader in promoting the breakdown of group life and the abandonment of the pursuit of the best."[19] Bibby's message found considerable support from the Alberta-based Reform Party and its leader, Preston Manning. In a series of 1991 broadsides, Reform called for dramatic changes in multiculturalism policies – most notably, the curtailment of funding for ethnocultural organizations.[20] Manning also called for changes in Canada's immigration and refugee policies, at the same time denying that he was anti-immigrant.[21]

Serious question about the implications of Canada's immigration and refugee policies were also raised by academic specialists.[22] One of the most comprehensive studies, *Economic and Social Impacts of Immigration* (1991), was prepared for the Economic Council of Canada. It emphasized the importance of adopting a broad perspective when evaluating the impact of immigration on Canadian society, and especially the need "to distinguish sharply between its effects on immigrants themselves and that on the host community, while acknowledging that once here, immigrants become part of the host community." Of special concern to these researchers was whether there was sufficient evidence to determine if immigrants had a positive or negative impact on Canada's economic prosperity and economic efficiency. Given the complexity of these questions, it is not surprising that the report's conclusions were ambivalent:

> With respect to per capita disposable incomes, an increase in immigration has a positive effect, but it is very small . . . .
>
> The impact of immigration on unemployment is almost certainly negligible, at least over the long term. Even temporary effects seem quite unlikely, unless immigration increases are very rapid . . . .
>
> If immigrants earn more than average this raises the combined average income of hosts and immigrants, but nothing is added to the income of hosts.
>
> The effects of immigration in filling labour market gaps, thereby enhancing efficiency, as compared with the alternative possibility of filling gaps by domestic market adjustments, are almost certainly exceedingly small.
>
> Immigrants who bring in human capital in the form of education obtained abroad gain economically from their education, but the balance of evidence suggests that no benefits accrue to existing residents.
>
> Immigrants who bring in monetary capital retain the title to their earnings of their capital, and existing residents are unlikely to benefit . . . .
>
> The spillover effects of immigrants are often believed to be positive, but there is no theoretical basis, and no empirical data to substantiate this view; and there is some empirical evidence against it.[23]

The Economic Council study did, however, factor into its analysis a variety of demographic, social, humanitarian, and political factors, which, it claimed, were sufficiently positive for the Council to recommend "that immigration be gradually increased above the average of the last 25 years to reach 1 per cent of the population, on a gross basis, by the year 2015."[24] This expansionist approach, it hastened to add, was only possible if Canada remained sufficiently tolerant to accept the inevitable "growth in the proportions of visible minorities, without a significant increase in social tensions."[25]

Projected increases in the number and percentage of visible minorities, the report suggested, would have the greatest impact on Canada's three largest metropoplitan centres, the destination of about 60 per cent of recent immigrants. It was estimated, for example, that a net immigration level of 0.8 per cent would expand Toronto's non-European population from 11 per cent in 1990 to 29 per cent in 2015, while Montreal's visible minority population would increase under this scheme from 4 per cent to 17 per cent.[26] The situation was deemed potentially more serious in Montreal since there existed an ongoing debate "between the principle of cultural convergence and the policy of cultural recognition of interculturalism" and a determination that Montreal not "lose its French character."[27] Canada's ability to absorb large numbers of non-traditional immigrants, the report concluded, largely depended on avoiding "dangerous circumstances" such as "a sudden, large increase in the proportion of visible minority immigrants, and deep economic recession."[28] This meant, above all, that Canada maintain control of its immigration system, at a time when "pressure from refugee claimants is high and growing."[29]

By 1992 the Canadian public was becoming increasingly anxious about the immigration "problem," especially as complaints about the inadequacy of the country's immigration determination system mounted. Among the media accounts, some of the hardest hitting exposés came from journalist Daniel Stoffman, whose articles were published in the *Toronto Star* under such provocative titles as "Fake Canadian Papers a Hot Item in Migrant Markets" and "The High Costs Of Our Refugee System: How Canada inadvertently encourages foreigners to claim refugee status as a way of jumping the immigration queues."[30] Stoffman was particularly critical of the Immigration and Refugee Board, created in 1989, which he denounced as expensive, inefficient, and corrupt, the happy hunting grounds for "unscrupulous entrepreneurs who make big profits selling false documents and tickets to people intending to make refugee claims in Canada."[31]

In 1992 there were renewed attempts by Canadian immigration officials to control the volume and composition of refugees as part of a general response to an international crisis. Germany, for example, with its half-million asylum seekers and its post-unification problems, had already begun to change its liberal refugee laws and to work with other members of the European Community to curb the movement of illegal workers.[32] Under the Dublin Convention of 1991, refugee determination systems were standardized, and common measures were adopted by EC countries to combat illegal immigration, terrorist organizations, and organized crime.[33]

Bill C-86 and Changes in Canada's Refugee and Immigration Laws

Many of the security provisions of the Dublin Convention would find expression in Bill C-86, which the Minister of Employment and Immigration introduced in July, 1992. The bill called for important changes in Canada's immigration priorities, expanded use of temporary employment visas, further encouragement for business and professional immigrants, and greater control over numbers admitted annually; it also proposed that certain immigrants be required to work in certain regions. All this, and more, was set forth in the speech of Immigration Minister Bernard Valcourt on July 27, 1992:

> Today the effectiveness of our immigration and refugee system is being severely tested by mounting international and domestic pressures. . . . We . . . must balance the needs of newcomers with those of the country itself. . . . Canada stands at the crossroads. . . . At the same time as Canadians debate the fundamental issue of national unity, they are also preoccupied by deep concerns about economic prosperity. . . . Without effective control over the number and categories of immigrants coming into our country, we cannot ensure immigration continues to best serve the interests of all Canadians. [34]

Significantly, one target group of Bill C-86 was the high number of semi-skilled immigrants who had come into Canada in ever-increasing numbers since 1976. This problem was outlined by the DEI Director of Strategic Planning and Research when he spoke about the qualities of the 250,000 immigrants admitted annually under the five-year plan:

> According to this plan we are to admit 100,000 persons in the family class, 50,000 persons on the humanitarian front, and some 37,000 immigrants whom we select in the skilled worker and business categories. . . . [But] there's a problem of immigration content. . . . On many fronts we find that today's immigrants don't enjoy the advantages enjoyed by earlier cohorts. The educational advantage, formerly enjoyed by the foreign-born, has largely disappeared, although we still import a significant number of highly educated and highly skilled people. The proportion of professionals and managers has dropped. Fewer immigrants are proficient in English or French and recent immigrants have been experiencing higher rates of unemployment and social assistance. . . . There are even some signs suggestive of maladjustment in the form of rising criminality, although it is still well below the Canadian average. [35]

Immigration officials also emphasized the need to channel more skilled workers and professionals away from metropolitan centres and toward smaller cities so "that all parts of Canada should have the opportunity to benefit from immigration." By adopting a modified contract labour approach, the department, they argued, would be able to provide badly needed skills and services and reduce congestion in Toronto, Montreal, and Vancouver.[36] These contract immigrants would be selected from "pools" of skilled workers, professionals, and business-men most likely "to make an economic contribution."[37]

One organization that strongly endorsed DEI efforts to make Canada's refugee system more occupationally selective was the Federation of Canadian Municipalities (FCM).[38] This was not surprising since many municipalities had experienced enormous demands on their social assistance resources, especially after the Mulroney government reduced many of its immigrant programs. In 1991, for instance, Metropolitan Toronto "paid $326 million for care of refugees at a time when local tax bases were hard hit by unemployment."[39] The situation was aggravated by DEI's refusal to give refugee claimants work permits and by individual and group sponsors reneging on their financial commitments. The FCM also alleged that welfare fraud was rampant, with many refugee claimants "acquiring multiple identities, allowing them to claim welfare under different names."[40]

As in previous inquiries, the activities of immigration consultants came under intense scrutiny by the parliamentary committee.[41] Although the Organization of Professional Immigration Consultants (OPIC) vigorously denied allegations of wrongdoing and denounced any attempt to interfere "with the legitimate business activities of highly trained and ethical consultants," they were clearly on the defensive.[42] The OPIC credibility was undermined when the RCMP presented its brief, which documented many instances of consultants breaking the law either by falsely representing absentee investor immigrants[43] or by encouraging their clients "to fabricate" their testimony in order to claim refugee status. From the RCMP perspective, the most serious development was the proliferation of criminal syndicates involved in "the trafficking or smuggling of humans." Such smuggling brought enormous profits – from $5,000 to $20,000 for each illegal immigrant. According to one of their investigations, Project Overflight, the scope of these operations had reached alarming proportions:

Thousands of customers were solicited directly in China or through relatives in the United States and Canada. . . . The illegal immigrants being smuggled were formed into groups of four or six for transportation to Canada. Each group was accompanied by an escort of the syndicate . . . responsible for bringing the illegals through a variety of European countries or cities – for example, Budapest, Helsinki, London, Amsterdam, Brussels and Zurich – using a variety of airlines, with the final destination being Canada. After serving its purpose, the fraudulent documentation used by the smuggling operation was recovered from the refugees and recycled for other operations.[44]

Criticism of Bill C-86 was extensive and well organized. Among those presenting briefs against the proposed changes in Canada's refugee procedures were the influential Canadian Labour Congress (CLC) and its president, Bob White. The CLC brief was blunt and to the point: "Bill C-86 . . . in our view will make Canada less caring, less compassionate and a less responsible member of the international community." According to White, the CLC did not see any reason for additional immigration controls: "We are quite unaware of our borders being flooded by prospective refugees. We are completely unaware of a ground swell of public opinion against the number of people we currently accept through normal immigration channels . . . ." If there was an enormous backlog of refugee cases the problem was departmental inefficiency "rather than too much accessibility."[45] Nor was White concerned that refugees or immigrants posed a threat to organized labour by taking low-paying and arduous jobs: "in the initial stages, some . . . move into those kinds of occupations, but you also see them moving out of those in a fairly short period of time. I can look to aerospace plants in Manitoba, for example, where a large Filipino population is employed. It is not all in the small, low-paying sectors. . . . The argument or the fear that somehow these people will create unemployment in the country just isn't the reality."[46]

White was more concerned about the implications of the Mulroney government's entrepreneur/investor program, which he dismissed as "overrated in terms of the jobs that are created."[47] He also criticized the increased emphasis on recruiting skilled immigrant workers, especially from eastern Europe:

My concern has always been – and I bargained with the auto industry for several years – that at least two of those companies did not accept the responsibilities in terms of training skilled workers, but would reach and pirate them from small employers or bring them in from somewhere else. . . . We are not saying there should not be provisions for skilled workers to come into the country. We are saying we have to make sure we are not going down that road again of not accepting our responsibilities in Canada to upgrade skills and to provide opportunities for younger people to move into the skilled job market today.[48]

On the civil liberties front, the CLC joined forces with other groups in attacking those sections of Bill C-86 dealing with subversion and criminality. White pointed out, for instance, that organizations such as the African National Congress, the CUT in Chile, and FENASTRA in El Salvador, all of which worked toward democratic goals, were once "illegal or banned within their own societies." Did this mean, he asked, that these democratic progressives would be excluded from Canada?[49] The basic tenets of the CLC position were endorsed by Rabbi Gunther Plaut and his colleagues from the Canadian Jewish Congress, who made a special plea for "the need to be compassionate toward the stranger" at a time when there was "rising intolerance and lack of understanding about the contribution immigrants make to Canadian society."[50] In Plaut's opinion Bill C-86 was a flawed document that did not reflect "the Canada we have come to know." More specifically, the CJC took exception to the narrow definition of who was a genuine refugee, the provisions against asylum shopping, and the abrupt and arbitrary means of processing refugee claimants.[51]

These criticisms were repeated and refined by other concerned organizations, most notably Amnesty International, the Canadian Civil Liberties Association, the Inter-Church Committee for Refugees, and the National Immigration Law Section of the Canadian Bar Association.[52] Some of the most emotional briefs came from organizations representing more recent refugees and immigrants. One of these was the Canadian Hispanic Congress (CHC), which spoke on behalf of the country's 400,000 Hispanics, many of whom had fled from authoritarian and brutal regimes. It attacked the security dimensions of Bill C-86 both by refuting charges about refugee criminality and by denouncing the fingerprinting proposal as "an odious police state measure that would create an inferior status for certain classes of persons legally residing in Canada." Such a measure would "exert mental anguish on refugees who may have suffered similar police controls under repressive regimes."[53] The CHC was most critical of the new guidelines for safe third countries, where asylum seekers could be returned or repatriated:

> Canada has recognized certain countries as members of a list of countries that protect or respect human rights in a loose definition of the Geneva Convention. . . . People coming through the United States would automatically be told to go back and be forced to undergo American refugee determination . . . the practice in the United States has been beneficial only to certain Latin American countries such as Cuba. . . . People coming from Central America . . . were, in fact, treated as illegal immigrants – Guatemalans, Salvadorians, Hondurans, etc. They came from countries that had military police alliances with the United States.[54]

No less biting was the brief submitted by the World Sikh Organization (WSO). It called C-86 a racist document that reinforced a system where "Justice is not the same for white Europeans as it is for so-called visible minorities." This was reflected, it argued, in the arbitrary powers given to immigration officials; the narrow definition of family members; the harassment of relatives on visitor visas; the refusal to grant work permits; and, above all, the government's failure to recognize that "in India Sikhs are presently being persecuted." The WSO saw the law-and-order thrust of Bill C-86 as an example of a "government too willing to cash in on the popular mood and take its cue from the Reform Party platform – blaming immigrants, especially refugees, for all the nation's ills."[55]

Additional flaws in Bill C-86 were highlighted in the testimony of the National Organization of Immigrant and Visible Minority Women of Canada (NOIVMW). While sharing the opposition of other groups toward the restrictive aspects of Bill C-86, NOIVMW concentrated its attack on two specific deficiencies. One of these was the failure to recognize "the realities of women who have experienced persecution in the form of sexual assault," and it called on the government to broaden the definition of "refugee" to include sex as one of the grounds of persecution for which a person can be recognized as a refugee. It also criticized the provisions of C-86 that would establish open refugee determination hearings on the grounds that these sessions would expose refugee women to a degrading and traumatic process. Nor was NOIVMW impressed with the proposal to curtail mobility opportunities for recent refugees, a restriction that would deprive the woman victim "of the type of social and psychological support systems which she could receive in the large urban centres." In closing, NOIVMW pointed out that immigrant women continued to be abused by the live-in requirements of the domestic employment authorization scheme, which created "more barriers, especially for women of colour who are trying to escape the pangs of poverty in their own countries."[56]

Postscript

Although Bill C-86 passed virtually intact, the Mulroney government did make one major concession. On March 9, 1993, the Immigration and Refugee Board issued its *Guidelines for Women Refugees Facing Gender-Related Persecution*, which acknowledged some of the arguments set forth in the NOIVMW brief. Most commentators praised the government's action as a "massive leap forward." But for conservatives such as writer Barbara Amiel, the change was a gimmick that threatened to inundate Canada with claimants who would "then turn around and sponsor husbands or family members whose approach to gender relations gave them refugee status in the first place."[57]

Other opponents of a generous refugee policy were heartened by the formation of a new Public Security portfolio in the summer of 1993, which placed the Immigration Branch alongside the Royal Canadian Mounted Police, the Canadian Security and Intelligence Service, and the Canadian Parole Board. Although Douglas Lewis, the Minister, tried to reassure ethnic and humanitarian organizations that his ministry remained committed to a vigorous immigration policy, his basic message emphasized the need for more rigorous enforcement and exclusion. One of the primary goals of his department, he argued, would be to control Canada's borders: "I know we both share the same anger when a foreign criminal slips through the system to claim the rights of Canadian citizenship. I know we share the same revulsion when an unscrupulous consultant is caught swindling defenceless migrants."[58]

Given the criticism of the Department of Public Security, the growing controversy over refugees, and the issue of annual immigration quotas, there were expectations that serious debate about Canada's immigration policy would take place during the October, 1993, federal election. This did not happen. Even the Reform Party, which had previously attacked high immigration levels and multicultural programs, rarely initiated discussion of the subject. This reticence on the part of federal politicians prompted *Globe and Mail* writer Michael Valpy to headline one of his articles: "IT'S NOT RACIST TO DISCUSS IMMIGRATION."[59]

Within a month of being elected, the Liberal government of Jean Chrétien dissolved the Public Security portfolio and, in November, 1993, created the Department of Citizenship and Immigration. On February 2, 1994, the Minister, Sergio Marchi, announced his intention to pursue "a dynamic immigration policy that balances humanitarian concerns, demographic and economic needs and our basic capacity to absorb newcomers."[60] Marchi's call for a comprehensive review of immigration policy through a series of public hearings was, however, overshadowed by several sensational homicides involving illegal immigrants and by reports of fraudulent refugee claims. Increasingly, there were demands for tougher deportation procedures and reductions in immigration quotas. The *Globe and Mail* added its editorial voice to the debate when it pointed out that Canada's level of immigration, at about 1 per cent of the population, was "the highest in the Western world . . . double that of Australia, New Zealand or the United States."[61]

On November 3, 1994, new immigration guidelines were established. The annual quota was dropped to about 200,000, with higher percentages coming from the independent and refugee categories and a reduction in the family-class group. Newcomers were also required to assume a greater portion of their settlement expenses; bonds were required for family-sponsored immigrants; and a knowledge of English or French was deemed "critical."[62] While the public response was generally favourable, some immigration advocacy groups denounced the policy on racial, gender, and political grounds, with one critic claiming there was "still a prevailing mind-set in this country that real Canadians are only those who are descended from British and French stock."[63] A more generous assessment came from consultant John Samuel, reflecting on his own experiences as an immigration official: "The backlash against immigration . . . arising from high profile crimes . . . the changing racial composition of the Canadian population, visible minorities becoming more bold in asserting their rights – has been building up for some time. Therefore, Marchi had a difficult political task, to say the least. The minister has tried his best to balance conflicting interests and viewpoints."[64]

Marchi's balancing act would subsequently involve his departmental status in the sweeping review of government services associated with the Liberal budget of February 27, 1995. Significantly, the most important changes were not drastic cutbacks in administrative personnel, but rather the cabinet's decision to impose a $975 right of landing fee on all adult immigrants applying for permanent resident status. Although critics denounced this "head tax" as unfair and arbitrary, the minister assured the *Globe and Mail* (March 1, 1995) that the policy was justified on the grounds that immigration was a right "that should be paid for by those who benefit."

Canada's immigration and refugee policies, problems of racism and discrimination, and the federal program of multiculturalism remain emotional subjects, and the debate has often been heated. During 1994, however, the quality of discussion was enhanced by the appearance of such scholarly works as Neil Bissoondath's *Selling Illusions: The Cult of Multiculturalism in Canada*,[65] Anthony Richmond's *Global Apartheid: Refugees, Racism, and the New World Order*,[66] Frances Henry's, *The Caribbean Diaspora in Toronto: Learning to Live with Racism*,[67] and *The Illusion of Difference: Realities of Ethnicity in Canada and the United States* by Jeffrey Reitz and Raymond Breton.[68] Although all of these books provide useful insights, *Selling Illusions* has been the most controversial, given the author's denunciation of multiculturalism as a divisive social policy and his plea for "a new vision of Canadian-ness . . . where no one is alienated with hyphenation."[69] At a time when concern over national unity and social stability runs deep, many Canadians have been attracted by Bissoondath's message that immigrants like himself are more concerned with individual integration and acceptance than with being placed within the "growing cult of racial and ethnic identity."[70] Others, including Sheila Finestone, Secretary of State for Multiculturalism, criticized Bissoondath for being intolerant and superficial.[71]

Ironically, in December, 1994, Finestone herself came under attack from a number of ethnic communities when she announced that the federal government would not provide redress, financial or otherwise, for those groups adversely affected by discriminatory government policies in the past. Her justification was simple: "We wish we could rewrite history. We cannot." This provided small comfort to Chinese Canadians, victimized by the racist head tax, or for those Canadians of Ukrainian, German, and Italian background who had been unjustly treated during the First and Second World Wars.[72]

This controversy provides a salutary reminder that Canada has often been a reluctant host – wary of those who did not meet its racial, ethnocentric, and class standards. Fortunately, there is little evidence that Canada will return to the exclusionist policies of the past.

Conclusion:
Reflections on Canada's Immigration Experience

In 1910, during the House of Commons debates on the Immigration Act, Conservative members charged that immigrants who had "come from Great Britain have not been treated as well as those from foreign countries, such as the Galicians and Doukhobors." Frank Oliver, in his rebuttal, felt compelled to point out that while his department sought men who would "secure the settlement of our vacant lands . . . in carrying out this policy we use due endeavour to secure the additions to our population from the people of our own blood . . . people of our own race."[1] A somewhat similar confrontation occurred in June, 1954, when Conservative immigration critic Davie Fulton assailed the Department of Citizenship and Immigration for its disastrous immigration policy, especially its failure to preserve "the ethnic balance within the country" and its "inability to work out an intelligent and vigorous application of the assisted passage loan scheme as applied to the United Kingdom so that we may encourage more immigration from there."[2]

Forty years later another heated debate over immigration priorities took place in the House of Commons, this time between the Liberal Minister of Citizenship and Immigration, Sergio Marchi, and Art Hanger of the Reform Party. At issue was Reform's question as to why Canada was still accepting, as a percentage of the population, "more immigrants than any other industrialized nation on earth." Marchi's response was emotional and direct: "Canada would not have flourished or progressed if we had locked ourselves into such a restrictive mind set that excluded the very people who have helped make us grow and prosper as a nation." He also indicated that Canada would be taking the lead in pushing for more generous refugee responses from the international community: "We will tell those countries locking their door that this is unacceptable and unfair to those countries whose doors are still open and whose door-steps are therefore crowded."[3]

In assessing these debates, it is important to remember that the background of immigrants coming to Canada is quite different in 1994 than it was in 1910 and in 1954. In both the earlier periods, the overwhelming majority of newcomers were of British or European background. In contrast, by the 1990s three of the five largest national groups were non-European: Hong Kong (14 per cent of the total), India (6.4 per cent), and the Philippines (5.1 per cent). Moreover, while the majority of Canada's immigrant population were born in Europe, the percentage from this region has declined from 62 per cent in 1986 to 54 per cent in 1991, while the percentage from Asia increased from 18 per cent to 25 per cent during this same period. Yet despite the change in ethnic composition, the proportion of the population of immigrant background has remained relatively constant since 1951, when 16 per cent of Canadians were born outside the country. However, now most immigrants (94 per cent) live in the provinces of Ontario, British Columbia, Quebec, and Alberta, with over half (57 per cent) in the three largest metropolitan areas (Toronto, Montreal, and Vancouver).[4]

Continuity and change in Canadian immigration policy has been the central focus of this book. One of the major continuities has been Canada's constant search for workers to take jobs at the bottom rungs of the occupational ladder. The recruitment of European unskilled workers was most pronounced during the Laurier/Borden years when Canada experienced massive economic growth. An immigration policy that gave priority to the imperatives of industrial capitalism and agricultural wage labour lasted until the advent of the Great Depression of the 1930s, which glutted the Canadian labour market. For fifteen years the voices of the immigration boosters were stilled. All this changed after 1946. The post-war economic recovery, which coincided with the presence of thousands of desperate European displaced persons, re-established a version of the earlier immigrant worker recruitment and placement system. Moreover, even before the DP pool was exhausted, immigrant workers from Italy, Portugal, and Greece were imported for work on the Canadian frontier. That most of these workers soon gravitated to urban jobs did not deter political and corporate immigration boosters. As late as 1966 Sidney Spivak, Manitoba's colourful Minister of Industry and Commerce, could argue that "without immigrants . . . cutting timber, mining, building hydro projects and transportation facilities, and carrying out work essential to the exploitation of remote resources . . . future major developments will be slow and costly."[5]

Representatives of extractive industries and agricultural organizations were even more resolute in their campaign for the open door. So, too, was the Canadian Manufacturers' Association, although in a somewhat different way – the

CMA wanted a higher ratio of skilled workers. But while many politicians and immigration bureaucrats were sympathetic to this campaign, they were also aware that organized labour was adamantly opposed to any plan to recruit skilled workers. The CMA, however, had one trump card: the need to replace the thousands of Canadian-born skilled workers who sought better jobs in the United States. This exodus southward caused considerable consternation during the 1920s; it became a national obsession during the 1950s as Canada's "brain drain" of professionals and scientists to the United States soared.

Throughout the twentieth century the Canadian government has assumed an important role in the recruitment of specific groups of immigrant workers. The most direct intervention occurred during the Laurier/Borden years when bonuses were paid to steamship companies and labour agencies for the recruitment of agriculturalists and domestics. At the same time, the virtual free hand given to the railway companies and labour-intensive industries to import labour was another form of state assistance. This silent partnership found full expression in the Railway Agreement of 1925. But the most extensive form of state involvement was the post-1945 DP Bulk Labour Program. Here the Canadian government provided the political/legal framework for the recruitment of Polish servicemen and displaced persons; it also actively recruited and screened these workers to ensure that they would be an economic asset. In addition, the state controlled the immigrant's ability to participate in the national labour market through a system of labour contracts reinforced by the threat of deportation.

Canada's immigration policy on occasion has departed from the goals of the capitalist labour market. Prior to 1914, captains of industry in British Columbia pushed hard for more Chinese workers. But the ferocious west coast anti-Oriental campaign, which found full expression in the 1907 Vancouver race riot, forced Ottawa to close the gates. During the Great War, federal authorities responded to security and patriotic arguments and began to monitor the use of enemy alien workers in various sectors, especially mining. The willingness of governments to avoid political controversy over the employment of immigrant workers was once again evident during the anti-alien hysteria in 1919 and was reflected in the 1919 amendments to the Immigration Act that barred German and Austrian immigrants until 1923.

In the study of chain migration from Britain, Europe, Asia, and the Caribbean, the role of the ethnic intermediary has been very important, whether he was a *padrone*, steamship agent, employment agent, village sponsor, or 1980s immigration consultant and lawyer. Throughout the twentieth century these agents have facilitated the movement of thousands of immigrants to Canada through the issuance of prepaid tickets, arrangement for employment, and, on occasion, circumvention of immigration regulations. The revelations of the 1904 Royal Commission to Inquire into the Immigration of Italian Labourers to Montreal, and Alleged Fraudulent Practices of Employment Agencies have striking parallels to the 1983 DEI *Report on Illegal Migrants in Canada*. In both cases, immigrant workers were bilked, and for similar reasons: "a willingness to place special trust in an adviser simply because of a shared language or cultural background."[6] Yet despite the potential for exploitation, ethnic intermediaries often performed a useful role in the chain migration process.

A much more important factor, however, was the government's decision after 1945 to give legal status to chain migration through the family reunification sponsorship system. Non-white immigrants, however, had only limited access until the 1960s. But for European immigrants the system operated admirably. During the difficult arrival period the newcomer could rely on family members for assistance in obtaining work and accommodation; ethnic connections also provided stability in an alien world. But to its critics, the sponsorship system had one major disadvantage – it dramatically increased the ratio of unskilled workers at a time when the Canadian economy was experiencing major structural changes. Yet periodic attempts to alter the system proved unsuccessful. The ability of ethnic organizations to use their political muscle and to make common cause with Anglo-Canadian immigration boosters, corporate and humanitarian, helps to explain why DEI bureaucrats were defeated in 1959, again in 1966, and once again in 1976. Clearly the days when bureaucrats such as F.C. Blair could act as personal immigration gatekeepers had long passed.

Canada's international commitment to the United Nations High Commission for Refugees, an integral part of the 1976 Immigration Act, provided additional insurance that the country will not repeat the tragic mistakes of the 1930s. Another form of insurance is the generally pro-refugee stance of the Department of External Affairs. This, however, was not always the case. During the interwar years, O.D. Skelton, undersecretary of state for external affairs, often reinforced Blair's exclusionist arguments; this was particularly evident when Armenian and Jewish refugees sought sanctuary. On the positive side, the External Affairs mandarins frequently assumed an important role in resolving Canadian-American border issues during the 1920s and in modifying deportation policies during the 1930s.

Canadian society did not indulge those immigrants who failed its winnowing tests. During periods of economic recession deportations were frequent. In practice the German *Gastarbeiter* system, the notion that "an expendable labour force takes its problems away with it when it is re-exported," had many Canadian adherents. Traditionally, governments in Canada have done little to help integrate different groups of immigrants into the civil life of the country. Prior to 1914 the task of Canadianizing the immigrant was left essentially to private agencies – Frontier College, the YMCA, and the Protestant churches. The voluntary agencies had to make it on their own, as Ottawa and the provinces squabbled, in true Canadian fashion, over whose jurisdiction encompassed the responsibility for immigrant education. Moreover, in attempting to inculcate

Anglo-Canadian and Protestant values the voluntary agencies, however well intentioned, often offended the immigrants' sense of their own cultural identification – a pride that was perhaps their most important asset in dealing with the vicissitudes of life in a land that at once promised and threatened.

The Canadian Trades and Labour Congress, with its exclusive craft orientation, was no more successful in reaching non-British immigrant workers. While occasionally the TLC might denounce the influx of large numbers of European unskilled workers, it never launched a systematic campaign against the practice. Few of the English-speaking among them, at least, were interested in the socially undesirable jobs to be found in the mines, in the lumber camps, and "at the end of steel." Nor were they particularly interested in bringing eastern and southern European workers into their craft unions. And Chinese and Japanese workers were almost totally excluded.

Shunned or patronized by traditional Canadian institutions, some alienated immigrant workers turned to groups that sought to transform Canadian life through revolution: the Industrial Workers of the World and the Communist Party of Canada. But even within these fringe organizations their deeply felt particularities could pose problems. Class and ethnicity proved as hard to reconcile in Canada as elsewhere.[7]

An even greater problem, however, was the hostility of the Canadian state. Although there had been periodic concern over radical activity among foreign workers prior to 1914, the war years and the Red Scare of 1919 greatly intensified the fear of the radical alien. Individuals and groups now tended to be deemed loyal or disloyal, law-abiding or revolutionary, according to their conformity to the norms of the Anglo-Canadian middle class. These same attitudes, particularly on the part of Canadian business groups and law enforcement officials, surfaced again during the Great Depression. Renewed efforts to contain the forces of radicalism culminated in August, 1931, in the arrest of Communist leaders and extensive use of section 41 of the Immigration Act to deport alien radicals. The advent of World War Two ushered in yet another phase in the continuing struggle between the left and the Canadian national security state. Nor did it end in 1945. The Cold War, with its intensified fear of the enemy within, produced even more rigorous immigration screening procedures. Not surprisingly, the RCMP played an important role in this search for subversives.

Although the security dimension of Canada's immigration policy remains important, there are more checks and balances to protect the rights of immigrants and refugees. Most of these were enshrined in the Immigration Act of 1976-77. Of particular importance is the refugee status determination system that provides for an elaborate investigation, the opportunity to appeal, and judicial review. This elevation of humanitarian considerations above security measures has not pleased the RCMP or the Immigration Branch. Their law-and-order arguments were forcefully presented during the 1992 debate on Bill C-86; they were also reflected in the 1993 creation of a Department of Public Security, which included the Immigration Branch.

Canadian immigration policy has evolved considerably since 1952. In part, this has reflected the transformation of Canada's resource and manufacturing economy to the post-industrial model, with the accompanying importance of high-technology jobs and the growth of the tertiary sector. These changes were particularly pronounced between 1971 and 1986, when the growth in the labour force of the primary sector was 6 per cent compared with a growth of 17 per cent in the secondary industries and a whopping 69 per cent increase in tertiary area employment. Significantly, the flow of immigrant workers into high-growth manufacturing jobs and into the tertiary sector was higher than for native-born workers. According to Anthony Richmond the seven fastest-growing economic sub-sectors "accounted for 43 percent of the total labour force in 1986 and almost half of the immigrants from nontraditional source countries."[8] He also acknowledged that while many of these jobs carried high status, others were "subject to seasonal fluctuations, high unemployment and traditionally low wages."[9] Recent immigrants from non-European countries, most of whom were visible minorities, experienced the greatest pay differentials. In 1985, for example, they received an average of 21.2 per cent less for men than did the traditional European immigrant groups and 10.7 per cent less for women. The vast majority of these people worked in the twenty-five census metropolitan areas.[10]

Do immigrants take jobs from Canadians? Are they a drain on the country's welfare system? These questions have been asked with varying degrees of intensity since the turn of the century. But in recent years the debate has gained momentum, in part because of the federal government's commitment to large-scale immigration during an economic recession. One recent study has concluded that while evidence had been found "of immigrant employment substitution for non-immigrant workers in certain industries, particularly those which are heavily capitalised and characterized by either highly skilled or unskilled work forces . . . there is no strong evidence that immigrants significantly displace non-immigrants from jobs across the economy as a whole." The authors concede, however, that certain economic sectors may benefit from "low skill wage immigrants (often illegal) to assist particular firms to adjust to increasing competition." They also remain ambivalent as to whether the aggregate level of economic consequences of immigrant workers was more than "marginally positive" but note that other considerations – social, demographic, humanitarian – should also be considered and "should form the main agenda in which the immigration debate and policy formulation are conducted."[11]

Another dimension of the contemporary debate over the status of immigrant workers has been their labour market participation. Most studies have concluded that, in general, immigrant workers have a higher level of employment than the Canadian-born, although country of origin and length of residence are significant factors in determining job levels, as is the concentration of recent immigrants in Canada's metropolitan centres, where overall employment is relatively high. Other surveys have demonstrated, however, that job opportunities and earnings can often be adversely affected by discrimination, especially during the first years in Canada.[12] According to sociologists Raymond Breton and Jeffrey Reitz this was particularly true for non-European or visible minority immigrants, who "earn substantially less than they would be expected to earn on the basis of their job qualifications, such as education, knowledge of English (French) and work experience."[13]

By the 1960s Toronto, not Winnipeg, was Canada's premier immigrant city. While ethnic relations have been generally quite harmonious, Toronto did have some serious racial incidents during the 1970s and 1980s. The Pitman report *Now Is Not Too Late* (1976) provided a graphic account of how and why this racially inspired violence occurred. *Equality Now* (1984) urged Canadians to overcome their prejudices against visible minorities. A more positive message came from a 1988 study by Jeffrey Reitz that compared contemporary patterns of racism in Toronto and London and Birmingham, England. While Reitz found that discrimination against visible minorities in Britain and Canada was "remarkably similar" in terms of employment opportunities, he concluded that racial conflict in Britain was more pervasive largely because it was reinforced "by institutionally derived perceptions of immigrants as a potential social burden." In contrast, the fact that Canadians had "more positive institutionally-sanctioned perceptions of immigrants as an economic asset helped to dilute social conflict." Or put another way, British immigration policy was driven by "the obligations of a declining imperial power to former colonial territories"; in Canada, non-white immigration had occurred "within the context of a long-term program of national development."[14]

Canada's rejection of its racist immigration legacy after 1966 greatly affected the character of Canadian society. So, too, did the country's commitment to multiculturalism in 1971. The inclusion of a continuous and substantial obligation to refugees in the Immigration Act of 1976 was another landmark. As well, the extension of Canada's welfare state to newcomers should not be minimized. These policies have gone far to differentiate contemporary Canadian attitudes toward immigrants, especially non-Europeans, from earlier decades. Canada has also not adopted the western European model of the guest worker instead of accepting immigrants. And despite allegations that Canada's immigration policy retains certain racist elements, this infection appears situational rather than systemic.[15]

A more positive profile of Canada's performance over the past thirty years emerges if a comparative approach is adopted. Australia, Germany, Great Britain, and the United States are all immigrant nations, in reality if not in law.[16] But none has demonstrated the same level of generosity toward diverse groups of immigrants and refugees as has Canada, especially since 1990. That does not mean that Canadians should be smug or complacent. The country still has a long way to go before it can achieve the model society described in this 1862 colonization pamphlet sent to prospective German settlers:

> Canada is the land of peace, order and abundance.... The immigrant when he arrives is protected and guided by government officials.... Canada is about the only country in which the ... immigrant practically as well as before the law is seen as immediately equal to the native born.[17]

Acknowledgements

This book is the product of more than twenty years of intermittent involvement in the fields of Canadian immigration, ethnic, and labour history. My earlier arguments, as embodied in *"Dangerous Foreigners": European Immigrant Workers and Labour Radicalism in Canada, 1896-1932* (1979), have been refined and expanded. New themes have been added, such as the experiences of immigrant professionals, which reflect my current research interests.

In preparing this study for publication I owe a special debt to my wife, Dr. Irmgard Steinisch, who has been a constant source of inspiration and a discerning but compassionate critic. Scholarly assistance has also been forthcoming from my colleagues and friends at the University of Western Ontario, most notably Peter Neary and Donald Cartwright, and from Raymond Breton of the University of Toronto, and Bruno Ramirez of the University of Montreal. I would like to thank the staff of McClelland & Stewart for shepherding the manuscript through its various stages, Michael Harrison for helping to launch the project, and Richard Tallman for his editorial work. Carrie Jeneroux and my son, Richard Avery, undertook the arduous task of compiling the book's index.

I am also grateful to the Social Sciences and Humanities Research Council and the University of Western Ontario for financial support, and to the secretaries of the UWO History Department for their hard work on my behalf.

Over the years, my research has been greatly facilitated by the staff of many archives and libraries in Canada and the United States. I owe a special debt to the National Archives of Canada.

Readers will note that chapters 1, 3, and 4 are based on sections of *"Dangerous Foreigners."* In each instance, however, the arguments have been reinforced by new research and by incorporating relevant interpretations of other immigration scholars. Quite a modified version of Chapter 2 was published in 1978 in the *Journal of Canadian Studies* as a joint article with Peter Neary, who has graciously allowed me to incorporate that material into this text. Chapter 3 has also benefited from some of the data that appeared in an article with Bruno Ramirez; this was published in 1994 in a collection edited by Dirk Hoerder *et al.*, *Roots of the Transplanted.*

241

Chapters in Part One of *Reluctant Host* are all based on extensive archival research. In contrast, Part Two is a broad survey of the elements of continuity and change in Canada's immigration policy since 1952 and the social implications associated with the arrival of diverse groups of immigrant workers. Because of the scope of this undertaking, both chronologically and thematically, most of the information has been obtained from contemporary government reports, parliamentary hearings, and a wide range of secondary sources.

Notes

Introduction

1. Frances Henry, "Caribbean Migration to Canada: Prejudice and Opportunity," in Barry Levine, ed., *The Caribbean Exodus* (New York, 1987), 218.
2. Alan Anderson and James Frideres, *Ethnicity in Canada: Theoretical Perspectives* (Toronto, 1981), 273.
3. G.M. Wrong, *The Canadians: The Story of a People* (Toronto, 1938); Chester Martin, *Foundations of Canadian Nationhood* (Toronto, 1938); R.G. Trotter, *Canadian Federation: Its Origin and Achievement: A Study in Nation Building* (London, 1924); Carl Berger, *The Sense of Power: Studies in the Ideas of Canadian Imperialism, 1867-1914* (Toronto, 1970); Thomas Chapais, *Cours d'histoire du Canada*, 8 vols. (Quebec, 1919-33).
4. Helen Cowan, *British Emigration to British North America* (Toronto, 1928); Norman Macdonald, *Canada, Immigration and Colonization, 1841-1903* (Toronto, 1968); Rudolph Vecoli, "European Americans: From Immigrants to Ethnics," *International Migration Review*, VI, 4 (Winter, 1972), 403-34.
5. Edmund Bradwin, *The Bunkhouse Man* (Toronto, 1928); J.W. Dafoe, *Clifford Sifton and His Times* (Toronto, 1931); James Fitzpatrick, *University in Overalls* (Toronto, 1920); C.A. Dawson, *Group Settlement: Ethnic Communities in Western Canada*, Vol. VII in W.A. Mackintosh and W.L.G. Joerg, eds., Canadian Frontiers and Settlement Series (Toronto, 1936); Robert England, *The Central European Immigrant in Canada* (Toronto, 1929) and *The Colonization of Western Canada* (Toronto, 1936); Kate Foster, *Our Canadian Mosaic* (Toronto, 1926); Dr. R.P. Bryce, *The Value to Canada of the Continental Immigrant* (Toronto, 1928); W.G. Smith, *Building the Nation* (Toronto, 1922); Arthur Morton, *History of Prairie Settlement* (Toronto, 1938); John Murray Gibbon, *Canadian Mosaic* (Toronto, 1938); Charles Young, *The Ukrainian Canadians: A Study in Assimilation* (Toronto, 1931).
6. J.T.M. Anderson, *The Education of the New Canadian* (Toronto, 1918); W. Bridgman, *Breaking Prairie Sod* (Toronto, 1920); J.S. Woodsworth, *Strangers Within Our Gates* (Toronto, 1909) and *My Neighbour* (Toronto, 1911); Charles Magrath, *Canada's Growth and Some Problems Affecting It* (Ottawa, 1910).
7. Books dealing with immigrants from Asia ranged from sympathetic studies, such as

C.H. Young and H.R.Y. Reid, *The Japanese Canadians* (Toronto, 1938), and C.J. Woodsworth, *Canada and the Orient* (Toronto, 1941), to polemics, such as H. Glynn-Ward, *The Writing on the Wall* (Vancouver, 1921), and F. Leighton Thomas, *Japan: the Octopus of the East and Its Menace to Canada* (Vancouver, 1932). There were, however, important books written from the perspective of these ethnic groups themselves, such as Cheng Tien-Fang, *Oriental Immigration in Canada* (Vancouver, 1931). One of the most important of the liberal revisionist studies was by the sociologist Forrest LaViolette, *The Canadian Japanese and World War II: A Sociological and Psychological Account* (Toronto, 1948).

8. Simon Belkin, *Through Narrow Gates: A Review of Jewish Immigration, Colonization and Immigrant Aid Work in Canada 1840-1940* (Montreal, 1966); Joseph Kage, ed., *With Faith and Thanksgiving: The Story of Two Hundred Years of Jewish Immigration and Immigrant Aid Effort in Canada, 1760-1960* (Montreal, 1962).

9. John Gellner and John Smerek, *The Czechs and Slovaks in Canada* (Toronto, 1968); David Rome, ed., *Jews in Canadian Literature* (Montreal, 1962); Vladimir Kaye, *Early Ukrainian Settlements in Canada, 1895-1900* (Toronto, 1964); J.M. Kirschbaum, *Slovaks in Canada* (Toronto, 1967); John Kosa, *Land of Choice: The Hungarians in Canada* (Toronto, 1957); W.J. Lindal, *The Icelanders in Canada* (Ottawa, 1967); Vera Lysenko, *Men in Sheepskin Coats: A Study of Assimilation* (Toronto, 1947); B.G. Sack, *History of the Jews in Canada* (Montreal, 1945); Victor Turek, *Poles in Manitoba* (Toronto, 1967) and *The Polish-Language Press in Canada: Its History and a Biographical Sketch* (Toronto, 1962); O. Woycenko, *The Ukrainians in Canada* (Ottawa, 1967); Paul Yuzyk, *The Ukrainians in Manitoba: A Social History* (Toronto, 1953).

10. David Corbett, *Canada's Immigration Policy: A Critique* (Toronto, 1957); Julian Park, ed., *The Culture of Contemporary Canada* (Ithaca, N.Y., 1957); Harry Hawthorn, ed., *The Doukhobors of British Columbia* (London, 1955); Peter Russell, ed., *Nationalism in Canada* (Toronto, 1966); Anthony Richmond, *Post-War Immigrants in Canada* (Toronto, 1967); J.F.C. Wright, *Slava Bohu: The Story of the Doukhobors* (New York, 1940); Arthur Chiel, *The Jews of Manitoba* (Toronto, 1961).

11. Two broader studies that demonstrated this new social science approach were Anthony Richmond, *Immigrants and Ethnic Groups in Metropolitan Toronto: A Preliminary Study*, Paper for the York University Institute of Behavioral Research (1967); and Freda Hawkins, *Canada and Immigration* (Montreal, 1972). This interdisciplinary approach was also evident in the study of some of Canada's ethno-religious groups: E.K. Francis, *In Search of Utopia: The Mennonites of Manitoba* (Altona, Manitoba, 1955); George Woodcock and Ivan Avakumovic, *The Doukhobors* (Toronto, 1968); Victor Peters, *All Things Common* (Minneapolis, 1965).

12. Historians such as Marcus Lee Hansen and Oscar Handlin, sociologists such as Robert Park and Everett Hughes, and anthropologists such as Herbert Gans and Thomas and Znaniecki had previously made American ethnic studies a legitimate field of scholarly endeavour.

13. Irving Abella and Harold Troper, *None Is Too Many: Canada and the Jews of Europe 1933-1948* (Toronto, 1982); Gerald Dirks, *Canada's Refugee Policy: Indifference or Opportunism* (Montreal, 1987); Freda Hawkins, *Critical Years in Immigration: Canada and Australia Compared* (Montreal, 1989); Alan Green, *Immigration and the Postwar Canadian Economy* (Toronto, 1976); Richmond, *Postwar Immigrants in Canada*; Reg Whitaker, *Double Standard: The Secret History of Canadian Immigration* (Toronto, 1987).

14. The Generations Series, funded by the Multiculturalism Directorate, produced a number of ethnic histories by 1988: Grace Anderson and David Higgs, *A Future to Inherit: The Portuguese Communities of Canada* (Toronto, 1976); Karl Aun, *The Political Refugees: A History of the Estonians in Canada* (Toronto, 1986); Norman Buchignani and Doreen Indra, with Ram Srivastava, *Continuous Journey: A Social History of South Asians in Canada* (Toronto, 1986); Baha Abu-Luban, *An Olive Branch on the Family Tree: The Arabs in Canada* (Toronto, 1980); Peter Chimbos, *The Canadian Odyssey: The Greek Experience in Canada* (Toronto, 1980); Gulbrand Loken, *From Fjord to Frontier: A History of the Norwegians in Canada* (Toronto, 1980); N.F. Dreisziger *et al.*, *Struggle and Hope: The Hungarian-Canadian Experience* (Toronto, 1982); Manoly Lupul, ed., *A Heritage in Transition: Essays in the History of Ukrainians in Canada* (Toronto, 1982); Henry Radecki and Benedykt Heydenkorn, *A Member of a Distinguished Family: The Polish Group in Canada* (Toronto, 1976); Anthony Rasporich, *For a Better Life: A History of the Croatians in Canada* (Toronto, 1983); Stanford Reid, *The Scottish Tradition in Canada* (Toronto, 1976); Edgar Wickberg, ed., *From China to Canada: A History of the Chinese Communities in Canada* (Toronto, 1982); Herman Ganzevoort, *A Bittersweet Land: The Dutch Experience in Canada, 1890-1980* (Toronto, 1988); Jean R. Burnet with Howard Palmer, *"Coming Canadians": An Introduction to a History of Canada's Peoples* (Toronto, 1988). The Canadian Historical Association booklet series on Canada's ethnic groups is also a useful source.

15. See Alan Anderson and James Frideres, *Ethnicity in Canada: Theoretical Perspectives* (Toronto, 1981); Norman Buchignani, *Cultures in Canada: Strength in Diversity* (Regina, 1984); Raymond Breton, *The Governance of Ethnic Communities: Political Structures and Processes in Canada* (Westport, Conn., 1991); Burnet with Palmer, *"Coming Canadians"*; Leo Dreidger, *Ethnic Canada: Identities and Inequalities* (Toronto, 1987); Jean Elliott, ed., *Two Nations, Many Cultures* (Scarborough, 1983); W.W. Isajiw, ed., *Identities: The Impact of Ethnicity on Canadian Society* (Toronto, 1977); Peter Li, ed., *Race and Ethnic Relations in Canada* (Toronto, 1990); Subhas Ramcharan, *Racism: Non-Whites in Canada* (Toronto, 1982); Jeffrey Reitz, *The Survival of Ethnic Groups* (Toronto, 1980).

16. Raymond Breton *et al.*, *Ethnic Identity and Equality: Varieties of Experience in a Canadian City* (Toronto, 1990); Augie Fleras and Jean Leonard Elliott, *Multiculturalism in Canada* (Scarborough, 1992); Robert Harney and Harold Troper, *Immigrants: A Portrait of the Urban Experience, 1890-1930* (Toronto, 1975); K. Victor

Ujimoto and Gordon Hirabayashi, *Visible Minorities and Multiculturalism: Asians in Canada* (Toronto, 1980); John Mallea and Jonathan Young, *Cultural Diversity and Canadian Education: Issues and Innovations* (Ottawa, 1984).

17. See Evelyn Kallen, *Ethnicity and Human Rights in Canada* (Toronto, 1982); Howard Palmer, *Patterns of Prejudice: A History of Nativism in Alberta* (Toronto, 1982); Harold Troper and Morton Weinfeld, *Old Wounds: Jews, Ukrainians and the Hunt for Nazi War Criminals in Canada* (Markham, 1989); Wilson Head, *Adaptations of Immigrants: Perceptions of Ethnic and Racial Discrimination* (Toronto, 1981); Peter Ward, *White Canada Forever: Popular Attitudes and Public Policy towards Orientals in British Columbia* (Montreal, 1978); Robin Winks, *The Blacks in Canada* (Toronto, 1971).

18. Books dealing with the Chinese-Canadian experience include Wickberg, ed., *From China to Canada*; Anthony Chan, *Gold Mountain* (Vancouver, 1983); Peter Li, *The Chinese in Canada* (Toronto, 1988). The Japanese-Canadian experience has been analysed by Ken Adachi, *The Enemy That Never Was: A History of the Japanese Canadians* (Toronto, 1976); A. Sunahara, *The Politics of Racism: The Uprooting of the Japanese Canadians During the Second World War* (Toronto, 1981). For aspects of the East Indian experience, see Hugh Johnston, *The Voyage of the Komagata Maru: The Sikh Challenge to Canada's Colour Bar* (Delhi, 1979); Joan Jensen, *Passage from India: Asian Indian Immigrants in North America* (London, 1988). Books about more recent immigrants from Asia have also appeared. For example, Louis-Jacques Dorais *et al.*, *Exile in a Cold Land: A Vietnamese Community in Canada* (New Haven, 1987). There has also been an increase in the number of books dealing with African Canadians. These include W.W. Anderson, *Caribbean Immigrants: A Socio-Demographic Profile* (Toronto, 1993); Wilson Head, *The Black Presence in the Canadian Mosaic: A Study of Perception and the Practice of Discrimination Against Blacks in Metropolitan Toronto* (Toronto, 1975); Dennis Magill, *Nova Scotia Blacks: A Historical and Structural Overview* (Halifax, 1970); Frances Henry, *The Caribbean Diaspora in Toronto: Learning to Live with Racism* (Toronto, 1994).

19. Some of the more outstanding are included in the Generations Series. Useful additions are Lubomyr Luciuk and Stella Hryniuk, eds., *Canada's Ukrainians: Negotiating an Identity* (Toronto, 1991); Bruno Ramirez, *Les Premiers italiens de Montréal: l'origine de la Petite Italie du Québec* (Montréal, 1984); Roberto Perin and Franc Sturino, eds., *Arrangiarsi: The Italian Immigration Experience in Canada* (Montreal, 1989); John Zucchi, *Italians in Toronto: Development of a National Identity* (Montreal, 1988).

20. See Sheila Arnopoulos, *Problems of Immigrant Women in the Canadian Labour Force* (Ottawa, 1979); Jean Burnet, ed., *Looking into My Sister's Eye: An Exploration in Women's History* (Toronto, 1986); Betty Boyd Caroli *et al.*, *The Italian Immigrant Woman in North America* (Toronto, 1978); Ruth Frager, *Strife, Class, Ethnicity, and Gender in the Jewish Labour Movement of Toronto, 1900-1939*

(Toronto, 1992); Franca Iacovetta, *Such Hardworking People: Italian Immigrants in Postwar Toronto* (Montreal, 1992); Varpu Lindstrom-Best, *Defiant Sisters: A Social History of Finnish Immigrant Women in Canada* (Toronto, 1988); Roxanna Ng, *The Politics of Community Services: Immigrant Women, Class and the State* (Toronto, 1987); Frances Swyripa, *Wedded to the Cause: Ukrainian Women and Ethnic Identity, 1891-1991* (Toronto, 1993).

21. Traditional accounts include Robert England, *The Central European Immigrant in Canada* (Toronto, 1929); Harold Troper, *Only Farmers Need Apply* (Toronto, 1972).

22. The first major study on the topic was D.C. Masters, *The Winnipeg General Strike* (Toronto, 1950). While Masters ignored the role of the immigrant workers, this can be excused given the level of scholarship about Canada's ethnic communities at the time. More puzzling is why David Bercuson, in *Confrontation at Winnipeg* (Montreal, 1974), chose only to consider the Anglo-Canadian leaders of the strike. Nor has Bercuson made any attempt to remove this deficiency in the recent reprint of *Confrontation*.

23. Ian Radforth, *Bushworkers and Bosses: Logging in Northern Ontario 1900-1980* (Toronto, 1987); Terry Copp, *Anatomy of Poverty: The Condition of the Working Class in Montreal, 1897-1917* (Toronto, 1974); Jorgen Dahlie and Tissa Fernando, *Ethnicity, Power and Politics in Canada* (Toronto, 1981); Bruno Ramirez, *On the Move: French Canadian and Italian Migrants in the North Atlantic Economy, 1860-1914* (Toronto, 1991); Vic Satzewich, *Racism and the incorporation of foreign labour: Farm labour migration to Canada since 1945* (London, 1991).

24. Some of the more notable are John Kolasky, *The Shattered Illusion: The History of Ukrainian Pro-Communist Organizations in Canada* (Toronto, 1979); Li, *The Chinese in Canada*; Erna Paris, *Jews* (Toronto, 1980); Rasporich, *For a Better Life*; Frances Swyripa and John Herd Thompson, eds., *Loyalties in Conflict: Ukrainians in Canada During the Great War* (Edmonton, 1983); and the seminal article by Robert Harney, "Montreal's King of Italian Labour: A Case Study of Padronism," *Labour/Le Travailleur*, 4 (1979), 57-84. The previously mentioned studies by Ruth Frager, Franca Iacovetta, and Varpu Lindstrom-Best on immigrant women workers are also outstanding.

25. Irving Abella, ed., *On Strike: Six Labour Struggles in Canada* (Toronto, 1974); Craig Heron, *Working in Steel: The Early Years in Canada, 1883-1935* (Toronto, 1988); Gregory Kealey, *Toronto Workers Respond to Industrial Capitalism, 1867-1892* (Toronto, 1980); A. Ross McCormack, *Reformers, Rebels and Revolutionaries: The Western Canadian Radical Movement* (Toronto, 1978); Bryan Palmer, *Working-Class Experience: Rethinking the History of Canadian Labour, 1800-1991* (Toronto, 1992); Joan Sangster, *Dreams of Equality: Women on the Canadian Left, 1920-1950* (Toronto, 1989).

26. W.R. Bohning, *The Migration of Workers in the United Kingdom and the European Community* (London, 1972). See also Stephen Castles and Godula Kosack, *Immigrant Workers and Class Structure in Western Europe* (Toronto, 1973).

27. H.C. Pentland, "The Development of a Capitalistic Labour Market in Canada," *Canadian Journal of Economics and Political Science*, XXV (November, 1959), 450, 460.

28. Edna Bonacich, "Advanced Capitalism and Black/White Relations in the United States: A Split Labour Market Interpretation," *American Sociological Review*, 41 (February, 1976), 34-51.

29. *Ibid.*, 36.

30. Terry Boswell, "A Split Labour Market Analysis of Discrimination Against Chinese Immigrants, 1850-1882," *American Sociological Review*, 51, 3 (September, 1986), 353-56.

31. John Porter, *The Vertical Mosaic* (Toronto, 1965), 73.

32. Thomas Archdeacon, "Reflections on Immigration to Europe in Light of U.S. Immigration History," *International Migration Review*, XXVI, 2 (1992), 526.

33. Bruno Ramirez has provided an excellent analysis of this topic for the early twentieth century in *On the Move*. See also Jose Igartua and Marine De Freminville, "Les Origines des Travailleurs de l'Alcan au Saguenay, 1925-1939," *Revue d'histoire de l'amérique française* (September, 1983), 255-76.

Chapter One

1. O.J. Firestone, *Canada's Economic Development, 1867-1953* (London, 1958), 65; *Census of Canada*, 1911 (Ottawa, 1913), 2, 42-44; Robert England, *The Central European Immigrant in Canada* (Toronto, 1929); George Haythorne and Leonard Marsh, *Land and Labour: A Social Survey of Agriculture and the Farm Labour Market in Central Canada* (Toronto, 1941), 213-30.

2. National Archives of Canada (NAC), Immigration Branch (IB), 571672, W.F. McCreary to J.A. Smart, 21 June 1897.

3. Pentland, "The Development of a Capitalistic Labour Market," 450.

4. *Ukrainian Rural Settlements, Report of the Bureau of Social Research* (Winnipeg, January 25, 1917); Dafoe, *Sifton*, 318-19; Canada, *House of Commons Debates*, (hereafter *Debates*), 1905, 7686; *ibid.*, 1911, 1611. There are also extensive references to this trend in IB, 29490, and IB, 195281.

5. M.C. Urquhart and K.A.H. Buckley, eds., *Historical Statistics of Canada* (Toronto, 1965), Series A, 133-142, 19.

6. Berger, *The Sense of Power*.

7. *Ibid.*, 143-54; Canada Manpower and Immigration, *Immigration and Population Statistics*, vol. 3 of *Canadian Immigration and Population Study* (also known as "The Green Paper on Immigration" (Ottawa, 1974), 7-15.

8. David Frank, "Company Town/Labour Town: Local Government in the Cape Breton Coal Towns, 1917-1926," *Social History/Histoire sociale*, 17 (May, 1981), 177-96;

David Frank and Nolan Reilly, "The Emergence of the Socialist Movement in the Maritimes," *Labour/Le Travailleur*, 4 (1979), 111-15.

9. Bruno Ramirez, "Migration and Regional Labour Markets, 1870-1915: The Quebec Case," in Deian Hopkin and Gregory Kealey, eds., *Class, Community and the Labour Movement: Wales and Canada, 1850-1930* (Aberystwyth and St. John's, 1989).

10. Bradwin, *Bunkhouse Man*; Bruno Ramirez, "Brief Encounters: Italian Immigrant Workers and the CPR, 1900-30," *Labour/Le Travail*, 17 (Spring, 1986), 9-28.

11. Donald Avery, "Canadian Immigration Policy and the Alien Question in Canada, 1896-1919: The Anglo-Canadian Perspective" (Ph.D. thesis, University of Western Ontario, 1973), 16-25.

12. Dafoe, *Sifton*, 95-100.

13. *Sessional Papers*, 1902, No. 13, 7; *ibid.*, 1896, no. 13, 7; Dafoe, *Sifton*, 319.

14. Emerson Hough, *The Sowing* (Winnipeg, 1909), 27, 62; *Sessional Papers*, 1910, no. 25, 110.

15. Haythorne and Marsh, *Land and Labour*, 181-92. The census of 1911 showed that there were 142,384 farm labourers in Canada; of these, 58,132 were immigrants. *Census of Canada*, 1911, vol. VI, 30-31.

16. IB, 741096, W.S. Herron to W.D. Scott, 6 November 1907.

17. Norman Macdonald, *Canada: Immigration and Colonization, 1841-1903* (Toronto, 1968), 95-100, 200-09; IB, 321912, John Dyke to T.M. Daly, Minister of the Interior, 28 April 1893.

18. IB, 48176, W.F. McCreary to secretary, Department of the Interior, 8 December 1897.

19. IB, 113228, No. 4, James A. Smart to Clifford Sifton, 13 July 1900; *ibid.*, J.A. Smart to the North Atlantic Trading Company, 17 July 1900. Between 1899 and 1906 this mysterious syndicate of European agents had a virtual monopoly on the recruitment of agriculturalists for Canada in central Europe and the Scandinavian countries. Despite an official inquiry of its operation by the House of Commons Select Committee on Agriculture and Colonization in 1906, neither James A. Smart, former deputy minister of the interior, nor W.T.R. Preston, former superintendent of emigration in London, England, would divulge the names of the directors of the North Atlantic Trading Company. "Evidence," Select Committee on Agriculture and Colonization, 1906, 231-32; W.T.R. Preston, *My Generation of Politics and Politicians* (Toronto, 1927), 125-222. IB, 113228, No. 11, F.C. Blair to Dr. Edwards, 24 October 1921.

20. IB, 17480, No. 1, L.M. Fortier, acting superintendent of Immigration Branch, to W.W. Cory, acting deputy minister of the interior, 21 September 1907; IB, 946587, No. 1, Report of Immigration Account to W.C. Black, deputy minister of immigration and colonization, 31 March 1922; *Proceedings of the Trades and Labour Congress*, 1908, 48.

21. IB, 389803, J.A. Smart to W.D. Scott, 31 May 1905; *ibid.*, Scott to Frank Oliver, 14 July 1905; *ibid.*, Smart to Oliver, 10 January 1907.

22. IB, 595173, No. 4, W.D. Scott to W.W. Cory, 16 January 1912.

23. Lloyd Reynolds, *The British Immigrant* (Toronto, 1935), 46, 289, 306; "Report of W.T.R. Preston," *Sessional Papers*, 1900, No. 13, 13; NAC, Sir Wilfrid Laurier Papers, 72945, Reverend Charles Gordon to Laurier, 7 May 1903; IB, 595173, J. Obed Smith to Scott, 12 February 1907.

24. George Haythorne, "Harvest Labor in Western Canada: An Episode in Economic Planning," *Quarterly Journal of Economics* (1932-33), 533-44; IB, 29490, No. 3, J. Obed Smith to Scott, 8 July 1909; NAC, Sir Thomas Shaughnessy Papers, microfilm, Shaughnessy to Alfred Jones, 3 August 1906.

25. Ottawa *Free Press*, 17 July 1911; IB, 29490, Smith to Pedley, 15 October 1901; *Debates*, 1904, 7302.

26. *Ukrainian Rural Settlements*, 4-6. See also William de Geldwr, *A Dutch Homesteader on the Prairies*, trans. Herman Ganzevoort (Toronto, 1973), 12-13.

27. Philip Taylor, *The Distant Magnet: European Emigration to the U.S.A.* (New York, 1972), 80; Francis Hyde, *Cunard and the North Atlantic, 1840-1973: A History of Shipping and Financial Management* (London, 1975), 140-92.

28. H.A. Innis, *A History of the Canadian Pacific Railway* (Toronto, 1971), 139, 170, 224, 264; Shaughnessy Papers, Shaughnessy to Archer Baker, 5 August 1908; *ibid.*, Shaughnessy to Robert Rogers, 2 December 1911. With the absorption of the Allan Line into the newly created Canadian Pacific Ocean Steamship service in 1915, an additional eighteen ships were added to the Atlantic service. The Pacific fleet, which dated back to 1889, was also expanded during this period. The CPR also benefited from lucrative mail subsidies from both the Canadian and imperial governments. See also Thomas Appleton, *Ravenscrag: The Allan Royal Mail Line* (Toronto, 1974), 120-30.

29. Hough, *The Sowing*, 92.

30. Shaughnessy Papers, Archer Baker to Shaughnessy, 5 August 1908; Innis, *Canadian Pacific*, 263-64.

31. IB, 39145, McCreary to Smart, 17 May 1900. See also James Hedges, *Building the Canadian West* (New York, 1939), 129-30; Harold Innis, *Settlement and the Mining Frontier* (Toronto, 1936), 370-75.

32. The term "navvy" or "navigator" was derived from the British experience in railway-building during the early nineteenth century. D. Brooke, "Railway Navvies on the Pennines, 1841-71," *Journal of Transport History*, 3 (February, 1975), 41-53.

33. IB, 39145, Smart to McCreary, 15 June 1900; *ibid.*, Blake Robertson to Oliver, 10 October 1907.

34. Sifton Papers, 82801, H.A. McKibbon, sec., Port Arthur Board of Trade, to Sifton, 5 November 1901. See also A.R.M. Lower, *Settlement and the Forest Frontier* (Toronto, 1936), 22, 134.

35. Paul Phillips, *No Power Greater: A Century of Labour in B.C.* (Vancouver, 1967), 45, 77; Haythorne and Marsh, *Land and Labour*, 200-25; Innis, *Mining Frontier*, 173, 221.

36. *Sessional Papers*, 1899, vol. 33, no. 70, "Report of Mr. R.C. Clute on the Commission to Inquire into the Death of McDonald and Fraser on the Crow's Nest Pass Railway," 16.

37. IB, 39501, Shaughnessy to James A. Stewart, 27 October 1897. See also F.A. Talbot, *The Making of a Great Canadian Railway* (London, 1912), 133-59, 238-76.

38. IB, 39145, Smart to D. McNicoll, 2nd vice president, CPR, 12 May 1903.

39. IB, 39145, Smith to Pedley, 1 July 1901; Mackenzie King to Thomas Shaughnessy, 3 July 1901, cited by John Wilson, *The Calcium Light: Turned on by a Railway Trackman* (St. Louis, 1902), 46; Sifton Papers, 83178, McCreary to Sifton, 3 July 1901.

40. Cordasco was a successful steamship agent, banker, and director of a labour bureau; he also controlled the Montreal newspaper *Corriere del Canada*. See Harney, "Montreal's King of Italian Labour," 57-84.

41. *Report, Royal Commission to Inquire into the Immigration of Italian Labourers to Montreal, and Alleged Fraudulent Practices of Employment Agencies* (Ottawa, 1904), 25, 95, 144.

42. Laurier Papers, 160620, Charles Hays to Laurier, 4 October 1909; IB, 594511, No. 3, J.O. Reddie to W.D. Scott, 1 April 1910; *Labour Gazette*, 12 (June, 1912), 721; IB, 594511, Survey of Labour Needs of Railroad Contractors, memorandum, W.D. Scott, 5 April 1909; IB, 39145, J. Bruce Walker, Winnipeg commissioner, to Scott, 19 May 1908; *Labour Gazette*, 1906-07, 261. IB, 594511, No. 3, Survey of Railroad Contractors, in 1910 revealed that of twenty-seven major companies the average wage varied from $1.50 per diem in New Brunswick to $2.50 in British Columbia.

43. University of Toronto Archives, James Mavor Papers, Mavor to George Cox, 2 April 1907; IB, 809068, W.W.B. McInnes to Scott, 5 April 1909; Scott to M.J. Reid, 18 September 1910; *Christian Guardian*, 2 April 1913.

44. IB, 594511, Scott memorandum, 5 April 1909; IB, 39145, J. Bruce Walker, Winnipeg commissioner, to Scott, 19 May 1908.

45. IB, 594511, No. 3, J.M. Langley, chief of police, to mayor of Victoria, 28 August 1911; *ibid.*, J. Bruce Walker to Scott, 12 March 1912. Extensive correspondence by immigration officials on the problem of restriction is located in IB, 594511, Nos. 2-6. What also troubled Canadian immigration officials was the difficulty of returning to the United States immigrants who had not been naturalized there and who were "undesirable." IB, 594511, No. 3, F.H. Larned, acting commissioner-general, Immigration and Naturalization, U.S. Government, to Scott, 16 June 1909.

46. Laurier Papers, 182131 Duncan Ross to Laurier, 27 February 1911; IB, 594511, W.W. Cory to Scott, 16 July 1910; NAC, Mackenzie King Diary, 10 January 1911; NAC, Mackenzie King Papers, 1910, memorandum of B. Robertson, July, 1910.

47. IB, 594511, No. 5, Donald Mann to W.D. Scott, 6 August 1912; *ibid.*, Timothy Foley to Robert Rogers, 27 March 1912.

48. IB, 594511, No. 4, W.D. Scott to Dr. W.J. Roche, 18 January 1913; *ibid.*, No. 6, Scott to R.H. Chadwick, secretary, Trades and Labour Council, Moose Jaw, 22 May 1915; *Christian Guardian*, 2 April 1913.

49. Innis, *Canadian Pacific*, 146, 164; Martin Robin, *The Rush for Spoils: The Company Province, 1871-1933* (Toronto, 1972), 111, 125-30.

50. *Sessional Papers*, 1910, No. 25, 41, 42, cited in Innis, *Mining Frontier*, 307.

51. Shaughnessy Papers, Shaughnessy to William Whyte, 3 August 1900; *Report of the Alberta Coal Commission, 1925* (Edmonton, 1926), 183-90.

52. Shaughnessy Papers, Shaughnessy to Thomas Skinner, 20 January 1906; *ibid.*, Shaughnessy to William Whyte, 26 November 1908; Innis, *Mining Frontier*, 293-314; Phillips, *No Power Greater*, 55-57.

53. Professor Arthur Coleman, "Address," 29 February 1912, *Empire Club of Canada: Addresses... During the Session of 1911-12* (Toronto, 1913), 163; *Canadian Mining Journal*, 15 June 1907, 195.

54. *Census of Canada*, 1911, vol. V, vi, xviii, xx, 7, 74, 88, 155; Report of Superintendent of New Ontario, "Acts and Proceedings of the General Assembly of the Presbyterian Church in Canada," 1914, 20.

55. *Labour Gazette*, September, 1904, 262; *Report of the Ontario Commission on Unemployment* (Toronto, 1916), 121. Most of these agencies were located in large transportation centres: Toronto (24), Montreal (18), Winnipeg (17), Edmonton (14), Vancouver (13), and Sudbury (11). Major companies such as the Central Employment Agency and the Star Employment Agency had branches in several cities, as did the employment arms of the Canadian Pacific Railway, the Grand Northern, and the Grand Trunk Pacific. (IB, 801518, Inventory of Employment Agencies licensed under PC 1028 and PC 1064 in the year 1913.)

56. IB, 801518, Henry Stanford to W.D. Scott, 25 January 1908.

57. *Royal Commission... Italian Labourers*, 1904, 155; IB, 775789, cited in letter of J.G. Young, immigration agent, Sydney, to Scott, 10 November 1913; IB, 819863, W.D. Scott to Robert Rogers, 5 December 1911.

58. *Statutes of Canada*, 1897, 60-61, V, c.11, 1; James J. Atherton, "The Department of Labour and Industrial Relations, 1900-1911" (M.A. thesis, Carleton University, 1972), 240-60.

59. Sifton Papers, 103827, W.L. Hagler to Minister of Labour, 18 January 1902; Clute, Royal Commission on Mining Conditions.

60. Laurier Papers, 85632, E. Kirby to T.L. Blackstone, 31 January 1901; Andrew R. McCormack, "The Origins and Extent of Western Canadian Labour Radicalism: 1860-1919" (Ph.D. thesis, University of Western Ontario, 1973), 103-18; King Diary, 1901, 276.

61. Shaughnessy Papers, Shaughnessy to William Whyte, 10 December 1908.

62. United States Immigration Commission, *Report of the Immigration Commission*, 61st Congress, 3rd session (Washington, 1911), vol. 1, 185, 190, 493-99; vol. 2, 375-85; vol. 18, 331-71; vol. 19, 17-34.

63. *Ibid.*, vol. 1, 46-50; E.G. Hartmann, *The Movement to Americanize the Immigrant* (New York, 1967), 80-130; Walter Nugent, *Crossings: The Great Transatlantic Migrations, 1870-1914* (Bloomington, Ind., 1992), 149-67.

64. Peter Ward, *White Canada Forever: Popular Attitudes and Public Policy toward Orientals in British Columbia* (Montreal, 1978); Li, *The Chinese in Canada.*

65. IB, 39145, #1, J. Obed Smith to Frank Pedley, 25 June 1901; Wilson, *The Calcium Light.*

66. *Labour Gazette*, September, 1904, 262.

67. Marilyn Barber, *Immigrant Domestic Servants in Canada*, CHA Booklet No. 16 (Ottawa, 1991); Barbara Roberts, "'A Work of Empire': Canadian Reformers and British Female Immigration," in Linda Kealey, ed., *A Not Unreasonable Claim: Women and Reform in Canada, 1880s-1920s* (Toronto, 1979).

68. In 1890, faced with an irate labour movement, the government appointed a Select Committee of the House of Commons to investigate charges that skilled workers had been imported from Great Britain, Europe, and the United States to break strikes in Canada. This inquiry produced a strong demand for legislation making it illegal to recruit alien workers by contract or other financial inducement. *Report of the Select Committee to Prohibit the Importation of Immigration of Foreigners and Aliens Under Contract Or to Perform Labour in Canada* (Ottawa, 1890).

69. Statutes of Canada, 1897; W.D. Atkinson, "Organized Labour and the Laurier Administration" (M.A. thesis, Carleton University, 1957), 35-55.

70. King Diary, 20 September 1906; *ibid.*, 18 October 1906; *Debates*, 1905, 7424, 8177.

71. Preston had been appointed to his position by Clifford Sifton as part of his promotional campaign. By 1905 Sifton had resigned from cabinet. W.T.R. Preston, *My Generation of Politics and Politicians* (Toronto, 1927), 125-222; *Proceedings of the TLC*, 1906, 30-45; *Industrial Canada* (October, 1904), 151.

72. To monitor the situation the TLC sent an official delegate to Great Britain annually between 1908 and 1910. This in turn brought an angry response from CMA president C.M. Murray, who charged in 1910 that the TLC was interfering with the recruitment of British skilled workers and should be prosecuted under the 1905 amendment to the Immigration Act covering misrepresentation. *Proceedings of the TLC*, 1907, 52; *ibid.*, 1908, 39; IB, 195281, #3, Murray to W.D. Scott, 12 April 1910.

73. Laurier Papers, 95153, A.F. Just to Laurier, 23 October 1905; *Proceedings of the TLC*, 1906, 9; *Industrial Canada*, August, 1906, 13; King Diary, 19 October 1906.

74. *Proceedings of the TLC*, 1910, 41-42; *ibid.*, 1913, 58-65; Lawrence Fric, "The Role of Commercial Employment Agencies in the Canadian Labour Market" (Ph.D. thesis, University of Toronto, 1973).

75. The *Report of the Royal Commission to Inquire into the Immigration of Labourers to Montreal, and alleged Fraudulent Practices of Employment Agencies* (Ottawa, 1904), prepared by Judge Winchester, forced the Laurier government to strengthen the Alien Labour Act. The 1905 legislation made it illegal to import under promise or offer of employment. An aroused business community was able, however, to water down the bill so that it applied only to the United States, where similar legislation was already in force in relation to Canada. The bill was further emasculated in the Senate, where penalties were applied not only to those who induced immigration by misrep-

resenting conditions in Canada, but also to anyone who tried to discourage immigration. Canada, Senate, *Debates*, 1904, 1223-30; *Proceedings of the TLC*, 1905, 9-12.

76. *Answers* (London, England), 23 April 1910.

77. *Royal Commission . . . Italian Labourers*; Montreal *Star*, 1 June 1904; *Debates*, 1904, 7898.

78. IB, 686314, Dr. Freyesleben to Oliver, 28 June 1907.

79. *Ibid.*, testimony of Franciszek Wlodzniski of Sokal, Galicia; *ibid.*, copy of agreement issued by Davis & Nagel Company to Carl Ditnar, 4 May 1907; *ibid.*, "Report of Immigration Inspector Henry Stanford to W.D. Scott," 14 November 1907; *ibid.*, testimony of Max Rabin, enclosed in letter sent by Dr. Freyesleben to Oliver, 28 June 1907; *ibid.*, Edward Bayley to Colonel A.P. Sherwood, commissioner of the Dominion Police, 13 August 1907; *ibid.*, W.W. Cory to J.J. Foy, Ontario Attorney General, 27 September 1907.

80. The Department of Labour had the responsibility of enforcing the Fair Wages Regulation of 1900, which imposed minimum standards on employers who were receiving federal subsidies. As a private company, the CPR was not covered by these regulations and on at least one occasion Thomas Shaughnessy expressed surprise at the "exorbitant money" the company doctors were charging the workers. Bradwin, *Bunkhouse Man*, 81, 144-53; *Sessional Papers*, 1907, "Report of the Deputy Minister of Labour," 64-67; *Labour Gazette*, July, 1912, 40-42; Shaughnessy Papers, Shaughnessy to William Whyte, 15 May 1907.

81. Lakehead University Archives, Diary of Mr. Angus Bell of the contracting firm of Bell & McMillan, sub-contractors on the Foley, Welsh & Stewart portion of the National Transcontinental in 1913 between Cochrane and Harriganaw River, Quebec.

82. Statistics tabulated from *Sessional Papers*, 1913, No. 36, "Report of the Deputy Minister of Labour," 72; Bradwin, *Bunkhouse Man*, 153, 200, 212.

83. See *Sessional Papers*, 1907-08, No. 25, pt. 2, "Report of the Superintendent of Immigration"; *ibid.*, 1915, No. 25, pt. 2, "Report of the Superintendent of Immigration."

84. *Eastern Labour News*, 24 May 1913; Bradwin, *Bunkhouse Man*, 234.

85. *Sessional Papers*, 11912, No. 36, 88-100; IB, 686314, "Report of Henry Stanford to W.D. Scott," 14 November 1907; *Eastern Labour News*, 24 May 1913; Bradwin, *Bunkhouse Man*, 234. *Alberta Coal Commission, 1925*, 183, 220-30; W.H.P. Jarvis, *Trials and Tales in Cobalt* (Toronto, 1908), 110; Innis, *Mining Frontier*, 320-28.

86. *British Columbia Federationist*, 7 June 1918.

87. W. Burton Hurd, *Racial Origins and Nativity of the Canadian People*, Census Monograph No. 4 (Ottawa, 1937), 586; NAC, Frontier College Collection, Twelfth Annual Report.

Chapter Two

1. By 1921, Ontario had 14 per cent of the Chinese population, Alberta 9 per cent, Saskatchewan 7 per cent, Quebec 6 per cent, and Manitoba 3 per cent. Li, *The Chinese in Canada*, 51.

2. Terry Boswell, "A Split Labor Market Analysis of Discrimination Against Chinese Immigrants, 1850-1882," *American Sociological Review*, 51, 3 (1986), 352-73.

3. See, for example, Stanford Lyman, *The Asian in North America* (1977); James Morton, *In the Sea of Sterile Mountains: The Chinese in British Columbia* (Vancouver, 1974).

4. It is notable that as late as 1906 not a single homestead entry had been made by an Asian. In 1914 the total was still very low: five Chinese, three Japanese, and four East Indians. *Sessional Papers*, 1906-07, no. 25, Pt. 1, xxiii; *ibid.*, 1915, no. 25, Pt. 1, xxi.

5. *Report of the Royal Commission on Chinese Immigration* (Ottawa, 1885), xix.

6. Phillips, *No Power Greater*, 9.

7. *Ibid.*, 12-13.

8. Woodsworth, *Canada and the Orient*, 26.

9. G. La Forest, *Disallowance and Reservation of Provincial Legislation* (Ottawa, 1955), 89-97, 114-15.

10. NAC, John A. Macdonald Papers, 144771, Onderdonk to Macdonald, 14 June 1882; Woodsworth, *Canada and the Orient*, 41.

11. Commissioner Gray, taking a eugenics approach, was contemptuous of the charge that the Chinese presented a threat to Anglo-Canadians when he asked why "the strong, broad shouldered superior race, superior physically and mentally, spring from the highest types of the old world and the new world [should be] expressing a fear of competition with a diminutive, inferior, and comparatively speaking, feminine race." *Debates*, 1885, 3006; Statutes of Canada, 1884-1885, chap. 71, "An Act to Restrict and Regulate Chinese Immigration Into Canada"; *Royal Commission on Chinese Immigration* (1885), 69; Kay Anderson, "The Idea of Chinatown: The Power of Place and Institutional Practice in the Making of a Racial Category," in Ian McKay, *The Challenge of Modernity* (Toronto, 1992), 156-86; Margaret Ormsby, *British Columbia: A History* (Vancouver, 1958), 303, 306, 332. *Report of the Royal Commission on Chinese and Japanese Immigration* (Ottawa, 1902), 145, 276-77.

12. Harry Keith Ralston, "The 1900 Strike of Fraser River Salmon Fishermen" (M.A. thesis, University of British Columbia, 1965), 49-51, 57, 66; "Report of the Executive Committee of British Columbia," in *Proceedings of the Nineteenth Annual Convention of the Trades and Labour Congress* (Toronto, 1903), 30; Laurier Papers, Charles Hope to Laurier, 16 May 1903; *ibid.*, F. Angus, manufacturing agent, to Laurier, 5 June 1903.

13. Ward, *White Canada Forever*, 54-75.

14. NAC, Canadian Pacific Railway President Letterbooks, 1890-97, Sir William Van Horne correspondence; *ibid.*, Sir Thomas Shaughnessy correspondence, 1899-1914; Patricia Roy, "The preservation of peace in Vancouver: the aftermath of the anti-Chinese riot of 1887," *B.C. Studies*, 31 (1976), 45-59; John Munro, "British Columbia and the Chinese evil: Canada's first anti-Asiatic immigration law," *Journal of Canadian Studies*, 6 (1971), 42-51.

15. Van Horne correspondence, Van Horne to J.C. McLagan, 17 July 1896.

16. *Ibid.*

17. *Ibid.*, Shaughnessy correspondence, Shaughnessy to Laurier, 26 January 1900.

18. *Ibid.*, Shaughnessy to W.T. Payne, Traffic Manager, Japan, 15 February 1900; *ibid.*, Shaughnessy to William Whyte, 3 December 1901; *ibid.*, Shaughnessy to Laurier, 21 March 1907.

19. King Papers, C-8675, T.R.E. McInnes to Laurier, 20 October 1907.

20. Canadian Pacific Collection, Glenbow Institute, J.S. Dennis to Shaughnessy, 5 April 1907.

21. *Report of the Royal Commission on Methods by Which Oriental Labourers Have Been Induced to Come to Canada* (Ottawa, 1908), 13-15.

22. Woodsworth, *Canada and the Orient*, 45-71; H.A. Logan, *Trade Unions in Canada: Their Development and Functioning* (Toronto, 1948), 68-69.

23. Woodsworth, *Canada and the Orient*, 49.

24. *Ibid.*, 57; H.L. London, *Non-white Immigration and the 'White' Australia Policy* (New York, 1970), 11.

25. Woodsworth, *Canada and the Orient*, 48-71.

26. *Royal Commission on . . . Oriental Labourers* (1908), 18-19.

27. *Ibid.*

28. Laurier Papers, A.W. Venheim and Gordon Grant to Laurier, 9 September 1907.

29. Woodsworth, *Canada and the Orient*, 80.

30. Laurier Papers, McInnes to Laurier, 11 September 1907.

31. Woodsworth, *Canada and the Orient*, 80.

32. *Royal Commission on . . . Oriental Labourers* (1908), 54.

33. Laurier Papers, Albert Healey to Laurier, 10 September 1907; Adachi, *The Enemy That Never Was*, 12-85; Ward, *White Canada Forever*, 36-76.

34. NAC, Rodolphe Lemieux Papers, report enclosed in Lemieux to Grey, 12 January 1908.

35. *Ibid.*

36. Public Record Office, London, England, Foreign Office (hereafter FO) 371/474, 45533, Hayashi to MacDonald, 23 December 1907, included in FO memorandum, 16 December 1908.

37. The American background is explained in T.A. Bailey, *Theodore Roosevelt and the Japanese-American Crises* (Stanford, Calif., 1934).

38. Elting E. Morison, ed., *The Letters of Theodore Roosevelt*, 8 vols. (Cambridge, Mass., 1952, etc.), VI, 1432. The account of the King-Roosevelt meetings given here

is, except where otherwise indicated, based on a forty-one-page confidential report prepared by King that is now in the Public Record Office (FO 371/471, 4810).

39. Roosevelt claimed it was King who made this prediction (Morison, ed., *Roosevelt Letters*, VI, 919-20). In his diary, King attributed the statement to Roosevelt. King Diary, 25 January 1908.

40. FO 371/471, 4810, confidential report by Mackenzie King.

41. *Ibid.*, 371/473, 5206, Bryce to Grey, 5 February 1908.

42. The British naval attaché in the Washington embassy, Commander Hood, reported that the American fleet would be at a strategic disadvantage in any naval conflict with Japan beyond the Pacific coast of the United States. FO 371/473, 5206, Bryce to Grey, 6 February 1908; *ibid.*, 6592, Grey to Bryce, 25 February 1908.

43. FO 371/473, 7715, memorandum by Ralph Smith. Smith, the member of Parliament for Nanaimo, was one of the Canadians who visited Roosevelt.

44. NAC, Papers of the 4th Earl of Grey, Bryce to Grey, 5 June 1908.

45. *Canadian Annual Review* (hereafter *CAR*), 1908, 119-20.

46. Robert MacGregor Dawson, *William Lyon Mackenzie King: A Political Biography* (Toronto, 1958), 162-66.

47. Shaughnessy correspondence, Shaughnessy to George Bury, 12 November 1912; *Vancouver News Advertiser*, 7 September 1911; G.R. Stevens, *Canadian National Railways* (Toronto, 1960), 11; Woodsworth, *Canada and the Orient*, 101.

48. Laurier Papers, Hays to Laurier, 4 October, 19 November 1909; Laurier to Hays, 12 November 1909.

49. *Debates*, 1910-11, 9831, 9833; *ibid.*, 1911, Second Session, 285-86.

50. King Diary, 29 August 1908, 219; *Proceedings of the Twenty-Seventh Annual Convention of the Trades and Labour Congress* (1911), 13-15, 52-53; *ibid.* (1914), 119-20.

51. Woodsworth, *Canada and the Orient*, 84.

52. Robin, *The Rush for Spoils*, 105, 115.

53. Roger Graham, *Arthur Meighen*, vol. II (Toronto, 1963), 66-86.

54. Phillips, *No Power Greater*, 57-58.

55. NAC, Robert Borden Papers, George Foster to Borden, 26 September 1913.

56. *Ibid.*, T.R.E. McInnes to Borden, 9 August 1913. For details on the California situation, see Carey McWilliams, *Factories in the Field* (Boston, 1939), 111.

57. Borden Papers, Borden to Pope, 20 August 1913; Ward, *White Canada Forever*, 79-93; Joan Jensen, *Passage from India: Asian Indian Immigrants in North America* (New Haven, 1988), 42-162; Johnston, *The Voyage of the Komagata Maru* (Delhi, 1979).

58. Borden Papers, Governor General Connaught to the Colonial Office, 15 August 1913; *ibid.*, Borden to W.J. Roche, 26 September 1913.

59. *Ibid.*, T.R.E. McInnes to Borden, 27 April 1914.

60. *Ibid.*, Borden to W.J. Roche, 10 December 1913.

61. *Ibid.*, W.D. Scott to Mitchell, 30 September 1913.

62. *Ibid.*, Borden to W.J. Roche, 10 December 1913.

63. *Ibid.*, Governor General Connaught to Colonial Office, 16 October 1913.

64. *Ibid.*, Nakamura to Borden, 24 December 1913.

65. *Ibid.*, Blake Robertson to Borden, 26 June 1914.

66. *Debates*, 1914, 4214, 4296, 1562, 4565.

67. *CAR*, 1914, 116-19.

68. Ward, *White Canada Forever*, 36-52; Wickberg, ed., *From China to Canada*, 42-90.

69. Anderson, "The Idea of Chinatown," 157.

70. According to Peter Li, organized labour in British Columbia in its desperate attempt to enrol more workers "often used the Chinese question to recruit popular support." The Trades and Labour Congress also utilized anti-Oriental policies "in promoting a national union between 1880 and 1900." Li, *The Chinese in Canada*, 39.

71. Chan, *Gold Mountain*, 67, 75.

72. *Ibid.*, 66.

73. Cited in Li, *The Chinese in Canada*, 19.

74. David Chuenyan Lai, *Chinatowns: Towns Within Cities in Canada* (Vancouver, 1988), 72-73.

75. Boswell, "Split Labor Market," 352-54.

76. B. Singh Bolaria and Peter Li, *Racial Oppression in Canada*, second edition (Toronto, 1988), 111.

77. In 1901, when Wellington Collieries was owned by the Dunsmuir family, 63 per cent of the surface workers were Asians. In 1911, when the mines were sold to the railroad entrepreneurs Donald Mackenzie and Donald Mann (and renamed Canadian Collieries), Asian surface workers declined to 57 per cent and underground workers to 14 per cent. *Report of the Minister of Mines, Province of British Columbia, 1901* (Victoria, 1902), 1208; *ibid., 1911*, 232; *ibid., 1913*, 348.

78. In 1909, when fifty-seven miners had been killed at the Extension Mine of Wellington Collieries, the union had initiated a legal suit charging the company with negligence for ignoring safety regulations. *British Columbia Federationist*, 14 November 1913, 1; Phillips, *No Power Greater*, 55-57.

79. Between 1912 and 1914 the number of Asians certified as miners at the Wellington Collieries increased by ninety-three, almost a 100 per cent increase. The *Federationist* claimed that the McBride government was working with Canadian Collieries to drive white miners out of the Vancouver Island mines, especially after the UMWA called for a district-wide strike on May 1, 1913. *British Columbia Federationist*, 10 May 1913; *ibid.*, 22 August 1913. *Annual Report of the Minister of Mines, Province of British Columbia, 1914*, 348-50; *Canadian Mining Journal*, 1 October 1913, 601.

80. *Report of the Royal Commission in the Matter of the Coal-Mining Labour Troubles on Vancouver Island*, submitted by Commissioner S.R. Price, August, 1913; Phillips, *No Power Greater*, 52-60.

81. Chan, *Gold Mountain*, 66, 89, 119.

82. Jin Guo, ed., *Voices of Chinese Canadian Women* (Toronto, 1992), 19.

83. Between 1886 and 1894 revenue from the head tax reached $624,679; during the next ten years it was $2,374,400; and during the period 1905-14 it amounted to $13,845,977. Li, *The Chinese in Canada*, 38, 61.

84. Life in Canada was particularly grim for Chinese prostitutes, who were often sold by their families "into the flesh market . . . [in] the last desperate attempt to keep the remaining members of the family together." Nor was "the inequality and brutal use of women," which this traffic represented, opposed by the Chinese community. Chan, *Gold Mountain*, 82.

85. Margaret Chan returned to Canada in 1934 and again worked in a fruit store despite her extensive teaching experience. Cited in Jin Guo, ed., *Chinese Canadian Women*, 27-29.

86. Since after 1897 Ottawa used the provincial voters' lists, this meant that Chinese residents were also excluded from federal elections. Although the number of Chinese paying the head tax from 1905 to 1914 declined to 27,578 from 32,457 in the previous decade, the $500 levy increased the amount of revenue six times. After 1903, Victoria shared the tax revenues equally with Ottawa. Li, *The Chinese in Canada*, 28-29, 38.

87. In 1885 the number of British Columbia Chinese engaged in laundry and restaurant work was less than 5 per cent; by 1921, 32 per cent were involved in these fields. *Ibid.*, 46-54.

88. In 1921 the Chinese population of Canada was 39,587; the ratio of males to females was 1,533:100. *Ibid.*, 60-61.

89. Peter S. Li, "Chinese Immigrants on the Canadian Prairie, 1910-47," *Canadian Review of Sociology and Anthropology*, 19 (1983), 527-40; Howard Palmer, "Anti-Oriental sentiment in Alberta 1880-1920," *Canadian Ethnic Studies*, 2 (1970), 31-57.

90. Wickberg, ed., *From China to Canada*, 118-33; Jensen, *Passage From India*, 194-269; Ward, *White Canada Forever*, 123-30.

Chapter Three

1. Oscar Handlin, *The Uprooted* (Boston, 1951), 90-105; John Higham, *Strangers in the Land* (New York, 1966), 50-165; John Brodar, *The Transplanted: A History of Immigrants in Urban America* (Bloomington, Ind., 1987), 104-16; Gad Horowitz, *Canadian Labour in Politics* (Toronto, 1968); Martin Robin, *Radical Politics and Canadian Labour 1880-1930* (Kingston, 1968); Gerald Rosenblum, *Immigrant Workers: Their Impact on American Labour Radicalism* (New York, 1973), 60-82, 124-39, 146-75.

2. Lysenko, *Men in Sheepskin Coats*, 101.

3. Porter, *The Vertical Mosaic*, 60.

4. See the annual reports of the Immigration Branch, *Sessional Papers*, 1890-1905;

Dafoe, *Sifton*, 132-44, 318-23; Macdonald, *Immigration and Colonization*, 240-80.

5. Toronto *Empire*, 2 October 1890.

6. Toronto *Mail and Empire*, 10 April 1899. The author has examined some twenty-two daily newspapers that commented negatively on the influx of Ukrainian immigrants between March and May, 1899. See IB, 60868, No. 1.

7. *The Independent* (Vancouver), 23 July 1904.

8. C.A. Magrath, *Canada's Growth and Some Problems Affecting It* (Ottawa, 1910), 53, 71-74; Henry Vivian, "City Planning," Address to the Ottawa Canadian Club, 22 October 1910, *Addresses Delivered before The Canadian Club of Ottawa, 1910* (Ottawa, 1911), 1; Dr. Charles Hodgetts, "Unsanitary Housing," Quebec City, 17 January 1911, *Addresses to the Second Annual Meeting of the Commission on Conservation* (Ottawa), 32-42; J.S. Woodsworth, *My Neighbour* (Toronto, 1911), 28-156.

9. Annual Report of the Commissioner of the RNWMP, A. Bowen Perry, *Sessional Papers*, 1904-14. This viewpoint was confirmed by the municipal police chiefs, especially at the 1913 annual convention. *Chief Constables Association, Ninth Annual Convention*, Halifax, 25-27 June 1913, IB, 813739, No. 11.

10. Ralph Connor, *The Foreigner* (Toronto, 1909), 34.

11. Woodsworth, *Strangers Within Our Gates*, 136, 195, 226; *The Christian Guardian*, 8 September 1909; *ibid.*, 16 July 1913; Handlin, *The Uprooted*, 94.

12. Joseph Barton, *Peasants and Strangers: Italians, Rumanians and Slovaks in an American City, 1890-1950* (Cambridge, Mass., 1975), 9-77; Brodar, *The Transplanted*; M.H. Marunchak, *The Ukrainian Canadians: A History* (Winnipeg, 1970), 99-114; Peter Stearnes and Daniel Walkowitz, eds., *Workers in the Industrial Revolution* (New Brunswick, N.J., 1914), 25-34, 72-82; Thomas Childers, "The Austrian Emigration: 1900-1914," in Donald Fleming and Bernard Bailyn, eds., *Dislocation and Emigration: The Social Background of American Immigration*, Perspectives in American History, vol. VII (Cambridge, Mass., 1973), 275-375.

13. Childers, "Austrian Emigration," 325.

14. *Ibid.*, 321; Vladimir Kaye, *Early Ukrainian Settlement in Canada* (Toronto, 1964), 5-27, 34, 47-50, 126-33.

15. John S. Macdonald and Leatrice D. Macdonald, "Chain Migration, Ethnic Neighbourhood Formation and Social Networks," *Milbank Memorial Fund Quarterly*, 52 (January, 1964), 82-97; Charles Tilly and C. Harold Brown, "On Uprooting Kinship, and the Auspices of Migration," *International Journal of Comparative Sociology* (1967), 138-64; Ramirez, *On the Move*.

16. *Ukrainian Rural Settlements, Report of the Bureau of Social Research* (Winnipeg, 25 January 1917), 4-6, 59; Reino Kero, "The Return of Emigrants from America to Finland," presentation at the Conference on the Finnish Experience in the Western Great Lakes Region: New Perspectives, 26 April 1974, 19; Report, Royal Commission to Inquire into the Immigration of Italian Labourers . . . (Ottawa, 1904), 25, 95, 144; Harney, "Montreal's King of Italian Labour," 57-84.

17. Childers, "Austrian Emigration," 362; U.S. Immigration Commission, *Report of the Immigration Commission*, vols. IV, XXXVII (Washington, 1911); Charlotte Erickson, *American Industry and the European Immigrant: 1860-1885* (Cambridge, Mass., 1957), 77-82; Kero, "Return of Emigrants," 16-19.

18. Donald Avery, "Dominion Control over the Recruitment and Placement of Immigrant Industrial Workers in Canada, 1890-1918," paper presented at the Conference on Canadian Society in the Late Nineteenth Century, 18 January 1975.

19. Public Archives of Manitoba (PAM), Report on the Housing Survey of Certain Selected Areas of Winnipeg, made March and April, 1921 (City of Winnipeg Health Department).

20. Woodsworth, *My Neighbor*, 43-155; George Prpic, *The Croatian Immigrants to America* (New York, 1971), 153-54.

21. A.R. McCormack, "Cloth Caps and Jobs: The Ethnicity of English Immigrants in Canada 1900-1914," in Jorgen Dahlie and Tissa Fernando, eds., *Ethnicity, Power and Politics in Canada* (Toronto, 1981), 38-55; Lloyd Reynolds, *The British Immigrant: His Social and Economic Adjustment in Canada* (Toronto, 1935).

22. That is not to say, however, that all British workers demonstrated the same level of class consciousness and involvement in socialist movements. As Deian Rhys Hopkin has pointed out, new model unionism made little headway in Wales during the second half of the nineteenth century, and "when most Welsh skilled workers emigrated . . . there was little tradition of trade unionism to take with them." Deian Rhys Hopkin, "Welsh Immigrants to the United States and Their Press, 1840-1930," in Christiane Harzig and Dirk Hoerder, *The Press of Labor Migrants in Europe and North America, 1880s to 1930s* (Bremen, 1985).

23. Between 1900 and 1914 over one million people migrated from the United Kingdom to Canada, representing about 40 per cent of the total immigration into the country for that period of time. Brinley Thomas, *Migration and Economic Growth: A Study of Great Britain and the Atlantic Economy*, 2nd ed. (Cambridge, 1973), 256-58.

24. Charlotte Erickson, *Invisible Immigrants: The Adaptation of English and Scottish Immigrants to Nineteenth Century America* (London, 1972); Rowland Berthoff, *British Immigrants in Industrial America* (Cambridge, 1953), 88-90; Clifford Yearley, *Britons in American Labor: A History of the United Kingdom Immigrants in American Labor, 1820-1914* (Baltimore, 1957), 27-103; John Laslett, *Labor and the Left: A Study of Socialist and Radical Influences in the American Labor Movement, 1881-1924* (New York, 1970), 144-91.

25. Keir Hardie toured Canada in 1907 and 1908, John Burns came in 1906, and Tom Mann in 1913. A.R. McCormack, "British Working Class Immigrants and Canadian Radicalism: The Case of Arthur Puttee," *Canadian Ethnic Studies*, 10 (1978), 65-86; Allen Seager, "Socialists and Workers in the Western Canadian Coal Mines, 1900-21," *Labour/Le Travail*, 16 (Fall, 1985), 23-59.

26. One of the most interesting of these British radicals was Sam Scarlett, a major organizer of the American-based IWW between 1911 and 1917. After his arrest and

subsequent deportation from the United States in 1923, he carried his IWW message to the mining regions of western Canada. In the late twenties he shifted his allegiance to the Communist Party of Canada and soon gained a reputation for being one of the Party's most effective union organizers. Donald Avery, "British-born Radicals in North America, 1900-1941: The Case of Sam Scarlett," *Canadian Ethnic Studies*, 10 (1978), 65-86.

27. Ralph Smith was born in the British coal-mining region of Newcastle-on-Tyne and migrated to Canada in the 1880s. As a representative of the Nanaimo coalminers, Smith was president of the national Trades and Labour Congress between 1894 and 1898. Arthur Puttee, a printer by trade, had emigrated to North America in 1888 and eventually made Winnipeg his home. He was a key participant in the movement to found a labour party in the city and edited the local TLC newspaper, *The Voice*, from 1897 until 1918. Seager, "Socialists and Workers"; McCormack, "Arthur Puttee," 23.

28. Another divisive element among west coast socialists was the controversy over the status of Chinese, Japanese, and Sikh workers. At the 1909 annual convention of District 18 of the United Mine Workers of America a resolution was passed deploring racial discrimination against Oriental workers. However, when District 28 attempted to make a concerted effort to challenge the large coal companies on Vancouver Island their failure to draw the Chinese and Japanese workers into their cause was a major reason for their disastrous defeat in the bloody strikes of 1913 and 1914. A.R. McCormack, *Rebels, Reformers and Revolutionaries: The Western Canadian Radical Movement, 1899-1919* (Toronto, 1977), 50-120; Seager, "Socialists and Workers"; Phillips, *No Power Greater*, 52-58.

29. Erickson, *American Industry and the European Immigrant*, 77-82; Walter Nugent, *Crossings: The Great Transatlantic Migrations, 1870-1914* (Bloomington, Ind., 1992), 41-164.

30. Ethnic churches were the first and most easily understood form of organization immigrants brought from the Old World to the New. Many of the mutual aid societies were associated with churches; others were secular, and often socialist. Rudolph Vecoli, "Prelates and Peasants: Italian Immigrants and the Catholic Church," *Journal of Social History* (Spring, 1969), 217-68; Brodar, *The Transplanted*, 144-68; Franca Iacovetta, *Such Hardworking People: Italian Immigrants in Postwar Toronto* (Montreal, 1992), 3-19; Maranchuk, *Ukrainian Canadians*, 154-73.

31. Jewish immigrants, for example, located in Montreal, Toronto, and Winnipeg, were kept informed about American socialist activities by the New York-based *Jewish Daily Forward* and *Freiheit*; after 1910 the Montreal *Eagle* and the Toronto *Hebrew Journal* provided a Canadian perspective on important Jewish and socialist issues.

32. Before 1931, the Canadian census does not provide ethnic or nationality breakdowns of the enumerated work force. This, coupled with the fact that the schedules relating to the post-1901 decennial censuses cannot be accessed, has made it difficult for

labour and urban historians to reconstruct, let alone measure, the distribution of immigrant workers within the Canadian occupational structure.

33. Robert Harney and Vincenza Scarpaci, eds., *Little Italies in North America* (Toronto, 1981).

34. Bruno Ramirez, "Brief Encounters: Italian Immigrant Workers and the CPR, 1900-1930," *Labour/Le Travail*, 17 (Spring, 1986). A similar scenario emerges from Craig Heron's study of the Canadian steel industry. See *Working in Steel*, 76-87.

35. George E. Pozzetta, *The Immigrant World of Ybor City* (Urbana, Ill., 1987); Donna Rae Gabaccia, *Militants and Migrants: Rural Sicilians Become American Workers* (New Brunswick, N.J., 1988).

36. Ramirez, *Les premiers italiens*, 112.

37. Bruno Ramirez, "Montreal Italians and the Socioeconomy of Settlement, 1900-1930," *Urban History Review*, IX (June, 1981); John Zucchi, *Italians in Toronto: Development of a National Identity, 1875-1935* (Montreal and Kingston, 1988).

38. The more politicized response of Jewish immigrants can be associated with the importance of the pre-migration experiences and their occupational activity in Canada. Many of the eastern European Jews had previously participated in socialist movements, and they often regarded socialism as a vehicle for ethnic emancipation. Unlike Italians, or most other immigrant groups, they had already known (and often fought against) the reality of being an oppressed ethnic minority. Another important factor was the considerable number of educated skilled workers and craftsmen in their midst, many of whom had already gained extensive experience with garment and other labour organizations in the Old World. Irving Abella, "Portrait of a Jewish Professional Revolutionary: The Recollections of Joshua Gershman," *Labour/Le Travailleur*, 2 (1977); Jacques Rouillard, "Les travailleurs juifs de la confection à Montréal, 1910-1980," *Labour/Le Travailleur*, 8-9 (Fall-Spring, 1981); Ruth Frager, *Sweatshop Strife: Class, Ethnicity, and Gender in the Jewish Labour Movement in Toronto, 1900-1939* (Toronto, 1992).

39. David Brody, *Labor in Crisis: The Steel Strike of 1919* (New York, 1965), 40-43; Rosenblum, *Immigrant Workers*, 32-87; Heron, *Working in Steel*.

40. Donald Avery, "Canadian Immigration Policy and the 'Foreign Navvy,'" Canadian Historical Association, *Historical Papers* (1972), 135-56.

41. Seager, "Socialists and Workers," 23-59; C. Kerr and A. Siegel, "The Inter-Industry Propensity to Strike: An International Comparison," in A. Kornhauser *et al.*, eds., *Industrial Conflict* (New York, 1954), 191-93; Victor Greene, *The Slavic Community on Strike: Immigrant Labor in Pennsylvania Anthracite* (South Bend, Ind., 1968), 50-121, 207-16.

42. The tradition of cultural hostility among different groups of workers was clearly evident during the 1840s and 1850s when Irish canal workers were divided into rival Protestant and Catholic camps, while bloody clashes also occurred between Irish and

French-Canadian navvies. Ruth Bleasdale, "Class Conflict on the Canals of Upper Canada in the 1840s," *Labour/Le Travailleur*, 7 (1981), 9-39.

43. Lysenko, *Men in Sheepskin Coats*, 53.

44. Mark Rosenfeld, "'It was a Hard Life': Class and Gender in the Work and Family Rhythms of a Railway Town, 1920-1950," Canadian Historical Association, *Historical Papers* (1988), 272-79; Michael Kaufman, ed., *Beyond Patriarchy: Essays by Men on Pleasure, Power and Change* (Toronto, 1987).

45. Eric Hobsbawm, *Primitive Rebels: Studies in Archaic Forms of Social Protest Movements in the 19th and 20th Centuries* (Toronto, 1959), 32; Lawrence Schofer, "Patterns of Worker Protest: Upper Silesia, 1865-1914," in Peter Stearnes and Daniel Walkowitz, *Workers in the Industrial Revolution: Recent Studies of Labor in the United States and Europe* (New Brunswick, N.J., 1974), 32; Edward Shorter and Charles Tilly, *Strikes in France, 1830-1968* (London, 1974), 16; Richard Pipes, *Social Democracy and the St. Petersburg Labor Movement, 1885-1897* (Cambridge, Mass., 1963), 1-16.

46. In September, 1907, a group of Italian navvies at Nanton, Alberta, threatened violence unless the CPR improved their working conditions. IB, 801181, Constable Carvan to Colonel Sherwood, Commissioner of the Dominion Police, 9 July 1908; NAC, Royal Canadian Mounted Police Records (hereafter RCMP Records), 321, Sgt. W.J. Redmond to Inspector Davidson, 41; *ibid.*, vol. 1605, Sgt. Piper to Supt. Primrose, 24 and 28 September 1907.

47. Melvyn Dubofsky, *We Shall Be All: A History of the Industrial Workers of the World* (Chicago, 1969), 4-35.

48. A.R. McCormack, "The Industrial Workers of the World in Western Canada: 1905-1914," Canadian Historical Association, *Historical Papers* (1975), 167-91; *British Columbia Federationist*, 5 April 1912.

49. One of the most successful attempts to organize immigrant workers into lasting industrial unions was made by the United Mine Workers of America, most notably in District 18, which encompassed the Rocky Mountain coal-mining region. By 1912 most of the miners in the region were foreign-born, and the membership of the UMWA realized that unless they successfully appealed to the immigrant workers they would "go out of existence."

50. Most lumber companies operating in northern Ontario tended to regard French Canadians as the best woodworkers "on account of their skills and docility." Finns were equally prized because of their industriousness and consistency. By 1914, however, many companies began to regard their Finnish workers as being "very susceptible to all labour movements and untrustworthy where they are in a majority." This concern became even more pronounced when Finnish IWW organizers began to organize the bush camps and working-class communities of northern Ontario. Radforth, *Bushworkers and Bosses*, 33-34.

51. Robin, *Radical Politics and Canadian Labour*; Norman Penner, *The Canadian Left: A Critical Analysis* (Toronto, 1977), 1-124.

52. Mauri Jalava, "The Finnish-Canadian Cooperative Movement in Ontario," Douglas Ollila, Jr., "From Socialism to Industrial Unionism (I.W.W.): Social Factors in the Emergence of Left-Labor Radicalism among Finnish Workers of the Mesabi, 1911-1919," both in Michael Karni *et al.*, eds., *Finnish Experience in the Western Great Lakes Region: New Perspectives* (Turku, 1975).

53. *Western Clarion*, 16 November 1907, cited in Varpu Lindstrom-Best, "The Socialist Party of Canada and the Finnish Connection, 1905-1911," in Dahlie and Fernando, eds., *Ethnicity, Power and Politics in Canada*, 113-22. Varpu Lindstrom-Best, "'Defiant Sisters': A Social History of Finnish Women in Canada, 1890-1930" (Ph.D. thesis, York University, 1986). By 1911 most Finnish socialists had parted company with the SPC and were instrumental in creating the Social Democratic Party of Canada.

54. Frager, *Sweatshop Strife*, 149, 212-14.

55. Rebecca (Becky) Buhay came to Canada in 1912 and became active in the Amalgamated Clothing Workers of America and the Ladies' Garment Workers prior to 1922, when she joined the CPC. Annie Buller also came out of Montreal's Jewish socialist movement; during the 1920s she was an important organizer for the CPC-dominated Industrial Union of Needle Trades Workers. *Ibid.*, 130-34, 177; William Rodney, *Soldiers of the International: A History of the Communist Party of Canada, 1919-1929* (Toronto, 1968), 164; Joan Sangster, *Dreams of Equality: Women on the Canadian Left, 1920-1950* (Toronto, 1989).

56. IB, 800111, J.H. Ashdown to Frank Oliver, 9 April 1908.

57. During the 1910 session of the House of Commons the member for West Huron, E.L. Lewis, introduced a private member's bill calling for the restriction of immigration from the area of Europe south of 44° north latitude and east of 20° east longitude in order to prevent Canada from becoming "a nation of organ grinders and banana sellers." *Debates*, 1909-10, 3134; *ibid.*, 1914, 140.

58. *Labour Gazette*, 1914, 286-332, 820-21.

59. *Robotchny Narod*, 14 March 1914. On November 12, 1913, the *Guardian* reported that over 3,000 Bulgarian navvies had returned to Europe during the fall of that year.

60. *Census of Canada*, 1911 (Ottawa, 1913), vol. II, 367; *CAR*, 1915, 353.

61. Revised Statutes of Canada, 1927, Chapter 206, vol. IV, 1-3; *Canadian Gazette*, 15 August 1914; Borden Papers, 56666, C.H. Cahan to C.J. Coherty, 14 September 1918.

62. Canadian citizens of African, Chinese, Japanese, East Indian, and Aboriginal background also encountered discrimination during the war years. One of the most blatant was how volunteers from these groups were treated by the Canadian military establishment. Although about 5,000 Native Canadians, 1,000 blacks, and several hundred Chinese and Japanese enlisted in the Canadian forces, they were predominantly assigned to low-status jobs in the construction or forestry units overseas. Most blacks and Aboriginals were assigned to their own segregated battalions, with white

officers. An offer by Japanese Canadians to form a separate battalion was rejected. In addition to their racial bias, Canadian politicians were reluctant to encourage large-scale military participation of these groups because it might lead to renewed demands for full civil rights. In contrast, the persistence of these groups "in volunteering, their insistence upon the right 'to serve', their urgent demand to know the reasons for their rejection, all suggest that 'visible' minorities had not been defeated by the racism of white society. . . ." James Walker, "Race and Recruitment in World War I: Enlistment of Visible Minorities in the Canadian Expeditionary Force," *Canadian Historical Review*, LXX, 1 (March, 1989), 26.

63. Major-General W.D. Otter, Internment Operations, 1914-20 (Ottawa, 30 September 1920), 2, 6, 12; *CAR*, 1916, 433.

64. *CAR*, 1916, 433; Joseph Boudreau, "The Enemy Alien Problem in Canada, 1914-1921" (Ph.D. thesis, University of California, 1964), 50-103.

65. *Canadian Ruthenian*, 1 August 1914.

66. NAC, Department of Militia and Defence Headquarters (hereafter DND), file C-965 #2, Report, Agent J.D. Sisler, 9 August 1914. There were numerous other reports in this file.

67. Some of the strongest support for internment camps came from prominent citizens in heterogeneous communities. In Winnipeg, for example, J.A.M. Aikins, a prominent Conservative, warned that the city's enemy aliens might take advantage of the war "for the destruction of property, public and private." Borden Papers, 106322, Aikins to Borden, 12 November 1914.

68. *Canadian Mining Journal*, 15 August 1914.

69. IB, 775789, T.D. Willans, travelling immigration inspector, to W.D. Scott, 9 June 1915; Borden Papers, 106499, H. McInnes, Solicitor, D.H. McDougall, Dominion Iron and Steel Corporation, to Borden, 17 May 1915.

70. *The Northern Miner* (Cobalt), 9 October 1915; *CAR*, 1915, 355; DND, file 965, No. 9, Major E.J. May to Colonel E.A. Cruickshank, district officer in command of military district #13, 28 June 1915.

71. Otter, Internment Operations, 6-12; NAC, Arthur Meighen Papers, 106995, Meighen to Borden, 4 September 1914. The European dependants of these alien workers obviously had to live on even less because after August, 1914, it was unlawful to send remittances of money out of the country. Chief Press Censor, 196, Livesay to Chambers, 4 December 1915.

72. British Columbia Provincial Police (BCPP), file 1355-7, John Simpson, Chief Constable of Greenwood, to Colin Campbell, supt. of the BCPP, 26 January 1916.

73. IB, 29490, No. 4, W. Banford, Dominion immigration officer, to W.D. Scott, 13 May 1915; McBride Papers, McBride to Premier Sifton (Alta.), 30 June 1915. About 20,000 Canadian troops had also been used in gathering the harvest during 1915.

74. IB, 29490, No. 6, W.D. Scott, "Circular Letter to Canadian Immigration Agents in the United States," 2 August 1916.

75. NAC, Sir Joseph Flavelle Papers, 74, Scott to Flavelle, director of imperial munitions, 11 August 1916; IB, 29490, No. 6, J. Frater Taylor, president of Algoma Steel, to Flavelle, 17 August 1917. The number of American immigrants entering the country was 41,779 in 1916 and 65,739 in 1917.

76. China provided over 50,000 labourers to the Allied cause. They were transported from Vancouver to Halifax in 1917 for service in France. *British Columbia Federationist*, 18 January 1918; Vancouver *Sun*, 7 February 1918; Wickberg, ed., *From China to Canada*, 119.

77. IB, 75789, A. Macdonald, Employment Agent, Dominion Coal Company, to Scott, 25 July 1916.

78. *CAR*, 1918, 330; *ibid.*, 1916, 325-28; Statutes of Canada, 9-10 Geo. V, xciii. The reaction of the Trades and Labour Congress to the treatment of enemy alien workers varied. On one hand they endorsed the "patriotic" dismissals in 1915 and supported the scheme to relocate enemy aliens on homesteads on the uncultivated lands of "New" Ontario. In June, 1916, however, the Congress executive, concerned over the possibility that the government intended to use large numbers of enemy aliens in the mines of northern Ontario, strongly protested the practice of forced labour. *Proceedings of the Thirty-First Annual Session of the Trades and Labour Congress of Canada* (1915), 16-17; *ibid.* (1916), 43.

79. Otter, Internment Operations, 9-14; NAC, Secretary of State Papers, Internment Operation Section, file 5330, No. 7, Major Dales, Commandant Kapuskasing, to Otter, 14 November 1918; Desmond Morton, "Sir William Otter and Internment Operations in Canada During the First World War," *Canadian Historical Review* (March, 1974), 32-58.

80. Borden Papers, 43110, Mark Workman to Borden, 19 December 1918; *ibid.*, 43097, Borden to A.E. Blount, 1 July 1918.

81. *CAR*, 1915, 354; Internment Operation Papers, Otter to F.L. Wanklyn, CPR, 12 June 1916.

82. Robin, *Radical Politics*, 138-39; McCormack, *Rebels, Reformers and Revolutionaries*, 143-216; Francis Swyripa and John Herd Thompson, eds., *Loyalties in Conflict: Ukrainians in Canada During the Great War* (Edmonton, 1983).

83. DND, C-2665, Major-General Ketchen, officer commanding Military District 10, to secretary of the Militia Council, 7 July 1917; NAC, Department of Justice Papers, 1919, file 2059, Registrar of Alien Enemies, Winnipeg, to Colonel Sherwood, Dominion Police, 17 August 1918; NAC, Chief Press Censor Branch, 144-A-2, Chambers to secretary of state, 20 September 1918.

84. Borden Papers, 56656, C.H. Cahan to Borden, 20 July 1918; *ibid.*, 56668, Cahan to Borden, 14-20 September 1918. The fourteen illegal organizations also included the IWW, the Group of Social Democrats and Anarchists, the Chinese Nationalist League, and the Social Democratic Party; the latter organization was removed from the list in November, 1918. *Ibid.*, 56698, Cahan to Borden, 21 October

1918; Statutes of Canada, 1919, 9-10 Geo. v, lxxi-lxxiii.

85. James Eayrs, *In Defence of Canada: From the Great War to the Great Depression* (Toronto, 1967), 30.

86. *Winnipeg Telegram*, 28 January 1919.

87. Internment Operations, file 6712, Major-General Otter to Acting Minister of Justice, 19 December 1918; Justice Records, 1919, vol. 227, Report, chief commissioner, Dominion Police, for director of public safety, 27 November 1918.

88. Borden Papers, 83163, Sir Thomas White to Borden, February 21, 1919. On February 28, 1919, the German government lodged an official complaint with British authorities over "the reported plan of the Canadian government to deport all Germans from Canada." IB, 912971, Swiss ambassador, London, England, to Lord Curzon, 28 February 1919.

89. *Vancouver Sun*, 26 March 1919; Mathers Royal Commission on Industrial Relations, "Evidence," Sudbury hearings, 27 May 1919, testimony of J.L. Fortin, 1923, Department of Labour Library.

90. Montreal *Gazette*, 14 June 1919.

91. In April, 1918, an amendment to the Dominion Land Act denied homestead patents to non-naturalized residents; the subsequent amendments to the Naturalization Act in June, 1919, also made it extremely difficult for enemy aliens to become naturalized. Justice Papers, 1919, file 2266, Albert Dawdron, acting commissioner of the Dominion Police, to the Minister of Justice, 28 July 1919. Statutes of Canada, 1918, 9-10 Geo. v, c. 19, s. 7; *Debates*, 1919, 4118-33.

92. Chief Press Censor, 196-1, E. Tarak to Chambers, 11 January 1918 (translation), 91. IB, 963419, W.D. Scott to James A. Calder, Minister of Immigration and Colonization, 11 December 1919; *Toronto Telegram*, 1 April 1920; Meighen Papers, 000256, J.A. Stevenson to Meighen, 24 February 1919; *Canadian Ruthenian*, 5 February 1919.

93. IB, 963419, W.D. Scott to James A. Calder, Minister of Immigration and Colonization, 11 December 1919; *Toronto Telegram*, 1 April 1920; Meighen Papers, 000256, J.A. Stevenson to Meighen, 24 February 1919; *Canadian Ruthenian*, 5 February 1919.

94. Mathers Royal Commission, "Evidence," Victoria hearings, testimony of J.O. Cameron, president of the Victoria Board of Trade; *ibid.*, Calgary hearings, testimony of W. Henderson; *ibid.*, testimony of Mortimer Morrow, manager of Canmore Coal Mines.

95. Alan Artibise, *Winnipeg: A Social History of Urban Growth 1874-1914* (Montreal, 1975), 223-45; *Manitoba Free Press*, 3 November 1918.

96. DND, C-2665, Secret Agent No. 47, Report (Wpg.), to Supt. Starnes, RNWMP, 24 March 1919.

97. *Winnipeg Telegram*, 29 January 1919.

98. PAM, OBU Collection, R.B. Russell to Victor Midgley, 29 January 1919.

99. *Manitoba Free Press*, 7 May 1919; *Western Labor News*, 4 April 1919. The Alien Investigation Board was legitimized by the passage of PC 56 in January, 1919, which transferred authority to investigate enemy aliens and to enforce PC 2381 and PC 2384 from the Dominion Department of Justice to the provincial attorney general. Between February and May the board processed approximately 3,000 cases; of these, 500 were denied certificates. RCMP Records, Comptroller to Commissioner Perry, 20 March 1919; *Manitoba Free Press*, 7 May 1919; Meighen Papers, 000279, D.A. Ross to Meighen, 9 April 1919.

100. D.C. Masters, *The Winnipeg General Strike* (Toronto, 1959), 40-50; David Bercuson, *Confrontation at Winnipeg* (Montreal, 1974), 103-95.

101. Murray Donnelly, *Dafoe of the Free Press* (Toronto, 1968), 104; RCMP Records, 1919, vol. 1, Major-General Ketchen to secretary of the Militia Council, 21 May 1919; *The Citizen* (Wpg.), 5-20 June 1919.

102. *Manitoba Free Press*, 22 May 1919.

103. Borden Papers, 61913, Robertson to Borden, 14 June 1919; Diary of Sir Robert Borden, 13-17 June 1919; RCMP, CIB, vol. 70, J.A. Calder to Commissioner Perry, 16 June 1919; IB, 961162, Calder to Perry, 17 June 1919.

104. Tom Moore to E. Robinson, 24 June 1919, cited by *Manitoba Free Press*, 21 November 1919; Borden Diary, 20 June 1919; Borden Papers, 61936, Robertson to Acland, 14 June 1919; *Manitoba Free Press*, 18 June 1919.

105. *Ukrainian Labor News*, 16 July 1919; Norman Penner, ed., *Winnipeg 1919: The Strikers' Own History of the Winnipeg General Strike* (Toronto, 1973), 175-81; IB, 912971, No. 3, T.J. Murray, telegram to J.A. Calder, 30 October 1919; Justice Records, 1919, file 1960, deputy minister of justice to Murray and Noble, 5 November 1919.

106. In October, 1918, the United States Congress had passed an amendment to the "Act to Exclude and Expel from the United States Aliens Who Are Members of the Anarchist and Similar Classes"; Emma Goldman, Alexander Berkman, and 247 other "Reds" were deported to Russia under this measure in December, 1919. John Higham, *Strangers in the Land* (New York, 1966), 308-24; IB, 961162, No. 1, F.C. Blair, secretary of immigration and colonization, memorandum to J.A. Calder, 24 November 1919; *ibid.*, John Clark, American consul-general, Montreal, to F.C. Blair, 19 June 1920.

107. *Ibid.*, A.J. Cawdron to supt. of immigration, 24 June 1919; *ibid.*, assistant director, CIB, RCMP, to F.C. Blair, 4 August 1920.

108. In addition to the pressure to exclude enemy aliens and pacifists, there was considerable support for the suggestion that Canada should not accept immigrants from certain regions because of their alleged racial deficiencies. Hume Conyn, MP for London, Ontario, cited the writings of eugenicist Madison Grant as justifying the exclusion of "strange people who cannot be assimilated." Higham, *Strangers in the Land*, 308-24; *Debates*, 30 April 1919; 1 May 1916; 9 May 1919, 2280-90.

109. *Industrial Canada* (July, 1919), 120-22.

110. After the merger in 1919 of the RNWMP and the Dominion Police, the joint force was renamed the Royal Canadian Mounted Police in 1920. Surveillance of Communist infiltrators continued throughout the 1920s. NAC, Department of Justice, 1926, file 293, C. Starnes to deputy minister of justice, 27 October 1926. Ivan Avakumovic, *The Communist Party in Canada: A History* (Toronto, 1975), 1-53; Barbara Roberts, *Whence They Came: Deportation from Canada 1900-1935* (Ottawa, 1988), 71-97, 125-58.

Chapter Four

1. *Debates*, 1919, 771, 1867-73, 2280-90; *CAR*, 1919, 503-21.

2. Figures compiled from the *Royal Commission on Bilingualism and Biculturalism, Book Four* (Ottawa, 1968), 238-46; Robert England, *Colonization of Western Canada* (London, 1936), 313-14; *Select Standing Committee on Agriculture and Colonization: Minutes of Proceedings and Evidence and Report*, 1928, Appendix No. 8 (Ottawa, 1928). Hereafter, *Select Committee*, 1928.

3. W. Burton Hurd, "Racial Origins and Nativity of the Canadian People," *Census of Canada*, 1931, vol. XIII, Monographs (Ottawa, 1942), 537-818; Floyd Alvin Farrar, "Migration and Economic Opportunity in Canada, 1921-1951" (Ph.D. thesis, University of Pennsylvania, 1962), 20-53; Leonard Marsh, "The Problem of Seasonal Unemployment," unpublished typescript, Research Project No. 22, McGill Social Research Series. Of the 215,978 immigrants from central and southern Europe who arrived in Canada between 1925 and 1931, the largest numbers were Ukrainians (57,657), Poles (30,649), Hungarians (28,624), Jews (22,107), Slovaks (19,167), and Italians (11,608). England, *Western Canada*, 312-13.

4. "An Act to amend an Act of the present session entitled An Act to amend The Immigration Act 1919," Statutes of Canada, 1919, 9-10 Geo. V, ch. 26, s. 41.

5. *Ibid.*; IB, 72552, No. 6, F.C. Blair, secretary, Immigration and Colonization, to deputy minister, 11 August 1921.

6. PC 1203 and PC 1204 were enacted June 9, 1919. Statutes of Canada, 1919, 9-10 Geo. V, vols. I-II, X. See Woodcock and Avakumovic, *The Doukhobors*, 240-56.

7. Wellington Bridgman, *Breaking Prairie Sod* (Toronto, 1920), 256. During the 1920s European immigrants were officially categorized as "preferred" and "non-preferred" immigrants. Not surprisingly, the application of the non-preferred label aroused deep resentment on the part of many European governments. IB, 28885, No. 6, F.C. Blair to J.A. McGill, general agent, CPR, 21 November 1923.

8. *Maclean's*, August, 1919, 46-49.

9. IB, 651, No. 3, Blair to McFadden & McMillan Lumber Company, Fort William, 27 August 1919.

10. *Ibid.*, 28885, No. 5, Blair to president of Algoma Steel Corporation (Sault Ste. Marie), 20 September 1920.

11. The luminaries who attended the 1912 London meetings of the International Eugenics Congress included Winston Churchill, Sir William Osler, Leonard Darwin, and Charles Eliot, former president of Harvard University. Angus McLaren, *Our Own Master Race: Eugenics in Canada, 1885-1945* (Toronto, 1990), 23.

12. Those attracted to the Canadian eugenics movement during the 1920s included prominent medical researchers such as Drs. Helen MacMurchy, Madge Macklin, Charles Macklin, Peter Bryce, William Hutton, Charles Hastings; industrialist A.R. Kaufman and magistrate D.B. Harkness were also active. Many of these people were also involved with organizations such as the Canadian National Committee on Mental Hygiene. The Eugenics Society of Canada was founded in November, 1930. *Ibid.*, 112-16.

13. *Ibid.*, 60.

14. *Ibid.*, 52-55.

15. *Sessional Papers*, 1920, vol. LVI, no. 18, "Annual Report of the Superintendent of Emigration for Canada in London, England, Lt. Colonel J. Obed Smith," 30-32; IB, 2183, No. 2, J. Obed Smith to F.C. Blair, 28 February 1921.

16. IB, 651, No. 3, P.C. Walker, agent for Shepard & Morse Lumber Company, to Blair, 14 October 1919.

17. IB, 775789, R.M. Wolvin, president, Dominion Steel Corporation, to W.R. Little, 24 September 1920.

18. *Canadian Mining Journal (CMJ)*, 25 February 1920.

19. Provincial Archives of Ontario (PAO), Ontario Department of Labour, 1920, "Report of Labour Conditions in Gold and Silver Mining Districts in Northern Ontario, October, 1920"; deputy minister of labour to W.R. Rollo, Minister of Labour, 15 October 1920; *CMJ*, 15 October 1920.

20. IB, 594511, C.P. Riddell, general secretary, Railway Association, to Sir George Foster, Acting Prime Minister, 23 February 1920.

21. *Ibid.*, Blair to Riddell, 9 April 1920; *ibid.*, Blair to Minister of Immigration and Colonization, 22 April 1920.

22. *Vancouver Sun*, 10 July 1920; Vancouver *World*, 17 August 1920.

23. Department of Labour, *Annual Report* 1927-28; *Labour Gazette*, December, 1920, 1630-34.

24. *Sessional Papers*, 1922, vol. XV, "Report of the Superintendent of Emigration for 1921," 24-25; England, *Western Canada*, 75-90.

25. PC 183, January 31, 1923, cited in *Select Committee*, 1928, 818-20.

26. Statutes of Canada, 1923, 13-14 Geo. V, ch. 28, section 5, "Chinese Immigration Act, 1923"; *CAR*, 1923, 45-46; Toronto *Globe*, 7 August 1923; IB, 9309, *passim;* Patricia Roy, "The Oriental 'Menace' in British Columbia," in Michiel Horn and Ronald Sabourin, eds., *Studies in Canadian Social History* (Toronto, 1974), 287-97.

27. Although the Chinese were not legally prevented from becoming Canadian citizens, naturalization became even more difficult after 1923, with many magistrates arbitrarily dismissing applications. Li, *The Chinese in Canada*, 30-31.

28. Wickberg, ed., *From China to Canada*, 137.

29. In Vancouver and Victoria there was considerable public agitation over the entry of Chinese illegals, largely because of a number of sensationalist articles in local newspapers. *Ibid.*, 136.

30. During the 1921 federal elections, Liberal and Conservative candidates in British Columbia had accused each other of showing favouritism toward Asians. *Ibid.*, 138.

31. Chinese organizations had used the good offices of consul-general Tsur to bring their civil status into line with that of other immigrant groups. They also insisted that Canadian-born Chinese should immediately be enfranchised. *Ibid.*, 139-43.

32. The Chinese Immigration Act reduced the flow of Chinese immigrants to under 700 by 1924; it also reinforced the sex imbalance, which was 1,241 males to 100 females in 1931. Total Chinese population actually decreased, from 39,587 in 1921 to 32,528 in 1941. *Ibid.*; Li, *The Chinese in Canada*, 60-61.

33. Robin Winks, *Blacks in Canada: A History* (New Haven, 1971); Howard and Tamara Palmer, "Urban Blacks in Alberta," *Alberta History*, 29 (1981), 8-18; James Walker, *Racial Discrimination in Canada: The Black Experience*, CHA Booklet No. 41 (Ottawa, 1985).

34. In 1911, the Canadian government had created a special program to recruit domestics from Guadeloupe for placement in Quebec homes. Agnes Calliste, "Race, Gender and Canadian Immigration Policy: Blacks from the Caribbean, 1900-1932," *Journal of Canadian Studies*, 28, 4 (Winter, 1993-94), 131-48.

35. During the 1920s the CNR adopted the practice of the CPR in excluding blacks from the dining cars and preventing promotion from porter to conductor. Agnes Calliste, "Sleeping Car Porters in Canada: An Ethnically Submerged Split Labour Market," in Laura Sefton MacDowell and Ian Radforth, eds., *Canadian Working Class History: Selected Readings* (Toronto, 1992), 675-77, 688.

36. Immigration officials seemed only concerned that the CPR recruitment campaign might increase Canada's black population. This was evident when in August, 1943, the district superintendent of immigration in Winnipeg wrote: "I do not think we would want to add to our coloured population and I do not believe that the arrangement with the Canadian Pacific Railway for the admission of these coloured porters contemplated the entry of their families. We have been discouraging their admission as visitors or otherwise, by every means possible here on this assumption." *Ibid.*, 682.

37. The situation did not improve for black porters until 1955, when the Brotherhood won the right to promotion to sleeping car conductor by appealing to the Ontario Fair Employment Practices Act of 1953. *Ibid.*, 680, 683.

38. Deputy minister W.J. Egan, assistant deputy minister F.C. Blair, and J. Bruce Walker, director of immigration in London, shared the problems approach to immigration. In

November, 1924, for example, Blair warned his minister, James Robb, of the danger of adopting a humanitarian criterion: "we are only making trouble for ourselves by admitting a few and keeping out the multitudes." Cited in Isabel Kaprielian, "Canada, the Nansen Passport, and Refugees," unpublished paper, 18.

39. It is estimated that during the 1920s Canada accepted about 34,000 Mennonite, Jewish, Armenian, and Russian refugees. *Ibid.*, 22.

40. Both the 200,000 Russians and 500,000 to 1,000,000 Armenians were categorized as stateless people by the League of Nations and its affiliate, the Refugee Service of the International Labour Office. Dr. Nansen of Norway, the first High Commissioner for Refugees, directed these humanitarian efforts. *Ibid.*, 1-5. In assisting the entry of about 10,000 Jewish refugees, Canada's Jewish community often sponsored groups and individuals and posted bonds of as high as $1,000 that these people would not become public charges. *Ibid.*, 25; Simon Belkin, *Through Narrow Gates* (Montreal, 1966), 134-35, 141, 146, 150.

41. Isabel Kaprielian, "Armenian Refugees and their Entry into Canada: 1919-30," *Canadian Historical Review*, LXXI, 1 (1990).

42. Instructions were also issued to immigration officials that the regulations could be waived when immigrants of the "right class" sought entry. Kaprielian, "Nansen Passport," 18-20.

43. In contrast, Armenians viewed themselves as Caucasians, speaking an Indo-European language. *Ibid.*, 20.

44. The Armenian Relief Association of Canada was founded in 1917. Among its board members were Governor General Lord Byng, the Most Reverend Neil McNeil, Archbishop of Toronto, Archdeacon H.J. Cody, the Hon. Sir William Mulock, and Toronto Mayor T.L. Church. *Ibid.*, 23, 31.

45. Despite his instructions to avoid any commitment for Canada, J. Bruce Walker, director of immigration, signed the agreement. As a result, the Canadian government was hard-pressed to justify its insistence on the provision that refugees could be deported within five years of arrival. Canada's image was also at stake since in 1925 Senator Raoul Dandurand had been elected chairman of the Assembly of the League of Nations. *Ibid.*, 6-12.

46. Dr. O.D. Skelton, under-secretary of state for external affairs, shared the Canada First views of immigration officials. *Ibid.*, 8, 14.

47. *Annual Departmental Reports* (hereafter ADR), 1924-25, vol. III (Ottawa, 1926).

48. ADR, 1925-26 (Ottawa, 1927), *Report of the Deputy Minister of Labour*, 6; *ibid.*, *Reports of the Department of Immigration and Colonization, 1921-29, passim.*

49. *Sessional Papers*, 1914, PC 1028; IB, 785450, M.B. Scarth to W.D. Scott, 9 December 1913. In Ontario there had been fifty-six convictions for violation of the law between May and December, 1914. *Report of the Ontario Commission on Unemployment* (Toronto, 1916), 121-22.

50. *CAR*, 1918, 490.

51. *Debates*, 1918, 841, 1034-38; *Annual Reports of the Department of Labour,*

Employment Service Branch, 1921-31, *passim*, 28. PAO, Ontario Department of Labour, Office of the Deputy Minister, L.G. Clarke to J.A. Mille, Toronto, 21 October 1919; Lawrence Fric, "The Role of Commercial Employment Agencies in the Canadian Labour Market" (Ph.D. thesis, University of Toronto, 1973), 42-68. In 1924 the Trades and Labour Congress called on the government "to place amongst the prohibited classes labour hired to replace strikers, or those hired without the sanction of the Employment Service." *Proceedings of the TLC*, 1924, 42.

52. *Debates*, 1919, 1870-90; *CAR*, 1920, 242-45; Reynolds, *British Immigrant*, 50-116; W.G. Smith, *A Study in Canadian Immigration* (Toronto, 1920), 150-85.

53. IB, 2446, No. 8, Egan to Robert Forke, 2 August 1927; *United States Daily*, 13 May 1927. The emigration of Canadian citizens to the U.S. averaged about 100,000 a year throughout the 1920s.

54. Ramsay Cook, ed., *The Dafoe-Sifton Correspondence, 1919-27* (Altona, Manitoba, 1966), 41-42, Sifton to Dafoe, 18 November 1920; IB, 28128, No. 4, Blair to W.C. Kennedy, 7 December 1920. England, *Western Canada*, 90-98.

55. *Grain Growers' Guide*, 21 January 1925; *ibid.*, October, 1928. The British and Canadian governments subsidized the transportation costs of British harvesters who came to Canada in the fall of 1923. George Haythorne, "Harvest Labour in Western Canada: An Episode in Economic Planning," *Quarterly Journal of Economics*, 47 (1932), 533-44.

56. *Grain Growers' Guide*, 23 December 1925; Hurd, "Racial Origins," 708-15; Reynolds, *British Immigrants*, 95-98.

57. Barber, *Immigrant Domestic Servants in Canada*, 14-19.

58. Varpu Lindstrom, "The Peoples of Canada: An Encyclopedia for the Country. The Finnish Canadian Community," unpublished manuscript, 22; Lindstrom-Best, *Defiant Sisters*.

59. The Emergency Immigration Restriction Act of 1921 passed the House without a recorded vote, and the Senate passed it 78 to 1. It was signed into law by President Warren Harding in May, 1921. Michael LeMay, *From Open Door to Dutch Door: An Analysis of U.S. Immigration Policy Since 1820* (New York, 1987), 78-82.

60. *Ibid.*, 80.

61. Overall European immigration declined from over 800,000 in 1921 to less than 150,000 by the end of the 1920s. *Ibid.*, 89.

62. Studies dealing with earlier movement of Canadians to the United States include Alan Brookes, "The Golden Age and the Exodus: The Case of Canning, King's County," *Acadiensis*, XI, 1 (Autumn, 1981); and Ramirez, *On the Move*.

63. Kenneth Lines, *British and Canadian Immigration to the United States Since 1920* (San Francisco, 1978), 18-26, 114-16.

64. Montreal *Gazette*, 14 June 1922.

65. IB, 2446, Black to Husband, 28 April 1922; *ibid.*, 653, Commissioner W.R. Little to Deputy Minister Cory, 17 May 1921.

66. IB, 2446, #6, Esme Howard to Lord Byng, 26 April 1924.

67. NAC, Flavelle Papers, Box 11, Flavelle to Lionel Hitchens, 14 April 1924. Flavelle was president of National Trust, a major Toronto-based financial institution, and a prominent supporter of the Conservative Party.

68. *Ibid.*, Flavelle to Frederick Hyde, Director, Midland Bank, London, England, 24 December 1924. *Industrial Canada*, the organ of the Canadian Manufacturers' Association, went one step further, blaming the loss of Canadian workers on the failure of the King government to support Canadian industry through either tariff protection or an active immigration policy. *Industrial Canada*, 26 April 1924.

69. King Papers, 86458, Tom King, External Affairs, Washington, to Mackenzie King, 11 April 1924. He also reported that there was growing pressure to extend this privilege "to the other American republics."

70. *Ibid.*, Report of the Secretary of Labor, December, 1924, cited in letter, Tom King to Mackenzie King, 29 April 1925.

71. King Papers, 95490, Governor General Byng to Esme Howard, 8 June 1925. By July, 1928, provision had been made for the admission of all Canadian Indians. IB, 2446, Vincent Massey to O.D. Skelton; *ibid.*, Massey to Skelton, 7 July 1928.

72. IB, 2446, G.F. Plant to W.R. Little, 23 May 1924; *ibid.*, Little to Plant, 27 May 1924.

73. For example, on September 12, 1923, Canadian immigration officers at Ellis Island received warnings from Ottawa that large numbers of Italian immigrants destined for Canada "propose getting off the train in that country [the U.S.] while en route . . . from New York." *Ibid.*, S. Meconi, circular letter.

74. Although some voices in the U.S. government advocated restriction of Mexican immigration, powerful agricultural interests in the Southwest exerted considerable pressure for a continuation of the influx. Harvey Levenstein, "The AFL and Mexican Immigration in the 1920s: An Experiment in Labour Diplomacy," *Hispanic American Historical Review*, 48, 2 (1968), 206-19.

75. IB, 2446, #7, J.R. Johnson, secretary ATLAO, to Mackenzie King, 31 January 1925. In January, 1925, Representative Box of Texas had introduced a bill that "strongly advocated making the quota provisions apply to Canada." It died in committee. IB, 2446, #7, M.M. Mahoney (Washington) to W.H. Walker, Acting Under-Secretary of State for External Affairs, 26 January 1925.

76. *Ibid.*, F.J. Mitchell to Mackenzie King, 20 January 1925.

77. NAC, CNR Colonization Records, vol. 8486, file 33852, C.W. Peterson to Colonel Dennis, 23 March 1926; *CAR*, 1922, no. 269.

78. England, *Western Canada*, 78-86; *ADR*, 1924-25, 20-33; King Papers, 71356, W.A. Buchanan to King, 14 December 1923.

79. *Canadian Mining Journal*, 5 October 1923.

80. IB, 216882, No. 1, W.J. Egan to Edward Beatty, 29 July 1925; King Papers, 94852, Beatty to King, 18 August 1925; *ibid.*, 94859, Beatty to King, 18 August 1928.

81. King Papers, 94824, Beatty and Thornton to King, 14 February 1925.

82. *Ibid.*, King to Beatty, 7 August 1925; *ibid.*, Beatty to King, 27 August 1925.

83. IB, 94861, 216882, No. 1, F.C. Blair, memorandum, 10 September 1925; James Hedges, *Building the Canadian West* (New York, 1939), 360-90.

84. IB, 216882, No. 1, Blair to Egan, 10 September 1925; IB, 926, No. 2, W.D. Black, director of colonization, CNR, to Blair, 1 March 1926.

85. Calgary *Herald*, 27 April 1925; John Irmie, editor of Edmonton *Journal*, to C.A. Macgrath, 9 June 1925, cited in Howard Palmer, *Patterns of Prejudice: A History of Nativism in Alberta* (Toronto, 1982), 82. Pro-business service clubs such as the Kiwanis International hailed the agreement as a major step in lifting Canada out of the economic recession. PAO, Howard Ferguson Papers, 1925, Immigration File, E.A. Cunningham, chairman of Kiwanis, to Ferguson, 29 October 1925.

86. Calgary *Herald*, 27 April 1925.

87. *Canadian Congress Journal*, June, 1922, 287.

88. *Grain Growers' Guide*, 21 January 1925. See Palmer, "Nativism and Ethnic Tolerance," 89; Hedges, *Canadian West*, 360-65.

89. IB, 216882, No. 1, W.J. Egan to J. Bruce Walker, Winnipeg commissioner, 21 October 1925; Egan to J. Robb, Minister of Immigration, 26 August 1925.

90. D.H. Miller-Barston, *Beatty of the C.P.R.: A Biography* (Toronto, 1951), 50-55; IB, 216882, No. 5, W.J. Black to Blair, 30 May 1927; Hedges, *Canadian West*, 257, 35-55, 361-86; CNR Records, vol. 842, Johnson to Black, 2 December 1927; *ibid.*, vol. 5629, file 5121-1, F.B. Tomanek, Catholic Czechoslovakian Immigration Society, to Black, 5 November 1928.

91. Canadian Pacific Railway Colonization Records, Glenbow Institute, Calgary, file 740, J. Colley, assistant supt. of colonization, to C.A. Van Scoy, 9 January 1929; *ibid.*, file 682, Colley to Van Scoy, 7 October 1927.

92. Hedges, *Canadian West*, 366-90; CNR Records, vol. 5629, file 5121-1, W.J. Black to F.J. Freer, CNR supt. of land settlement, Winnipeg, 13 July 1927; IB, 216882, No. 6, Blair to Egan, 5 October 1927. There was a preponderance of single and unaccompanied males who came to Canada from continental Europe. In 1926, for example, out of a total of 38,028 immigrants, 28,979 or 76 per cent were males; in 1927 the figure was 78 per cent. This trend was especially pronounced among immigrants from Czechoslovakia (92 per cent), Yugoslavia (90 per cent), Austria (85 per cent), Lithuania (80 per cent), Poland (78 per cent), Hungary (76 per cent), and Romania (74 per cent). *Select Committee*, 762-63.

93. *Ibid.*, 1039, Colley to J. Schwartz (labour agent), 21 March 1931; IB, 216882, No. 5, Walter Woods, district supt., Land Settlement Branch, to Major John Barnett, superintendent, 18 May 1927.

94. IB, 216882, No. 6, memorandum F.C. Blair, 7 June 1927.

95. CPR Records, 1039, Colley to M. Bosworth, 7 November 1930; Miller-Barston, *Beatty of the C.P.R.*, 53-65.

96. IB, 216882, No. 7, Supt. J.G. Rattray, Land Settlement Branch, to W.J. Egan, 10 January 1928; *ibid.*, No. 10, W.S. Woods to Rattray, 30 January 1929.

97. *Alberta Labor News*, 27 March 1926.

98. Provincial Archives of Alberta (PAA), Dept. of Labour, 1927 files, Report, Provincial Dept. of Labour for Premier Brownlee, 11 March 1927.

99. PC 534, 8 April 1926, cited in *Select Standing Committee on Agriculture and Colonization: Minutes of Proceedings* (Ottawa, 1928), 820; *ADR*, 1926-27, 59.

100. IB, 594511, Black to Egan, 4 June 1926.

101. *Ibid.*, Egan to Black, 7 September 1926.

102. IB, 216882, No. 6, Blair to Egan, 15 June 1927.

103. *Ibid.*, No. 3, J.H. McVety, general supt. of Labour Bureau, to A.D. Skinner, division commissioner, 25 December 1926; *ibid.* No. 5, W.R. Clubb, Manitoba Minister of Labour, to King, 25 May 1927.

104. *Ibid.*, No. 6, Blair to Egan, 15 June 1927; *ibid.*, Blair to Charles Stewart (Minister of Immigration), 27 May 1927; *Select Committee*, 1928, 409-21.

105. CNR Records, vol. 8386, file 33852, Colonel J.S. Dennis to Black, 23 February 1926.

106. *Ibid.*, C.W. Peterson to Dennis, 23 March 1926; *ibid.*, Dennis to George Walker, CPR solicitor, Calgary, 9 March 1926.

107. IB, 216882, No. 6, Blair to Robert Forke, Minister of Immigration, 1 August 1928; *ibid.*, Edward Beatty to Charles Stewart, 30 June 1928; Haythorne, "Harvest Labor in Western Canada," 533-44.

108. IB, 907095, T.W. Bell, chairman, Grand Lodge of British America, Immigration Department, Toronto, to Lodge #1895, Coleman, Alberta, 12 September 1928; Montreal *Star*, 8 August 1928; *Grain Growers' Guide*, 1 October 1928.

109. *TLC Proceedings*, 1928, Resolution of the Ontario Provincial Council of Carpenters (#61). The TLC had also severely criticized the 1923 movement of British harvesters. King Papers, 76789, Tom Moore to King, 10 September 1923.

110. *ADR*, 1928, 49-50; IB, 216882, No. 9, W.S. Woods, Supt. of Land Settlement, to Col. Rattray, 5 June 1928.

111. IB, 348818, Leask, Saskatchewan, to Blair, 11 June 1928; Toronto *Telegram*, 13 September 1928.

112. *CAR*, 1928-29, 162-63; *Canadian Congress Journal*, March, 1928. UCA, Board of Home Missions, file 7-8, F. Albert Moore, Secretary, United Church of Canada, to J.H. Edmison, 11 October 1926; *ibid.*, Moore to Dr. C.E. Manning, 22 April 1927.

113. *Grain Growers' Guide*, 1 June 1928.

114. IB, 348818, Resolution of the Prince Albert NAC, 21 May 1928. NAC, R.B. Bennett Papers, 241067, Resolution, Assembly #2, Native Sons of Canada, November, 1930. The *Orange Sentinel* (Toronto) also maintained a fierce anti-alien position as well as charging that Canadian immigration policy was determined by the Roman Catholic hierarchy. *Sentinel*, 12 May 1927; *ibid.*, 28 February 1929.

115. The defeat of the Gardiner government in the 1929 provincial election, largely on religious and immigration issues, did much to force the King government to reassess its immigration policy. Patrick Kyba, "The Saskatchewan General Election of 1929" (M.A. thesis, University of Saskatchewan, 1964), 23.

116. Saskatoon *Star*, 5 June 1928.

117. Saskatoon *Beacon*, 28 December 1928; *Orange Sentinel*, 12 May 1927; Regina *Star*, 2 January 1929.

118. *TLC Proceedings*, 1928, 164-68.

119. *Ibid.*

120. *Grain Growers' Guide*, 1 May 1928; Resolution, Lethbridge UFA Local, cited in Palmer, "Nativism and Ethnic Tolerance," 97

121. Toronto *Globe*, 9 February 1928.

122. *Debates*, 1928, 3924.

123. IB, 216882, No. 8, F. Franke, Austrian consul-general, to Forke, 15 August 1928; *ibid.*, No. 10, A.V. Seferovitch, consul-general Serbes, Croates and Slovenes, to Forke, 6 June 1929; Albert de Haydin, Hungarian consul-general, cited in Calgary *Herald*, 12 August 1927.

124. *Select Committee*, 1928, 347-48. Sir Henry Thornton was somewhat more cautious, and he admitted that it was not always possible "to make a good Canadian out of the first foreigner" who arrived in Canada. *Ibid.*, 328.

125. *Ibid.*, 367-407.

126. *Ibid.*, 670-80; Regina *Leader*, 24 November 1927; Ottawa *Citizen*, 13 February 1928.

127. *Select Committee*, 1928, x-xi.

128. IB, 216882, No. 8, A.L. Jolliffe to Egan, 14 August 1928; Department of Labour, file 617 (24-2), Egan to H.H. Ward, deputy minister of labour, 15 January 1930.

129. *CAR*, 1928-29, 158-59; Department of Labour, file 617 (24-2); IB, 216882, No. 11, Egan to Stewart, 19 February 1930.

130. *CAR*, 1929-30, 86, 94-102; IB, 216882, No. 12, W.A. Gordon to Thornton and Beatty, 31 October 1920; Bennett Papers, 241109, W.A. Gordon, letter to the provincial premiers, 14 February 1931.

131. "Annual Review by L.W. Simms, president of the CMA," Annual Meeting, Halifax, 4-6 June 1929, 9.

Chapter Five

1. Donald Avery, *"Dangerous Foreigners": European Immigrant Workers and Labour Radicalism in Canada* (Toronto, 1979).

2. Gerald Dirks, *Canada's Refugee Policy: Indifference or Opportunism?* (Montreal, 1974), 255.

3. Abella and Troper, *None Is Too Many*, 281.

4. CMA Annual Meeting, 2 June 1930, Toronto, "Annual Review by President R.J. Hutchings," 9.

5. Winnipeg *Tribune*, 30 January 1930; "Votes and Proceedings of the Legislative Assembly of Manitoba, 3 February 1930," Department of Labour, 617, 24-2.

6. PAO, Howard Ferguson Papers, 1930, Ferguson to A.J. Moore, 6 January 1930.

7. Avery, *"Dangerous Foreigners,"* 109-12.

8. Department of Labour, 617, 24-2, "Minutes of an Interview of Representatives of Certain Municipalities in Ontario, Manitoba, Saskatchewan, Alberta and British Columbia and of the Provincial governments of Manitoba, Saskatchewan, Alberta and British Columbia with the Cabinet, 26 February 1930, Ottawa, 1 March 1930." PAM, John Bracken Papers, 1933, City of Winnipeg Unemployment Relief Dept.

9. Montreal *Gazette*, 4 February 1930.

10. CNR Records, 8386, file 3600-20, manager of Eastern District to Black, 17 December 1929; *ibid.*, Robert England, Winnipeg manager of colonization, to Black, 2 September 1930; *ibid.*, 7 October 1930.

11. Ontario Department of Labour, 1931, James Gallagher, N. Bay, to Minister of Labour, 12 May 1931.

12. *Ibid.*, W.C. Dobbs, supt. of employment agencies, to H.C. Hudson, deputy minister of labour, 24 March 1931.

13. *Ibid.*, affidavit, John Kostiuk and William Pendryk, Sudbury, March, 1932, enclosed in letter, Hudson to Dr. J.D. Monteith, minister, Department of Public Works and Labour, 9 March 1932.

14. Bracken Papers, 1933, "City of Winnipeg Unemployment Relief Report."

15. Henry Blank, "Industrial Relations in Sarnia, Ontario, with Specific Reference to the Holmes Foundry Strike of March, 1937" (M.A. thesis, University of Western Ontario, 1975), 115-18; Sarnia *Observer*, 7 May 1932; *ibid.*, 27 February 1933.

16. W.B. Hurd, *Racial Origins and Nativity of the Canadian People* (Ottawa, 1942), 586, 698, 699, 719.

17. IB, 216882, No. 9, Wasyl Czaban (Mundare, Alberta), enclosed in letter from Woods to Blair, 13 December 1939; Radecki and Heydenkorn, A *Member of a Distinguished Family*, 192-93.

18. University of British Columbia Archives, Papers of Simon Fraser Tolmie, vol. 8, file 8-32, Stephen Raymer, J.P., memorandum to Tolmie, 7 April 1932.

19. LeMay, *From Open Door to Dutch Door*, 86-95; E.P. Hutchinson, *Legislative History of American Immigration Policy, 1798-1965* (Philadelphia, 1981), 474-78.

20. LeMay, *From Open Door to Dutch Door*, 92.

21. The Mexican percentage of total immigration into the U.S. declined from 11.2 per cent during the 1920s to 4.2 per cent in the 1930s. *Ibid.*

22. The Canadian percentage of immigrants to the U.S. was 22.5 per cent during the 1920s; it was 20.5 per cent during the 1930s. *Ibid.* IB, 2664, #9, Massey to Skelton, 30 December 1929.

23. Consul H.F. Hawley found these accusations exaggerated and ridiculous. After checking out real estate sales, he concluded that only a few Detroit citizens had relocated in the Windsor region. Nor did this surprise him given the more expensive costs of living, the absence of entertainment, grim Sundays under Ontario's Lord's Day Act, and the fact that "most American parents would prefer that their children gain

their education in the United States." The Ambassador Bridge opened November 15, 1930. U.S. National Archives, State Department, 150.01, Hawley to State, 16 December 1929.

24. Martel also claimed that General Order No. 86 had "hardly put a dent in the traffic of aliens from Windsor"; instead, he claimed, "it had simply legitimized commuters."

25. The *News* also cited Detroit councilman Fred W. Castator, who claimed that if the jobs of the 8,000 daily commuters were given to Detroit residents "we might cut the number of the relief roll in half." *Detroit News*, 4 March 1929.

26. On February 26, 1930, Detroit city council ordered the immediate dismissal of 1,689 aliens, including "a large proportion of . . . Canadians." Faced by intense criticism from groups within the city and from the border cities, council unanimously agreed to rescind its order on March 31. IB 2664, #8, Massey to Skelton, 26 February 1930. According to an April 2 editorial in the *Border City Star*, another factor was the realization "that the removal of Canadians would seriously handicap various civic services."

27. The Spolansky Act was roundly denounced by various groups in Detroit, ranging from the American Civil Liberties Union to the Detroit Chamber of Commerce. In December, 1931, a panel of three judges ruled it unconstitutional. Thomas Klug, "Labor Market in Detroit: The Curious Case of the 'Spolansky Act' of 1931," *Michigan Historical Review*, 14 (Spring, 1988), 1-32.

28. NAC, Department of External Affairs (DEA), file 1574, H.M. Wrong to O.D. Skelton, 19 August 1930.

29. *Ibid.*, Wrong to Skelton, 21 January 1931. In September, 1931, the American consul in Toronto asked the Ontario attorney general "for any information arising out of the prosecution of the Communist leaders that [would] help . . . to counteract Communist propaganda in the United States." DEA, file 1574, Report, T.S. Belcher, assistant commissioner, RCMP, to O.D. Skelton, 3 September 1931.

30. See Robin, *Radical Politics and Canadian Labour*; Stuart Jamieson, *Times of Trouble: Labour Unrest and Industrial Conflict in Canada, 1900-66* (Ottawa, 1968), 1-276; William Rodney, *Soldiers of the International: A History of the Communist Party of Canada, 1919-1929* (Toronto, 1968); Avakumovic, *Communist Party*.

31. Tom McEwen, *The Forge Glows Red: From Blacksmith to Revolutionary* (Toronto, 1974), 85-137; Tim Buck, *Thirty Years, 1922-1952: The Story of the Communist Movement in Canada* (Toronto, 1952), 1-106; Irving Abella, *Nationalism, Communism and Canadian Labour* (Toronto, 1973), 1-22, 66-85.

32. Jerry Petryshyn, "A.E. Smith and the Canadian Labour Defence League" (Ph.D. thesis, University of Western Ontario, 1977), 100-83.

33. McEwen, *The Forge Glows Red*, 172-85.

34. Toronto *Mail and Empire*, 6 September 1929; *ibid.*, 12 October 1929; *Debates*, 1931, 17 May 1931.

35. J.E. Rae, "The Politics of Class: Winnipeg City Council, 1919-1945," in Carl Berger and Ramsay Cook, eds., *The West and the Nation: Essays in Honour of W.L. Morton*

(Toronto, 1976), 232-49; Bennett Papers, 94478, Webb to Bennett, 16 April 1931; *ibid.*, Webb to Bennett, 29 May 1931.

36. Bennett Papers, 94763, Premier Tolmie to Bennett, 13 June 1931.

37. *Ibid.*, 95663, Honore Raymond, Montreal, to Bennett, 12 May 1931; IB, 563263, Charles Lanctot, attorney general, to W.A. Gordon, 5 May 1931.

38. NAC, Department of Justice, 1929, file 293, Ferguson to King, 11 August 1929; Ferguson Papers, 1930, Ferguson to Tolchard, 10 May 1930.

39. The total number deported from Canada rose from 1,886 persons in 1927-28 to 7,025 in 1931-32. Ontario and Manitoba most dramatically increased the level of expulsions: in Ontario, from 646 to 2,828 and in Manitoba, from 279 to 1,014. *Report of the Department of Immigration and Colonization for the Fiscal Year Ending 31 March 1936* (Ottawa, 1936), 77.

40. IB, 274585, deputy minister to C. Starnes, 13 April 1929. Attempts were made in April, 1930, to prevent Tom Sula, a prominent member of the Sudbury local, from getting back into the country. Ferguson Papers, 1930, Immigration File, Charles Stewart to Ferguson, 25 April 1930.

41. *Senate Debates*, 1931, May 21, 140, June 11, 225-47; PAM, Minutes of the City Council of Winnipeg, 14 July 1931. Parliament was adjourned on July 23 before the bill could come to a vote; of course, some nineteen days later the Communist Party was declared an illegal organization.

42. IB, 817510, Thomas Gelley, Winnipeg commissioner, to A.L. Jolliffe, 5 September 1931; *ibid.*, Jolliffe to Gelley, 2 October 1931. The number of immigrants deported for criminality or other civil reasons increased from 673 in 1927-28 to 1,276 in 1931-32. Unfortunately, immigration records do not specify exactly how many of these people were deported under sections 40 and 41. The Canadian Labour Defence League, however, regularly published lists of Communists who were being deported for "political reasons." *Report on Immigration and Colonization 1936*, 77; University of Toronto Library, Robert Kenny Collection, "Statistics on Cases Handled by the C.L.D.L., 1929-Feb. 1930."

43. Those arrested were Tim Buck, Party secretary, Tom McEwen, A.T. Hill, John Boychuk, Sam Carr, Mike Cacic, Malcolm Bruce, Mathew Popovich, and Mike Golinsky, who was later released. Of the Toronto Eight, all but Cacic received five-year sentences. Buck, *Thirty Years*, 75-102; Avakumovic, *Communist Party*, 85-87.

44. IB, 513116, Comm. Starnes, RCMP, to Superintendent of Immigration, 21 November 1931. Arvo Vaara was the most controversial member of the group, largely because of the following editorial in *Vapaus* in 1929, when King George V was on his deathbed: "Will the King die, it does not matter to us. The social order will be equally oppressive to the poor, whoever is king." For his "indiscretion" Vaara was found guilty of seditious libel and sentenced to six months in jail and a fine of $1,000. *Debates*, 1931, 2354; *The Worker*, 5 September, 5 October 1931.

45. Buck, *Thirty Years*, 90-118; Petryshyn, "Canadian Labour Defence League," 100-42; Avakumovic, *Communist Party*, 91-95; *Parliamentary Guide*, 1935

(Ottawa, 1935), 243-340; Abella, *Nationalism, Communism and Canadian Labour*, 1-22.

46. Prior to 1928, 17,519 Russian Mennonites had emigrated to Canada, in part because Soviet authorities were prepared to allow Canadian doctors to inspect prospective immigrants. This arrangement ended in 1928, when the two countries broke off diplomatic relations. Frank Epp, *Mennonite Exodus: The Rescue and Settlement of the Russian Mennonites Since the Communist Revolution* (Altona, Manitoba, 1962), 223-35. See also Henry Paetkau, "Separation or Integration: The Russian Mennonite Immigrant Community in Ontario, 1924-45" (Ph.D. thesis, University of Western Ontario, 1986).

47. Epp, *Mennonite Exodus*, 247.

48. The Canadian position was strongly influenced by the arguments of O.D. Skelton and F.C. Blair. Skelton warned King that more generous refugee guidelines would only encourage the Nazis to persecute and expel more German Jews. In contrast, Blair viewed the movement of refugees as part of a long-term plan by the Canadian Jewish community to bring their co-religionists from Germany, Austria, and eastern Europe. Abella and Troper, *None Is Too Many*, 27-33.

49. Dirks, *Canada's Refugee Policy*, 44-98; Francis Carsten, "German Refugees in Great Britain 1933-1945," in Gerhard Hirschfeld, ed., *Exile in Great Britain: Refugees from Hitler's Germany* (Atlantic Highlands, N.J., 1984), 15-16; Lewis Coser, *Refugee Scholars in America: Their Impact and Experiences* (New Haven, 1984).

50. NAC, Privy Council Papers, vol. 779, Proceedings of the First Meeting of the Canadian National Committee on Refugees, 6 December 1938.

51. King Papers, memorandum to Mackenzie King prepared jointly by the Departments of External Affairs and Mines and Resources, 29 November 1938. Statement to cabinet by T.A. Crerar, 12 December 1938, cited in Dirks, *Canada's Refugee Policy*, 57.

52. Australia's more positive response toward Jewish refugees has often been compared to Canada's negative stance. There was, however, strong opposition to the Australian government's offer in 1938 to bring in 15,000 refugees over a period of three years. In June, 1939, for example, the American consul-general in Sydney reported to his superiors that this plan "faced organized and stubborn resistance" and that there was a distinct possibility "that a serious flare up against the Jew may take place in centres where he is seeking to establish himself." Faced with this opposition, Australian authorities only admitted 6,425 Jewish refugees prior to 1945. U.S. National Archives, State Department Decimal files, 840.48 (Refugees), report, Thomas Wilson, 15 June 1939. Egon Kunz, *Displaced Persons: Calwell's New Australians* (Sydney, 1988), 6.

53. During the late 1930s the Canadian Jewish Congress was ineffectual in its attempts to get more Jewish refugees into the country. Its profile did improve, however, when the dynamic Montreal businessman Sam Bronfman became its president in 1939. Irving Abella and Harold Troper, "Canada and the Refugee Intellectual, 1933-1939," in Jarrell Jackman and Carla Borden, *The Muses Flee Hitler: Cultural Transfer and*

Adaptation, 1930-1945 (Washington, 1983), 26; Michael Marrus, *Mr. Sam: The Life and Times of Samuel Bronfman* (Toronto, 1992), 258-63.

54. The role of F.C. Blair in keeping Jewish refugees out of Canada has been extensively discussed in Abella and Troper, *None Is Too Many*. While they provide abundant evidence to support their contention that the director of the Immigration Branch was "an anti-Semite" perhaps they do not place sufficient emphasis on Blair as "a narrow-minded bureaucrat" who saw his job as primarily keeping all immigrants out of Canada during the Great Depression.

55. IB, file 28-2-2, Jolliffe to F.G. Green (NRC), 13 April 1939; *ibid.*, Dr. Boyle to S.J. Cook, 15 April 1939.

56. *Nature*, 23 December 1933, 954. On May 3, 1934, in an article in *The Times*, Rutherford made an impassioned appeal to the world's scientific community.

57. In 1935 it became the Society for the Protection of Science and Learning. Funding was provided by private donations, from corporate sources (Imperial Chemicals donated £2,500), and above all, by the Carnegie Endowment. About 500 German refugee scientists and other scholars found permanent homes in Britain. See Gustav V.R. Born, "The Effect of the Scientific Environment in Britain on Refugee Scientists and Their Effects on Science in Britain," *Berlin Wissenschaftsgesch*, 7 (1984), 129-43.

58. A survey of October, 1933, showed that more than 2,000 out of a total of 27,000 university teachers had been released from the faculties of 240 U.S. institutions. At the same time, thousands of new Ph.D.s were coming into the academic job market. See Gerald Holton, "The Migration of Physicists to the United States," in Jackman and Borden, *Muses*, 169-88; Nathan Reingold, "Refugee Mathematicians in the United States, 1933-1941: Reception and Reaction," *ibid.*, 205-32.

59. Reingold, "Refugee Mathematicians," 206-21; F. Thomas Carroll, "Immigrants in American Chemistry," in Jackman and Borden, *Muses*, 189-203.

60. The Rockefeller Foundation aided foreign scientists in a variety of ways prior to 1939. One of these was through the award of Rockefeller Fellowships in the natural sciences, which enabled nearly 1,000 scientists to carry out their research abroad; one-third came to the United States. Officials of the Rockefeller Foundation were also instrumental in the formation of the Emergency Committee in May, 1934. Bolton, "Physicists," 177.

61. Significantly, neither MIT nor Harvard immediately supported the Emergency Committee. In the case of Harvard, the president, James Conant, in 1933 warned against any tendency "to mix up charity and education." According to historian James Hershberg, "this initial cold-blooded indifference showed Conant's serious underestimation of the contributions these refugees from Hitler would make to American scholarship." James Hershberg, *James Conant* (New York, 1993), 85.

62. NAC, Gerhard Herzberg Papers, vol. 2, Herzberg to the Academic Assistance Council, London, 25 June 1934.

63. John Spinks, *Two Blades of Grass: An Autobiography* (Saskatoon, 1980), 40-50.

64. According to Spinks he cabled Herzberg a modest offer, "thinking that if things were bad enough in Germany it would seem attractive and that once he got here there would be two possibilities: if Dr. Herzberg fitted in as well as I was sure he would, the university would quickly raise his salary, and if not, he could certainly go elsewhere for more money." Spinks observed that Herzberg's appointment "could only have happened under a fairly autocratic system with a president like Dr. Murray who trusted his own judgement, was filled with the milk of human kindness, and was prepared to take a bit of a gamble." *Ibid.*, 43-44, 45. See also Lawrence Stokes, "Canada and an Academic Refugee from Nazi Germany: The Case of Gerhard Herzberg," *Canadian Historical Review*, LVII (June, 1976), 150-70.

65. University of Toronto Archives (UTA), Cody Papers, Cody to Lord Rutherford, 22 March 1935.

66. The hiring of Haurwitz was strongly endorsed by John Patterson of the Ottawa Meteorological Observatory, who argued that Canada should not miss the opportunity of obtaining outstanding scientists since this was "not likely to occur again in our lifetime." After six academic years as lecturer in the Department of Physics, Haurwitz joined the Meteorological Service of the Department of Transport in 1941. That same year, he was offered a position of associate professor at the MIT Department of Meteorology; he accepted. *Ibid.*, Patterson to Dr. Sigmund Samuel, 8 December 1934; *ibid.*, Cody to Dr. J.M. Russell, Carnegie Corporation, New York City, 31 January 1935; *ibid.*, vol. 45, Haurwitz to Cody, 8 May 1941.

67. Michael Bliss, *Banting: A Biography* (Toronto, 1984), 252.

68. McGill Archives, President's Papers, vol. 47, Mackay to Currie, 23 April 1926.

69. Mackay also warned about having "the medical and especially the legal profession . . . overcrowded with Jewish practitioners." *Ibid.*, Mackay to Currie, 21 July 1933.

70. Currie did, however, authorize a survey of the ratio of Jewish faculty at McGill. The report of September, 1933, showed that there were eleven full-time and eleven part-time Jewish faculty out of 549 total faculty. Report of the Office of the Principal and Vice-Chancellor, 20 September 1933, *ibid.*, Box 47, file 443.

71. Currie also acknowledged that there were "men among those displaced who, as scholars and research workers, have a contribution to make." *Ibid.*, Currie to Edward R. Murrow, assistant to Stephen Duggan, ECADGS, 26 June 1933.

72. *Ibid.*, Conant to Douglas, 28 January 1939 (the letter was actually addressed to President W.H. Brittain).

73. Douglas, an American-born economist, was appointed principal in 1937. With the outbreak of war in September, 1939, he resigned and returned to the U.S. Douglas was also concerned when John Meakins, director of medicine at McGill, reported that the Royal Society of Canada was preparing to debate this issue. In addition, he was advised by Rector Monseigneur Olivier Maurault of Laval about the need for caution. *Ibid.*, Douglas to Maurault, 20 February 1939; Meakins to Douglas, 21 April 1939.

74. Irving Abella and Harold Troper, "Canada and the Refugee Intellectual, 1933-1939," in Jackman and Borden, *Muses*, 261.

75. Although many of the responses claimed that economic conditions and the high unemployment of Canadian graduates still mitigated against accepting refugee scientists, others emphasized how these newcomers could develop new technology and establish new companies. IB, vol. 166, file 28-2-2, Boyle to S.J. Cook, 15 April 1939.

76. Banting had previously supported the work of the Canadian National Committee on Refugees, formed in December, 1938. Bliss, *Banting*, 252; IB, vol. 166, file 28-2-2, cited in S.J. Cook to Blair, 31 August 1939.

77. The Sudeten German Social Democrats had strongly resisted Nazism, but it was a losing cause. Their fate was sealed when the region was given to Germany as part of the Munich Agreement of September, 1938. The British government tried to place these refugees in Canada through persuasion and by the use of $260,000 from its Czech Refugee Trust Fund. Jonathan Wagner, "British Columbia's Anti-Nazi Germans: The Tupper Creek Refugees," *B.C. Studies*, 39 (Autumn, 1978), 3-19; Andrew Amstatter, *Tomslake: History of the Sudeten Germans in Canada* (Saanichton, B.C., 1978).

78. The CPR provided land for the settlement in the Peace River region of northern British Columbia. The relationship between the refugees and the company was not very cordial, especially after its representatives issued them brown parkas during the winter of 1939-40, which were reminiscent of the garb worn by Nazi stormtroopers. Amstatter, *Tomslake*, 95.

79. U.S. National Archives, State Department Papers, vol. 846, Joseph Kennedy to American Secretary of State, 25 October 1938.

80. State Department Papers, 840.48; Michael Marrus, *The Unwanted: European Refugees in the Twentieth Century* (New York, 1985), 190-93.

81. King Papers, C-565668, Vincent Massey to O.D. Skelton, 23 February 1939; NAC, Immigration Records, 665668, memorandum for Prime Minister, 6 March 1939.

82. *Ibid.*, Blair to Skelton, 9 March 1939.

83. As early as 1936 the Canadian government had sought to deal with the threat of Fascist and Nazi subversive activity. But it was not until the appointment of the Committee on the Treatment of Aliens and Alien Property in the spring of 1938 that sustained planning occurred. NAC, Norman Robertson Papers, vol. 12, O.D. Skelton to Commissioner of the RCMP, 26 March 1936; *ibid.*, file 134, memorandum, 24 May 1939. J.L. Granatstein provides a brief but informative account of these developments in *A Man of Influence: Norman Robertson and Canadian Statecraft, 1929-68* (Toronto, 1981), 80-91. The threat of Nazi and Fascist subversion has been the subject of a number of articles and books. See Robert Keyserlingk, "'Agents within the Gates': The Search for Nazi Subversives in Canada during World War II," *Canadian Historical Review*, LXVI (June, 1985), 211-38; Jonathan Wagner, *Brothers Beyond the Seas: National Socialism in Canada* (Waterloo, 1982); John Zucchi, *Italians in Toronto:*

Development of a National Identity, 1875-1935 (Montreal and Kingston, 1988).

84. Barbara Roberts, *Whence They Came: Deportation from Canada 1900-1935* (Ottawa, 1988), 125-58.

85. Reg Whitaker, "Official Repression of Communism during World War II," *Labour/Le Travail*, 17 (Spring, 1986).

86. NAC, Canadian National Committee on Refugees Papers, Proceedings of Conference, 6-7 December 1938, résumé of interview with the Hon. T.A. Crerar.

87. Early in 1939 the nationalist St. Jean Baptiste Society submitted a petition against Jewish immigration to Canada signed by 127,364 people. Lita-Rose Betcherman, *The Swastika and the Maple Leaf: Fascist Movements in Canada in the Thirties* (Toronto, 1975), 32-44, 128-35.

88. This allegation was repudiated by the Committee on Gentile-Jewish Relations, which claimed that of the approximately 15,000 members of the Communist Party of Canada only about 450 were Jewish. *Globe and Mail*, 15 November 1937. Avakumovic, in *The Communist Party in Canada*, estimated that about 15 per cent of Party membership was Jewish during the late 1930s, while Erna Paris, *Jews: An Account of Their Experience in Canada* (Toronto, 1980), 145-46, put the figure at 20 per cent. Harvey Klehr, *The Heyday of American Communism: The Depression Decade* (New York, 1984), 163, says that 19 per cent of the U.S. Party was Jewish in 1931.

89. The report "Nazi-Fascist Activity and the Naturalization Act" was prepared for cabinet consideration. It outlined in some detail how the Naturalization Act could be used as a security device. Robertson Papers, vol. 12.

90. *Ibid.*, Tim Buck to Prime Minister King, 23 February 1939. One person who kept Norman Robertson informed about Fascist and Nazi activities in Canada was Fred Rose, a prominent Montreal Communist and subsequent member of the House of Commons.

91. King Papers, C-257904, report, "On a Wartime Intelligence Service"; Robertson Papers, vol. 12, Robertson to Skelton, 28 August 1939; King Papers, C-153968, Walter Turnbull to King, 6 December 1939.

92. NAC, J.L. Cohen Papers, file 2761, Rex vs. Arthur Bortolotti, Cohen to J.S. Woodsworth, 29 November 1939; *ibid.*, Cohen to Oscar Kitching, president of the Windsor Trades and Labour Council, 1 March 1940; *ibid.*, petition, February, 1940; *ibid.*, Cohen to T.A. Crerar, 16 May 1940.

93. *Toronto Star*, 13 February 1940. Emma Goldman, the famous anarchist writer and organizer, assumed a major role in the defence of Bortolotti and her other "boys." After three years of trying to raise money for the Loyalist cause in Spain, she had returned to Toronto and become involved in this, her last crusade. She died in Toronto on May 14, 1940. Candace Falk, *Love, Anarchy and Emma Goldman* (New York, 1984).

94. Robertson Papers, vol. 12, Blair to Skelton, 6 March 1939; *ibid.*, Skelton to Blair, 6 March 1939.

95. Loring Christie, the Canadian chargé d'affaires in Washington, reported that "no person has been deported from the United States under the present administration to a totalitarian country if he would suffer there for his political convictions." Cohen Papers, Blair to Cohen, 29 April 1940; Robertson Papers, vol. 12, Christie to Robertson, 12 March 1940.

96. Robertson Papers, vol. 12, Report of the Inter-Departmental Committee on Alien Propaganda, 30 July 1939; *ibid.*, Report of the Committee on the Treatment of Aliens and Alien Property, August, 1939; *ibid.*, Robertson to Skelton, 24 October 1939; *ibid.*, Skelton to Commissioner Wood, 11 December 1939.

97. At this meeting Commissioner S.T. Wood of the RCMP complained that the Force was not receiving the "full cooperation and information in regard to refugees entering Canada." IB, vol. 856, file 555-4, A.L. Jolliffe memorandum, 27 May 1940.

98. Robertson Papers, vol. 12, Robertson to Dr. E. Coleman, undersecretary of state, 1 August 1940.

99. Between 1940 and October, 1942, 250 men and women associated with the Canadian Communist movement were arrested. Most were placed in internment camps. William and Kathleen Repka, *Dangerous Patriots: Canada's Unknown Prisoners of War* (Vancouver, 1982); William Kolasky, *The Shattered Illusion: The History of Ukrainian Pro-Communist Organizations in Canada* (Toronto, 1979), 26-88. Although an active campaign was launched by the Canadian Civil Liberties Union and its allies to obtain the immediate release of interned Communists, little could be achieved until June, 1941. Yet even when the Soviet Union became Canada's wartime ally, the King government was slow to release leftist internees or to restore confiscated property despite mounting popular pressure. In October, 1942, for example, a massive petition, signed by a large number of "respectable" Anglo-Canadians, including Premier Mitchell Hepburn of Ontario, was sent to Ottawa calling for the removal of all disabilities. Federal authorities were sufficiently impressed to release the Communists; they did not, however, remove the ban against the movement until October, 1943, or agree that confiscated property should be restored. For the ULFTA, return of all their halls would take almost another two years.

100. IB, file 673931, #1, Blair to Jackson, 21 February 1941.

Chapter Six

1. Abella and Troper, *None Is Too Many*, 281.

2. Reg Whitaker, *Double Standard: The Secret History of Canadian Immigration* (Toronto, 1987), 103.

3. David Wyman, *Abandonment of the Jews: America and the Holocaust, 1941-1945* (New York, 1984), 5, 11.

4. Ronald Stent, *A Bespattered Page: The Internment of His Majesty's 'most loyal enemy aliens'* (London, 1980), 27-28.

5. Michael Seyfert, "His Majesty's Most Loyal Internees," in Hirschfeld, ed., *Exile in Great Britain*, 163.

6. A survey of the King Papers revealed seventy-eight petitions from veterans organizations, forty-one from municipal councils, twenty-two from boards of trade, seventeen from service clubs, twenty-two from patriotic organizations, and eleven from various citizen meetings. The majority of the petitions came from Ontario (seventy) and British Columbia (sixty-five). King Papers, C-257922-50.

7. The federal government made it clear that vigilante action by patriotic organizations would not be tolerated. Canada, House of Commons, *Debates*, 803; King Papers, C-257918, memorandum for Prime Minister, 27 May 1940.

8. King Papers, C-239972, memorandum for Prime Minister, 27 June 1940. This report not only criticized various private organizations for over-reacting to the situation, but also charged that Premier Mitchell Hepburn of Ontario had made irresponsible statements. In defending their position, federal authorities emphasized that "no single serious act of sabotage has yet occurred in Canada." See J.L. Granatstein, *Canada's War: The Politics of the Mackenzie King Government, 1939-1945* (Toronto, 1975), 76-93.

9. Kolasky, *Shattered Illusions*, 35-80; Granatstein, *Man of Influence*, 80-92.

10. In 1939 Germans were the third largest ethnic group in the country; the vast majority were Canadian citizens. Of the 90,000 German immigrants who came during the interwar years, only a small number had been German nationals. Perhaps this explains why the overt pro-Nazi movements in Canada numbered less than 800. It was primarily these people who were interned. Robert Keyserlingk, "Breaking the Nazi Plot: Canadian Government Attitudes Towards German Canadians, 1939-1945," in Norman Hillmer, ed., *On Guard For Thee: War, Ethnicity, and the Canadian State, 1939-1945* (Ottawa, 1988), 53-70; John Herd Thompson, *Ethnic Minorities During Two World Wars*, CHA Booklet No. 19 (Ottawa, 1991), 10-18.

11. Bruno Ramirez, "Ethnicity on Trial: The Italians of Montreal and the Second World War," in Hillmer, ed., *On Guard*, 71-84; Joseph Ciccocelli, "The Innocuous Enemy Alien: Italians in Canada During World War II" (M.A. thesis, University of Western Ontario, 1977).

12. The internment of the Canadian Japanese has been extensively discussed. Since the vast majority of the Canadian Japanese (over 90 per cent) were citizens and few if any Japanese refugees were admitted during either the pre-war or war years, their experiences have not been discussed here. See Adachi, *The Enemy That Never Was*; Barry Broadfoot, *Years of Sorrow, Years of Shame* (Toronto, 1977); Ann Gomer Sunahara, *The Politics of Racism: The Uprooting of Japanese Canadians During the Second World War* (Toronto, 1981); Ward, *White Canada Forever*; Patricia Roy *et al.*, *Mutual Hostages: Canadians and Japanese during the Second World War* (Toronto, 1990).

13. As early as 1938 the Interdepartmental Committee on Orientals and the Interdepartmental Committee on the Treatment of Aliens and Alien Property had considered the threat of subversion in British Columbia. So, too, had the October, 1940, Joint Canada-United States Basic Defence Plan. RCMP officials, however, remained unconcerned about possible espionage or subversion by Japanese Canadians, in part because of their limited capacity to gather intelligence; but no evidence was produced during the war linking Japanese Canadians with subversive activity. Roy, *Hostages*, 50-56; Granatstein, *Man of Influence*, 157-67; Thompson, *Ethnic Minorities*, 19-20.

14. Canadian authorities also used the expertise of the Polish and Czechoslovak consuls in gathering information about Nazi and Communist activities among their nationals in Canada. Robertson Papers, vol. 13, Skelton to Commissioner Wood, RCMP, 21 December 1939. Christopher Andrew, *Secret Service: The Making of the British Intelligence Community* (London, 1985), 448-97; Keyserlingk, "Search for Nazi Subversives"; C.V. Harvison, *The Horsemen* (Toronto, 1967), 86-101; John Sawatsky, *Men in the Shadows* (Toronto, 1980), 60-80.

15. NAC, Norman Robertson Papers, vol. 13, memo of 15 June 1940.

16. *Ibid.*, Skelton to Blair, 29 March 1940.

17. The case of Father Dom Odo, Duke of Wuerttemberg, who sought sanctuary in the Benedictine monastery, Muenster, Saskatchewan, also challenged Canadian officials, especially since the Duke's entry was strongly supported by Cardinal Villeneuve of Quebec and German Catholics in western Canada. For reasons that remain obscure, his application was rejected. *Ibid.*, Blair to Skelton, 8 November 1940; *ibid.*, Skelton to K.M. Mahoney, chargé d'affaires, Washington, 2 December 1940.

18. A similar case occurred in March, 1942, when Lester B. Pearson, Canadian ambassador in Washington, reported that Professor Louis Rougier, "an active Vichy propagandist" in the United States, was trying to get permission to visit Quebec. There is also an interesting parallel with the post-war controversy over the entry of Count de Bernonville, a prominent Vichy collaborator, who sought sanctuary in Quebec in 1946. His deportation occurred only after much national and international pressure. *Ibid.*, Skelton to Commissioner Wood, 22 October 1940; DEA, vol. 2168, Pearson to H.M. Wrong, 13 March 1942; Whitaker, *Double Standard*, 125-29.

19. Robertson Papers, vol. 13, Blair to Skelton, 8 November 1940; *ibid.*, Skelton to K.M. Mahoney, 2 December 1940.

20. David Wyman, *Paper Walls: America and the Refugee Crisis, 1938-1941* (New York, 1968), 184-85.

21. *Ibid.*, 186-87; Henry Feingold, *The Politics of Rescue* (New Brunswick, N.J., 1970), 14, 130-35.

22. Robertson Papers, vol. 13, Mahoney to Skelton, 24 June 1940. The Smith Act went further than previous American laws dealing with sedition since it applied in peace as well as in wartime. It was used only twice during World War Two. In 1949 it was used

in the prosecution of the eleven top leaders of the American Communist Party. Sanford Unger, *FBI* (Boston, 1975), 131.

23. Canadian diplomats had previously criticized the "witch-hunt" tactics of the recently created House Committee on Un-American Activities. Robertson Papers, vol. 13, Skelton to Chief of the General Staff, 30 November 1939; Wyman, *Paper Walls*, 187.

24. In many ways Breckinridge Long was similar to F.C. Blair in his determination to keep Jews and other "troublesome" refugees out of the country. See Wyman, *Paper Walls*, 193; Feingold, *The Politics of Rescue*, 191.

25. Wyman, *Paper Walls*, 189-205.

26. *Ibid.*, 205.

27. Refugees from Nazi and Soviet persecution arrived in Shanghai in several waves between 1933 and 1941, when the Japanese eventually imposed their full authority. Between 1939 and 1941 F.C. Blair used security arguments to prevent the entry of some 300 Polish rabbinical students and their teachers (the Yeshiva boys) who had gained temporary sanctuary in Japan. IB, 673931, Wrong to Robertson, 31 May 1941. Marrus, *The Unwanted*, 180; Renata Berg-Pan, "Shanghai Chronicle: Nazi Refugees in China," in Jackman and Borden, *Muses*, 283-89; Abella and Troper, *None Is Too Many*, 85-95.

28. Stent, *Bespattered Page*, 1-70.

29. J.P. Fox, "Germany and German Emigration to Great Britain," *Weiner Library Bulletin*, XXVI (October, 1972), 55; Stent, *Bespattered Page*, 20-220.

30. Andrew, *Secret Service*, 479-81.

31. Stent, *Bespattered Page*, 200-60; Paula Jean Draper, "Muses Behind Barbed Wire: Canada and the Interned Refugees," in Jackman and Borden, *Muses*, 271-79.

32. Between June, 1940, and July 1, 1941, General Panet and Colonel H. Stethem supervised these internment camps. DEA, 621-BF-40, Hayes to Panet, 9 August 1940; Eric Koch, *Deemed Suspect: A Wartime Blunder* (Toronto, 1980), 222.

33. Canadian authorities were extremely critical of the British removal policy. See DEA, 11252, file 11-1-5, Skelton to General Panet; King Papers, C-248518, Robertson memorandum for King, 10 October 1940.

34. Among those released in December, 1940, was Dr. Klaus Fuchs, who later was a member of the British scientific team that had access to atomic bomb secrets. In 1950 Fuchs was exposed as a Soviet spy. A second group of 274 internees was returned to Britain in February, 1941, and an additional batch of 330 on June 26, 1941. King Papers, C-248516, Report of the Cabinet Sub-Committee dealing with internees from Great Britain, 12 September 1940. A complete inventory of "the academic talent" is provided in Koch, *Deemed Suspect*, 146-73; Montgomery Hyde, *The Atom Bomb Spies* (London, 1980), 93-116.

35. By PC 4568 of June 25, 1941, the position of Commissioner of Refugee Camps was created, and Colonel R.W.S. Fordham was named to the post. DEA, vol. 6577, file 1-2-10, memo, Military Intelligence, District 3, 15 January 1941.

36. King Papers, C-248516, Report of the Cabinet Sub-Committee, 12 September 1940.

37. DEA, vol. 6577, file 1-2-10, Stethem to W.G. Scully, 21 May 1941.

38. Between 1941 and 1943 the Canadian National Committee on Refugees pressured the Canadian government to adopt a more humane approach toward the internees. One hurdle was overcome when in January, 1941, it was decided that the British Home Office would issue certificates to "stateless internees" to make it possible for them to emigrate to the United States or remain in Canada on a temporary basis. CNCR Papers, vol. 5, Constance Hayward to Dr. Muriel Roscoe, 6 January 1941; DEA, 6577, file 1-2-10, Blair to Robertson, 31 January 1941.

39. IB, 673931, F.C. Blair to N.H. Vernon, associate director general, Industrial Security Branch, Department of Munitions and Supply, 10 September 1942.

40. *Ibid.*, Jolliffe to Robertson, 27 October 1943.

41. Some, however, elected to return to Britain and serve in the non-combatant Auxiliary Military Pioneer Corps. Koch, *Deemed Suspect*, 190-91.

42. *Ibid.*

43. Throughout the winter of 1942 military officials and university authorities grappled with the question of whether internee students should be required to take military training. Robertson warned King that the issue might "spur the latent xenophobia in this country, and easily take on an anti-semitic twist because a large proportion of recent immigrants ineligible for naturalization (and therefore for military service), are Jewish refugees from Europe." NAC, Department of National Defence Records (DND), vol. 2159, file 54-27-35-60-1, President Cody to J.L. Ralston, 4 December 1942. King Papers, C-239998, Robertson memo, 14 November 1941.

44. *Debates*, 22 February 1943; *ibid.*, 7 April 1943; DND, 2159, 54-27-35-60-1, Church to Ralston, 25 March 1943; *ibid.*, Ralston to Church, 17 March 1943; *ibid.*, Ralston to Cody, 14 April 1944.

45. One celebrated case involved a young refugee mathematician Professor J.L. Synge of the University of Toronto wanted to use in his war-related research. He was unsuccessful. The record shows that Canada did not use its refugee scientists as extensively as either the U.S. or Britain. NAC, National Research Council Papers (NRC), vol. 170, 32-1-54, Mackenzie to General Panet, 19 August 1940; *ibid.*, vol. 170, 32-1-97, Synge to Dr. W.L. Webster, NRC, 13 January 1943; *ibid.*, Mackenzie to Synge, 18 February 1943.

46. All of the executives within the Nationalities Branch were Anglo-Saxons: the director was Professor George Simpson of the University of Saskatchewan's History Department; his special adviser was Tracy Phillips, a former adviser to the British Foreign Office. One of the consultants was Professor Watson Kirkconnell of McMaster University, whose 1941 pamphlet *Canadians All* raised the alarm "that the Soviets and Nazis were seeking converts among eastern European groups in Canada." N.F. Dreisziger, "The Rise of a Bureaucracy of Multiculturalism: The Origins of the Nationalities Branch, 1939-1941," in Hillmer, ed., *On Guard*, 1-30; William R. Young, "Chauvinism and Canadianism: Canadian Ethnic Groups and the Failure of Wartime Information," *ibid.*, 31-52.

47. The Ukrainian Canadian Committee was created at a conference in Winnipeg in November, 1940, as an attempt "to provide a faction-ridden community with an umbrella organization that could speak for the community while helping to preserve its identity." All major groups except the pro-Communists were included. Oleh W. Gerus, "The Ukrainian Canadian Committee," in Lupul, ed., *A Heritage in Transition*, 195-205.

48. Donald Avery, "Canadian Communism and Popular Front Organizations, 1935-45," paper presented at the meetings of the Canadian Political Science Association, June, 1983, Vancouver.

49. Robertson was quick to assure the Director of Prisoners of War that complete security checks would be conducted. DEA, 621, AF-40, memorandum, 13 October 1943; *ibid.*, Robertson to Colonel Streight, 29 October 1943.

50. Hermann Bondi was a young scientist who later became a leading British scientific adviser.

51. DEA, 621-AC-40, Pearson to Robertson, 22 August 1944.

52. IB, 673931, #3, Robertson memo, 15 October 1944; Dirks, *Canada's Refugee Policy*, 93-95; Abella and Troper, *None Is Too Many*, 142-58.

53. King Papers, C-292985, Robertson memorandum, 10 June 1943; DEA, 5127-EA-40, memorandum, 28 August 1943; IB, 673931, #9, Jolliffe to the Hon. J.A. Glen (the new Minister of Immigration), 17 July 1945.

54. In June, 1941, the Czechoslovakian consul-general in Ottawa was able to secure the entry of some skilled technicians who had been stranded in Vichy France. IB, 673931, #1, Blair memorandum, 29 April 1941; *ibid.*, 673931, #1, Dr. F. Pavasek to F.C. Blair, 17 July 1941.

55. Dirks, *Canada's Refugee Policy*, 91.

56. IB, 673931, #1, Blair memorandum, 29 April 1941; *ibid.*, Blair to Robertson, 16 September 1941.

57. *Manitoba Free Press*, 17 June 1943.

58. IB, 673931, #3, Blair to Alfred Rive, External Affairs, 17 February 1943; Abella and Troper, *None Is Too Many*, 157-62.

59. Dirks, *Canada's Refugee Policy*, 93-95.

60. In October, 1943, the Canadian government reopened its immigration office in Lisbon and once again appointed Odilon Cormier. When examining Polish refugee technicians he was instructed to pay particular attention to "their technical abilities and their political views." IB, 673931, #3, Blair to Rive, 17 February 1943; Abella and Troper, *None Is Too Many*, 164.

61. Despite the provocation, Sam Bronfman, president of the Canadian Jewish Congress, did not confront Duplessis, "pleading rather for the recognition of Jewish patriotism, and commitment to the war effort." Montreal *Gazette*, 10 March 1944; Michael Marrus, *Mr. Sam: The Life and Times of Samuel Bronfman* (Toronto, 1992), 310.

62. The editor of the paper, Joseph Menard, had been associated with the Quebec fascist

movement prior to the war. IB, 673931, #3, *Le Bavard*, 26 November 1943 (translated and summarized by the RCMP).

63. Strong opposition to the entry of large numbers of refugees was also evident in the House of Commons. On April 6, 1944, Robertson wrote Pearson in Washington "that various members, principally from Quebec, have tabled petitions received from their constituencies expressing opposition to post-war immigration.... In many cases also there is mingled with this an opposition to allowing entry of refugees in which it would not be too unjust to suspect an anti-Semitic bias." DEA, 5127-40. Herbert Quinn, *The Union Nationale* (Toronto, 1963).

64. IB, 673931, #3, report of Superintendent Duncan, RCMP, 23 November 1942.

65. *Ibid.*, Assistant Commissioner F.J. Mead to Blair, 2 February 1943; *ibid.*, Duncan to Blair, 13 March 1943.

66. DEA, 5127-40, Commissioner Wood to Louis St. Laurent, 1 June 1944.

67. *Ibid.*, St. Laurent to Robertson, 7 June 1944; *ibid.*, Robertson to St. Laurent, 10 June 1943; *ibid.*, Robertson to A.L. Jolliffe, Director of Immigration, 21 July 1944.

68. IB, 673931, #9, Robertson to Jolliffe, 13 November 1944.

69. *Ibid.*, Jolliffe to Robertson, 23 March 1944; *ibid.*, Jolliffe memorandum, 22 September 1944; *ibid.*, Jolliffe to J.A. Glen, 17 July 1945.

70. *Ibid.*, Commissioner Wood to Jolliffe, 29 December 1944; *ibid.*, Jolliffe to Wood, 7 February 1945.

71. Whitaker, *Double Standard*, 22.

72. IB, vol. 800, 547-5-513, memorandum, 20 June 1949; NAC, Privy Council Papers (PCO), vol. 103, S-100-1, security panel meeting, 13 July 1946; *ibid.*, security panel meeting, 19 August 1946.

73. PCO, vol. 103, S-100-1, security panel meeting, 19 December 1946; IB, vol. 889, 547-5-513, Commissioner Wood to Jolliffe, 27 January 1947.

74. After 1946 it was extremely difficult for Canadian citizens with "left-wing tendencies" to sponsor relatives from Europe. IB, vol. 889, 547-5-513, Escott Reid, External, memorandum, 23 September 1948; PCO, vol. 103, S-100-1, security panel meeting, 22 May 1947.

75. Colonel Fortier would become deputy minister of immigration in 1950. Whitaker, *Double Standard*, 31, 57-82.

76. Allied compromises at Yalta and Dumbarton Oaks that legitimized the Soviet Ukraine and provided for its membership in the United Nations were regarded by the mandarins of External Affairs as enhancing the allied coalition. They also believed this might "drive from the nationalists' minds the mirage of absolute Ukrainian independence and in this way hasten the process of [Canadian] assimilation." Thomas Prymak, *Maple Leaf and Trident: The Ukrainian Canadians during the Second World War* (Toronto, 1988), 121.

77. The propaganda war was primarily conducted in the rival Ukrainian-language newspapers. In some communities, however, pitched battles between the two sides also occurred; one of the worst incidents was the October 8, 1950, bombing attack of a

ULFTA hall in Toronto. Kolasky, *Shattered Illusion*, 100-10; Donald Avery, "Divided Loyalties: The Ukrainian Canadian Left and the Canadian State," in Lubomyr Luciuk and Stella Hryniuk, eds., *Canada's Ukrainians: Negotiating an Identity* (Toronto, 1991), 284.

78. IB, vol. 856, 555-13, Commissioner Wood to A. MacNamara, deputy minister of labour, 23 January 1950.

79. Avery, "Divided Loyalties," 284-85.

Chapter Seven

1. Hugh L. Keenleyside, *Memoirs of Hugh L. Keenleyside*, vol. II (Toronto, 1982), 298.

2. Robert Bothwell, Ian Drummond, and John English, *Canada Since 1945: Power, Politics and Provincialism* (Toronto, 1981), 1-21.

3. J.L. Granatstein, *Canada's War: The Politics of the Mackenzie King Government, 1939-1945* (Toronto, 1975), 212-60.

4. The United Nations defined refugee and displaced person as follows:

   "The term 'refugee' is intended to apply to a person who had left, or is outside of, his country of nationality or of former habitual residence, and who is a victim of the nazi, fascist or falangist regimes or who was considered a refugee before the outbreak of the Second World War for reasons of race, religion, nationality or political opinion. The term 'displaced person' is intended to apply to an individual who has been deported from his country of nationality or of former habitual residence to undertake forced labour, or has been deported for racial, religious or political reasons."

   Yearbook of the United Nations, 1946-47 (New York, 1947), 808.

5. Marrus, *The Unwanted*, 229.

6. *Ibid.*, 344-345.

7. Dirks, *Canada's Refugee Policy*; Milda Danys, *DP Lithuanian Immigration to Canada After the Second World War* (Toronto, 1986); Whitaker, *Double Standard*; Abella and Troper, *None Is Too Many*.

8. In 1947 Saskatchewan passed an even more comprehensive law that prohibited discrimination in accommodation, employment, occupation, land transactions, education, and business. Enforcement of both the Ontario and Saskatchewan Acts was left to the police and the courts. Daniel G. Hill, *Human Rights in Canada: A Focus on Racism* (Toronto, 1977), 23.

9. The image of Canada's Chinese community had greatly improved during the war both because China was a gallant ally and because of the contributions of the community "volunteering service overseas, joining the Red Cross, and participating in loan drives for the war effort." The fact that the United States had in 1943 repealed its

Chinese Exclusion Act and made provision for the admission of 105 Chinese annually also had an impact. Li, *The Chinese in Canada*, 89.

10. At the end of the war 10,397 Japanese Canadians had agreed to voluntary repatriation; but by December, 4,720 of these people had changed their minds. At this stage the King government was not prepared to listen. Swayed by bureaucratic arguments and political pressure from British Columbia, it passed three orders-in-council that would have continued the deportations. Outraged by this decision, a variety of civil liberties organizations, most notably the recently formed Cooperative Committee on Japanese Canadians, strongly supported by liberal newspapers such as the Winnipeg *Free Press* and *Toronto Star*, carried out a vigorous campaign against forcible repatriation. Reference was made to Canada's commitments to the United Nations, to the implications of the Canadian Citizenship Act of 1946, and to the fact that Japanese Americans could use the U.S. Bill of Rights to prevent their deportation. By January, 1947, after review by the Canadian Supreme Court and Judicial Committee of the Privy Council, the King government capitulated. Dispersal, not deportation, was now the government's policy. In early 1949, the British Columbia legislature, without dissent, voted to enfranchise Japanese Canadians. Pat Roy *et al.*, *Mutual Hostages: Canadians and Japanese during the Second World War* (Toronto, 1990), 166-91; Adachi, *The Enemy That Never Was*.

11. Cited in Susan Armstrong-Reid, "Canada's Role in the United Nations Relief and Rehabilitation Administration 1942-1947" (Ph.D. thesis, University of Toronto, 1982), 135.

12. *Ibid.*, 181-239; G. Woodbridge, *UNRRA, A History* (New York, 1950), I, 430-70; J. Vernant, *The Refugee and the Post War* (New Haven, 1952), 20-355.

13. In September, 1945, there were approximately one million Poles left in western Europe, plus some 170,000 Balts, 100,000 Yugoslavs, and 54,000 Soviet citizens. Mark Wyman, *DP Europe's Displaced Persons, 1945-1951* (Philadelphia, 1989), 69.

14. *Ibid.*, 55.

15. Under Allied guidelines, the DPs were to receive the equivalent of 2,000 calories a day. To prevent epidemics, UNRRA doctors carried out an active campaign against typhus, typhoid, and various skin diseases. *Ibid.*, 44-57.

16. Allied complicity in the forcible repatriation of millions of people, labelled Soviet citizens, has been discussed in a number of studies. See Mark Elliott, *Pawns of Yalta: Soviet Refugees and America's Role in Their Repatriation* (Urbana, Ill., 1982); Nikolai Tolstoy, *Victims of Yalta* (London, 1977).

17. By the time of the final vote on the constitution of the IRO in December, 1946, it was obvious that Communist bloc countries would not join the organization. Although the Canadian government deplored this exclusion, it accepted the IRO as "the best compromise that could be achieved." Armstrong-Reid, "Canada's Role," 310; Dirks, *Canada's Refugee Policy*, 99-163; Louise Holborn, *The International Refugee Organization: A Specialized Agency of the United Nations, Its History*

and Work, 1946-1952 (London, 1956), 29-46; *Debates*, 30 June 1947.

18. The ICR had been formed after the 1938 Evian Conference to care for Jews and other refugees from Fascism. The transition from UNRRA to the IRO was facilitated by the work of the London-based Preparatory Commission for IRO. In 1951, the United Nations High Commission for Refugees and the Intergovernmental Committee for European Immigration were established with the primary purpose of protecting and relocating European refugees. Malcolm Proudfoot, *European Refugees, 1939-1952: A Study in Forced Population Movement* (Evanston, Ill., 1956); Dirks, *Canada's Refugee Policy*, 176-89.

19. Gerhard Bassler, "German Immigration to Canada 1945-1950: Issues and Questions," *Annals*, German-Canadian Studies (Montreal, 1988), 168-79.

20. Dirks, *Canada's Refugee Policy*, 124-35.

21. In a House of Commons speech in December, 1945, Glen did, however, emphasize that no major revisions of Canada's immigration policies could be considered while the government was preoccupied with the repatriation and re-establishment of Canadian veterans. *Debates*, 1945, vol. 3, 3536; PCO, vol. 83, 1-50-2, J.A. Glen to cabinet, 15 October 1945.

22. The 4,527 Polish veterans sent to Canada in 1946 and 1947 were members of the Second Polish Corps that had fought as part of the British Eighth Army in the Italian campaign. After 1945 Britain had, because of its wartime commitments and labour shortages, accepted approximately 88,000 of these soldiers and their dependants. Vic Satzewich, *Racism and the incorporation of foreign labour: farm labour migration to Canada since 1945* (London, 1991), 85.

23. DEA, 1946, 358, R.G. Riddell (External) to Acting High Commissioner, G.B., 3 July 1946; *ibid.*, 377, H.H. Wrong, acting undersecretary, DEA, to Humphrey Mitchell, Minister of Labour, 14 May 1946.

24. *Ibid.*, 1946, 363, Aide-Memoire/Government of Great Britain of Canadian Govt., 26 July 1946; *ibid.*, 366, Wrong to Acting Prime Minister, 29 July 1946.

25. PCO, vol. 83, 1-50-2, Pearson to Secretary of State for External Affairs, 31 May 1946.

26. DEA, 1946, 353, Memorandum Second Division External, 3 January 1946; *ibid.*, 395, A. Fiderkiewicz to Secretary of State External Affairs, 11 September 1946; Pedro Cabric, Yugoslav chargé d'affaires, to Pearson, 13 November 1946.

27. Winnipeg *Tribune* 26 July 1946; *Globe and Mail*, 29 July 1946; Owen Sound *Sun Times*, 8 August 1946.

28. In June, 1946, by order-in-council, arrangements were made for the admission of 4,000 male Polish veterans to work on Canadian farms for two years under contract. After three more years in Canada they could apply for Canadian citizenship. Satzewich, *Racism*, 87.

29. Senate Standing Committee on Immigration and Labour (Senate Committee, 1946), Minutes of Proceedings and Evidence, 1946, Recommendations, August, 1946.

30. The 1944 convention of the TLC had accepted a resolution affirming "that a policy of accepting immigrants into this country be pursued as long as such a policy in no way adversely affects living standards or the welfare of the Canadian population." The CCL had adopted a similar position, with perhaps more opposition to the recruitment of skilled workers. Dirks, *Canada's Refugee Policy*, 129; Senate Committee, 1946, 219-22.

31. PCO, vol. 82, I-50, cabinet report, 12 August 1946.

32. Founded in October, 1938, the CNCR's mandate was "to coordinate all efforts in Canada on behalf of refugees, to promote public education and discussion of the refugee problem, and to maintain contact with the Canadian government." Dirks, *Canada's Refugee Policy*, 62.

33. Senate Committee, 1946, 3.

34. Satzewich, *Racism*, 85.

35. Until 1947, immigration to Australia had been almost exclusively from Great Britain and great emphasis had been placed on "the virtues of ethnic homogeneity." Post-war support for large-scale immigration from Europe was associated with concern that Australia's small population made the country vulnerable to military aggression and industrial stagnation. Egon Kunz, *Displaced Persons: Calwell's New Australians* (Sydney, 1988), 3-9.

36. Of the 170,000 admitted to Australia, the largest groups were Poles (63,394), Yugoslavs (23,543), Latvians (19,421), Ukrainians (14,464), Lithuanians (9,906), Czechs (9,142), and Estonians (5,329). Calwell took special care "to keep Jewish immigration within 15,000 limit set at Evian by the Lyons government, lest anti-semitic sentiments should jeopardize his immigration programme." *Ibid.*, 17, 45-47.

37. IRO officials were rather dismayed by the self-interest demonstrated by the Australians, who, it was claimed, "skimmed the cream and got the best immigrants"; in addition, it cost the IRO a lot to ship migrants to Australia. Canada's response was also viewed as essentially pragmatic, not humanitarian. *Ibid.*, 48; Wyman, *DP*, 190-204.

38. Abella and Troper, *None Is Too Many*, 200-40; Keenleyside, *Memoirs*, 289-309; NAC, Department of Labour Papers, vol. 280, Gardiner to Glen, 25 September 1947.

39. PCO, vol. 83, 1-50-7, Report of Dept. of Labour for the Cabinet Committee on Immigration, 1 October 1946.

40. According to Lewis Clark, American chargé d'affaires in Ottawa, King's speech was inconclusive: "While it broadens considerably the present narrow restrictions, it is not a very sweeping program, and is, in a practical sense, uncertain of any large accomplishment in the near future." U.S. National Archives, State Department Papers, 842.5500, Clark to State, May, 1947.

41. *Debates*, 1947, 2644-2646; Montreal *Star*, 15 August 1946.

42. On October 2, a report from the U.S. embassy in Ottawa commented on differences among Canadians on the immigration issue: "Canadians of British stock hope

particularly for Anglo-Saxon immigration, while the French do not want any immigration, as it would be difficult to get more French, and besides being basically isolationist, they do not wish to reduce the pressure of their tremendously growing numbers." State Department Papers, Clark to State, 18 October 1946; *Debates*, 1946, vol. 1, 532.

43. The U.S. embassy was also impressed with Drew's initiative and commented that it had "been generally acclaimed throughout the country, except in the province of Quebec." *Ibid.*, report, Harrington to State, 26 August 1947.

44. In May, 1947, the American embassy reported that Louis St. Laurent, Minister of External Affairs, was "fearful of opposition from labor groups to large increases of available cheap European labor." Particular reference was also made to the controversy in Quebec over the decision to allow Liberal MP Ludger Dionne "to recruit in person in Europe 100 textile workers for his mills." State Department Papers, Report of Julian Harrington, May, 1947.

45. Dirks, *Canada's Refugee Policy*, 147-60; Alan Green, *Immigration and the Post-War Canadian Economy* (Toronto, 1976), 20-35. In August, 1948, Hugh Keenleyside, deputy minister of immigration, did call upon the cabinet to initiate a "basic" revision of the Immigration Act. Hearings were conducted throughout 1951 and the Immigration Act was revised in 1952; however, very few changes were made in either the admissions standards or administrative procedures.

46. PCO, vol. 53, Report of the Dept. of Labour, 4 March 1947. On April 19, 1947, PC 1329 facilitated the use of contract immigrant labour; on May 20, 1947, the immediate entry of 5,000 workers under the Bulk Labour Program was authorized. *Ibid.*, I-50-D.

47. Keenleyside, *Memoirs*, 304.

48. Department of Labour, vol. 279, I-26-6, V.C. Wansborough, Executive Director, CMMA, to Deputy Minister Arthur MacNamara, 17 July 1947. Similar arrangements were made in other sectors of the economy. For example, in August, 1948, the Immigration-Labour Committee established the following quotas under the group movement:

Woods workers	3,750
Clothing	2,695
Domestics	12,500
Heavy labourers	3,041
Building construction	1,000
Hydro construction	2,000
Furniture Workers	35
Agricultural	3,360
Metal miners	2,722
Textile workers	311
Boot and shoe workers	100

49. *Ibid.*, vol. 282, 1-26-20-3, John Sharrer, employment adviser, Department of Labour, 4 April 1948. Sharrer gave an extended account of how the mining scheme had worked and concluded with the comment that "without exception mine managers expressed their entire satisfaction with the work performed by these new Canadians." In general, organized labour went along with the various refugee schemes. The only exceptions were left-wing unions such as the Canadian Mine, Mill and Smelter Workers, who charged that the DP workers were driving Canadian workers out of the mines. There was also some dissatisfaction from French-Canadian miners, most notably those located in the gold-mining district of western Quebec.

50. *Ibid.*, vol. 279, 1-26-6, W.K. Leadbeatter, chief resettlement officer, to Chief of IRO, Vienna, 28 September 1948; *ibid.*, Peter Gibson, chief, Dept. Re-Establishment, IRO, to Director of Resettlement, IRO Headquarters, Geneva, 2 October 1948.

51. The 1947 meeting of the Canadian Jewish Congress was informed by its president, Sam Bronfman, that Ottawa had agreed to accept 1,000 Jewish war orphans, close relatives of Canadian citizens, and selected Jewish workers in the needle and fur trades. Marrus, *Mr. Sam*, 332.

52. Department of Labour, vol. 280, 1-26-10-5, Saul Hayes, secretary, Canadian Jewish Congress, to Arthur MacNamara, 11 May 1950; Abella and Troper, *None Is Too Many*, 252.

53. *Ibid.*, 246.

54. Avery, *"Dangerous Foreigners,"* 1-38, 90-115; Palmer, *Patterns of Prejudice*, 90-122.

55. *Northern Miner*, 12 February 1948.

56. Department of Labour, vol. 280, 1-26-6, V. Wansborough to W.W. Dawson, Dept. Labour, 28 April 1948; *ibid.*, Dawson to IRO Resettlement Branch, 23 October 1950.

57. Marrus, *The Unwanted*, 332-33. Australia also gained notoriety with IRO officials because of its rigorous medical screening. They were particularly vigilant when interviewing Jewish applicants. As well, Jews tended to avoid Australia's bulk labour scheme "with its contract obligation, relying instead on assistance given by Jewish organizations ... to provide for their passage." Kunz, *Displaced Persons*, 45.

58. Australia adopted a similar system of ethnic preference. Arthur Calwell was insistent that the first group of 726 men and 114 women were Balts: 440 Lithuanians, 262 Latvians, and 138 Estonians. Kunz, *Displaced Persons*, 44-48.

59. Department of Labour, vol. 280, 1-26-10-5, W.W. Dawson to A. MacNamara, 11 May 1950; *ibid.*, 1-26-20, Report, John Sharrer, 4 April 1948.

60. *Ibid.*, vol. 277, 1-26-2-I, A.H. Brown to G.V. Haythorne, 7 June 1947.

61. *Ibid.*, vol. 280, 1-26-6, Wansborough to MacNamara, 25 August 1950.

62. Whitaker, *Double Standard*, 105-13.

63. PC 1373 of April, 1946, reaffirmed their exclusion as enemy aliens; PC 4850 of November, 1947, maintained the ban. Bassler, "German Immigration," 168-70.

64. Angelika Sauer, "A Matter of Domestic Policy? Canadian Immigration Policy and

the Admission of Germans, 1945-50," *Canadian Historical Review*, LXXIV, 2 (June, 1993), 226-63.

65. The CCCRR was formed in June, 1947, largely through the efforts of T.O.F. Herzer, general manager of the Canada Colonization Association, a CPR subsidiary. Herzer acted as an effective liaison between the Mennonite, Lutheran, and German Catholic and Baptist churches, on the one hand, and the Immigration Branch and the Department of External Affairs, on the other hand. He also benefited from the financial resources and placement facilities that organizations such as the Mennonite Central Committee could provide. The political support of Saskatchewan Liberal MP Walter Tucker was an additional asset. Bassler, "German Immigration," 170-74.

66. The CCCRR wisely concentrated first on family reunification and then moved into the bulk labour movement, concentrating on *volksdeutsche* who could be classified as farm workers and domestics. By 1948, with the assistance of the CPR, it was able to move most of its refugees on the *S.S. Beaverbrae*.

67. IB, vol. 784, 541-1, Robertson, Canadian High Commissioner, to Pearson, under-secretary of state for external affairs, 17 January 1948; *ibid.*, Keenleyside to Pearson, 11 February 1948. Significantly, one prominent Czech Canadian, Tom Bata, expressed concern that some of the Czech refugees would be Communist agents.

68. IB, vol. 856, 554-33, John Decore, MP, Vegreville, to C.E.S. Smith, Commissioner of Immigration, 17 October 1949. Basil Dmytrychyn, "The Nazis and the SS Volunteer Division 'Galicia,'" *American Slavic and East European Review*, XV, 1 (1956). Canada accepted about 40,000 Ukrainian displaced persons. See Lubomyr Luciuk, "Unintended Consequences in Refugee Resettlement: Post-War Ukrainian Refugee Immigration to Canada," *International Migration Review*, XX, 2 (1986), 467-82; Luciuk, "'Trouble All Around' – Ukrainian Canadians and Their Encounter with the Ukrainian Refugees of Europe, 1943-1951," paper presented at the Canadian Ethnic Studies Conference, Calgary, October, 1989.

69. IB, vol. 856, 554-33, Secretary, Ukrainian Canadian Committee, to Minister of Immigration, 28 September 1947; *ibid.*, Keenleyside to Jolliffe, 15 October 1947; Whitaker, *Double Standard*, 132-38.

70. Green, *Immigration and the Post-War Canadian Economy*, 20-30; RG 76, vol. 856, Arnold Heeney, PCO, to Laval Fortier, Minister of Citizenship and Immigration, 25 October 1950.

71. IB, 76, vol. 856, E.J. Bye, security officer, RCMP, to Canadian Immigration Mission, Karlsruhe, 18 December 1951. A number of recent books claim there was a deliberate decision to ignore the Nazi background of many of the refugees of this period. See Tom Bower, *Blind Eye to Murder: Britain, America and the Purging of Nazi Germany – A Pledge Betrayed* (London, 1981); John Loftus, *The Belarus Secret* (New York, 1982). More recently, in Canada the Commission of Inquiry on War Criminals (Ottawa, 1985) has provided extensive evidence of how former Nazis were able to gain entry into Canada between 1950 and 1954. Whitaker, *Double Standard*, 105-15.

72. CNCR, vol. 5, minutes of IRO meeting, 26 September 1947, report of Wing

Commander Innes; *ibid.*, A. Vermeulen, specialized resettlement officer, IRO, to Constance Haywood, 17 October 1947.

73. In Australia only about 25 per cent of the DP professionals eventually succeeded in being accredited. Kunz, *Displaced Persons*, 153-62.

74. Keenleyside, *Memoirs*, 306.

75. *Canadian Medical Association Journal*, 61 (July, 1949), 214.

76. Statement by Dr. A.D. Kelly, 22 September 1947, cited in Danys, *DP*, 253.

77. According to Egon Kunz, the Australian Medical Association used its "political power and influence . . . to arouse distrust and fear of foreign doctors in the public mind." It did not, however, oppose their being employed in the outback regions. Danys, *DP*, 254; Kunz, *Displaced Persons*, 186-88.

78. The actual screening of DP professionals was carried out by officials from External Affairs, Labour, Immigration, and Trade and Commerce.

79. IB, Report of Professional Refugees in IRO Assembly Centres, September, 1948; *ibid.*, Olga Hyka, specialist, IRO Resettlement Branch, to Keenleyside, 30 June 1949.

80. These views were actively presented by a number of the major Canadian civic organizations, most notably the Rotary Club and the Kiwanis, both of which indicated that they would be willing to sponsor some of these professional displaced persons. So, too, was the Canadian Jewish Congress in its June 3, 1949, submission to the Immigration Branch. "The Forgotten Elite."

81. Canada continued to drive a hard bargain, and the IRO was forced to pay both the ocean and inland transportation of the white-collar DPs.

82. In July, 1947, the Corporation of Professional Engineers of Quebec warned the Immigration Branch "that the foreign engineers, presently concerned, and the firms to which they are destined, might find themselves in an embarrassing position if the matter of qualifying for practice under the terms of our Act was overlooked or improperly timed." IB, vol. 279, 1-26-8, Marc Boyer, registrar, to C.E.S. Smith, commissioner of immigration, 9 July 1947.

83. IB, vol. 668, file C31120, pt. 1, minutes of an interdepartmental meeting, 5 July 1949; *ibid.*, Keenleyside to Dr. T.C. Routley, 6 July 1949. Report of A.L. Jolliffe of meeting, 4 August 1949, which discussed what role Canadian voluntary organizations such as the Rotary and Kiwanis would assume in helping to place DP professionals.

84. The Deschenes Commission of Inquiry on War Criminals (Ottawa, December 30, 1986) ordered an investigation of fifty-five of the seventy-one German scientists and technicians who had been admitted under the "Matchbox" recruitment program. Only one person was found who had Nazi connections. IB, vol. 649, B6737, pt. 1, B.R. Hayden, assistant director, Industrial Development Branch, Trade and Commerce, to P.T. Baldwin, assistant commissioner, Immigration Branch, 16 October 1950. Whitaker, *Double Standard*, 51-52, 104, 273-74; Bassler, "German Immigration," 176.

85. This criterion was evident when Mackenzie considered the case of physicist Dr. Kurt

Starke of the University of Heidelberg, who arrived in Canada in August, 1948, on a six-month minister's permit and almost immediately joined the McMaster University faculty. In the fall of 1950, while still on temporary permits, he became a research assistant in chemistry at the University of British Columbia. IB, vol. 649, B6737, pt. 1, Mackenzie to Pearson, 11 October 1946.

86. *Ibid.*, Mallory to Jolliffe, 6 November 1946. Eight Canadian companies had indicated an interest in securing German technicians. *Ibid.*, Heeney to J.A. Glen, 14 November 1946.

87. The University of British Columbia was one of the few Canadian universities to hire German scientists, largely through the efforts of Professor G.M. Schrum, head of its physics department, who argued that since "quite a number of German scientists have been taken to Great Britain, the United States, and, I believe, Australia . . . I feel that, if we can get men of the right calibre, this country would benefit very greatly by bringing them in as immigrants." *Ibid.*, G.M. Schrum to Keenleyside, 11 September 1948.

88. Robertson also explained that since many German scientists were "dissatisfied with their present employment," they might be "persuaded through German intermediaries acting for the Soviet Union to cross the inter-zonal frontier and be employed either in the Soviet Zone or in the Soviet Union." IB, vol. 649, B6737, pt. 1, Robertson to St. Laurent, 27 November 1946.

89. PCO, file 225-1-43, "Memorandum to the Privy Council Committee on Scientific and Industrial Research on Entry into Canada of Selected German Scientists," 29 April 1947. While the transportation costs of the German scientists were advanced by the Canadian government, these expenses were later recovered from "the eventual employer of the German's services." The employer also had the responsibility of finding "suitable accommodation" and had to submit monthly reports "in respect of the ability and conduct of German employees." If these reports were favourable, provisions could be made for the family of the scientist to come to Canada.

90. *Ibid.*, Circular from the German Department of the Board of Trade, enclosed in letter of R. Ridell, undersecretary of state for external affairs, to Jolliffe, 22 November 1946.

91. In 1945 the British and Americans had agreed to channel the applications of all German scientists through the Joint Staff Liaison in Washington so that competition for these men could be minimized. In some instances the competition was resolved "simply by spinning a coin." *Ibid.*, Robertson to St. Laurent, 27 November 1946.

92. Throughout 1947 and 1948 various Canadian trade unions, most notably the Mine, Mill and Smelter Workers and the United Packinghouse Workers of America, protested against "employers having rights of selection of immigrants to this country" and claiming that many of the DP workers were "fascists." IB, vol. 279, 1-26-8, K. Smith, secretary, MMSW, to Mackenzie King, 9 February 1948; *ibid.*, report, F.W. Smelts, Regional Advisory Board, Department of Labour, 26 February 1948.

93. *Ibid.*, Jolliffe to Commissioner S.T. Wood, 16 November 1946. *Ibid.*, Pearson to Jolliffe, 8 February 1947.

94. IB, vol. 649, B6737, pt. 1, Robertson to St. Laurent, 16 December 1946.

95. Tom Bower, *The Paperclip Conspiracy: The Battle for the Spoils and Secrets of Nazi Germany* (London, 1987), 273-312.

96. In 1948 there were allegations that one of the technicians, Robert Funke of Dusseldorf, had been a "No. 1 Nazi in the dental trade prior to the war." Subsequent investigations did not, however, provide any hard evidence and Funke was admitted. Gerhard Bassler has argued that "Canadian security screening procedures appear to have been more meticulous than that of other countries recruiting immigrants at that time." IB, vol. 279, I-26-8, Smith to Commissioner Wood, RCMP, 19 January 1948; Bassler, "German Immigration," 176.

97. IB, O.M. Solandt, Director-General of Defence Research, to undersecretary of state for external affairs, 14 February 1947.

98. Bower, *Paperclip Conspiracy*, 311.

99. Labour shortages were particularly acute in the western Canadian sugar-beet industry. Labour officials, however, believed that this industry offered a great opportunity for the newcomer to start as a farm hand, then save enough money to first rent and then buy a few acres of his own, and then eventually become an employer of farm labour himself. Danys, *DP*, 165.

100. Satzewich, *Racism*, 89.

101. In April, 1956, deputy minister Laval Fortier informed RCMP Commissioner L. Nicholson that with the shortage of farm workers "the Minister has asked the Immigration branch to do whatever may be possible to . . . secure our selection abroad of farm workers. Germans from the East Zone are one of the main sources. . . . Although the delays in obtaining clearance for security on persons coming from West Germany has been shortened considerably, there is still a delay of a few weeks and the Minister thought it would be advisable to waive security in those cases." Danys, *DP*, 92; Satzewich, *Racism*, 104.

102. Protestant domestics were given preference over Catholics, while Jewish domestics were "considered unsuitable because they had not traditionally worked as domestics." Barber, *Immigrant Domestic Servants in Canada*, 19-22; Danys, *DP*, 133-53.

103. Kunz, *Displaced Persons*, 23, 133.

104. *Ibid.*, 53; Wyman, *DP*, 108-30.

105. Department of Labour, vol. 282, I-26-2-3, enclosed in petition of DP workers in St. Paul d'Ermite, Quebec, 7 January 1952.

106. CNCR, vol. 5, Montreal branch to Hon. Paul Martin, 21 July 1948.

107. *Ibid.*, Constance Hayward to King, 7 October 1950.

108. Much the same thing happened in Australia, where the term "DP" joined other traditional xenophobic epithets such as "pommy," "scowegian," and "reffo." As in Canada, however, many Australians combatted this bigotry and criticized

the government for its perpetuation of the contract system. Kunz, *Displaced Persons*, 166.

109. Department of Labour, vol. 280, 1-26-10-9, Keenleyside to MacNamara, 28 March 1949; *ibid.*, 1-26-6, Wansborough to MacNamara, 15 December 1950.

110. Green, *Immigration and the Post-War Economy*, 20-30.

Chapter Eight

1. Freda Hawkins, *Canada and Immigration: Public Policy and Public Concern*, 2nd edition (Montreal, 1988), 92-93.

2. *Ibid.*, 95; *Debates*, vol. 3, 1949, 2284-97.

3. This was done by order-in-council, September 14, 1950 (PC 4364); Japanese remained, however, as enemy aliens until July, 1952.

4. But the numbers were minuscule: 150 for India, 100 for Pakistan, and forty for Ceylon.

5. In 1955-56 the Immigration Branch had approximately 2,054 employees; of these, 417 were stationed abroad. Hawkins, *Canada and Immigration*, 246; D. Corbett, *Canada's Immigration Policy* (Toronto, 1957), 92.

6. Recruitment of new staff was done on the basis of a Grade 12 education, with war service being an important asset. Many within the Branch criticized the failure to establish an immigration foreign service career officer similar to those developed by External Affairs. But the immigration foreign service officers who staffed the European visa offices did not enjoy much prestige with their counterparts in External Affairs or Trade and Commerce.

7. Hawkins, *Canada and Immigration*, 253.

8. Corbett, *Immigration Policy*, 101.

9. Statutes of Canada, Immigration Act of 1952, section 61; Corbett, *Immigration Policy*, 70.

10. Some ministers, notably J.W. Pickersgill, felt that the discretionary powers meant an "inexorable flow of individual cases across the Minister's desk preventing constructive administrative action." Hawkins, *Canada and Immigration*, 103.

11. *Debates*, 26 June 1954, 6787-6803.

12. Hawkins, *Canada and Immigration*, 106.

13. *Debates*, 28 February 1955. In June, 1954, Davie Fulton and George Drew of the Progressive Conservative Party and M.J. Coldwell of the CCF had attacked the government's immigration policy. *Ibid.*, 26 June 1954, 6787-6802.

14. Howard Adelman, "Canadian Refugee Policy in the Post-war Era," in Adelman, ed., *Refugee Policy: Canada and the United States* (Toronto, 1991), 190.

15. *Ibid.*, 192.

16. There was little opposition to this importation of a high percentage of skilled and

professional refugees, or to the decision by the federal government to subsidize their transportation costs and initial adjustment expenses. *Ibid.*, 244.

17. Whitaker, *Double Standard*, 85.

18. J.W. Pickersgill, *My Years with Louis St. Laurent: a political memoir* (Toronto, 1975), 245.

19. Under the Act persons who had been associated "at any time" with organizations "likely to engage in espionage, sabotage or any other subversive activity" were prevented from entering Canada. *Ibid.*, 240-41; Whitaker, *Double Standard*, 135.

20. The Interdepartmental Committee, set up in 1951 to review cases the RCMP felt were security risks, discriminated against eastern European immigrants. Of the 1,874 applications under review, 83 per cent of them were from this region. Of these, 48 per cent were rejected. Although the government temporarily opened the gates to Czechoslovakian refugees in 1968, entry from eastern Europe still remained difficult. Whitaker, *Double Standard*, 83-84.

21. The Bureau of Immigration and Naturalization was also busy keeping Canadian "leftists" out of the United States. During the 1950s those on the prohibited list included filmmaker John Grierson, writer Farley Mowat, and academic Pierre Elliott Trudeau. Whitaker, *Double Standard*, 150-98.

22. This ban was incorporated into the 1952 Act. By the early 1960s the RCMP had files on over 9,000 suspected homosexuals in the country. *Ibid.*, 37; Philip Girard, "From Subversion to Liberation: Homosexuals and the Immigration Act 1952-1977," *Canadian Journal of Law and Society*, 2 (1987), 3-12; Girard, "The Queer Career of Homosexual Security Vetting in Cold-War Canada," *Canadian Historical Review* (forthcoming).

23. The Banks case was the focus of a rousing debate in the House of Commons in June, 1954, when George Drew asked why a convicted felon, who had "already broken our laws," should be allowed to remain in Canada. Drew also made reference to an exposé of Banks's activity by journalist Blair Fraser in a March 15, 1952, article in *Maclean's* magazine. *Debates*, 26 June 1954, 6799-6802.

24. Exposure of this traffic was carried out most extensively by U.S. authorities. Hawkins, *Canada and Immigration*, 132.

25. Pickersgill had also been concerned that some of these Chinese illegals were "secret agents" who would be involved in espionage or subversive work in Canada and the United States. The RCMP found no evidence to validate this suspicion. In 1955 he was criticized in the House of Commons by Conservatives Davie Fulton and John Diefenbaker for his anti-Chinese policies. *Ibid.*, 234.

26. This aroused intense antagonism within Canada's Chinese communities, especially when European illegals were not subject to such close scrutiny. *Ibid.*, 131-34.

27. Franca Iacovetta, *Such Hardworking People: Italian Immigrants in Postwar Toronto* (Montreal, 1992), 48.

28. Immigration authorities recognized that they could not prevent the entry of

unmarried children, spouses/fiancées, parents, or orphaned nieces or nephews; their target was married children and other family members. Between December, 1955, and February, 1959, the backlog had increased from 77,158 to 131,787 overall, with the number from Italy expanding from 12,000 to about 63,000. *Ibid.*, 50; Valerie Knowles, *Strangers at Our Gates: Canadian Immigration and Immigration Policy, 1540-1990* (Toronto, 1992), 140.

29. For Italian and Greek sponsored immigrants, more than 54 per cent were distant relatives; only 2.4 per cent in the case of Italy, and 5.3 per cent in the case of Greece, met the occupational standards. The proportion of unskilled workers from Italy was 43.2 per cent, from Portugal 22.7 per cent, from Greece 6.6 per cent, and for all other countries 5.3 per cent. Hawkins, *Canada and Immigration*, 48.

30. Fairclough, elected as a Conservative in Hamilton in the 1957 election, served as Minister of Citizenship and Immigration from May, 1958, to August, 1962.

31. Freda Hawkins claims that despite the Pickersgill-Fairclough confrontation there was no fundamental difference in the immigration policies of the St. Laurent and Diefenbaker governments. "Whichever party was in power was obliged to do something about the escalation of the sponsored movement." Hawkins, *Canada and Immigration*, 124-27.

32. Pickersgill claimed that the restriction came about "when the government realized that more people of Italian origin than people from the United Kingdom came in last year, and they got in a panic." He also alleged that the hidden agenda was to import more skilled workers. This charge helped mobilize trade union opposition to the order-in-council and arouse the ire of immigration boosters such as the Toronto *Globe and Mail*, which charged that Canadians "rattle around in an empty country while the world's masses cry for living room." A third criticism was the secrecy surrounding the changes. *Debates*, 1959, 2711; Hawkins, *Canada and Immigration*, 125; Knowles, *Strangers*, 145.

33. Fairclough took Pickersgill to task for not having immigration processing facilities in Spain, Turkey, Mexico, and the countries of Central and South America. *Debates*, 1959, 2934.

34. The author of this report was George Davidson, former director of the Canadian Welfare Council, and deputy minister of DCI after 1960. Richard Bell, MP for Ottawa, presided over efforts to make the department's operation more racially inclusive. He did not, however, introduce legislation for a new Immigration Act. Hawkins, *Canada and Immigration*, 128-31.

35. Iacovetta, *Hardworking People*, 33-51.

36. *The Migration of Professional Workers Into and Out of Canada, 1946-1960*, Economics and Research Branch, Department of Labour (Ottawa, 1961), 1, 10.

37. The influx of British professionals peaked in 1956-57 after the Suez Crisis, when British professionals were 62.2 per cent of the total. Most of the Hungarian professionals also came at this time, as a result of the abortive 1956 uprising. Almost all of the Polish professionals entered the country as displaced persons. The high point for

German professionals was in 1951, when they were 11.9 per cent of the total. Professionals from the United States ranged from a high of 36.5 per cent in 1946 to a low of 7.2 per cent in 1957. *Ibid.*, 13-15.

38. Much was made of the fact that the great influx of immigrant professionals after 1951 "met exactly a need for increasing the number of professionals because of economic expansion . . . and that the growing demand . . . coincided with the decline in Canada of university graduations. This decline was attributable to . . . the virtual disappearance of the veteran graduate . . . and a diminished college-age population, during these years, that had originated from a fall in the birth rate in the 1930's." *Ibid.*, 45.

39. *Ibid.*, 11, 45.

40. This report, *Engineering and Scientific Manpower Resources in Canada: Their Earnings, Employment and Education, 1957*, Department of Labour (Ottawa, 1959), provided a useful data base for assessing comparative professional salaries in Canada and the United States.

41. Higher incomes in the U.S. were regarded as the most important incentive. *The Migration of Professional Workers*, 25. Since the Canadian Immigration Branch did not keep emigration figures, most statistics were drawn from U.S. census reports and from specialized surveys conducted by the National Research Council and the Department of Labour. In the academic year 1955-56 there were 4,900 Canadian graduates; 5,379 in 1956-57; 5,271 in 1957-58; 5,430 in 1958-59; and 5,691 in 1959-60. In addition, the Department of Labour circulated its list of Canadian students among the major employers of professional graduates in Canada, as well as inviting graduating students to return to Canada. *Ibid.*, 26-32.

42. Between 1953 and 1960, 5,013 American immigrants indicated manager as their intended occupation compared with 3,412 who emigrated from Great Britain. *Ibid.*, 40.

43. *Ibid.*, 45.

44. In the case of Germany, for instance, the number of professionals declined from a high of 640 in 1952 to 304 in 1960. Although an increase in the number of Canadian-trained professionals was predicted, the importance of maintaining a steady supply of foreign-trained professionals was emphasized, if only to replace those Canadians seeking better opportunities in the United States. *Ibid.*, 14, 45.

45. See Green, *Immigration and the Post-War Canadian Economy*, 169, 187.

46. Green's figures for his rest-of-the-world professional category showed an average influx of 600 during the 1950s to 3,200 by the late 1960s. He also suggested, however, that in a competition for Asian health professionals Canada "comes out second best to the United States." *Ibid.*, 223, 206.

47. Economic Council of Canada, First Annual Review, *Economic Goals for Canada to 1970* (Ottawa, 1964), 160.

48. Born and educated in England, Kent had been general editor of the *Winnipeg Free Press* between 1954 and 1959; during the next seven years he worked as a Liberal Party organizer, consultant, and speech writer. Tom Kent, *A Public Purpose: An*

Experience of Liberal Opposition and Canadian Government (Montreal, 1988).

49. *Ibid.*, 407.

50. Kent also claimed that the existing sponsorship system was biased against immigrants from Asia and the Americas who could sponsor fewer family members. Nor did British or American immigrants extensively utilize the sponsorship system. *Ibid.*, 410-11.

51. *White Paper on Immigration* (October, 1966), 5-7.

52. Special Joint Committee on Immigration, Hearings, 16 February 1967, 319.

53. *White Paper*, 7, 11-15.

54. There was also a proposal to fingerprint immigrants suspected of illegal entry despite "a natural repugnance to this type of identification." *Ibid.*, 32.

55. The White Paper adopted a more enlightened approach to medical disabilities than had been the case with the 1952 Act, and proposed that the blanket exclusion of homosexuals, beggars, vagrants, or alcoholics "by virtue simply of their personal failings" be abolished. *Ibid.*, 26.

56. Reference was also made for the need to screen more effectively the approximately 34 million non-immigrants who entered the country annually, especially "the abnormally large number of visitors here who have sought immigrant status." *Ibid.*, 21-22.

57. *Ibid.*, 34-35.

58. Nor did Marchand seem impressed when told that Greek and Italian organizations were angry that the White Paper was "based upon assumptions as to the difficulties of assimilation and not based upon actual studies of the employability of those who come as sponsored immigrants but perhaps without skills." Special Joint Committee on Immigration, Hearings, 17 November 1966, 18-19.

59. Marchand explained that the small number of French immigrants was due to three factors: their reluctance to leave France, the opposition of the French government, and the greater appeal of the United States. *Ibid.*, 26.

60. The CNTU made specific reference to the 1946-47 case involving about 100 Polish refugee women who were exploited by a textile plant owner in Quebec, who was also the Liberal MP for Beauce. *Ibid.*, 22 February 1967, 457-75, 488-94.

61. The CLC was particularly critical of the continued refusal of Canadian employers to engage in job-training and their proclivity to recruit "a ready supply of already trained workers whose training has occurred elsewhere at someone's else's expense." *Ibid.*, 2 March 1967, 616-45.

62. *Ibid.*, 620, 625.

63. Among its members were some of the most powerful companies in the country – Algoma Steel, Cominco, Falconbridge, Inco, Hollinger, Noranda, and Rio Algom.

64. Being well educated, MAC representatives argued, was usually a liability in becoming a good miner since most of the work was repetitive and only required "strength, endurance, manual dexterity and the proper attitude." *Ibid.*, 16 February 1967, 269.

65. The MAC also claimed that its members had tried to use native Canadians, but were hampered by the fact that "the average Indian thinks he would be foolish to work like

whites for six days a week when he can get a cheque from welfare without doing any work." *Ibid.*, 268-71.

66. Byrne also claimed that during the past year his company had employed "30 landed immigrants representing about 12 different nationalities, and 90 per cent of them had never seen a mine and knew nothing about it." Even more important, he added, was that "90 per cent are still with us after one year"; the combination of high wages and low cost of living meant that even "the lowest paid employee can save $1,800 a year." *Ibid.*, 269.

67. The MAC gave assurances that its members were prepared to co-operate with federal labour and immigration officials in the selection of immigrant miners, to provide on-job training, to give language training, "and generally to assist the immigrant to adapt himself to his new environment." *Ibid.*, 320.

68. The Federation also claimed that its members had attempted to hire Aboriginal workers, but with limited success since "not a single Indian beet worker employed during the 1954-66 period has moved to the crop share category to say nothing of tenant or owner group." *Ibid.*, 18 April 1967, 965.

69. Spivak charged that the province had actually been cheated by Ottawa out of at least 10,000 immigrant workers who were badly needed in the mining and garment industries. He, too, sought to explain why more Aboriginal workers were not employed in the northern extractive industries.

70. The NDP immigration critic, David Orlikow (Winnipeg North), also suggested more Canadian workers would be attracted to Manitoba's mining and garment industries if the companies paid decent wages and offered better working conditions. *Ibid.*, 213-16.

71. Another supporter was the Canadian Chamber of Commerce, which endorsed the educational criteria and urged "that efforts be made to attract and secure immigrants with special skills by offering employment opportunities to be arranged through direct contacts with Canadian employers, assisted whenever possible, by Chambers of Commerce and Boards of Trade and other community organizations." *Ibid.*, 23 February 1967, 523.

72. *Ibid.*, 16 February 1967.

73. *Ibid.*, 21 March 1967, 811. Discussion of immigration issues, especially the licensing and professional status of foreign-trained doctors, was quite pronounced in the *Canadian Medical Association Journal* throughout 1966-67. Dr. Leslie Iffy, a Budapest-trained specialist in obstetrics and gynecology, was one of the most strident critics of the "old boy" discrimination against foreign-trained doctors, a practice he equated with the "ancient Egyptian priest-physicians, whose rules forbade the disclosure of medical knowledge to persons outside their ranks." *Canadian Medical Association Journal*, 96 (1967), 286, 487.

74. The CMA brief also noted that between 1960 and 1964 some 2,230 medical immigrants had entered the country, while during the same period 1,975 foreign-trained medical doctors had been certified. Of these, 57 per cent came from Britain, 4 per

cent from the United States, and 37 per cent from other countries. Special Joint Committee, Hearings, 21 March 1967, 812, 842.

75. Dr. Roy claimed that doctors from the Philippines were most likely to use Canada as a "stepping stone to the States." *Ibid.*

76. Statement by Saul Hayes, vice-president, CJC. *Ibid.*, 22 February 1967, 407. According to Hayes, about 76,000 Jewish immigrants had entered Canada since 1945.

77. Nor was the CJC impressed with the White Paper's reference to a literacy standard, which, it claimed, had an unfortunate legacy since countries such as Australia had used such measures as "an attempt to keep out Asiatics." It also argued that Jewish immigrants, victimized by Nazi or Soviet oppression, should receive special consideration. *Ibid.*, 408.

78. Saul Hayes made specific reference to six individuals who "were guilty of the atrocities in connection with the death camps in Latvia." *Ibid.*, 408, 418.

79. Briefs by the Canadian Lithuanian Community, the Canadian Hungarian Federation, and the Estonian Central Council in Canada were quite similar, although each had its own special agenda.

80. Two Polish organizations presented briefs: the Canadian Polish Congress and the Association of Polish Engineers in Canada. Former group captain Stefan Sznuk of the Polish Air Force, who had come to Canada in 1941 as head of the Polish military and air mission, presented his own personal brief. *Ibid.*, 13 March 1967, 681-83; 11 April 1967, 899.

81. Both the Order of the Sons of Italy of Ontario and the Italian Immigrant Aid Society criticized the educational criteria and the nebulous and unwieldy concept of "adaptability." In their opinion, the White Paper intended to undermine the sponsorship system and bring "a very heavy decline" in the number of Italian immigrants. *Ibid.*, 16 March 1967, 728, 773, 731.

82. Di Lorenzo came to Canada during the 1950s. He was a strong opponent of Canadian trade unions that, he claimed, would impede occupational mobility and force the Italian immigrant to remain "a labourer for the rest of his life." *Ibid.*, 701-09.

83. The Alliance had been chartered in September, 1952. Ernst Zuendel (Zundel), a post-war immigrant from Germany who would gain notoriety in the 1980s as a publisher of neo-Nazi tracts, presented a private brief in which he deplored the "veritable wave of anti-German sentiment expressed by the news media, radio, television and especially the film industry." *Ibid.*, 23 February 1967, 567.

84. *Ibid.*, 16 March 1967, 770.

85. Reference was made to the fact that the level of Chinese immigration still remained low: 876 in 1963, 1,571 in 1964, and 3,200 in 1965. *Ibid.*, Submission of the Mon Sheong Foundation of Toronto, 21 March 1967, 831-37. It was also pointed out that many Canadian organizations, particularly trade unions, were still reluctant to "accept people of Chinese origin."

86. There was obvious bitterness about the 1962 British immigration restrictions. *Ibid.*, 24 February 1967, 582. All of the groups who appeared spoke on behalf of the 10,000

West Indians in Montreal. The Negro Citizenship Association, created in 1952, was the oldest; the Jamaica Association was founded in 1962 and the Trinidad/Tobago Association three years later.

87. It was estimated that of 2,345 Caribbean immigrants who came in 1965 about 561 were professionals, and 618 were white-collar workers. Figures were also cited to show that in 1965 there were six times more West Indian immigrant professionals than Greeks, despite the fact that the Greek immigration level was higher. *Ibid.*, 574-76.

88. *Ibid.*, 582.

89. *Ibid.*, 17 February 1967, 333.

90. The IIMT took particular exception to the disparity in the standards of the citizenship courts, which undermined the "value and privilege attached to Canadian citizenship," and reported that in 1966 it had provided services to over 51,900 new Canadians, of whom 900 received intensive counselling, 12,000 participated in specialized group activities, and 7,000 were given language training. *Ibid.*, 333, 335-37, 379.

91. There was, however, quite a range of opinion between these organizations. Some were more inclined toward the IIMT emphasis on social and cultural integration; others endorsed a more pluralistic approach.

92. Kent, *Public Purpose*, 410. In addition, ten points were awarded for competence in English and French, with another ten if the applicant had arranged employment. Five points were given if the applicant went to a region of high general unemployment and another five if he/she had a sponsor. Independent immigrants were admitted if they achieved fifty points. More distant relatives were now placed in a new nominated class and given special concessions; they had to meet fewer occupational requirements and were given bonus marks if their nominator was a close relative and a Canadian citizen.

93. *Ibid.*, 411-13.

94. *Report of the Royal Commission on Security* (abridged) (Ottawa, June, 1969), 45-49.

95. Under the Citizenship Act of 1952, non-British applicants were required to meet a number of standards, including security clearance. Those rejected on security grounds had no access to the Citizenship Appeal Board. The Registrar of Canadian Citizenship of the Department of Secretary of State was duly informed of the decision. *Ibid.*, 54-57.

96. Since passports were only issued to native-born and naturalized Canadians the Commission called for continued vigilance especially since "hostile intelligence services have concentrated on the acquisition of Canadian documentation because of its relative ease of procurement." The Commission did, however, concede that Communist intelligence services had various ways of getting passports other than through the time-consuming citizenship route. *Ibid.*, 54-61.

97. To avoid appearing discriminatory, the Commission recommended that all prospective immigrants be fingerprinted. It also urged a tough policy toward visitors who

applied for landed immigrant status, thereby avoiding security checks in their country of origin. *Ibid.*, 47-49.

98. Hawkins, *Canada and Immigration*, 46.

99. In 1970 approximately 45,000 visitors to Canada applied for landed immigrant status, or one-sixth of all applicants. Between January and August, 1972, there was an average of 4,500 applicants per month; by October, this number arrived at Toronto International Airport one weekend. *Ibid.*, 46.

100. *Ibid.*, 47, 48. At the end of the program, about 39,000 people from 150 different countries were granted landed immigrant status.

101. By 1984 the number of workers coming under the Employment Authorization Program increased to 143,979, compared to only 38,500 workers who arrived as immigrants. Daniel Kubat, ed., *The Politics of Migration Policies: The First World in the 1970s* (New York, 1979), 30; B. Singh Bolaria and Peter Li, *Racial Oppression in Canada*, second edition (Toronto, 1988), 226-32.

102. Hawkins, *Canada and Immigration*, 52.

103. *Immigration Policy Perspectives* (Ottawa, 1974), 59-60.

104. *Debates*, 3 February 1975, 2819.

105. Between 1968 and 1973 only 29 per cent of the nominated class were classified as skilled. *Immigration Policy Perspectives*, 23, 34.

106. The Canadian migrant worker system was deemed superior to the European guest worker system, where millions of immigrants occupied jobs "that citizens of these nations regard as 'undesirable,'" and which led to "a heavy toll of social distress and antagonism." In contrast, the Canadian system was praised for its recruitment process, which required the DMI to demonstrate that no Canadian-born or landed immigrant workers were available before an employment visa was issued. *The Immigration Program*, vol. 2, Green Paper (Ottawa, 1974), 186-89.

107. *Ibid.*, 32.

108. In 1968 the Quebec government created its own Department of Immigration "with both recruitment and settlement functions." According to the Green Paper, this initiative was directly related to the decline in the birth rate of the province and to the "direct tendency of immigrants to become assimilated within the anglophone rather than the francophone community." *Ibid.*, 56.

109. Brief reference was also made to the controversy over the brain drain, especially the concern of Third World Countries "about the loss of trained people whose talents their societies may desperately require." The Report recommended that both the Department of Manpower and Immigration and the Canadian International Development Agency ensure that Canadian immigration policies did not subvert Canada's international social development programs. *Ibid.*, 47-70.

110. According to Freda Hawkins the presentation of the Green Paper was flawed for several reasons: the lack of sensitivity by senior DMI officials "to immigration's special sensitivities"; the failure to use either academic experts or the DMI Advisory

Council; and Robert Andras's determination to introduce the bill to the House of Commons as quickly as possible. *Canada and Immigration*, 52.

111. Peter Dobell and Susan d'Acquino of the Parliamentary Centre in Foreign Affairs and Foreign Trade praised the Committee for its collective ability, cohesiveness, and commitment in a special study, *The Special Joint Committee on Immigration Policy 1975: An Exercise in Participatory Democracy, Behind the Headlines* (Toronto, 1976).

112. The response of the provinces to the federal invitation to participate in bilateral or multilateral discussion on future population trends was generally one of indifference; only Quebec and Alberta gave any positive response. Hawkins, *Canada and Immigration*, 68-71.

113. Canada, Statutes of 1976-77, C-52, Immigration Act, 1976, 1197-98. By 1985 subsection (f) had been changed to read: "that do not discriminate in a manner inconsistent with the *Canadian Charter of Rights and Freedoms.*" Revised Statutes 1985 (Ottawa, 1989), 7-8.

114. Freda Hawkins, *Critical Years in Immigration: Canada and Australia Compared* (Montreal and Kingston, 1989), 64-74.

115. Between 1980 and 1984 family class immigrants averaged 50,000 or about 50 per cent of the total; but when other dependants were added, the total usually exceeded 60 per cent. Hawkins, *Canada and Immigration*, 87.

116. The new policy excluded many more immigrants from the points system; it also placed more emphasis on practical training and experience rather than on formal education. On the positive side, it established designated occupations and regions to meet specific shortages of skilled labour. The new provisions also reduced the importance of the screening process or personal assessment by overseas immigration officers. Hawkins, *Critical Years*, 77-78.

117. The definition of the 1951 UN Convention and its 1967 Protocol were adopted in section 2(1) of the Act, the designated class in section 6(2). The three categories of designated classes were political prisoners and oppressed persons (which in 1978 specified refugees from four Latin American countries – Chile, El Salvador, Guatemala, and Uruguay), the self-exiled persons, and Vietnamese refugees. The first category had to prove they had been detained, had been subject to some form of penal control, or have "a well founded fear of persecution." The second category, the self-exiles, dealt primarily with those fleeing from Communist countries; they did not have to establish "a well founded fear of persecution." The Vietnamese refugees only had to show that they left their country after April 30, 1975.

118. In 1980-81, for example, it was projected that 60,000 Vietnamese refugees would be admitted, of whom 26,000 would be government assisted and 34,000 privately sponsored. Hawkins, *Critical Years*, 185.

119. Once an applicant claimed refugee status the case was reviewed by the Minister, by the Refugee Status Advisory Committee, by the Special Review Committee, by the

Immigration Appeal Board, and, possibly, by the Federal Court of Appeal. *Ibid.*, 193.

120. House of Commons, Minutes and Proceedings and Evidence of the Standing Committee on Labour, Manpower and Immigration, Respecting Bill C-27, An Act to establish the Department of Employment and Immigration, the Canada Employment and Immigration Commission and the Canada Employment and Immigration Advisory Council, to amend the Unemployment Insurance Act, 1971, and to amend other statutes in consequence thereof. Bill C-24, "An Act Respecting Immigration to Canada."

121. Standing Committee on Labour, 2 June 1977, 62-67.

122. The Canadian mining companies claimed they "had to interview 22,000 people a year to get 2,000," and that very poor results were achieved in recruiting miners from Atlantic Canada: "The retention rate was nil. They came to the mining area, they worked . . . a few days to a few weeks . . . and then returned home." *Ibid.*, 24 May 1977, 44.

123. Sugar-beet growers, vegetable farmers, and tobacco interests were, however, satisfied that the flow of temporary workers from the West Indies and Mexico under Employment Visa Regulations met most of their needs. *Ibid.*, 15 June 1977, 36-17.

124. The CLC insisted on the importance of developing a comprehensive set of guidelines to govern the selection and movement of temporary workers in Canada. "Submission by the Canadian Labour Congress to the Standing Committee on Labour, Manpower and Immigration on Bill C-24, An Act Respecting Immigration to Canada," 15 June 1977, 36A 1-11.

125. Standing Committee on Labour, 7 June 1977, 28-29.

126. The Alliance was formed in 1975 in response to "a rising tide of aggressive behaviour" against visible minorities in Toronto. It was represented by Dr. Wilson Head, a long-time African-Canadian activist, and by Mrs. Sharon Lax. *Ibid.*, 6 June 1977, 4-38, 31A, 1-5.

127. Reference was also made to the scarcity of immigration officers of visible minority background, particularly at high-volume reception centres such as Pearson International Airport. *Ibid.*, 31, 17.

128. Dr. Head mentioned the results of a local poll indicating that only 7 per cent of the black population of Toronto preferred to live in the U.S. rather than in Canada. *Ibid.*, 31, 24-26.

129. Committee member MacDonald tried to mute this charge by suggesting that Canada, unlike the United States, had little experience in living in "a kind of multi-racial society" and that the social implications of new immigration patterns had not received sufficient public debate in English Canada. *Ibid.*, 31, 26.

130. In many ways it was unfortunate that Employment and Immigration was only one of seven groups under the Commission and that the new Canadian Employment and Immigration Advisory Council was less informed and influential than its predecessor. In addition, the removal of the Foreign Immigration Branch and its placement

with External Affairs adversely affected both planning and morale. Hawkins, *Critical Years*, 76-82.

131. Under the 1978 Regulations the general structure of the points system remained intact. But there was much less emphasis on formal education (a decline from 20 to 12 points) and an increase in vocational training and experience to 23 points. Extra points were also awarded for "designated occupations" and for going to "designated areas." The subjective assessment of the overseas immigration officer about the personal suitability of the candidate was further reduced. *Ibid.*, 78.

132. There were four ministers between 1976 and 1984: Bud Cullen (September, 1976-June, 1979), Ron Atkey (June, 1979-March, 1980), Lloyd Axworthy (March, 1980-August, 1983), John Roberts (August, 1983-September, 1984). Despite some instances of vacillation, Axworthy was the most enterprising and successful in this period.

133. Hawkins, *Critical Years*, 86.

134. The sample was based on 2,036 immigrants who had responded to all four surveys; their average age was twenty-nine, and average level of education was 11.4 years. Thirty-nine per cent of the sample were in the managerial, professional, and technical occupations. By the end of their third year in Canada, 69 per cent were in the occupations they intended to follow when they arrived in Canada. *Three Years in Canada: First report of the longitudinal survey on the economic and social adaptation of immigrants* (Ottawa, 1974), 32, 139-41.

135. The study also showed that during the first year, nominated immigrants had an unemployment level two and a half times higher than the independent group. After three years, however, the level of unemployment was virtually the same for each group; it was also comparable to the Canadian average. About 90 per cent of the sample felt that they had been well accepted in their new Canadian environment. *Ibid.*, 6-12.

136. T. John Samuel, *Family Class Immigrants to Canada, 1981-1984: Labour Force Activity Aspects*, Population Working Paper No. 5, 1-20. This study was based on a sample of 1,400 respondents who had come to Canada between 1981 and 1984.

137. *Ibid.*, 12.

138. Heln Buckley and Soren Nielsen, Strategic Planning and Research Division, *Immigration and the Canadian Labour Market*, 26 April 1976, 12-15. Overall, the number of professionals in the Canadian labour force expanded from 6 per cent in 1949 to almost 15 per cent by 1974.

139. The flow of workers across the U.S.-Canada boundary was the focus of a DEI study that showed that in 1980 there were 843,000 Canadian-born residents in the United States, or 3.5 per cent of the 1981 population of Canada. In contrast, the number of American-born in Canada was 312,000, or 1.3 per cent of the Canadian total. Roderic Beaujot and Peter Rappak, "Emigration from Canada: its importance and interpretation," Population Working Paper No. 4, Employment and Immigration (Ottawa, 1987), 10, 35, 57.

140. The report also noted that three occupations – physicians (19 per cent), mechanical engineers (18 per cent), and architects (15 per cent) – continued their consistently high foreign-born representation between 1961 and 1971. In the case of university teachers, this decade saw spectacular increase in the number of foreign-born; by 1971 they represented 32 per cent of the total. *Ibid.*, 23-25.

141. Aside from the controversy over American war resisters in Canada during the late 1960s, there has been little discussion about the some 300,000 American-born in Canada prior to 1978. The only exception was the controversy over the number of American-born academics teaching in Canadian universities. Monica Boyd, "The American Emigrant in Canada: Trends and Consequences," *International Migration Review*, XV, 4 (Winter, 1981), 651.

142. Canadian nurses were also being recruited in large numbers. *CMA Journal*, May 21, 1977, 116; *ibid.*, January 21, 1978, 175.

143. One of these Canadian transplants, Dr. Paul Leroux, formerly an obstetrician-gynecologist in Cornwall, Ontario, expressed the attitudes of many when asked whether he felt any sense of obligation to the Canadian government and taxpayer who helped finance his education. "Every time I received an OHIP cheque," he wrote, "I felt that I had more than compensated.... I owe them nothing. Not one iota." *CMA Journal* (vol. 116), 1171, 1309.

144. The AMI, along with its competitors, Hospital Corporation of America, American Medicorps, Humana, and Medenco, exploited the fact that on average American medical incomes were about $20,000 higher than in Canada. *Ibid.*, 118 (1978), 176, 980.

145. U.S. statistics indicated that 222 physicians migrated from Canada to the United States in 1974; 298 in 1975; 425 in 1976; and about 500 in 1977. *Ibid.*, 175.

146. Canadian doctors had a decided advantage over other foreign-trained medical workers in obtaining visas, work permits, state licensing, and permanent resident status. This was particularly true in states such as Texas, Arizona, Massachusetts, and California. *Ibid.*, 175-76.

147. Hawkins, *Critical Years*, 79, 90, 256.

148. During the late 1980s a number of highly qualified immigrants from Hong Kong selected the family category rather than the independent class "because of the priority this gives them in gaining an immigration visa." Diana Lary *et al.*, "Hong Kong: A Case Study of Settlement and Immigration," in Howard Adelman *et al.*, eds., *Immigration and Refugee Policy: Australia and Canada Compared* (Toronto, 1994), 407-08.

149. Under this program, investor immigrants were given considerable leeway in terms of continuous residence. In 1987 the investment level was reduced from $250,000 to $150,000. Knowles, *Strangers at Our Gates*, 178.

150. Cited in Iacovetta, *Hardworking People*, 200.

Chapter Nine

1. The federal government's policy of multiculturalism also included a commitment to combat racism by encouraging, through education, "respect for and observance of human rights and civil liberties." *Canadian Council for Multiculturalism and Inter-cultural Education*, 14 May 1984; Augie Fleras and Jean Leonard Elliott, *The Challenge of Diversity: Multiculturalism in Canada* (Toronto, 1992).

2. By 1975 all provinces had human rights commissions to administer anti-discriminatory legislation, and two years later the Canadian Human Rights Act established a comparable federal commission. The Charter, however, went much further in creating guidelines to protect the rights of individuals. *Ibid.*, 85-91.

3. Pickersgill got himself into a political controversy when, in a speech in Victoria, B.C., he stated that "the best kind of immigration was the cradle." Opposition newspapers interpreted this as meaning that "no immigrant no matter where he came from was as good as a Canadian baby." He was also attacked in the House of Commons. *Ibid.*, 236.

4. Canada, Manpower and Immigration, *Immigration Statistics 1970*, 22. These figures are based on country of birth. See Anthony Richmond, *Post-War Immigrants to Canada* (Toronto, 1967), 1-6.

5. Richmond, *Post-War Immigrants*, 30-32.

6. *Ibid.*, 70-72.

7. For instance, the average number of years of education among British immigrants was 10.7, with only 8 per cent having less than nine years of schooling – the benchmark of being poorly educated. *Ibid.*, 78-85.

8. Most of the post-war British immigrants were from middle-class or upper working-class backgrounds, with very few coming from the semi-skilled or unskilled categories. Richmond provides two major reasons to explain this phenomenon: the traditional reluctance of the British lower working class to leave their locality and the greater attraction of Australia, "where an almost free passage is provided." Among skilled immigrants, 70 per cent of the British sample retained their former occupational status, while only 42 per cent of those from other countries were so fortunate. *Ibid.*, 106, 111.

9. Richmond made special reference to the problems of refugee lawyers and doctors. *Ibid.*, 111, 116.

10. Like his predecessors in the portfolio, Pickersgill discovered "how easy it was for the Opposition to take opposite positions on immigration. While Diefenbaker talked about non-discrimination, Fulton and Churchill complained there was not enough discrimination in favour of British immigration." Pickersgill, *Years with St. Laurent*, 237-40.

11. Pickersgill also claimed that King's famous 1947 "absorptive capacity" speech was based on a preferential system on the basis of adaptability, not race. *Ibid.*, 238.

12. *Ibid.*, 245.

13. The first were primarily single agricultural workers; these were followed by married families. William Petersen, *Planned Migration: The Social Determinants of the Dutch-Canadian Movement* (Berkeley, Calif., 1955), 174-76.

14. The CNR Colonization Department had also assumed an important role in recruiting and placing Dutch farmers. The strong ties that developed between Canada and the Netherlands during the war and the arrival in Canada of thousands of Dutch war brides were also assets. *Ibid.*, 173.

15. Prominent among the boosters were the CMA, the CPR, and the Port Arthur, Ontario, contracting company R.F. Welch, which had been founded in 1905 by two brothers from Calabria, Vincenzo and Giovanni Veltri. Iacovetta, *Such Hardworking People*, 23.

16. Fortier had replaced Hugh Keenleyside as deputy minister in the fall of 1949. After returning from Italy, he noted that it would be possible to select "a much better type of migrant" around Rome and in the northern regions. *Ibid.*, 27.

17. By 1951 over 20,000 Italians entered the country, and this level was maintained throughout the decade. *Ibid.*, 28.

18. The Immigration-Labour Committee, chaired by Arthur MacNamara, expected a ratio of 70 per cent northerners to 30 per cent southerners. Only 117 of the 1,500 bulk order were northerners. *Ibid.*, 30.

19. Canadian officials preferred young, single, healthy men who would remain in their assigned jobs for at least one year. The costs of transportation were advanced, under the 1951 assisted passage loan scheme; inland transportation costs were assumed by the employer, who secured repayment through monthly deductions. *Ibid.*, 29.

20. Another factor was the positive reaction in Quebec to the performance of 237 Italian farm workers sent out in June, 1950. *Ibid.*

21. Canadian unions had little reason to be concerned since most employers were reluctant to hire Italian tradesmen because of language problems and their demand for high wages and decent working conditions. Reports about the exploitation of their nationals prompted Italian authorities to seek redress from the IRO. In June, 1951, IRO authorities forwarded the complaint to Ottawa. *Ibid.*, 33-35.

22. In the fall of 1951 the Canadian Metal Mining Association complained that many of its members had lost Italian workers before they had repaid the travel loans, and that attempts to apprehend and deport these defaulters had been unsuccessful. *Ibid.*, 42.

23. Chimbos, *The Canadian Odyssey*, 45-46.

24. Department of Citizenship and Immigration, Deputy Minister's Records, 1957, File 3-33-14, cited *ibid.*, 46.

25. Cited *ibid.*, 59.

26. *Ibid.*, 33-34.

27. *Ibid.*, 53.

28. Between 1950 and 1969 about 61,755 Portuguese came to Canada. This represented about 5.5 per cent of total emigration from Portugal in this period. Grace Anderson

and David Higgs, *A Future to Inherit: Portuguese Communities in Canada* (Toronto, 1976), 24, 42-43.

29. Farmers coming from the Azores found themselves at a disadvantage when exposed to Canadian farm machinery and farming techniques. Those entering the Lake Erie fishing industry were more successful. *Ibid.*, 30, 61-63.

30. Vic Satzewich, *Racism and the incorporation of foreign labour: Farm labour migration to Canada since 1945* (London, 1991), 149.

31. *Ibid.*, 148-50. Canadian officials neglected to mention that plans had been made to import over 3,000 American migrant tobacco workers for the Ontario harvest. Almost all of these workers were white. After 1957 organizations such as the Ontario Field Crops Association began an intensive lobbying campaign for the admission of· "300 coloured workers from the West Indies for a period of approximately six months each summer."

32. *Ibid.*, 126-27. A January, 1955, immigration policy statement also claimed that West Indian migrants did "not assimilate readily and pretty much vegetate to a low standard of living . . . many cannot adapt themselves to our climatic conditions."

33. Memo from R. Curry, assistant deputy minister, to Kent, 21 January 1966; Briefing Paper on Immigration from the West Indies, no date, cited in Satzewich, *Racism*, 139.

34. Memo from assistant deputy minister to deputy minister, 13 January 1965, cited *ibid.*, 175.

35. In contrast, the Department of Labour remained obdurate, convinced that the growers' demands were unjustified and unacceptable. *Ibid.*, 164, 167.

36. Certain changes were later implemented, such as the guarantee of a minimum weekly wage of $50. The high costs of the return fare, in the short run, deterred many growers from hiring Caribbean workers during the 1966 harvest. *Ibid.*, 170.

37. During this same period the total number of immigrants destined for the agricultural sector was 3,153 in 1966, or 3.2 per cent of the total number of immigrants destined for the Canadian labour force. Donald Dawson and David Freshwater, *Hired Farm Labour in Canada*, Report of the Food Prices Board (Ottawa, 1975), 12-14.

38. Cited in Robert Chodos, *The Caribbean Connection* (Toronto, 1977), 229.

39. Representatives of the growers' association argued that federal standards for the accommodation of such short-term labour placed "the small producer at a definite disadvantage as he cannot always afford to provide adequate accommodation which will be used only one or two months in the year." *Ibid.*, 12; *Debates*, 20 July 1973, 5838.

40. The research teams visited 629 farms, of which 145 hired foreign workers; they recorded a total of 471 workers, of whom 142 were illegals. All of the illegals had their status "regularized" by the issuance of employment visas. *Report on Migrant Farm Labour Investigation, Southwestern Ontario, 27 August-12 September 1973*, Department of Manpower and Immigration (Ottawa, 5 October 1973), 3-4.

41. The report noted about one-third of the labour force were illegals. It also claimed that

the Mexican Mennonites were primarily from the northern provinces of Chihuahua and Durango. They had been coming north for seasonal work, in family units, for decades. *Ibid.*, 6, 8-9.

42. The bellicose nature of the report was evident from its complaint that "the Department of Manpower and Immigration has been taking it on the chin for all the ills said to be plaguing agriculture" and that it was time the department take the initiative "to damn well work out some solutions." *The Seasonal Farm Labour Situation in Southwestern Ontario: A Report* (Ottawa, 11 August 1973), 2-4.

43. Most of the Portuguese workers were from the Azores and were lured to Canada by immigration brokers: often their wages were significantly diminished by paying a broker's fee, "usually a standard $500." *Ibid.*, 21.

44. By 1973 the Caribbean Program provided for an hourly wage of $1.80 or $72 for a forty-hour week, return air fare to the West Indies, and "the provision of decent, inspected . . . accommodation." *Ibid.*, 16.

45. The report also mentioned the existence of Ontario-based brokers who were recruiting these Mexican workers: "a bus has been leaving El Paso, Texas on the U.S.-Mexico border, for several months on a daily basis, carrying Mexicans to work in Ontario." *Ibid.*, 19.

46. It was estimated that by the mid-1970s there were over six million migrant workers in western Europe. By the end of 1975 there were about 770,000 Yugoslavian workers in western Europe with another 200,000 having emigrated to other parts of the world. This meant "that for every 100 persons employed in Yugoslavia there are some 20 who work abroad." Joel Martin Halpern, "Yugoslav Migration and Employment in Western Europe," in Hans Christian Buechler and Judith-Maria Buechler, *Migrants in Europe: The Role of Family, Labor, and Politics* (New York, 1987), 106-08.

47. By 1975 France had about four million foreigners, or about 6.5 per cent of the total population. Unlike many of its neighbours, however, France had a long experience with immigrant workers; for example, in 1936 the ratio of foreign-born was about the same as in 1975. The major difference was that in the 1970s most of the immigrant workers were non-white, primarily from Africa. Jacques Barou, "In the Aftermath of Colonization: Black African Immigrants in France," *ibid.*, 77-90.

48. See Ursula Mehrlander, "Germany," in Daniel Kubat, ed., *The Politics of Migration Policies* (New York, 1979), 145-62, A. Ersan Yucel, "Turkish Migrant Workers in the FRG," in Buechler and Buechler, *Migrants*, 121. From 1945 to 1974, West Germany received nine million refugees and emigrants from East Bloc countries, plus four million guest workers and their families.

49. After 1974, when the legal movement of guest workers was curtailed, the German government was faced with the dilemma of how to integrate the thousands of Turks, Yugoslavs, and other *Gastarbeiter* into German society. Programs of integration included improved housing, language classes, occupational training programs, and the controversial issue of naturalization; for guest workers who wished to return home, generous assistance was provided. Mehrlander, "Germany," 154.

50. Between 1951 and 1961 the enumerated population of West Indians in Britain increased from 15,300 to 171,800; those of Indian origin from 30,800 to 81,400; those of Pakistan origin from 5,000 to 24,900; and those from the Far East from 12,000 to 29,600. Gary Freeman, *Immigrant Labor and Racial Conflict in Industrial Societies: The French and British Experience 1945-1975* (Princeton, N.J., 1979), 45; Elizabeth Thomas-Hope, *Explanation in Caribbean Migration: Perception and the Image: Jamaica, Barbados and St. Vincent* (London, 1992), 59.

51. This absorptive capacity argument was vigorously challenged by Labour Party leader Hugh Gaitskell, who called on the government to act responsibly when dealing with the problems of the inner city rather than resorting to the tools of racial intolerance and discrimination. Ironically, three years later, in August, 1965, the Labour government of Harold Wilson totally excluded unskilled Commonwealth immigrant workers and reduced the skilled quota to 8,500. The reluctance of the powerful Trade Union Congress to criticize this policy attracted many unfavourable comments. On the positive side, the Wilson government did pass the Race Relations Act of 1965, which outlawed discrimination in public places, prohibited incitement to racial hatred, and set up a Race Relations Board. Freeman, *Immigrant Labor*, 51, 54; Sheila Patterson, *Immigration and Race Relations in Britain, 1960-1967* (London, 1969), 44-47; Paul Foot, *Immigration and Race in British Politics* (London, 1965), 127.

52. Despite being publicly chastised by his leader, Edward Heath, Powell's ability to mobilize public opinion strongly influenced the policies of the Labour government at a time when it had to deal with the exodus of large numbers of East African Asians holding British passports. In 1968 a bill was introduced "which took away the right of free entry from all those possessing citizenship in the U.K. and colonies but who lacked a substantial personal connection with the country – either by birthplace, parents or grandparents. . . . It was overtly racially discriminatory since through the device of the grandfather clause the descendants of white colonialists could enter the country freely, but Asian passport holders whose spouses were living in Britain had to queue up for years in some cases." Freeman, *Immigrant Labour*, 59.

53. Although the grandfather clause was removed from the final bill because of its similarity with the tactics used by southern American racists to prevent blacks from voting, in 1973 it was reinserted. The Tory government also claimed that its immigration policies were now primarily based on manpower considerations, which meant that few unskilled or semi-skilled immigrant workers would be required. Although the government did agree to accept over 28,000 Asians expelled from Uganda, further measures were adopted to eliminate any future influx. *Ibid.*, 66-69.

54. The report noted that most workers in Canada holding low-paying jobs were either nationals or landed immigrants who would be adversely affected by the entry of guest workers "because their wages would rise less than they would have risen otherwise." It also compared the booming European economies of the 1960s with a Canadian economy characterized by high unemployment and high labour turnover. *Ibid.*, 62-66.

55. Lloyd Wong, "Canada's Guestworkers: Some Comparisons of Temporary Workers in Europe and North America," *International Migration Review*, XVIII, 1 (1984), 85-97. The charges were disputed in a hard-hitting article that pointed out that many employment authorizations (over half between 1977 and 1983) were issued for social and humanitarian reasons, not because of labour market demand. Monica Boyd *et al.*, "Temporary Workers in Canada: A Multifaceted Program," *ibid.*, XX, 4 (1986), 929-49.

56. Ronald Labonte, "Racism and Labour: The Struggle of British Columbia's Farm-workers," *Canadian Forum* (June/July, 1982), 9-11.

57. Labonte described instances where planes sprayed fields with pesticides while the workers and their families were still in them. One particularly toxic pesticide was the fungicide Captan, which had "been shown to cause cancer, birth defects and genetic damage in laboratory animals." *Ibid.*

58. In British Columbia, workers' compensation coverage by agricultural concerns was optional. *Ibid.*

59. The specific problems faced by visible minority farmworkers, especially in Ontario and British Columbia, were discussed by the 1983 Special Parliamentary Committee on Participation of Visible Minorities in Canadian Society. While the Committee acknowledged that many employers were fair and humane, it was concerned about the vulnerability of these workers "to both physical danger and economic exploita-tion." *Equality Now*, 29-43, 135-36.

60. R.C. Cecil and G.E. Ebanks, "The Human Condition of West Indian Migrant Farm-Labour in Southwestern Ontario," *International Migration Review*, XXIX, 3 (Sep-tember, 1991), 389-405; Elizabeth Payne, "The Newcomers Struggle," *Toronto Star*, July 28, 1994.

61. German and Dutch domestics viewed domestic service as a temporary expedient to escape from troubles at home. The recruitment of Spanish domestics was also unsuc-cessful, but for other reasons: Spanish officials were insistent that they be placed only in Catholic homes, while most of the employers were Protestant. Barber, *Immigrant Domestic Servants in Canada*, 22.

62. The scheme was cancelled in April, 1952, after only 357 women had arrived. *Ibid.*

63. Emigration of their daughters could relieve Greek families of dowry burdens either because of the money earned in Canada or because of marriage in Canada. Daughters could also sponsor other members of the family after three years. *Ibid.*, 23.

64. *Ibid.*

65. In his memo to the deputy minister of Citizenship and Immigration, the director also noted that when the Caribbean domestics were "superior types they are unlikely to remain in domestic service." Cited in Satzewich, *Racism*, 143.

66. *Ibid.*, 144.

67. In January, 1966, the assistant deputy minister advised that the quota for West Indian domestics be combined with the overall quota for domestics as a means of reduc-ing West Indian numbers. By this stage over 2,690 domestics had been admitted

from the region. *Ibid.*, 142; Barber, *Immigrant Domestic Servants in Canada*, 23.

68. According to Barber, domestic women of colour "also suffered from continuing racism which stereotyped them as inferior and immoral. They endured abuses ranging from the curtailment of the wages and leisure time stipulated in the contract to sexual harassment and rape." *Ibid.*

69. In 1980, 3,031 or 28 per cent of the total came from Great Britain, 1,878 or 17.3 per cent from the British West Indies, and 1,299 or 12 per cent from the Philippines. In addition, there were 295 domestics from Finland. *Domestic Workers on Employment Authorizations: A Report of the Task Force on Immigration Practices and Procedures* (Ottawa, 1981), 51.

70. *Ibid.*, 12.

71. *Ibid.*, 29.

72. Arnopoulos, *Problems of Immigrant Women*, 55.

73. *Domestic Workers on Employment Authorizations*, 8.

74. Mirjana Morokvasic, "Birds of Passage Are Also Women," *International Migration Review*, XVIII, 4 (1984), 886-95.

75. The situation was much better for those coming from Britain or western Europe and for those with professional standing who could more readily gain entry to well-paying white-collar jobs than for those coming from eastern or southern Europe or from Asia or the Caribbean. Monica Boyd, "At a Disadvantage: The Occupational Attainments of Foreign Born Women in Canada," *ibid.*, 1107, 1092. See also Tania Das Gupta, "Political Economy of Gender, Race, and Class: Looking at South Asian Immigrant Women in Canada," *Canadian Ethnic Studies*, XXVI, 1 (1994), 59-73.

76. Dionne Brand, "Black Women and Work," *Fireweed*, 25 (Fall, 1987), 35.

77. Local 79, with its 8,000 members, was the largest municipal local in Canada; it was also the first to organize a bargaining unit composed entirely of casual workers. Ronnie Leah, "Linking the Struggles: Racism, Feminism and the Union Movement," Queen's University Industrial Relations *Reprint Series*, No. 93 (1990), 3.

78. According to Leah, "union struggles against racism and sexism have proceeded in separated spheres: women's committees have organized against sexism, focusing on women's rights; race relations or human rights committees have organized against racism focusing on minority workers' rights. . . . This division has been especially harmful to women of colour. . . ." *Ibid.*, 1.

79. *Special Inquiry . . . to investigate and report upon the state and management of the Department of Manpower and Immigration* (Ottawa, 1976), 22.

80. *A Report . . . on Illegal Migrants in Canada*, from W.G. Robinson, Special Advisor, June, 1983, and *The Exploitation of Potential Immigrants by Unscrupulous Consultants. . .*, April, 1981.

81. *Illegal Migrants*, 29. For Australian policies, see pp. 6-10.

82. In 1979, fifty-one employers were charged and forty-two convicted; in 1982, fifty-eight were charged and only twenty-nine convicted. Part of the problem was the difficulty of proving that businessmen "knowingly" hired an illegal; another was that

both the RCMP and the courts gave these cases very low priority. In addition, the Immigration Branch only had about 100 investigation officers, and they did not have the power to initiate a search. *Ibid.*, 95-102.

83. The lottery winner subsequently made application to enter Canada as an entrepreneur. *Ibid.*, 98.

84. Contrary to popular belief, 41 per cent of the illegals were women. *Ibid.*, 12, 28.

85. Although consideration was given to making relatives criminally responsible for aiding illegals and targeting those groups that provided a high ratio of illegals, including "infiltration and raids," these measures were not recommended. Large-scale fingerprinting was also rejected. *Ibid.*, 90.

86. *Ibid.*, 18.

87. The lure of a "fast buck" helped swell the number of immigration consultants during the 1980s. Part of the problem was that proposals to establish an effective licensing system and to make misrepresentation and fraud separate offences under the Immigration Act did not materialize. *Exploitation of Potential Immigrants*, 4, 12-17.

88. Victor Malarek, *Heaven's Gate: Canada's Immigration Fiasco* (Toronto, 1987), 177, 200.

89. Raids were made in Trois-Rivières, Quebec City, Ottawa, Peterborough, Sarnia, Windsor, Toronto, London, Kingston, Winnipeg, Regina, Edmonton, Calgary, Prince George, Vancouver, and Victoria. Wickberg, ed., *From China to Canada*, 214-15.

90. *Debates*, 1960, 4723-24.

91. The Chinese Adjustment Statement Program, which was set up at this time, eventually regularized the status of over 12,000 Chinese before it was phased out in 1973. Wickberg, ed., *From China to Canada*, 216-17.

92. Allan Borowski *et al.*, "Immigration and Crime," in Howard Adelman *et al.*, eds., *Immigration and Refugee Policy: Australia and Canada Compared* (Toronto, 1994), 631-52.

93. Margaret Cannon, *China Tide: The Hong Kong Exodus to Canada* (Toronto, 1989), 215.

94. *Ibid.*, 204.

95. Diana Lary *et al.*, "Hong Kong: A Case Study of Settlement and Immigration," in Adelman *et al.*, *Australia and Canada Compared*, 413.

96. Immigration Canada, *Guidelines for the Immigrant Investor Program*, April, 1991 (Ottawa, 1992); Paul Miller, "The Earnings of Asian Male Immigrants in the Canadian Labor Market," *International Migration Review*, XXVI, 4 (1992), 1222-43; Martin Marger, "Ethnic Enterprise in Ontario: Immigrant Participation in the Small Business Sector," *ibid.*, 968-81.

97. Peter Li, "Ethnic Enterprise in Transition: Chinese Business in Richmond, B.C., 1980-1990," *Canadian Ethnic Studies*, XXIV, 1 (1992), 120-37.

98. Although Guyana is located on the mainland of South America, historically it has

had close links with the British Caribbean islands. Together with Trinidad and Tobago, Guyana experienced a large influx of South Asian indentured workers during the nineteenth century for work in the plantations. In contrast, Jamaica's population is largely of Afro-Caribbean and European descent. Anthony Richmond, *Caribbean Immigrants: A Demo-economic Analysis* (Ottawa, March, 1989), 1-9; Frances Henry, *The Caribbean Diaspora in Toronto* (Toronto, 1994), 27-54.

99. According to Richmond, Haitian immigration to Canada "peaked in 1974." He also noted that this cohort "had difficulty in obtaining recognition for their professional qualifications . . . despite the fact that, in general, their level of education was high. . . ." Richmond, *Caribbean Immigrants*, 7.

100. See Derek Cooper, "Migration from Jamaica in the 1970s: Political Protest or Economic Pull?" *International Migration Review*, XIX, 4 (1985), 728-43.

101. *Ibid.*, 742; Kristin Couper, "An Elusive Concept: The Changing Definition of Illegal Immigrant in the Practice of Immigration Control in the United Kingdom," *International Migration Review*, XVIII, 3 (1984), 437-51.

102. See Richmond, *Caribbean Immigrants*, xxx, 15, 19-22.

103. Richmond noted that at the time of the 1981 census, unemployment among Caribbean immigrants "was measurably higher than among comparable Canadian-born persons," and that among males, the average total income "was below that for those born in Canada, and substantially below that of other immigrants," despite the fact that Caribbeans "faced no linguistic barrier." The greatest disparity was among Caribbean males in Quebec, who were "earning only 60% as much as did corresponding Canadian-born men." *Ibid.*, 65, xxx, 23.

104. Richmond emphasizes the differences between the pre-1970 arrivals, whom he characterizes as being part of a Caribbean "brain drain," and those coming later, especially "less qualified" visitors, who took advantage of opportunities to become landed immigrants, and family class immigrants. *Ibid.*, 20.

105. See, for example, Austin Clarke, *In This City* (Toronto, 1992), 72.

106. The first serious incident occurred in May, 1976, when a fifteen-year-old black youth was knifed "merely because he was black." This coincided with "the highly emotional gatherings held in reaction to the Federal Government's Green Paper on immigration." Two of the more serious were the New Year's Eve attack on South Asians in the Toronto subway and the January, 1977, pitched battle between whites and South Asians on Weston Road. *Now Is Not Too Late*, Submitted to the Council of Metropolitan Toronto by Task Force on Human Relations (November, 1977), 22-26.

107. No attempt was made in the report to differentiate between the various South Asian groups. *Ibid.*, 40-41.

108. *Ibid.*, 109-11.

109. It was noted that although the number of black officers had increased in recent years, "South Asians, Chinese and Japanese are grossly under represented." Comments on Toronto police culture were drawn from the *1976 Report of the Royal Commission*

into Metropolitan Police Practices by Mr. Justice Morand, the *Task Force on Polic-ing in Ontario* (1974), and the *Metropolitan Toronto Review of Citizen-Police Com-plaint Procedures* (1975). *Ibid.*, 140-46.

110. There were eighty specific recommendations. *Equality Now* (Ottawa, 1984), 135-41. This report acted as a catalyst for other studies of employment bias. See especially Frances Henry and Effie Ginzberg, *Who Gets The Work? A Test of Racial Discrimi-nation in Employment*, The Urban Alliance on Race Relations and The Social Plan-ning Council of Metropolitan Toronto, January, 1985.

111. *Equality Now*, 1, 3.

112. The report cited statistics showing that even in ethnically diverse cities such as Toronto and Vancouver, visible minorities represented less than 3 per cent of the po-lice and were often excluded or discouraged "because of prejudice, the chill factor and artificial barriers to recruitment." The Committee called on the RCMP to become a role model in the recruitment of visible minorities. *Ibid.*, 65-87.

113. Recommendations for improvement included new awareness programs for immi-gration officers, especially when dealing with visible minority visitors who were often assumed, without any proof, to be illegal immigrants. In addition, the Canadian Human Rights Commission was urged to examine any evidence of "systemic dis-crimination" in the public service, Crown corporations, and private companies obtaining federal contracts. It also advocated the creation of a separate Ministry of Multiculturalism and a Standing Committee on Multiculturalism. Finally, it called on Parliament officially to acknowledge the mistreatment afforded Japanese-Cana-dians during World War Two. *Ibid.*, 47-62.

114. *Ibid.*, 19.

115. *Ibid.*, 139-41.

116. *The Report of the Race Relations and Policing Task Force* (Toronto, April, 1989).

117. Two fatal shootings involving Jamaican Canadians – Lester Donaldson and Michael Wade Lawson – brought renewed charges that the province's police forces were racist and trigger-happy. In preparing its full report, the Task Force held a number of public hearings in Toronto, Ottawa, Windsor, and Thunder Bay and heard testimony from over 100 individuals, community organizations, and police associations. *Ibid.*, 1, 15-16.

118. Nor was the Task Force diverted by police claims that many of their critics were "irre-sponsible activists"; these charges were dismissed as "defensive and ultimately self-defeating attempts to isolate such critics as troublemakers unworthy of attention." *Ibid.*, 12.

119. Albert Mercury, a retired businessman, claimed that he didn't think "there's any black that was born and raised in Toronto that doesn't know someone personally or hasn't personally experienced police harassment in some form or another." *Ibid.*, 155.

120. In the case of battered women, there were charges that "they receive less sensitivity from police than do white females who have been abused." *Ibid.*, 153.

121. *Ibid.*, 44-45.

122. A survey of ninety-nine municipal police forces, employing 18,283 officers, found that only twenty-two of these forces employed visible minority officers. Although Metropolitan Toronto led the way with 4.1 per cent, this was still well below the 20 per cent of the region's population that were visible minorities. Nor did the Ontario Provincial Police, with only 0.9 per cent of its officers being visible minorities, provide an inspiring role model. The report advised that recruitment would have to be done carefully since "many visible minorities harbour a deep reluctance to consider policing as an occupation or believe that they are not welcome within police institutions." *Ibid.*, 55-61.

123. *Ibid.*, 127-50.

124. In the first trial, the Los Angeles police officers were acquitted, despite vivid evidence of their acts of brutality. On May 3, a Toronto policeman shot and killed an alleged Jamaican drug dealer.

125. Austin Clarke, *Public Enemies: Police Violence and Black Youth* (Toronto, 1992), 2. Clarke remained optimistic, however, that multiculturalism could succeed in Toronto. A special report of the incident was prepared by veteran public affairs commentator Stephen Lewis, at the behest of Ontario Premier Bob Rae. Stephen Lewis, *Report on Race Relations in Ontario* (Toronto, 1992).

Chapter Ten

1. The five-year plan also emphasized the following goals: managing immigration; protection of society; economic immigration; the integration of immigrants. In its 1991-92 annual report DEI indicated that Canada would accept upwards of 30,000 refugees in the following year. It also announced that between January, 1986, and December, 1991, the Immigrant Investor Program had "attracted 7,593 applicants with investment subscriptions totalling $1.5 billion, creating an estimated 10,000 jobs in Canada." Department of Employment and Immigration, *Annual Report, 1991-92*, 17-18.

2. Osvaldo Nunez, *Debates*, 2 February 1992, 800-01.

3. *Ibid.*, 796-99, 802-04.

4. Those advocating more control often made use of equilibrium thermodynamics analogies portraying refugee policy as a type of hydroelectric dam. Critics viewed this concern for equilibrium not "as a goal but as part of the problem." Howard Adelman, ed., *Refugee Policy: Canada and the United States* (Toronto, 1991), 175-77.

5. Policy statement by Rafawl Girard of DEI, one of the authors of Bills C-55 and C-84. Cited *ibid.*, 202.

6. Christopher Wydrzynski, "Refugees and the Immigration Act," *McGill Law Journal*, XXV, 2 (1979), 191.

7. According to David Matas the refugee determination system was biased against the

claimant both at the initial stages, when he/she had to decide whether to claim in-status or out-of status, and during the investigation of the Refugee Status Advisory Committee. David Matas, *Close the Doors: The Failure of Refugee Protection* (Toronto, 1989), 88-92.

8. The overall level of acceptance ranged from about 20 per cent in France to 7 per cent in Germany and 3 per cent in Switzerland. In terms of naturalization, Germany had the lowest rate in the European Community with only "about 0.3 per cent" of alien residents becoming citizens each year. Dennis Gallagher, "The Evolution of the International Refugee System," *International Migration Review*, XXIII, 3 (1989), 593-94; Mark Miller, "Dual Citizenship: A European Norm?" *ibid.*, XXIII, 4 (1989), 945-50; Tugrul Ansay, "The New UN Convention in Light of the German and Turkish Experience," *ibid.*, XXV, 4 (1991), 840; Rosemarie Rogers, "The Future of Refugee Flows and Policies," *ibid.*, XXVI, 4 (1992), 1119-23; Gerald de Boer, "Trends in Refugee Policy and Cooperation in the European Community," *ibid.*, XXVI, 2 (1992), 668-74.

9. About 400,000 refugees came from Vietnam between 1975 and 1980. The largest influx from Cuba came during the 1980 Mariel crisis when the Castro government allowed over 125,000 to leave, some of whom came from Cuban jails and mental institutes. By 1990, immigrants in the United States numbered more than 17 million, more than at any time in the country's history.

10. The Refugee Act of 1980 improved on the previous commitment of the 1965 legislation to create a constant proportion of places (6 per cent of 290,000, or 17,400 a year) for refugees. Under the 1980 Act the target number was 50,000. Gil Loescher and John Scanlan, *Calculated Kindness: Refugees and America's Half-open Door, 1945 to Present* (New York, 1986), 155, 214.

11. Three to five million illegals were believed to be in the U.S. in 1986. Gary Freeman, "Migration Policy and Politics in the Receiving States," *International Migration Review*, XXVI, 4 (1992), 1146-49.

12. Alan Simpson (Chairman, U.S. Senate Subcommittee on Immigration and Refugee Policy), "The Politics of Immigration Reform," *International Migration Review*, XVIII, 3 (1984), 486-504; Vernon Briggs, Jr., "The 'Albatross' of Immigration Reform: Temporary Worker Policy in the United States," *ibid.*, XX, 4 (1986), 995.

13. The primacy of national self-interest was revived in the U.S. Immigration Act of 1990, which emphasized that future policies should elevate economic considerations, most notably the skill requirements of the present and future U.S. job market. This priority was reflected in the increase of the number of visas reserved for select occupations from 58,000 a year to 140,000. "Immigration Reform," in John Kromkowski, ed., *Race and Ethnic Relations 92/93* (Guilford, Conn., 1992), 57-62.

14. This was both an amnesty program for illegals already in the U.S. and a "gift" for southwestern growers who needed cheap agricultural labour. Briggs, "The 'Albatross' of Immigration Reform," 1015.

15. There was an enormous public reaction against the bogus claims of the 155 Sri Lanka Tamils who arrived in Newfoundland in August, 1986, and the 173 Sikhs who were dumped off the shores of Nova Scotia one year later. See Nobuaki Suyama, "Canada's Refugee Policy – In a right direction or not?," paper presented at the Canadian Ethnic Studies Association Conference, Calgary, 19 October 1989, 14, 21. See also Adelman, ed., *Refugee Policy*, 207-08.

16. The right of the refugee claimant to have an oral hearing had been ordered by the Supreme Court in the 1985 case *Singh v. Minister of Employment and Immigration*. *Refugee*, V, 1 (October, 1985), 5-6; *Globe and Mail*, July 31, 1989; *Saturday Night*, CIV, 1 (January, 1989), 11. See also *Globe and Mail*, editorial, February 20, 1988.

17. Former immigration ministers Lloyd Axworthy and Ronald Atkey, as well as Gordon Fairweather, chairman of the Immigration Appeal Board, were also targets of abuse. Doug Collins, *Immigration: Parliament Versus The People* (Toronto, 1987), 1-22.

18. Collins also denounced the "selling of landed immigrant status" to Hong Kong businessmen, the acceptance of thousands of phoney refugees, and the hypocritical views expressed in *Equality Now*, which was dismissed as "a fix from the start." *Ibid.*, 7, 18.

19. Reginald Bibby, *Mosaic Madness: The Poverty and Potential of Life in Canada* (Toronto, 1990).

20. Adelman *et al.*, eds., *Australia and Canada Comopared*, 398.

21. Art Hanger, the MP from Calgary Northeast, was a consistent critic after the 1993 election.

22. Four of the more important studies were Anthony Richmond, *Immigration and Ethnic Conflict* (London, 1988); Kathryn McDade, *Barriers to Recognition of the Credentials of Immigrants in Canada* (Ottawa, April, 1988); Charles Beach and Alan Green, eds., *Policy Forum on the Role of Immigration in Canada's Future* (Kingston, 1989); Roderic Beaujot, *Population Change in Canada: The Challenges of Policy Adaptation* (Toronto, 1991).

23. Neil Swan *et al.*, *Economic and Social Impacts of Immigration: A research report prepared for the Economic Council of Canada* (Ottawa, 1991), 131.

24. The report noted that the average level of immigration for the past twenty-five years had been 0.63 of the population – which would result in 168,000 immigrants in 1991, and then gradually rising to 340,000 by 2015. *Ibid.*, 134.

25. In its demographic section, the report proposed three different levels of immigration with the subsequent changes in Canada's population size and composition. Under scenario I, with no net immigration, Canada's population would increase marginally from 26,580,000 in 1990 to 28,314,000 in 2015. Under scenario II, with the existing net immigration rate of 0.4 per cent, Canada's population would increase to about 32 million by 2015. Under scenario III, with a net immigration rate of 0.8 per cent, the country would have about 36 million people in 2015. *Ibid.*, 132, 64-66.

26. Under this scenario, Vancouver's non-European population would increase from 11 per cent to 26 per cent; most would be of Asian background. In contrast, in Toronto Asian represented three-quarters of the non-European cohort, and in Montreal two-thirds. *Ibid.*, 66-68.

27. Jacques Henripin and François Vaillancourt of the University of Montreal described some of the consequences of "a low fertility and high immigration strategy" on Quebec society at a 1988 symposium. According to Henripin low fertility levels were particularly serious for Quebec, especially since the province was "losing 50% of its immigrants 20 years after their arrival." Statistics provided by Vaillancourt showed that between 1968 and 1985 Quebec's acceptance rate of immigrants ranged between 17 and 20 per cent of the national total, and that even by the 1980s less than 40 per cent of the immigrants going to Quebec spoke French. Beach and Green, eds., *Policy Forum on the Role of Immigration*, 94-95, 21-22.

28. *Ibid.*, 132. Beaujot's *Population Change in Canada*, 119, 136, 141, also emphasized that immigration was "likely to become the only source of population growth," and that the long-term implications of immigration, fertility, and mortality levels of the 1981-85 period "would produce a Canadian population that is about 23 per cent foreign born." He also noted that in 1990 about one-third of all immigrants spoke neither English nor French.

29. Beach and Green, eds., *Policy Forum on the Role of Immigration*, 132. According to Beaujot, *Population Change in Canada*, 144, refugees represented one-quarter of all immigrant arrivals between 1980 and 1987. Most of those admitted were not convention refugees, but rather those seeking asylum under Canada's unique policy of accepting "refugees as landed immigrants." He also pointed out that 80 per cent of the convention refugees were men, "while some 75 to 80 per cent of the world's refugees are women."

30. *Pounding At the Gates: A Study of Canada's Immigration System, Special Report by Daniel Stoffman* (Toronto, 1992).

31. Stoffman claimed that it cost Canada $50,000 to process each refugee claimant, largely because of the extended interview and appeal process. *Ibid.* 13-15.

32. Rogers, "The Future of Refugee Flows," 1118, 1127. In France, the racist Front National, led by Jean-Marie Le Pen, gained 15 per cent of the popular vote in the 1991 elections. Anthony Richmond, "Open and Closed Borders: Is the New World Order Creating a System of Global Apartheid?" *Refugee*, 13, 1 (April, 1993), 6-10.

33. Under the Convention only those asylum seekers with valid documents, and who could demonstrate that they had sufficient means to support themselves during their stay and who did not pose any threat to national security, would be allowed entry. Once admitted they could travel freely within the European Community, subject to special procedures that member nations might impose. The country that granted either an entry visa or residence permit was deemed responsible for that person. *Ibid.*

34. *Minutes of Proceedings and Evidence of Legislative Committee on Bill C-86, An Act*

to amend the Immigration Act and other Acts in consequence thereof, Third Session of the Thirty-fourth Parliament, 1991-92, 27 July 1992, 2-16.

35. *Ibid.,* 28 July 1992, 3-9.

36. Immigration officials also claimed that many of these designated immigrants would remain in the small centres, especially if the communities "create the type of welcoming environment which will cause the individual to set down roots." *Ibid.,* 27 July 1992, 9; 28 July 1992, 3:13.

37. Representatives of DEI emphasized the point that Canada had a "unique opportunity" to select the world's "best" immigrants. *Ibid.*

38. The FCM had, in addition to its fifteen provincial and territorial associations, over 560 municipal bodies representing "over 70% of the Canadian population."

39. Reference was made to the fact that Convention refugees were not eligible for the immigration adjustment assistance program after their first year of residence in Canada. This was changed in 1994. *Ibid.,* 29 July 1992, 44.

40. Representatives from Peel claimed that they and the Metropolitan Toronto municipalities had, since 1990, sent invoices to the Minister of Employment and Immigration to recover $225 million under the refugee assistance plan but had received nothing. *Ibid.,* 47, 48.

41. *Ibid.,* 30 July 1992, 112-13.

42. The OPIC claimed a membership of forty-two, most of whom were "ex-civil servants who, at one time, were responsible for the delivery of the immigration program, either in Canada as immigration officials, or overseas as visa officers." *Ibid.,* 11 August 1992, 80-91.

43. The RCMP claimed it was investigating over sixty organizations involved in the immigration traffic. It was careful, however, to emphasize that it was merely carrying out its responsibilities "for the criminal enforcement of the Immigration Act," and that policy decisions were the responsibility of Employment and Immigration. *Ibid.,* 10 August 1992, 6, 25.

44. RCMP evidence indicated that the syndicate most active in this operation was a well-known "Pacific Rim triad crime gang . . . involved in illegal narcotic, gambling, prostitution and a variety of other criminal activities." It had reportedly smuggled between 1,000 to 2,000 persons to Canada at an estimated profit "of 10 to 20 million dollars." *Ibid.,* 26-27.

45. The CLC claimed to represent 2.2 million Canadian workers. *Ibid.,* 12 August 1992, 8, 9-10.

46. White did concede, however, that some of his CLC colleagues, who had "a feeling of insecurity," were supportive of immigration restriction, but he noted that the CLC "in open debates at the convention . . . have gone completely in the opposite direction." *Ibid.,* 10-11.

47. *Ibid.,* 26.

48. White also rejected any provision that would require refugees, or any immigrants, to work in a specific region of the country. *Ibid.,* 13-14.

49. *Ibid.*, 21.

50. *Ibid.*, 15 September 1992, 6-7.

51. Reference was made to the changing status of Tamil refugees, whose claims had been initially rejected since Sri Lanka was considered a parliamentary democracy. In making his point about the vulnerability of refugees, Rabbi Plaut related his own pre-war experiences: "when I arrived as a refugee from Germany in 1935 and got off the train in Cincinnati, Ohio, with four of my colleagues, the news media were at the station, because we were the first refugees from Germany to arrive in that city, and none of us dared to speak to the media. We all had families back home." *Ibid.*, 10-14.

52. *Ibid.*, 29 July 1992, 4-113; *ibid.*, 11 August 1992, 26-112.

53. *Ibid.*, 11 August, 7-131.

54. *Ibid.* The CHC branded the proposal to send refugees to Canadian frontier regions as a thinly disguised *Gastarbeiter* system that would throw immigrants around "like so many cattle." In the case of Latin American refugees, it would be particularly onerous since 75 per cent had "at least a college degree."

55. The WSO claimed to represent 22,000 Sikhs in Canada. *Ibid.*, 30 August 1992, 4-14.

56. *Ibid.*, 8-14. NOIVMW, founded in Winnipeg in 1986, noted that about one-third of the 33,000 refugee claimants for 1991 were women.

57. Pro-refugee advocates ridiculed Amiel's suggestion that "immense numbers" of women, "fearing gender-related persecution," would flood Canada by pointing out that these women were "lucky to make it to the next country." *Maclean's*, March 29, 1993, 9; Leanne MacMillan, "Focus on Gender Issues and Refugee Law," *Refugee*, 13, 4 (July-August, 1993), 1-3.

58. Lewis also cited a report, prepared by the right-wing Fraser Institute of Vancouver, which claimed that the Canadian public would continue to view immigration as a liability until there were effective enforcement measures. Extract from a speech by the Honourable Douglas Lewis to representatives of ethnocultural agencies in Toronto, July 19, 1993.

59. *Globe and Mail*, September 15, 1993.

60. *Debates*, 2 February 1994, 797.

61. This editorial also stressed that Canada's level of acceptance of refugee claimants was 57 per cent, compared with an average level of 14 per cent for the sixteen Western countries that are the destination of asylum seekers. *Globe and Mail*, December 28, 1993.

62. *Toronto Star*, November 3, 1994; *Globe and Mail*, November 2, 1994.

63. *Toronto Star*, November 2, 1994.

64. *Ibid.*, November 3, 1994.

65. Neil Bissoondath, *Selling Illusions* (Toronto, 1994), 43, 170.

66. In a chapter titled "Immigrants and refugees in Canada and the Unites States: Policy dilemmas," Richmond criticized Bill C-86 for having given immigration bureaucrats more power, and he deplored the reduction in acceptance rates for the Convention

Refugee Determination Division from 70 per cent in 1990 to 54 per cent in 1993. Anthony Richmond, *Global Apartheid* (Toronto, 1994), 130-51.

67. While acknowledging the class divisions among Caribbean immigrants in Toronto and certain cultural traits that create barriers for incorporation into Canadian society, Henry blames most of the problems of adjustment on "the stresses of racism, which all Caribbean migrants face in varying degrees and forms." Frances Henry, *The Caribbean Diaspora* (Toronto, 1994), 272.

68. Reitz and Breton provide a comprehensive comparison of cultural pluralism and social mobility by minority groups in Canada and the U.S. Jeffrey Reitz and Raymond Breton, *The Illusion of Difference* (Toronto, 1994).

69. *Ibid.*, 224.

70. By December, 1994, Bissoondath's *Selling Illusions* had been on the Canadian best-seller list for over three months. *Ibid.*, 122.

71. *Globe and Mail* writer Bronwyn Draine was especially critical in her October 20, 1994, article "Bissoondath Selling Some Illusions of His Own."

72. The Chinese community sought repayment of the $23 million the federal government had collected in head taxes. The Ukrainian, German, and Italian communities primarily wanted a formal admission of government discrimination as well as symbolic redress. A request was also submited on behalf of the Sikhs and Jews who were turned away from Canadian shores in 1914 and 1939. *Toronto Star*, December 27, 1994.

Conclusion

1. *Debates*, 22 March 1910, 5850.

2. Fulton made specific reference to the figures for 1953, which showed 47,077 from the U.K., plus 9,000 from the United States; in contrast, there were 68,675 western Europeans, notably 35,015 Germans, and 43,737 others, including 24,219 from Italy. *Ibid.*, 26 June 1954, 6789.

3. *Ibid.*, 2 February 1994, 803, 797-98.

4. Swan *et al.*, *Economic and Social Impacts of Immigration*; Canada Employment and Immigration, *Immigration Statistics, 1991* (Ottawa, 1992).

5. Special Joint Committee on Immigration, Hearings, 31 January 1967, 206.

6. *Illegal Migrants in Canada*, 29.

7. Avakumovic, *Communist Party*; Nathan Glazer, *The Social Basis of American Communism* (New York, 1961); Kolasky, *Shattered Illusion*.

8. The growth fields were: business services, finance, insurance, real estate, accommodations and food services, health and welfare services, and amusement and recreation. Anthony Richmond, "Immigration and Structural Change: The Canadian Experience, 1971-1986," *International Migration Review*, xxvi, 4 (1992), 1200-21.

9. According to Richmond, recent immigrants were overrepresented in product fabricating and in service occupations because of language difficulties, non-recognition of qualifications, or lack of skill. *Ibid.*, 1213.

10. In 1986 the foreign-born represented 15.6 per cent of the Canadian population; in the twenty-five metropolitan areas the percentage was 21.2 per cent. In Metropolitan Toronto it was 36.3 per cent, one-quarter of whom arrived in the decade 1976-86. *Ibid.*, 1201, 1207.

11. William Foster *et al.*, "Economic Effects on the Host Community," in Adelman *et al.*, eds., *Australia and Canada Compared*, 465, 469.

12. Judith Sloan and François Vaillancourt, "The Labor Market Experience of Immigrants," *ibid.*, 482; Barry Chiswick, ed., *Immigration, Language and Ethnicity: Canada and the United States* (Washington, 1992).

13. The authors took particular exception to a 1991 Economic Council of Canada report that concluded there was "no significant difference against . . . coloured immigrants." Reitz and Breton, *The Illusion of Difference*, 101, 122-23.

14. Jeffrey Reitz, "The Institutional Structure of Immigration as a Determinant of Inter-Racial Competition: A Comparison of Britain and Canada," *International Migration Review*, XXII, 1 (1988), 117-45.

15. Many of the visible minority organizations that presented briefs to the House of Commons Standing Committee on Bill C-86 claimed that a double standard prevailed. Some academic commentators have also found serious fault with the administrative process of the Immigration Act. K.W. Taylor, "Racism in Canadian Immigration Policy," *Canadian Ethnic Studies*, XXIII, 1 (1991), 1-19; Li, ed., *Race and Ethnic Relations in Canada*, 13, 263-65.

16. Stephen Castles, "The Australian Model of Immigration and Multiculturalism: Is It Applicable to Europe?" *International Migration Review*, XXVI, 2 (1992), 549-65; Silvia Pedraza-Bailey, "Immigration Research: A Conceptual Map," *Social Science History*, 14, 1 (Spring, 1990), 43-67.

17. *Canada 1862. Zur Machricht fur Einwanderer.* (Located and translated by Dr. Irmgard Steinisch.)

Index